A
BONHOEFFER
LEGACY

A
BONHOEFFER
LEGACY

Essays in Understanding

Edited by
A. J. Klassen

WILLIAM B. EERDMANS PUBLISHING COMPANY
GRAND RAPIDS, MICHIGAN

Library of Congress Cataloging in Publication Data
Main entry under title:

A Bonhoeffer Legacy.

1. Bonhoeffer, Dietrich, 1906-1945—Addresses,
essays, lectures. I. Klassen, A. J.
BX4827.B57E87   230'.092'4   80-19427
ISBN 0-8028-3546-5

The editor and publisher wish to thank the following for
translating one or more of the essays in this book:

Geoffrey W. Bromiley
Leonard Olschner
Ted Plantinga
Larry Rasmussen
Ralph W. Vunderink

A special thanks goes to Clifford Green and Geffrey Kelly
of the International Bonhoeffer Society
for their invaluable assistance and encouragement.

"Bonhoeffer's Assertion of Religionless Christianity—Was He Mistaken?" has appeared in
Am gegebenen Ort, Aufsätze und Reden 1970–1979 under the title *"Christlicher Glaube
ohne Religion—Hat sich Dietrich Bonhoeffer geirrt?"* and is used by permission of
Christian Kaiser Verlag, Munich.

"Adolf Von Harnack and Bonhoeffer" first appeared in *Die Zeichen der Zeit,*
Evangelishe Verlagsansteit, Berlin.

CONTENTS

V. CHURCH AND WORLD

VI. RELIGION AND SECULARIZATION

VII. ETHICS

PREFACE

THE IDEA OF THIS BOOK on the legacy of Dietrich Bonhoeffer was conceived by intensive dialog with Eberhard Bethge, following my initial reading of his definitive biography in galley form. At that time we were struck by Bonhoeffer's apparent impact on the younger generation of scholars. In short order we compiled an impressive list of individuals who were in the process of writing or who had already completed full length dissertations on some aspects of the Bonhoeffer corpus. Would a symposium of critical essays summarizing the best insights of this research be a significant and appropriate tribute on the 70th anniversary of his birth?

The initial response to this proposal was overwhelming, and a number of essays were in fact available for that occasion. However, we did not anticipate the serious problems and subsequent delays that would arise in the process of completing the project. I am grateful to the contributors for their patience and encouragement along the way.

The beginning of this decade marks two milestones in the life of Dietrich Bonhoeffer: April 9, 1980 commemorated the 35th anniversary of his death; and February 4, 1981 celebrates the 75th anniversary of his birth. While there is still no agreement on the final meaning of his life and work, a general concensus has emerged in at least two important areas. Bonhoeffer was clearly a man of his time—a theologian whose thought was intimately related to the dramatic events of his life.

In many respects, however, Bonhoeffer was also ahead of his time. While some of his thinking was far from complete, and its meaning not immediately clear, few of the important issues in theology today have escaped the influence of his powerful pen. The years since their publication have established Bonhoeffer as one of the most creative minds in contemporary theology. And the basic questions he addressed are still as incisive and important as the day they were penned: "What is Christianity?" and "Who is Christ for us today?"

A. J. KLASSEN
April, 1980

vii

ABBREVIATIONS

MANY OF BONHOEFFER'S WORKS have appeared in several editions, often with different pagination, sometimes with additional material, and occasionally with revised translations. As an international group, the contributors have used various editions, details of which are given following the abbreviations.

Primary Sources

AB   *Act and Being*. New York: Harper & Row; London: William Collins, 1962. Trans. from *Akt und Sein* (see *AS* below).

AS   *Akt und Sein*. Munich: Christian Kaiser Verlag, 1956; 3rd ed., 1964 (originally published Gutersloh, 1931).

CC   *Christ the Center*. New York: Harper & Row, 1966; London: William Collins, 1966, entitled *Christology*. Fontana paperback edition, London: Collins, 1971 (with same pagination). New translation, London: Collins; San Francisco: Harper & Row, 1978 (paperback, pagination differs). Trans. from *Christologie (Gesammelte Schriften*, III, 166-242).

CD   *The Cost of Discipleship*. First edition abridged: London: SCM, 1948; New York: Macmillan, 1949. Second revised and unabridged edition: London: SCM; New York: Macmillan, 1959. Paperback of second edition: London: SCM; New York: Macmillan, 1963.

CFT   *Creation and Fall. Temptation*. London: SCM; New York: Macmillan, 1966. Both works originally published separately: *Creation and Fall*, London: SCM; New York: Macmillan, 1959; *Temptation*, London: SCM; New York: Macmillan, 1955. Trans. from *Schöpfung und Fall* (see *SF* below) and *Versuchung* (see *T* below).

CS   *The Communion of Saints.* New York: Harper & Row, 1964. *Sanctorum Communio:* London: Collins, 1963. Trans. from *Sanctorum Communio*, 3rd German ed. (see *SC* below).

E   *Ethics.* London: SCM; New York: Macmillan, 1955. Re-arranged edition, based on the sixth German edition: London: Collins (Fontana), 1964; New York: Macmillan (paperback), 1965. Hardcover version of the re-arranged edition published by SCM in 1971; pagination differs from Collins and Macmillan publications of this edition. Trans. from *Ethik* (see *Ek* below).

Ek   *Ethik.* Munich: Christian Kaiser Verlag, 1949. Re-arranged 6th ed., 1963.

GL   *Gemeinsames Leben.* Munich: Christian Kaiser Verlag, 1939, in the series Theologische Existenz heute, No. 61; many later editions.

GS   *Gesammelte Schriften.* Munich: Christian Kaiser Verlag, 1958-1961 (Vols. I-IV); 2nd ed., 1965-1966 (Vols. I-IV), 1972 (Vol. V), 1974 (Vol. VI).

LPP   *Letters and Papers from Prison.* London: SCM, 1953; New York: Macmillan, 1954, entitled *Prisoner for God. Letters and Papers from Prison* (1962 Macmillan paperback version, different pagination, entitled *Letters and Papers from Prison*). Second edition (not published in the United States): London: SCM, 1956. Third edition, revised and enlarged: London: SCM; New York: Macmillan, 1967 (Macmillan paperback edition, with different pagination, 1967; also Collins Fontana paperback edition, with somewhat different arrangement). Trans. from *Widerstand und Ergebung* (see *WE* below).

LPPE *Letters and Papers from Prison*, The Enlarged Edition. London: SCM, 1971; New York: Macmillan (paperback), 1972. Trans. from *Widerstand und Ergebung*, Neuausgabe (see *WEN* below).

LT   *Life Together.* London: SCM; New York: Harper & Row, 1954 (pagination differs in U.S. ed.) Also Harper paperback edition 1978, same pagination. Trans. from *Gemeinsames Leben* (see *GL* above).

N   *Nachfolge.* Munich: Christian Kaiser Verlag, 1937. Many later editions; 11th ed., 1976.

NRS   *No Rusty Swords. Letters, Lectures and Notes, 1928-1936.* Vol. I of selections from *The Collected Works of Dietrich Bonhoeffer.* London: Collins; New York: Harper and Row, 1965. Revised translation, paperback edition, same pagination: London: Collins, 1970;

WCOA Smith, Ronald Gregor, ed. *World Come of Age.* Philadelphia: Fortress Press; London: Collins, 1967.

Cleveland: Collins-World, 1977. Trans. from *Gesammelte Schriften* (see GS above).

PG   *Prisoner for God.* New York: Macmillan, 1954 (see above under *LPP*).

SC   *Sanctorum Communio.* Berlin: Trowitzsch, 1930. Reprinted Munich: Christian Kaiser Verlag, 1954 (pagination differs). Third German edition 1960 (restoring some original material omitted from previous printings), the basis of the English translation. Fourth German edition, 1969.

SF   *Schöpfung und Fall.* Munich: Christian Kaiser Verlag, 1933. Fourth German edition, 1958. Reprinted, together with *Versuchung*, 1968.

T   *Temptation.* London: SCM; New York: Macmillan, 1955. Trans. from *Versuchung* (Munich: Christian Kaiser Verlag, 1953).

WE   *Widerstand und Ergebung. Briefe und Aufzeichnungen aus der Haft.* Munich: Christian Kaiser Verlag, 1951. Many later editions, including revisions and additions (see especially *WEN* below).

WEN   *Widerstand und Ergebung . . . ,* Neuausgabe. Munich: Christian Kaiser Verlag, 1970.

WF   *The Way to Freedom. Letters, Lectures and Notes, 1935-1939.* Vol. II of *The Collected Works of Dietrich Bonhoeffer.* London: Collins; New York: Harper and Row, 1966. Paperback edition, same pagination: London: Collins, 1972; Cleveland: Collins-World, 1977. Trans. from *Gesammelte Schriften* (see *GS* above).

Secondary Sources

DB   Bethge, Eberhard. *Dietrich Bonhoeffer. Theologe, Christ, Zeitgenosse.* Munich: Christian Kaiser Verlag, 1967. 2nd ed., 1968; 3rd ed., 1970.

DBET   Bethge, Eberhard. *Dietrich Bonhoeffer. Man of Vision, Man of Courage.* London: Collins; New York: Harper and Row, 1970; paperback, same pagination, 1977. Trans. (abridged) from *DB* (see above).

MW   *Die Mündige Welt.* Munich: Christian Kaiser Verlag, 1955-1963 (Vols. I-IV), 1969 (Vol. V).

ThDB   Feil, Ernst. *Die Theologie Dietrich Bonhoeffers. Hermeneutik, Christologie, Weltverständnis.* Munich: Christian Kaiser Verlag, & Mainz: Matthias-Grünewald Verlag, 1971. 3rd ed., 1979.

WP   Fant, Clyde E. *Bonhoeffer. Worldy Preaching* (including trans. of Bonhoeffer's Finkenwalde lectures on homiletics). Nashville: Nelson, 1975.

I.
INTRODUCTION

BONHOEFFER'S ASSERTION OF RELIGIONLESS CHRISTIANITY— WAS HE MISTAKEN?

Eberhard Bethge

THIRTY YEARS HAVE PASSED since the theologian and political prisoner, Dietrich Bonhoeffer, died in Flossenburg.[1] Died, unnoticed, in what was then a little-known concentration camp. Died without the reason or purpose of his death being known to his church. Died without finishing his work and with no inkling of the effect of this unfinished work.

Today it is impossible to overlook the impact of such Bonhoefferian slogans as "costly grace," "religionless Christianity," and "the church for others." More recently, of course, massive criticism has also been leveled. This criticism claims that a surprising revival of the phenomenon of religion, both in theory and practice, has refuted Bonhoeffer's once fascinating analysis of a world that is becoming religionless. The revival has taken place at the very heart of technological western Europe and America, supported by an unprecedented facilitation of access to the fullness of the colorful religious life of the East and South. A verdict has quickly been reached that on this point at least Bonhoeffer was in error.

In 1973 the Synod of the German Evangelical Church issued an extensive report on the newly awakened religious movements of the time. Near the end, the author states that "from all indications Bonhoeffer was wrong in his prognosis of a world becoming religionless." The influential American theologian Harvey Cox, who was himself once inspired by Bonhoeffer, says in a recent book that "'religion' is a much more polyglot phenomenon than either its critics or its defenders of the past century supposed, much more complex than I thought during the height of my Bonhoeffer days. Not only is it more complex, it is also more persistent."[2] Contemporary programs of religious education rest almost exclusively on the theology of Paul Tillich. Tillich's positive evaluation of religion and his

3

discovery of it in every culture have proved to be more useful than Bonhoeffer's discovery of liberation from religion. The Christian philosopher of religion has for the moment carried the day against the christocentric theologian. The climate favors those who would gladly evade the critical claim of the phenomenon of Bonhoeffer.

Nevertheless, even if it be granted that the matter has been badly put, the terms "religionless Christianity" and "nonreligious interpretation" stand for facts that cannot be swept under the rug when the vocabulary is rejected. On the contrary, it is my contention that these facts still confront us intact. Harvey Cox and Helmut Aichelin, who made that report to the Synod, sense this clearly. Aichelin concluded his report as follows: "This [i.e., the picture of the religious and philosophical situation of our times] is the hour of Bonhoeffer,...of the Bonhoeffer who wrote concerning the future of the Christian faith: 'We ourselves are totally thrown back again upon the beginnings of understanding'—with all that this implies." Harvey Cox quotes again from Bonhoeffer's famous prison writings of 1944:

> What is bothering me incessantly is the question what Christianity really is, or indeed who Christ really is, for us today. The time when people could be told everything by means of words, whether theological or pious, is over, and so is the time of inwardness and conscience—and that means the time of religion in general. . . . What do a church, a community, a sermon, a liturgy, a Christian life mean in a religionless world? How do we speak of God—without religion, i.e., without the temporally conditioned presuppositions of metaphysics, inwardness, and so on?[3]

Even today Cox can say about these words: "This is still a powerful passage. Just rereading it today speeds my pulse . . . ," and again:

> Since then [i.e., since religion has slowly edged itself back into his thinking] I have never rejected the core of Bonhoeffer. I never will. He was looking for this—a worldly, politically viable, life-affirming expression of Christianity. For him that meant a new form that would leave behind most of what he associated with "religion." He was, and remains, right in his search, mistaken only in his terminology.[4]

What, then, did Bonhoeffer "associate" with religion? What did he really have in mind? And is there a terminology for it that is not problematic?

First, it must be stated firmly that the main theme of Bonhoeffer's life is not the quantitative or statistical role of religion or religionlessness; it is instead the question, Who is Christ for us today? In the recent upsurge of religion, however, religion has become the primary issue and the theme of Christ a subsidiary one, if it has not faded from view altogether. Granted, religious phenomena as such hardly had a place in Bonhoeffer's field of interest. He did little work in the history or sociology or psychology of religion. Today, however, we can hardly ignore these disciplines and we have to study them without being able to count on direct help from Bonhoeffer.

He himself, of course, would never have allowed himself to make his main theme—Who is Christ for us today?—into a subsidiary theme. In his thinking the analysis of religion or religionlessness was a specific tool but not the article on which he was working. Tools are exchanged and sharpened and adapted. This tool—the analysis of religionlessness—helped to bring Bonhoeffer to a better knowledge of Christ and a more concrete relationship with him. This was its function. Whether its rejection today would better serve the primary purpose is very questionable to me. It is more likely that Bonhoeffer's analysis of religionlessness still contains indispensable insights, which Christianity overlooks to its own detriment.

Naturally Bonhoeffer's analysis derives from a specific geographical and cultural framework. We must take a look, then, at the context in which this analytical tool belongs.

We may start with the two complexes that have most persistently impressed themselves on the discussion of Bonhoeffer during the thirty years since his death. The first is his so-called "nonreligious interpretation of the gospel in a world come of age." The second is his political participation in the conspiracy against Hitler.

The first complex, that of nonreligious interpretation, found an enthusiastic reception among the many who were seeking a helpful understanding of the gospel in the post-Enlightenment age without having to disavow (once again) the Enlightenment itself. It awakened mistrust, however, among those who saw in it a blurring of the biblical witness. For them, Bonhoeffer, who had once been a witness of radical Christian discipleship, had begun to tread the precipitous path of accommodation to modernism and was luring many onto this wrong path.

The second complex, that of political resistance, secured for Bonhoeffer a credibility in the East, the West, and the Third World that only a few German Christians have enjoyed and that still works to our advantage. But in this regard, too, he provoked a stubborn mistrust among those who closely guard the boundary between the church and the world, who arouse people's emotions by campaigning against the "politicization of the church," who, armed with the Lutheran doctrine of the two kingdoms, today advocate nonviolence, but have nothing to say about institutional violence.

The two complexes are very closely related even though they have been treated separately in the discussion thus far. They are related as theory is to practice, for in the nonreligious interpretation Bonhoeffer's concern is to understand the claim of Christ on the whole of human life and all its responsibilities, i.e., precisely in its areas of strength and not merely in its weak areas, in the remoter areas of life. The move to political conspiracy was his practical protest against the exclusion of faith from the life-and-death political process of the Germany of his day.

In both complexes, then, Bonhoeffer was fighting against the same concept and practice of Christian faith as a closed province separated from the totality of life. This paralyzing isolation of faith, which Christians had produced or permitted in a troubled history, occupied him for much of his life. For him the main mark of religion, to which faith had been reduced, is the separation in which religion has little contact with the real currents of life in action and guilt, responsibility and failure.

As this type of religion, Christian faith is restricted to "pure inwardness" and a realm of "metaphysics." At one point in his Tegel letters Bonhoeffer uses the concepts of inwardness and metaphysics to define the essence of religion. He thinks that religion as thus understood has had its day, and also that it contradicts everything that the biblical Christ is and does and desires. Christ does not let himself be restricted to reserved provinces of life. In no sense does he merely mediate expansions of consciousness and experiences of infinity—inducing "trips" is the job of religion. Christ hardly wanted to create the church as a stabilizer of the religious and social status quo or as a special department for the marginal zones of human existence. Bonhoeffer often said that he would rather find faith in Christ at the center of life and not on its borders, namely, where it claims, directs, and renews people, not in their weaknesses, but in their strength and responsibility.

A negative concept of religion was one of the tools that Bonhoeffer used to express all this. From the perspective of Christ as the Lord of all life he maintained that religion as he understood it had become a bastion of escape for drop-outs, the most refined of all human means to secure with piety and all kinds of deities the self-affirmation that is not to be secured in any other way.

Bonhoeffer did not invent these ideas. With Karl Barth he developed them at a particular point in the history of German theology. It happened like this. Only in the Enlightenment did religion become the dominant master concept for all manifestations of faith; it does not occur in the Bible. The concept had at that time a polemical and emancipatory character, making possible a detachment from the institutional churches and from allegiance to Jesus of Nazareth, but without entailing the socially disruptive sin of unbelief.

Yet with this movement of emancipation from institution and dogma faith strayed off into private inwardness. Schleiermacher developed religion positively as a "perceiving and feeling of the universe." Marx made private religion negatively into religion as a private concern and developed his criticism of it as a tool of injustice and social control in the hands of the ruling classes. For Freud religion became a symptom of regressive neurosis and a barrier to maturity.

Eventually the philosophical and emotional content of the concept of religion completely displaced that of faith. That is how Bonhoeffer experienced it in his ecclesiastical and theological origins. It was a feeling detached from the world, an individual orientation to the universal order of the cosmos, art, and culture—"cultural Protestantism." A countermove was due. The faith of the Bible and the Reformation could not be "religion" in this sense; it was not at all a private religious matter of individual inwardness.

It is important to note that changing the function of faith into this type of religion ran parallel with the development of political abstinence. As the theological doctrine of the two kingdoms strongly required, this Christian religion almost completely ignored the social questions of the century, gathered recruits for social reaction, and finally under Hitler rejected or neglected political activity in every form.

Karl Barth succeeded more than anyone else in severing Christian faith from this religious embrace. In so doing he adopted to a great extent the criticism of religion developed by Marx and Freud but strengthened and sharpened it in terms of his christocentric theology. He also opened up again for faith the possibility of better recognizing its political responsibility.

Bonhoeffer very early pledged himself to this radical separation of faith and religion, and in his own way he widened the gap. In two early observations he noted the compartmentalizing of religion and the way in which it had dropped out of the world. In an essay in 1932 he wrote:

> We are backwoodsmen or we are secularists. . . . We are backwoodsmen since we learned the evil trick of being religious and even "Christian" at the expense of the earth. . . . We neglect the present, we despise the earth, we are better than it is. . . . A church in the backwoods can be certain of winning over at once all weaklings, all who are glad to be lied to and deceived, all fantastics, all the unfaithful sons of the earth. . . . After all, man is weak, and this weakling called man is susceptible to the religion of the backwoods. . . . Or else we are children of the world. . . . We have fallen victim to secularism, namely, a pious Christian secularism. Not godlessness . . . but the Christian repudiation of God as Lord of the earth.[5]

And in his *Cost of Discipleship* he stated: "Yet the outcome of the Reformation [is] the victory not of Luther's perception of grace in all its purity and costliness, but of the vigilant religious instinct of man for the place where grace is to be obtained at the cheapest price."[6] Cheap grace—that is religion.

Bonhoeffer's independent contribution to the criticism of religion is twofold. First, he increasingly showed that when faith becomes religion it no longer fits the Christian's relation to the world. The person who adheres to Christ accepts, reconciles, and renews the world and will necessarily transcend a narrow interest within the boundaries of the province reserved for religion. Political and critical coresponsibility for and to the world is part of the discipleship of Christ. Along these lines Bonhoeffer still asks those who are enthusiastically reviving religion whether a religion that shuns responsibility or flees from the world has any future. Precisely this kind of religion failed utterly in the days of National Socialism. Harvey Cox does not want his new turning to the phenomenon of religion to be understood in this way either. On the contrary, he has tried to recapture with it the emancipatory elements in the concept of religion when it developed at the time of the Enlightenment. On page after page of his new book he issues warnings against the repressive and regressive dangers that arise with each religious discovery of the modern period.

Second, Bonhoeffer took an important step beyond Barth—and this, of course, is what complicates matters today. He analyzes religion not merely as a phenomenon that unavoidably accompanies faith, and that is naturally for him its perversion, but also as a characteristic element of an epoch that is drawing to a close. Theologians say that he does not treat it merely as a systematic problem, as Barth did, but as a movement in intellectual history as well. Is this where he went astray?

Looking more closely, we find that Bonhoeffer speaks of religion as a specific form of Christianity inherited by us. It developed ecclesiastically and theologically under the conditions of the past century, including the privileged status of the established institutions of that century and their administrators. He speaks, then, of "historically conditioned" and "transitory expressions" of faith, of its "clothing," of the "Western form" of Christianity, which shows itself today to be a "prelude to complete religionlessness."

It was for this reason that in Tegel in 1944 he tried to show how a Christianity of a post-religious if not totally religionless century would come on the scene at the close of a declining and heavily compromised religious epoch. He did not need to give the recipient—myself—any long explanation of the concept of religion he was using, for I, too, had been schooled in Barth's criticism of religion. But his expansion of this criticism was breathtaking.

Ideas of God are tottering: the *deus ex machina*; the God of the gaps; God as a working hypothesis; the God of inwardness. Tottering, too, is a Christianity that makes its own peace with the world by avoiding conflicts and finding for its concerns a special province. A Christianity is coming that critically examines the form that it has taken in hierarchical churches, that attacks offices and institutions that keep people in religious immaturity in order to share rule with the state, that abandons privileges that an emancipated society has long since been unwilling to tolerate any longer. A

Christianity is coming that will participate in God's suffering at the hands of the world and in the suffering of his creatures. This shows that for Bonhoeffer "nonreligious interpretation" is much more than a rhetorical explanation; it is the making of a decisive turn. One can see this in the sketch "Outline for a Book"[7] in the Tegel letters.

Bonhoeffer never thought that the transcending of religion in this sense would mean the end of all piety, liturgy, prayer, and devotional life, as if the practice of a personal relation to Christ and his gospel could fully disappear. He neither eliminated such things in his own life nor did he regard their elimination as the necessary result of a nonreligious interpretation. On the other hand, the form and supports of the life of faith would have to change in such a way as to take man seriously in his coming of age and to foster rather than thwart his emancipation with Christ for personal responsibility and actualization, the outworking of Christ's liberating power being man's own free decision "to live and suffer for others." Bonhoeffer's precise formulation is as follows: "a nonreligious interpretation of the biblical message in a world come of age." The most important implication of this expression is that through Christ we arrive at a free decision to be for others.

Not every modern rediscoverer of religion will want to go back behind this formula of liberation for himself and for others. Harvey Cox, for example, takes great pains to distinguish between repressive and liberating religion. For this reason he does not take issue with the substance of what Bonhoeffer says, but simply states that his "terminology" is "mistaken." But this terminology has a specific meaning in our Western tradition; it is hard, in fact, to replace it. I have never found anyone who has formulated the matter better than Bonhoeffer, i.e., in an equally demanding way.

To sum up, Bonhoeffer believed that Western religion (he did not speak of other religions) was reaching its end. Theologically he came to this conclusion in the name of the suffering and sympathy-creating Christ. Intellectually he did so as he wrestled with the consequences of the Enlightenment. For he was of the opinion 1) that medieval metaphysics, which had molded ideas of God and the hierarchy, was out of date with its basic concept of tutelage; 2) that the time of inwardness, which until now had almost exclusively influenced hymn-books, sermons, and the devotional life, but also killed off responsibility for the world, was now over; and 3) that the compartmentalizing of the Christian faith, which had domesticated it under the interdict of religion, would no longer be accepted. Harvey Cox, it is true, breaks a lance for a new "inwardness," but does he not mean by this something similar to what Bonhoeffer allows for either as maturity or as the undemonstrative devotional life that he twice describes as "arcane discipline"? Bonhoeffer did not live long enough to explain himself more clearly on this matter.

In conclusion we ask again whether his thesis is not still sound and only his terminology incorrect. Wilhelm Dantine, an Austrian Lutheran, wrote in the German periodical *Evangelische Kommentar*: "Not a few are trying to take refuge again in the many offerings of a world-renouncing religion that are all characterized by a lack of any ultimate meaning in their calling and work."[8] Cox, too, addresses the danger of dropping out, "the danger of a new quietism, a unilateral retreat from the kneel-in to the lotus position, from the picket line to the self-awareness group."[9] Such statements have an authentic Bonhoefferian ring. And when Cox summarizes his book in the thesis that the sickness of our time does not lie in the movement toward inwardness but in its disappearance, he may well be recalling that Bonhoeffer recommended those who cry out on behalf of the Jews to sing Gregorian chants as well, that he himself had times in which he sang many Gregorian chants, and that he had a high regard for this practice and did not describe it negatively as "religious." Today the time has certainly come to recapture the sovereign purposelessness of praising God.

Nevertheless, the essential elements in Bonhoeffer's analysis seem to me to be as true and valid as ever they were. Bonhoeffer is right to believe that a new epoch is starting for Christianity under the painful and humbling experiences of loss. The church and theology are ill-advised if they try to find in the greatly exaggerated revival of religion an excuse to evade once again the long delayed consequences of Bonhoeffer's announcement of a fundamental turn for Christianity.

Or are we already on the point of being persuaded that Bonhoeffer's analysis of religion and of other issues is off the mark? A newly revived orthodoxy and a newly awakened pietism are falling victim to the old sin that Bonhoeffer placed under the judgment of religion, namely, that of renewing "the—relatively mild—peace dictated by the world in the conflict between the church and the world"—a peace that (in the words of E. Feil) "Barth renounced, and the renewal of which Bonhoeffer considered out of the question."[10]

This may mean, however, that Bonhoeffer's mistake does not lie in his analysis of the religionlessness of our world; it may lie instead in his assumption that after what it experienced in the thirties the church could not really go back again to that well-regulated and restrictive peace with contemporary society. All the newly revived studies, experiments, needs, and satisfactions of religion do not refute Bonhoeffer (he finally finds a place for them in man's right to his maturity). The new unpolitical or apolitical peace of the churches with contemporary society, whether easily negotiated or won with difficulty, but either way carefully safeguarded on both sides—this constitutes a more powerful refutation, refuting as it does his optimistic assessment of the capacity of the churches for renewal during the last thirty years after their compromising catastrophe.

It may be, then, that Bonhoeffer's analyses—or those that others after him have developed and modernized—are not behind us but still before us.

Notes

1 The substance of this essay was given as an address on April 9, 1975 in commemoration of the thirtieth anniversary of Bonhoeffer's death.
2 *The Seduction of the Spirit* (New York, 1973), p. 141.
3 *LPPE*, pp. 279f. (*Seduction*, pp. 126f.)
4 *Seduction*, pp. 127f.
5 *GS*, III, 270f.
6 *CD* (London, 1959), p. 41.
7 *LPPE*, pp. 380ff.
8 January 1975, p. 17.
9 *Seduction*, p. 221.
10 *Stimmen der Zeit*, 10 (1974), 685.

II.
THEOLOGICAL METHOD—
HERMENEUTIC

THE FORMS OF JUSTIFICATION: ON THE QUESTION OF THE STRUCTURE IN DIETRICH BONHOEFFER'S THEOLOGY

Hans Pfeifer

A NUMBER OF YEARS after Hanfried Müller's *Von der Kirche zur Welt* was published,[1] Eberhard Bethge published his biography of Bonhoeffer,[2] and Ernst Feil published a presentation of his theology.[3] The latter two books represent important interpretive treatments of the life and work of Bonhoeffer. They attempt to portray the interrelationship of theology and practical action in Bonhoeffer's life and work, and give ample proof of it.

My goal in this essay is much more limited.[4] I intend to concentrate on the question of the immanent structure of Bonhoeffer's writings, which is really only half the picture. I am proceeding on the assumption that certain characteristics of Bonhoeffer's theology can only be understood if one pays attention to the core of his thinking. Defining that core is difficult insofar as Bonhoeffer's self-understanding cannot be allowed to remain unquestioned. The difficulty of defining that core will come as no surprise to those who are aware of the broad range of Bonhoeffer's theological and philosophical interests. Despite his close relationship with Karl Barth, his thinking never moved in the confining channels of any given school of theology. Bonhoeffer independently chose and assimilated concepts from many sources. Thus he was never a systematic theologian in the usual sense and was not sure of his own identity. However, there are certain continuous elements that determine his theological work. This I will attempt to show in this essay.

Paul Lehmann has defined Bonhoeffer's *Ethics* as an ethics of discipleship. He was thereby adopting a concept of Bonhoeffer's theology of which Bonhoeffer himself was somewhat critical, and it happens that most scholars are in agreement with Bonhoeffer in this regard. Nevertheless, there is good reason for Lehmann to point out that Bonhoeffer's ethics, like his entire theology, can only be properly understood when viewed as a new—though sometimes rather unconscious—interpretation of the doctrine of sanctification and justification.[5]

A survey of some of the basic terms characteristic of Bonhoeffer's theological ethics will clarify this matter. Discipleship, shaping, deputyship, preparation of the way, surrender—all these terms have this in common: they speak of an action of mankind that is not determined by the will of the active person himself but has its roots outside the doer. No other current ethical concept goes as far as Bonhoeffer's ethics in trying to avoid any trace of synergism. And when Bonhoeffer later criticized his own concept of discipleship, it was because the idea of discipleship still includes an element of human self-realization.

The Reformers' principle of justification was so basic and important to Bonhoeffer that it became the central focus of his anthropology and his ethics. The reason a new interpretation of justification could have such tremendous significance for Bonhoeffer's theology was that it was closely interrelated with his concept of God. The young scholar had already given predominant significance to the idea that God is immanent in Christ and that all other determinations of God, by way of contrast, are rather meaningless. His trinitarian beliefs could be framed in a this-worldly manner because they made use of the economic doctrine of the Trinity found in Hegel and some of the early church fathers. Similar observations could be made about his Christology, as we shall see later. In view of the fact that Bonhoeffer understood God's existence more and more as immanent or—as we could better express it—this-worldly, his interest in concrete forms of an existence determined not by the ego but by Christ is entirely understandable. In such forms of existence lies the peculiar unity of concrete revelation as well as the basis for justification. For Bonhoeffer, subsequent forms of Christian life have been the church, the "thou" (the Brother), Christ, the reality of the world, the basic terms of *Ethics* mentioned above, and probably also "coming of age," of which he speaks in his letters from prison.[6]

To demonstrate the forms of justified existence as Bonhoeffer understood them, it is necessary to trace the development of Bonhoeffer's concept of God. In the process some misunderstandings can be corrected. Bonhoeffer's talk of "the end of religion" must then indeed be understood in a radical sense as the end of a time in which God can be thought of as existing as such outside the world. This idea was probably communicated to Bonhoeffer through the Ritschlian school, although he did not conceive of Christian action as self-controlled. The Christian lives and acts out of his relationship to the living Christ, who is always man's opposite and limitation, according to Bonhoeffer. The Christian who has come of age is not a person who acts in place of the dead God. His decisions and will are enlisted by the coming Christ. In his knowledge of the ultimate, the

Christian is free to prepare the way in the penultimate. The Christian acts in the present, representing the coming Christ who has a claim on the present because the future belongs to him.

Thus Bonhoeffer's *Ethics* ultimately goes beyond the question of command or order or natural theology and ultimately also beyond the possibility of a situation ethics. In formal terms it comes close to Ritschl's ethics of the kingdom, but Bonhoeffer differs greatly from Ritschl regarding content by insisting on the reality of Christ's future as the basis of ethics.

I. The Contingency of Revelation and the Problem of the Reality of Justification

1. The Young Bonhoeffer's View of Luther's Concept of God

Throughout his life Bonhoeffer considered himself a Lutheran and viewed Luther as the most important theological authority next to the New Testament.[7] Holl and Seeberg, two of his teachers in Berlin, were therefore important to him above all in their interpretation of Luther. Both held the view that Luther understood God as *actus purus,* and both were likewise of the opinion that Luther understood *actus purus* as pure activity.[8] Bonhoeffer adopted this concept of God and its interpretation and even defended it as one of the propositions attached to his dissertation.[9] This view was significant for his concept of revelation.[10] In *Act and Being,* however, he attempted to create a broader basis for substantiating this concept of God by drawing on the notion of being as well as the notion of activity. In that book, he interprets activity and being as continuity and contingency.[11]

Parts of a surviving seminar paper by Bonhoeffer will be presented here as we seek a better insight into his perception of Luther's concept of God. The paper deals with Luther's concept of the Holy Spirit. It states, among other things, that for Luther the problem of the Spirit does not originate in the metaphysical question of the Trinity, as it does in Scholasticism.[12] He argues that for Luther, "faith and the awareness of conscience are seen as essentially belonging together, which invalidates any purely metaphysical-dogmatic reasoning."[13] Man's first encounter with the Holy Spirit, Bonhoeffer goes on to explain, is a confrontation with the judgment of the law, which he experiences as something opposing his own will.[14] Luther speaks of the ethical will that confronts man in such a case as the Holy Spirit "in his majesty."[15] According to Luther, this is an inadequate way of speaking of the Holy Spirit, for "the Holy Spirit acts not only as a 'gift' but also as a *deus,* as majesty."[16] Bonhoeffer continues: "In the notion of *majestas,* the Holy Spirit and God coincide for Luther."[17] The nature of faith, he says, is determined in the same way for Luther because he is able to equate *fides* and *Spiritus Sanctus.*[18] The Spirit provides not metaphysical but ethical judgment.[19]

At the end of the paper, Bonhoeffer discusses the question of Luther's teachings with regard to the Trinity. Luther, he argues, was interested in God's ultimate inscrutability, which was why he advocated an economic doctrine of the Trinity. "God the Father in his majesty sends the Son and the Holy Spirit as gifts (in the broader sense of the word) whose efficacy ends, however, with the end of the world, because in the *status perfectionis* we need neither Word nor Sacrament."[20] This paper clearly reveals that Bonhoeffer had adopted Holl's interpretation of Luther to a considerable extent.[21] This comes through above all in the insistence that Luther advocated an economic doctrine of the Trinity. Bonhoeffer here attributes his own preference for an economic doctrine of the Trinity to Luther.

2. Religion and Justification: Barth's Influence on Bonhoeffer as a Student

Bonhoeffer's first written encounter with Barth's theology occurs in a seminar paper he prepared as a student,[22] where he states: "The Scriptures are now the only source of revelation for us," for the simple reason that God speaks through them.[23] Any interpretation must take this principle as its point of departure because it is the only criterion appropriate for understanding Scripture.[24] All other criteria that have been applied to Scripture come to it from the outside. They fail to account for man's relationship to God because they overlook the *finitum incapax infiniti.*[25] Mankind cannot apprehend God unassisted; he cannot even apprehend God's revelation when confronted with it.[26] Like can only be known by like, which means that God can only be known by the Holy Spirit.[27] It is only possible for mankind to apprehend God if the Holy Spirit creates an organ for knowledge of God—faith.[28] The thought that man relies entirely on God's revelation for his knowledge of God because the finite cannot apprehend the infinite, and relies entirely on the gift of the Holy Spirit because God can be apprehended only through the Holy Spirit, appears repeatedly in the papers Bonhoeffer wrote as a student.[29] The thesis the young Bonhoeffer takes up and affirms, then, is none other than the cardinal thesis of Barth's theology.

At this stage Bonhoeffer gives every appearance of being an out-and-out Barthian. There is hardly a trace of critical reserve vis-à-vis Barth in the papers he wrote before his doctoral dissertation.[30] This is apparent, for example, in his readiness to concur with Barth that it is impossible to demonstrate the new ego.[31] This, in fact, is the very point that becomes the object of Bonhoeffer's criticism of Barth in *Act and Being.*[32] But the cardinal points of Barth's teachings on revelation are to be found in Bonhoeffer's student writings. He concurs with Barth in maintaining that the prerequisite for the doctrine of God's Word is the recognition of the infinite difference between man and God and of the consequent inability of

man to apprehend God in even the most imperfect way. Like Barth, Bonhoeffer uses the term "religion" to sum up mankind's attempt to apprehend
God without revelation. The reality of revelation and the indemonstrability
and inaccessibility of the new ego that has partaken of revelation are necessary constituents of the doctrine of God's Word, for it is only in such a
way that God's absolute sovereignty can be kept inviolate. Bonhoeffer
consequently affirms that man's reception of the Word is to be considered
the work of the Holy Spirit alone.[33]

3. Christ as the One and Only God: The Continuing Influence of Ritschl's Theology on Bonhoeffer's Concept of God

Since the young Bonhoeffer was under the influence of Barth's concept of
revelation, it is only natural that his concept of God should also change
considerably. The most important conclusion he reached in this regard was
his abandonment of the theory that the doctrine of the Trinity made a
division into three historical periods possible by virtue of the economy of
the three persons of the Godhead. The revelation in Christ had become so
important to him that he was inclined to interpret God's post-Easter activity
Christologically rather than pneumatologically.[34] Whereas Hegel[35] and subsequently Seeburg[36] regarded the church community as the abode of the
Holy Spirit, Bonhoeffer Christologically transformed this statement into
the proposition that formed the basic thesis for which he argued in his
doctoral dissertation, namely, that the church is Christ existing as community.[37] However, Bonhoeffer's critical dissociation from Harnack was
also a factor here, for it made any interpretation of church history as a
specific action of God untenable for him.[38]

A further indication that Bonhoeffer wished to interpret God's post-
Easter activity Christologically is the fact that for a long time he was at a
loss as to how to interpret "Christ in heaven." The second proposition
Bonhoeffer defended in his doctoral examination states that there is an
unresolved antithesis between Christ in heaven and Christ in the congregation.[39] In Act and Being, however, he is more careful in his formulation.[40]
In his Christology lecture and in his sermons, Bonhoeffer finally found a
way of interpreting the concept of Christ in heaven, namely, as Christ
ruling the world.[41] But in doing so, he discovered the possibility of construing this concept as a statement about the "this-worldliness" of Christ
after Easter, as the passages in question clearly indicate.[42]

In making this move, Bonhoeffer was well aware of a certain difficulty
that could not arise for Seeberg and Holl. The latter two saw no problem
in assuming the existence of God per se above and beyond his historical
acts; they were well able to distinguish an activity of God as his being from
the individual acts.[43]

It is significant that in *Act and Being* Bonhoeffer accuses both Barth and Seeberg of being unable to prevent their concept of God from breaking down when confronted with God's actual existence.[44] He therefore considered it necessary to pose the question of God's continuity anew: Assuming that God's activity consists in his acting in his own revelation, how can he be considered to be continuous? Bonhoeffer's answer, which we will consider at length later, was as follows: He is continuous in nonidealist, transsubjective forms of revelation. At this stage it is sufficient to point out that in his criticism of metaphysics, Bonhoeffer was guided by Ritschl's personal view of a metaphysical concept of God. Any existence of God beyond his historical activity Ritschl had dismissed as metaphysics. At first this led Bonhoeffer to consider the existence of Christ in the church as incompatible with his existence in heaven. It also led him to develop his own concept of God's transcendence: God's transcendence—or more precisely, his being *extra me*—cannot be understood transcendentally in the normal sense but can only be seen in personal terms as an encounter in the "thou" of one's fellow men.[45] Even in prison Bonhoeffer was able to say: "The transcendental sphere is not infinitely remote but immediately at hand."[46]

Although Bonhoeffer knew that he had been influenced by Ritschl's theology while he was a student in Berlin,[47] later he did not seem aware of the origin of his thinking. Indeed, he tried to derive his concept of God from Luther. In a lecture given in America, he presented his most detailed account of his interpretation of Luther's question of principle. In this lecture he claimed: "Luther recognized the insufficiency of the scholastic form of thinking for an interpretation of the facts of revelation. He sees in the notion of substance a great danger in making revelation static and depriving it of its actual livingness."[48] This clearly indicates that he believed he had found evidence—whether rightly or wrongly is beside the point—for Ritschl's denial of the being of God per se in Luther's writings. It is significant that some of Luther's statements that were originally of a more pastoral character became theological statements of principle in Bonhoeffer's interpretation. He liked to appeal to Luther, for example, in his interpretation of the ascension as a statement about God's proximity.[49]

Bonhoeffer often quoted Luther's statement, "God 'is' in faith alone."[50] He saw this statement, together with another statement to the effect that God is actually present in the sermon, as an indication that Luther viewed God as existing only in revelation.[51] This becomes even clearer in his report on his studies in the United States, where he writes that the pragmatism of William James is reminiscent of Luther's transcendentalism.[52] When Luther says that God is close to man—and not far away from him—Bonhoeffer takes this to mean that God is only God in his revelation and does not exist elsewhere per se. Even while he was in prison, he claimed to find support in Luther's writings for his statements about the "this-worldliness" of God.[53]

Bonhoeffer elaborated this interpretation of Luther independently; it went far beyond anything that Holl and Seeberg saw in Luther. In fact, Bonhoeffer explicitly distinguished between Holl's interpretation of Luther and his own, and he agreed with Gogarten when he criticized Holl for underestimating the importance Luther attached to Christ.[54] Therefore, it is not quite sufficient to say, as both Bethge and Moltmann do, that Bonhoeffer's Christology "was fundamentally rooted within the Lutheran Christology of condescension."[55] This assertion is defensible only if it is understood that Bonhoeffer interpreted the concept of condescension from an entirely Ritschlian point of view.

4. The This-worldliness of Revelation

Earlier we saw that Bonhoeffer was unable to accept the existence of God apart from revelation. If we are to understand his concept of revelation, we must take this conviction as our point of departure, for it was at this juncture that he felt obliged to differ from Barth. In *Act and Being,* in a critical commentary on Barth's theology, he writes:

> In revelation it is not so much a question of God's freedom beyond revelation, that is, of his eternal abiding in himself and of his aseity; rather, it is a question of God's emergence in revelation, of his given Word, of the covenant in which he has bound himself, and of his freedom, which is most strongly evidenced in his voluntarily having bound himself to man in history, in his having placed himself in the service of mankind. God is not free from man but for man.[56]

According to Bonhoeffer, Barth had expressed his concept of revelation too formally and had not given enough consideration to the fact that revelation represents a specific active relationship of God to man, namely, the justification of the latter.[57] Revelation must be interpreted in the light of justification—and not vice versa. From this point of view, the manifest God is defined as being *pro me.* To an ever-increasing extent, Bonhoeffer understood the *pro me* of God as the this-worldliness of God. Therefore, he stressed that Christ is actually present, *hic et nunc.*[58]

Bonhoeffer was capable of attaching great importance to the role of Jesus on earth. In passing I might mention that he criticized the Apostles' Creed for not paying enough attention to Jesus' life on earth. A lecture on Jesus Christ which Bonhoeffer gave in Barcelona in 1928 can, in fact, be regarded as an early contribution to the question of the historicity of Jesus Christ, which has become the subject of much controversy again in recent years.[59] A sermon he preached in Barcelona is characteristic of his thinking at the time. In it he says: "If you want God, restrict yourself to the earth. . . . Why minister to time? Because only in time can you find God and eternity."[60] He who flees the present flees the hour of God. God loved the earth and "made us out of earth. He who is our Father gave us the earth as our mother."[61] "God loves us in our time; in the very act of clinging to our mother earth and to her gifts in solidarity with the human race even in its frailty, in brotherly companionship with our fleeting and feeble time— God wants us."[62] Then he quotes the legend of Antaeus, commenting that "this legend of the giant Antaeus is extremely profound" because it expresses the thought that anyone who loses contact with the earth loses his strength.[63] Although this sermon reveals that while he was in Barcelona Bonhoeffer was strongly influenced by Nietzsche's philosophy (an influence which was not just temporary, according to Müller),[64] the decisive reason for the heavy emphasis on the this-worldliness of revelation is the nature of revelation itself. Revelation is not an encounter with the eternal and unattainable God; rather, it is an encounter with the God who establishes an active relationship to me personally in this world. God manifests himself by bestowing a new existence on me.

To sum up, we could say that Bonhoeffer, coming from the Ritschlian school, denied the existence of God apart from his actions; that is to say, he denied the existence of God per se. Influenced by Barth, he then interpreted God's actions as revelation in Christ. The problem he then faced was the question of the continuity of revelation, since justification by grace alone can only be maintained as long as the continuity of revelation is maintained. This view of Bonhoeffer remains to be discussed below.

II. Idea and Reality as a Theological Problem

1. Faith and Thought

Pannenberg is correct in pointing out that Bonhoeffer gave the problem of knowledge a great deal of attention.[65] Bonhoeffer repeatedly considered the significance of the doctrine of justification for theological epistemology. The subject he chose for his lectures at the University of Berlin testifies to this.[66] There is a statement of Luther that became extremely important for him in connection with this problem: Man is characterized by a *cor curvum in se*.[67] In Luther's writings this passage means that the totality of sin consists in man's inability to recognize his own egocentricity, which results in his being unaware that even when he enjoys God he does so for his own sake and not because of any awe of God. What these words meant primarily to Bonhoeffer is that man's self-conceit causes him to restrict everything—even God—to his own consciousness. Although this can perhaps be seen as purely purposive from the point of view of creation,[68] it is greatly affected by the fall into sin because the ego takes the place of the *extra me*. Self-reflection replaces thought.[69] From this point on, thought and faith are distinct from each other. Faith is the *actus directus*—pure contemplation of Christ.[70] Since the fall, thought has no longer been capable of this, for it shares in the boundlessness of sinful existence. Thought is boundless in sin because it is now only capable of being directed at objects that are immediately accessible to consciousness, which means that it remains within the realm of the possible. In spite of this, however, there is no point whatsoever at which thought cannot transcend its limitations.[71] Thought is given the ability to transcend all limitations by the ego of sin, which sets itself up as the source of thought and continually provides thought with further validity.[72]

It was for this reason that Bonhoeffer's criticism of idealism was so severe: he objected that idealism provided an immanent concept of the Spirit,[73] which meant that ultimately the whole of existence was supposed to be contained in human consciousness. For Bonhoeffer, then, idealism was the prime example of thought in sin. Its concept of the Spirit maintains the absolute value of the ego.[74] In idealism, thought overcomes the opposition of subject and object in the unity of the idea and is therefore able to prevail against everything that limits thought.[75] Thought is capable of conceiving of the absolute and therefore sets itself up as the absolute.

Bonhoeffer does not consider this to be a failing that is peculiar to idealism; rather, it is the fate of all theoretical philosophy.[76] More recent philosophy also overcomes the borderline situations of life by means of thought. For example, thought can undertake to overcome death, as Heidegger has shown.[77] Bonhoeffer was convinced that the physical limitations of life did not have to be an insuperable barrier to thought.[78]

It is here, however, that Bonhoeffer sees the proof that thought, together with the whole of existence, is sinful.[79] Even *ratio* is *in se ipsam incurva*.[80] On the other hand, sin has the effect of causing thought to be mistaken in its understanding of reality.[81] Thought is not capable of properly apprehending God, because it identifies him with the ego; nor is it capable of understanding the reality of creation and sin. It cannot recognize that it was created itself. In thought, reality becomes merely a possibility and ceases to have any ultimate validity. Expressed theologically, this means that in thought nothing can exist *extra me*. In this regard, thought is recognized by man as an attempt at self-justification and must be altered accordingly if it is to be used in theology. Since man's salvation is to be found outside himself in Christ, while thought, on the other hand, remains completely confined to the ego, theology has to guard against allowing its subject to turn into a mere product of thought. Theology is concerned with the reality of God—not with ideas.[82] Here Bonhoeffer, in his own way, has combined Ritschl's demand for nonmetaphysical theology with Barth's conception of theological thought as thought a posteriori.[83] For Bonhoeffer, the point the two have in common is their refusal to regard the subject of theology as something that can be analyzed intellectually in an a priori manner. Thinking is inadequate to the subject of theology, which, in any case, is not intended to be considered intellectually.[84]

The consequence of this conclusion for Bonhoeffer is that, in theology, thought has to refrain from seeking understanding and a grounding in terms of itself.[85] Once revelation is accepted as a reality that is and remains *extra me,* it must have methodological significance for thought. Thought must allow itself to be limited externally, that is, by a μετάβασις εἰς ἄλλο γένος.[86] Bonhoeffer is able to say that thought must be prepared to make a *sacrificium intellectus.*[87] In his Christology lecture[88] he demonstrates his conception of thought that waives its own potential and thus renounces the category of potentiality itself. The first sentence is characteristic: "The doctrine of Christ begins in silence."[89] Thought that begins in silence does not begin with itself.[90] In his description of Christ as the antilogos who cannot be fitted into man's system of the logos, he brings the incommensurability of Christ and thought to expression.[91] From this it follows that certain questions cannot be asked in theology—above all, the "what" question and the "how" question.[92]

The "how" question now becomes the "who" question.[93] Bonhoeffer was of the opinion that when thought was limited in this way, it could no longer reduce Christ to an idea.[94] This alone can preserve the *extra nos.* The contrast of the finite with the infinite, on the other hand, is insufficient to preserve the *extra nos,* since thought has infinite potential and can therefore conceive the infinite. Genuine transcendence must exist outside consciousness since only in that way can it have contingency and continuity.[95] A self-imposed delimitation of competence on the part of thought vis-à-vis God's transcendence will not suffice, for such a delimitation is ultimately based on thought itself and not on God.[96] Here again we see how Ritschl's criticism of metaphysics had an effect on Bonhoeffer. Statements describing a theological object as infinite or eternal are insufficient for the comprehension of true transcendence. Only the concrete person of Jesus Christ, about whom the question "Who is he?" can be asked, is *extra me.*

It can now be shown that this was exactly what Barth did not think. In a series of lectures at the Hochschulinstitut in Dortmund, Barth spoke on the basic philosophical problems in theology.[97] His point of departure in the lectures was that thought is subject to a twofold definition that it will ultimately always have to face.[98] The twofold definition stems from the fact that thought always presupposes itself and its object. How it is to be understood depends on whether greater importance is attached to the object of thought or to the powers of cognition inherent in thought. By using the terms "destiny" and "idea" to designate these two possibilities,

Barth intended to bring thought and life into a certain relationship. According to Barth,[99] the terms used to describe the contrast could just as well be reality and truth, concrete and abstract, existence and thought, nature and spirit, realism and nominalism. In the course of the lectures Barth himself substituted the term "reality" for "destiny,"[100] and "truth" for "idea."[101]

In defining the relationship between the two concepts, Barth shows that he is a philosophical disciple of critical philosophy. The relationship of reality to truth is such that the latter has the function of criticizing and correcting the former.[102] The idea, admittedly, is also criticized by reality, but this criticism is only applicable to the idea in the sense of absolute idealism. Barth describes thought as something that "reveals itself in its originality and superiority in comparison to mere existence."[103] He maintains: "Idealism is the discovery of the correlation between thought and truth, the discovery of the creative logos as the source of the correlation between subject and object."[104] Note that *this* philosophy and *this* thought process have to be corrected in the light of reality, for it has been stated that theology cannot permit God and idea to be identified with each other.[105] This criticism, unlike Bonhoeffer's, does not apply to all thought and philosophy; it applies only to the philosophies that attempt to enclose God in a system.[106] In other words, it is a criticism of absolute idealism. According to Barth, thought is entirely capable of setting itself bounds, of preventing itself—by means of critical reserve—from identifying God with the idea, with philosophical truth.[107]

Thereby thought is unreservedly assigned a decisive function, namely, that of criticism. Knittermeyer was correct in claiming in his review of *Act and Being* that Barth was a critical theologian.[108] Barth was not conscious of the fact that critical philosophy has a system, even though it stops short of a final identification of reality and truth. It seems to me that Bonhoeffer had a clear view of matters when he applied theological criticism not only to thought within idealism but to all thought. Barth's relatively unquestioning acceptance of thought[109] flies in the face of the truth that man in his totality is a sinner and therefore sins also in his thought. True, Barth does not equate God's truth and reality with man's truth and reality, but this limitation on his part does not lead to any particular criticism of thought. Thought which harbors a critical reservation about identifying this world's reality with truth is, as such, suitable for theology. Critical philosophy, then, clearly becomes a prerequisite for theology.

Despite all that has been said above, I believe that Bonhoeffer viewed himself as following Barth, particularly in his criticism of thought as such. His criticism of thought stems from revelation *extra me.* Thus he is able to point to Barth's own theological approach and demonstrate an inconsistency in the methodological foundations of his theology.

2. The Historicity of Man and the Question of Continuity

The Christian doctrine of man cannot do without terms that refer to mankind as a whole. If creation, sin, and redemption are illustrated only by means of individual examples, mankind's position with regard to these three basic states cannot be explained satisfactorily. However, if no convincing conceptual proof can be adduced to show that mankind cannot control his own destiny as created being, sinner, or redeemed being, his finite nature is annulled. Not even the philosophy of the I-Thou relationship can avoid this pitfall completely.[110]

This is why Bonhoeffer tried to find terms that apply to man universally. Yet he joined Ritschl and Seeberg in rejecting natural definitions of the human race.[111] If the concept of being is anthropologically founded, the individual assumes a position of secondary importance next to nature as a whole. For Bonhoeffer, however, the individual as an ethical being was intended by God as his counterpart.[112] Statements about human nature are not suitable for giving expression to the individuality of man because they do not explain man's temporality. According to Bonhoeffer, man can only be understood historically. "The *persona* always comes into being and passes away in time."[113] Given this perspective, universal statements about man become especially problematic. If man is seen as coming into being and passing away in time without enjoying a being beyond that, the danger of complete relativism looms large. All statements about man, therefore, seem to be restricted in their applicability to the time and place to which they refer.

Ritschl and Seeberg tried to understand historical continuity as community. "Mankind" is a term that refers not to the species but to the total community of people, some of whom live at one time and many at other times. Ritschl spoke of the kingdom of sin and the kingdom of God,[114] seeing in them the two main communities in which human life can occur. And it was in this connection that Seeberg developed the doctrine of the sociality of man and of the objective intellect.

Bonhoeffer also made his universal statements on man in the form of a doctrine of human communities.[115] The individual necessarily exists in a community. This "existing in" is the basis for all universal statements about mankind; it is as essential to the basic structure of mankind as coming into being and passing away in time. Time, which makes a human being's coming into being and passing away possible, is always qualified as either time of sin or time of Christ. Man lives in either Adam or Christ.[116] For his definition of the essential human communities, Bonhoeffer refers to the fifth chapter of Romans. God sees mankind as one person, as a collective thou in Adam or Christ.

The community has the character of transcendent temporality: "The profoundest significance of the character of transcendent temporality, which the community has in common with history, finds expression in the phrase 'from God to God.' "[117] The reason the community can become the basis for universal statements about man is not that it is possible to demonstrate empirically that the whole of the human race forms one single community but that the race has continuity which is determined by God.

The community has its beginning and end in God himself:

> God does not desire a history of individuals but rather the history of the community of man. However, what God wants is not a community that absorbs the individual but a community composed of individuals. In his eyes, the community and the individual are present in each other at one and the same time. The structure of the collective unit and the individual unit are identical to God.[118]

Bonhoeffer's idea that the community has the same structure in God's eyes as the individuals stems from the doctrine of monads.[119] He is thus able to describe the community as a collective person.[120] This applies in the first place to the original community, but as we shall see below, it also applies to the community in Christ. It even applies to sin, though not in the same way. To begin with, the inevitability of sin results from the fact that the objective intellect of the community of mankind was set on a sinful course by Adam.[121] Since man cannot become a person except in community, he is unable to overcome sin by himself. This is a consequence of his finite nature. The inevitability of sin is confirmed by God himself, however, for God imputes Adam's sin to the whole of mankind.[122] From this it follows that God addresses sinful mankind as thou.[123] The focus of sin is in the community of mankind. Therefore the term "collective person" can properly be applied to the sinful community.[124]

The conception of the sinful community as one person is important for Bonhoeffer above all, because it provides the only reasonable explanation for the doctrine of Christ's substitution.[125] On the one hand, sentence is passed on the whole of mankind in Adam when God reduces the sinful community in Adam to a single thou; on the other hand, redemption through a single person also becomes possible. What redemption consists of is that Christ, as substitute for the whole of mankind, accepts the punishment for the sins of mankind and bears that punishment on the cross.[126] Bonhoeffer refers explicitly to Ritschl's concept of substitution.[127] Christ takes Adam's place, suffers his punishment, and in his stead receives forgiveness for his sins. This substitution has the effect of introducing a new life into history—the life of love.[128] For Bonhoeffer, this is Christ's decisive act. Christ redeems mankind by restoring its community in God.[129] Christ acts primarily for mankind as a whole, and through him mankind in Adam is transformed into mankind in Christ.[130] At this point in the doctrine of redemption, Bonhoeffer's debt to Ritschl and Seeberg comes through most clearly. Christ does not bring salvation to a certain number of individuals; rather, he establishes mankind afresh. The individual is then added by the Holy Spirit.[131]

Christ's act for mankind is interpreted by Bonhoeffer in such a way that the new mankind actually exists in Christ. Contrary to Seeberg, it is reality—and not merely an idea. (There is no place for the concept of potential in theology.[132]) Bonhoeffer explains the continuity of the new mankind in the only possible way, that is, by justification through grace alone.

III. Concrete Forms of Justification

Before dealing with the question whether Bonhoeffer's theses expounded above recur at various stages of his theological development, I will formulate more precisely what was established above and make some generalizations. As we have seen, Bonhoeffer interprets revelation as both immanent and trans-subjective, thereby attempting a compromise between Ritschl and Barth. He characteristically prefers to speak of the worldliness of revelation rather than of its immanent nature. In terms of revelation, "worldliness" means that God "exists" only in the act of revealing himself: "A God who is, is not."[133] But God's act of self-disclosure is not to be understood as an unveiling of his pure being, his aseity, and the revelation of the Trinity as a being; rather, God's self-disclosure reveals God to us as the merciful Father, the justifying Lord, the one who actually renders a sinless life possible.

It was important to Bonhoeffer that systematic statements be excluded from theology, which was what Ritschl had demanded before him.[134] Moreover, Bonhoeffer was not afraid to name and label some concrete forms of revelation, that is, of justification, setting himself off clearly in this regard from Karl Barth, his actual teacher. The decisive factor for Bonhoeffer is not the basic incomprehensibility of revelation but rather the concrete proof that the forms of revelation justify man by taking him from his state of self-determination and placing him in a new, predetermined existence, an existence which he must allow himself to be given and which he is on no account able to create for himself.

Bonhoeffer was not satisfied with merely asserting in principle that revelation is inaccessible, which is what Barth had done. In accordance with the criticism he leveled at thought, he feared that a mere cognitive assertion to the effect that God is inaccessible was in actual fact nothing more than a limit set up within consciousness itself, a limit which could accordingly be changed or manipulated by consciousness. In Bonhoeffer's eyes, Barth's mere assertion of the "fact" of inaccessibility is revelational positivism. Revelation only becomes inaccessible through concrete forms of justification.

This conviction was by no means a constant preoccupation in Bonhoeffer's theological reflections. But it can be shown that in both *The Cost of Discipleship* and the fragments of his *Ethics* this thought continually influenced Bonhoeffer's Christology, his actions during the church struggle, and his ethics. It is for this reason that I speak of a structure in his theology.

1. The Church as the Extra Me of Justification

That the inaccessibility of revelation could be explained anthropologically, in man's historicity, might be considered an obvious approach. The very fact that revelation approaches man in his history means that it confronts him externally as a determining factor. Because of the historical uniqueness of revelation in Jesus Christ himself, man is denied access to it, one would then conclude. But on this point Bonhoeffer thought otherwise. His understanding of history was too much influenced by his abandonment of Harnack's liberal theology. For him history did not represent a true *extra me,* since it was prone to disintegration when exposed to the powers of reason. History only transcends consciousness at the present time. But what is the present time? Bonhoeffer had defined it as the *extra me.* But not even the individual "thou" of the other person is sufficient as a place for God's transcendence. As the inaccessible, God only encounters mankind in the church, the new mankind created by his revelation.[135]

What this statement represented for Bonhoeffer in the first place was the solution to the problem of God's inaccessibility, which had troubled him. However, it was also the reason for his discovering ecclesiology.[136] For him the church became both the answer to the question of the true passivity of the existence of faith[137] and the definition of God's *extra me.* "Thus all previous ideas are included in the concept of the church."[138] Bonhoeffer had learned from Barth that justification by grace alone can only be preserved as long as God's inaccessibility is preserved, which implies, however, a true concept of revelation. In Bonhoeffer's opinion, Barth had not preserved this inaccessibility in his early work because he had not occupied himself enough with the place of God's *extra me.* That place is the church, which must then, of course, be understood as *Sanctorum Communio.* Only in the true concept of communion is it possible to define revelation, justification, and even the true concept of God. Without a doubt, Bonhoeffer was influenced by Ritschl's doctrine of the kingdom of God. Just as Ritschl saw the common purpose of God and mankind in the kingdom of God,[139] the young Bonhoeffer discovered in the church the theological concept that denoted both the existence of revelation and the place of the Christian's new existence. He came particularly close to Ritschl in that he considered God's works to be conceivable only in particular historical forms—not per se.[140]

When Bonhoeffer identifies these forms with the purpose and destiny of mankind accorded to it by God, Ritschl's pattern of thought becomes clearly recognizable.[141] Yet the parallel does not extend beyond the formal framework. Influenced by the emphasis on God's sovereignty in Barth's early writings, Bonhoeffer hesitated simply to equate God's purpose with the purpose of mankind. Without stating anything about God's purpose, Bonhoeffer merely identified the concrete act of God in his revelation with the new existence of man.[142] But in the very act of revelation, God remains inaccessible because he is revealed to man in the form of another person.[143] This made it possible for him to identify God's revelation with man's salvation while retaining God's inaccessibility.[144] That was where Ritschl failed, for he forfeited God's sovereignty by assuming a purpose shared by God and mankind.

2. Christ as Concrete Limit to the Ego

In Bonhoeffer's Christology lecture of the summer of 1933, there is a definite change in his conception of the form of revelation. In the lecture he attempts to develop a Christology to precede ecclesiology. The question as to the form of Christ is still answered ecclesiologically: Christ is manifest in the word, in the sacrament, and in the community.[145] "As a person Christ is present in the church."[146] However, the person of Jesus Christ becomes the object of a special study revealing divine humanity as the special quality of his person.[147] Thus the second main section describes Christ as mediator.[148] Bonhoeffer categorically rejects a metaphysical definition of Christ's divine nature since he sees the divine nature and even God himself as existing within the limits of time and space.[149] Bonhoeffer attaches particular importance to the complete humanity of Christ.[150] The unique quality of this man is on the one hand that he is eternally present[151] and therefore cannot cease to be a person, and on the other hand that he is God for us. In this regard Christ's quality as a person is again decisive, since he can remain inaccessible only by the eternal confrontation with him, which means, however, that he is transcendental.[152]

As a person Christ is *extra me*, that is, God.[153] For Bonhoeffer the decisive criterion for judging something as God is whether it represents a truly unassailable counterpart to mankind. At the same time, however, the *pro me* is based on the *extra me*. This fact is reflected in the arrangement of the lectures. The whole first section consists of two parts dealing with Christ's transcendence and his "worldliness," that is, his soteriological significance,[154] which is all brought together under the heading "Christ in the Present: The *Pro Me*."[155] It is the second section that reveals that Bonhoeffer is trying to extend Christology beyond the bounds of ecclesiology. This section is divided into three parts: 1) Christ as the center of human existence; 2) Christ as the central point in history; and 3) Christ as the central point between God and nature.[156] The part about Christ as the center of human existence is the decisive one. All the statements it contains about the significance of the limits the ego experiences through the "thou," which in *The Communion of Saints* led to the determination of the individual through Christ via the detour of the community and the brother in Christ, are now released from the necessity of this mediation and refer directly to Christ.

Christ is the center of human existence because he restores the original human limitations.[157] The fact that Christ is both the center and the limit at the same time can be explained as follows. Man should not be the center of his own existence; rather, at the center of his existence, where the sinner has his ego, he finds Christ.[158] Thus the original state is restored. It becomes apparent that for Bonhoeffer justification is genuine recreation, as was implied above.[159] In spite of this, however, the church remains the concrete form of Christ; Christ exists for us in the church. In this Christology lecture it becomes much clearer than in Bonhoeffer's earlier writings that a distinction must be made between Christology and ecclesiology, because the former contains more extensive statements and affords the basis for ecclesiology.

3. Reality as the Place of Justification

In spite of what we saw above, Bonhoeffer did not remain satisfied with defining the place of revelation so narrowly. Ever since he had started working on the problems of ethics, he had been searching for a wider concept to affirm the universality of revelation. He found what he was looking for in the concept of reality.[160] In his lectures on the theology of crisis, he says that only a naive, unphilosophical realism could overlook the necessity of interpreting what we mean by "reality."[161] In ethics he had posed the question of what could be meant by a realistic action and had excluded the realism that consists in a servile attitude toward facts,[162] as Nietzsche had expressed it. However, Bonhoeffer was not just concerned with recognizing that the concept of reality poses a problem of comprehension, or that reality cannot be viewed as static because it also contains the element of life, of the dynamic;[163] he was concerned with developing his own theological concept of reality. Reality must be defined Christologically. Any concept of reality that does not include historical revelation is an abstraction in Bonhoeffer's eyes.[164]

Müller and Moltmann, independently of each other, have both pointed out this interpretation of reality in Bonhoeffer's writings.[165] Moltmann examines and delineates Bonhoeffer's concept of reality most thoroughly in the lecture he gave at the Bonhoeffer Conference in 1959.[166] In this lecture he states: "In the face of all tradition, Bonhoeffer undertakes to adopt as his point of departure 'one reality' and 'reality as a whole' as it exists in revelation, from which the miracle of the expiation of the world stems."[167] Again: "The revelation of Jesus Christ is not just revelation of God, of his being and his actions, but is at the same time a revelation of the reality of the world."[168] Moltmann, who was the first to take a closer look at Bonhoeffer's personalistic ideas,[169] accurately describes this concept of reality as personalistic in nature.[170] For Bonhoeffer, it is an essential part of the structure of reality that the world should be accepted—though at the same time changed—by God.[171]

Yet Moltmann has been criticized for his interpretation, and rightly so.[172] When we read his comments carefully, we see that he is unable to avoid positing a pattern of ideas and realization behind Bonhoeffer's concept of reality.[173] He may have seen it that way as a result of the slightly ambiguous statement about "above and below" that Bonhoeffer uses in *Ethics* in developing the concept of mandate.[174] Moltmann presumably understands the terms "above" and "below" as a metaphysical substantiation of the mandates. Barth understood this matter better: he called the expression slightly patriarchal,[175] for he recognized that it referred to an "above and below" purely within the world. Moltmann assumes that the platonic concept of *eidos* was behind Bonhoeffer's thinking.[176] It is therefore understandable that Moltmann should speak of an ahypostatization of the reality of the world in the Incarnation.[177] But by doing so Moltmann misunderstands Bonhoeffer's concept of reality in a crucial way. He distinguishes in the first place between the reality of the world and the extraterrestrial existence of God, and then he goes on to speak of the acceptance of the reality of the world in the Incarnation.

Yet Bonhoeffer does not recognize the existence of the reality of the world outside of revelation. What characterizes his concept of reality is his refusal to attribute the slightest quality of reality to the world without Christ.[178] "The world without Christ is enslaved in its own potential, has no true limit, and can therefore not exist in reality. Revelation, however, puts an end to all potential. . . . Through revelation there can only be a sinful existence or an existence in grace without potentiality."[179] Reality has its true antithesis in potential rather than in the idea; the idea, in essence, is nothing other than a potential of man. At the same time, however, revelation is antithetical to all potential in the world and in man. Revelation and reality are on one side,[180] while potential is on the other side. The potential of the world and of man leads to self-righteousness, while the reality determined by revelation is justification through grace alone.[181]

Reality is man's existence outside himself,[182] and potential is existence stemming from one's own consciousness.[183] In *Creation and Fall* Bonhoeffer shows that man's creaturehood consists in his existence being established outside himself.[184] Sin consists in mankind's taking possession of this *extra me* in order to exist totally in himself. But since man cannot provide his own *extra me,* the fall into sin is final. Only Christ can give him new limits that at the same time restore his creaturehood. Thus Bonhoeffer sees justification as the process of making just, and nothing else; a doctrine of justification as a mere forensic process is impossible from his point of view.[185] But since this event transfers mankind to reality, reality has the character of new existence. Reality is, "from the first beginning to the final end, not a neutral state but that which is real, namely, God become man."[186]

Bonhoeffer's unusually positive evaluation of reality can perhaps be traced back a little further. In his later years this concept probably took the place of a central concept of the Ritschlian school, namely, the concept of the kingdom of God. In Bonhoeffer's lecture "Thy Kingdom Come," it is immediately evident that the concept of the kingdom of God is closely connected to the world.[187] Similarly, in *The Cost of Discipleship* he speaks of the restoration of the world as the content of the kingdom of God.[188]

The restoration of mankind takes place in the church, while the restoration of the world takes place in the kingdom of God.[189] But it can also be shown that the definition of the kingdom of God as the restoration of the earth became important for Bonhoeffer's ethics. Very early, in a seminar paper, he says: "What is the purpose of Jesus' commandment of love? To bring the kingdom of God to earth."[190] Later, in a paper about an ecumenical youth meeting, Bonhoeffer says that in view of the ethical problems to be faced, the old theological question about the concept of the kingdom of God in Continental and Anglo-Saxon theology was of pressing importance.[191] As we saw above, Bonhoeffer resolutely denied that the kingdom of God was created or extended by human moral behavior.[192] The significance of the kingdom of God for ethics lies on another level. The idea that the kingdom of God also grows in history is given a Christological twist by Bonhoeffer. In his ethics he talks about Christ taking shape.[193] This comes about in the disciples' obedience. Though the concept of the kingdom of God becomes much less important in his *Ethics* and is replaced by the concept of reality, it is only possible to understand the singular importance of reality in Bonhoeffer's ethics when we see that "reality" replaced the kingdom of God. Bonhoeffer's ethics is ultimately an ethics of the kingdom of God.

4. Discipleship, Identity, and Deputyship as Forms of Justification in Ethics

The concept of reality presents itself as an important aid to understanding Bonhoeffer's ethics. His ethics is the place to look for a verification of my hypothesis that there is a basic structure in his theology, a structure that runs right through his whole theological work. Bonhoeffer tried to comprehend a Christian act first as discipleship, then temporarily as identity with the working Christ, and finally, above all, as a representative act. What these three concepts have in common is that they endeavor to establish acts beyond the subjectivity of the ethical individual. All three describe a doing that is determined by a relationship to another person (i.e., Christ). Christian ethics is founded on the concrete acts of the living Christ. The Christian approaches this activity by allowing himself to be included in Christ's acts. These acts can then be considered commensurate with reality.

If we seek any proper understanding of Bonhoeffer's work in the field of ethics, we have to bear in mind that we can then concern ourselves only with the question of new Christian obedience. The law is completely abolished for the Christian[194] and has no more significance for his actions. The distinction between the ultimate and the penultimate does not mean the antithesis between law and gospel.[195] This becomes clear as early as the lecture Bonhoeffer gave in Barcelona: "For a Christian the only law that exists is the law of freedom."[196] This sentence is fundamental also for all of Bonhoeffer's later work in ethics.[197]

All he discards later is the idea that the Christian creates his own new decalogues. One of Bonhoeffer's last works was a report on the *primus usus legis*. Its conclusions are extremely reserved, since it was written as a preparatory study for a synodical commission.[198] This makes it even clearer that Bonhoeffer categorically rejects the idea of a *primus usus*. He could no more accept the idea of a *primus usus* than he could accept the concept of the law of creation. The reason for this is that, for a Christian, Christ is the only legislator.[199] A Christian's actions are based on the awareness that God will not only re-create man but also the conditions in which he lives.[200] Christian ethics is only possible because Christ is not only Lord of his church but also Lord of the whole world.[201]

Christian ethics is possible because the kingdom of God will come.[202] One of the titles Bonhoeffer considered for his work on ethics was "Preparing the Way and Entry."[203] But he definitely did not want Christian ethics to be understood in a way that would suggest that it is the Christian's task to bring about the kingdom of God.[204] Rather, ethics presupposes Christ's sovereignty. At this point the concept of reality becomes particularly important. Several times Bonhoeffer defines what is to be understood as reality in the context of Christian ethics.[205] In *Ethics* he also proceeds from the idea that reality is what the sinner lacks: "In his knowledge of good and evil, man does not see himself in the reality of his dependence on the primal source, but in his potential, namely, to be good or evil."[206] Therefore, ethics first of all presumes a complete transformation of mankind; Adam, who has fallen into sin, must be overcome.[207] However, this is not something that still has to occur; it has already taken place on the cross.[208]

For that reason alone, Jesus' commandment makes sense and has concrete form: "Established in the reality of the earth which has been reconciled with God in Jesus Christ, Jesus' commandment gains sense and reality."[209] Reality without Christ is inconceivable: "Our conclusion from this must be that action which is in accordance with Christ is action which is in accordance with reality. This proposition is not an ideal demand, but it is an assertion which springs from the knowledge of reality itself."[210] The statement that the reality of the world consists in its being accepted by Christ is made many times:

> Jesus Christ said of Himself: "I am the life" (John 14:6 and 11:25), and this claim, and the reality which it contains cannot be disregarded by any Christian thinking, or indeed by any philosophical thinking at all. This self-affirmation of Jesus is a declaration that any attempt to express the essence of life simply as life is foredoomed to failure and has indeed already failed.[211]

Again:

> Good is life as it is in reality, that is to say, in its origin, essence and goal; it is life in the sense of the saying "Christ is my life" (Phil. 1:21).[212]

In adopting the reality of the world as its point of departure, Christian ethics is compassionate and takes the world and mankind very seriously.[213] It releases actions from all ideology[214] and thereby frees the world from being terrorized by these ideologies.[215] At the same time, Christian ethics alone contains a promise and proves its worth in times of terror.[216] A further reason for the importance attached to the concept of reality was that Bonhoeffer wanted to keep Christian deeds free from all preconceived opinions and thus make love their sole content.[217]

Christian love of the world is love that accepts the world as it is, thereby corresponding to Jesus' claim to the whole world. Bonhoeffer was supported by experience in this conviction: in view of the "deification of the irrational" under the National Socialist regime, and in view of an ideology that violated reality,[218] "reason, education, humanity, tolerance, and independence" had become allies of the church. In this he saw a return of these values to the primal cause.[219] Christ's claim to sovereignty over the whole world forbids the burdening of Christian ethics with principles, which in any case can be considered to be purely human potential, and his claim binds us to unconditional love.[220]

This does not mean, however, that a Christian is left to decide on his actions by himself. Thoughts of this nature that had been expressed in Bonhoeffer's lecture in Barcelona had been overcome by 1932. Christian action does not stem from the free activity of the ego; it is determined by reality.[221] Just as faith is basically distinct from all other mental activities, Christian action has to be seen as different from all other human activity. Christian actions are never to be understood as the applications of general principles. Bonhoeffer continually complained that ethics was not concrete enough.[222] God's commandment does not leave the process of concretizing rules for action to man; if understood correctly, God's commandment never exists as anything other than instructions for certain specific actions.[223] This means that man is passive with regard to his own actions;[224] he does not control them and has no right to decide for himself. Obedience, like faith, is *actus directus,*[225] that is, both are acts which the ego cannot simply perform of its own accord. Both need certain preconditions. Just as the church is the precondition for the act of faith, reality is the precondition for the act of obedience. If this is accepted, Bonhoeffer's strange statement that reality is the sacrament of ethics can be understood.[226] Bonhoeffer had increasingly stressed the sacraments, especially communion, in their significance for faith.[227]

Because the sacraments are concerned with concrete acts that cannot be questioned by reflection since they are a physical confrontation with the body of Christ, they express most clearly the nature of faith. Bonhoeffer discusses this matter in *The Cost of Discipleship.* In this work the question of how to follow the call, which had a rather concrete meaning for the first disciples, is answered with a reference to baptism.[228] The question can be understood just as concretely today and can be withdrawn just as fully from the doubtfulness of personal decision. At the moment of the completion of the sacrament, the discipleship becomes real. Ethics needs a sacrament in the same way; it needs an act of simple, concrete obedience.[229] Such an act is possible if the Christian makes reality the precondition of his action.

In Bonhoeffer's *Ethics* the concept of identity is used to make possible a more precise characterization of an activity that has been withdrawn from the individual's control.[230] The point of departure is the idea that both ethics and the church are concerned with the occurrence of revelation: "The problem of Christian ethics is the realization of God's reality of revelation in Christ among his creatures, just as the problem of dogmatics is the truth of God's reality of revelation in Christ."[231] In this respect ethics is also concerned with eschatology.[232] In a Christian act, it is a question of Christ's taking shape in the world.[233] The ethical form of Christ in the world is self-representation.[234] Bonhoeffer uses this concept to express Christ's act of expiation;[235] it is not primarily an ethical concept, for representation or deputyship is impossible for mankind. It is only possible when Christ takes shape in our deputyship. "Deputyship, and therefore also responsibility, exists only in the complete submission of one's own life to another person. Only those who are selfless live responsibly, which means only those who live selfless lives."[236] The second part of this quotation is based on the idea that man only finds reality—and with it, Christ—in the act of self-surrender in obedience: "The moment a person accepts responsibility for others—and only by doing so does he exist in reality—the truly ethical situation arises."[237]

Deputyship is of great importance for Bonhoeffer because it makes genuine obedience possible. Christian action must be freed from the subjective decision of the ego; it must be objectively grounded in reality to some extent. A person's actions can only be truly Christian if they are not determined by his own conscience, for the conscience and the knowledge of ethical principles and ethical maxims are susceptible to the arbitrary influence of the ego. According to Bonhoeffer, Christian ethics is based on a transsubjective reality, namely, that of Christ. We can share it for others and in the place of others. The reality in which the Christian acts is defined eschatologically.

A survey of Bonhoeffer's writings from his doctoral thesis to his treatise on ethics, which covers a fifteen-year period, demonstrates that there are certain problems, questions, and conclusions running all the way through. The justification of man, his new life, is based on the idea that the consciousness of the individual is limited from outside. The violation of these limits is the sin of the ego that sees itself as absolute: on this point Bonhoeffer disagrees completely with Tillich. In his theological work and in his activities in the church and the political arena, Bonhoeffer was always concerned to manifest the reality which is prescribed for each person and which makes Christian life possible, and to act in accordance with it. At the outset Bonhoeffer called this reality the *Sanctorum Communio,* in which revelation and justification play an important role. Later, he saw Christ himself as the form of justification. In his work on ethics, Bonhoeffer is able to view reality theologically as the structure of justification. Faith and obedience are the modes of behavior through which humans can share the new existence Christ has brought about in the church and in reality. In this connection, obedience is described as imitation, identity, or deputyship.

For Bonhoeffer, the overlapping contexts in which the Christian finds himself involved are church and reality—not church and society. Yet this position could be fruitfully explored in connection with the problem of church and society, which has considerable relevance for contemporary ethics. The discussion of Bonhoeffer's ethics stagnated for a long time because people were distracted by certain weaknesses in it, like the doctrine of the mandates and the reintroduction of the concept of authority. Much more important is that Bonhoeffer attempted a theological critique of consciousness that led him to formulate a theory of reality.

It is impossible to agree with Bonhoeffer about certain details without arousing suspicion to the effect that one supports a certain ideology. But his ethics is by no means as rigid as Moltmann, for example, believes it is; for the basis on which Bonhoeffer conceives his ethics is transsubjective. Here we have the possibility of a fruitful starting point, but, to my knowledge, very little discussion has taken place about it.

5. Coming of Age: The Actualization of the Christ

Bonhoeffer's preliminary studies for a Christian ethics remained inconsistent. He tried to cope with the subject by choosing various approaches, but this did not enable him to find ultimate clarity for himself. A contradiction remains unresolved: on the one hand, he wanted to desist from an ethics based on the natural order; on the other hand, he did not wish Christian action to be controlled by the ambivalent decisions of man's subjective conscience.[238] Here he deviated from his own position as expressed in his lecture in Barcelona. The two viewpoints found expression in various concepts. Bonhoeffer tried to develop a situation ethics on the basis of the history of the Western world, but on the other hand he was also capable of conceiving given structures for Christian action, for example, in the idea of mandates. He never managed an ultimate, deeper unification of these concepts.

This has become commonly accepted by Bonhoeffer scholars. There has been disagreement, however, about the interpretation of his last theological concept, which we have learned to speak of as "coming of age." Is coming of age determined through the death of God? A number of passages seem to point in this direction,[239] and it is certainly not by chance that the opponents of the ontological concept of God point to Bonhoeffer as one of their sources of inspiration. But isn't it possible that coming of age actually means something quite different, namely, the emancipation of human society from all theological and ecclesiastical tutelage? This would mean that every Christian, on the basis of his faith in the transcendent God, can act in this world entirely in accordance with reason and social necessity.[240] Hanfried Müller has attempted to develop the ideas along this line to be found in Bonhoeffer's letters from prison. Paul Lehmann, however, has pointed out that the idea of formation in accordance with the form of Christ has predominant significance. This means that Bonhoeffer, in his studies for a Christian ethics, and perhaps even as early as the beginning of the 1930s, tried to determine God's reality in the concrete acts of Christian existence. Christ would then become really existent just as much in a Christian's action as in the church.

In prison Bonhoeffer was emancipated from the idea of a Christian world view. This has implications for all ontological concepts, as well as all given structures that could determine a Christian's actions. Even the church became questionable for him as a structuring element.

It seemed clear to Bonhoeffer that reality itself, without mediation—that is, not determined by any theological criteria—is the decisive object of faith. In a time in which the ideological distortion of reality had horrible consequences, the return to reality was God's command. In view of National Socialistic racism, the mere *humanum* was the highest obligation. In Nazism Bonhoeffer could see nothing but a late form of the idealist self-conceit of the ego that he had already attacked in *The Communion of Saints*. A theology unprepared to leave this tradition would be ultimately unable to overcome Nazism. Therefore, there was to be no idealistic misunderstanding of the concept of discipleship or formation in accordance with the form of Christ. This concept does not abolish free arbitration for the Christian; rather, Christ gains reality in man's acting for mankind and for man's real nature. The real mankind, the real history, is the place of God. Perhaps the enigmatic expression "existing without God before God" can become clear through such an interpretation. In fact, a twentieth-century Christian must exist without God and therefore without a theologically shaped world view. However, he remains related to God as his opposite, bringing him back to himself out of alienation and making him truly human. "Coming of age" is a term for the unchecked acceptance of the reality of man because no one but Christ is the real man.

Christian ethics, then, has antipositivistic tendencies as well as anti-ideological tendencies. Despite all the brutal facts, the Christian must never give up hope. Like Antaeus, he remains deeply rooted in the earth. Neither ideology nor positivism is capable of grasping mankind's reality. It would be interesting to inquire further to determine whether this approach must remain a mere postulate. Or could it be that it finds meaning in the life of the church today?

Notes

1 Hanfried Müller, *Von der Kirche zur Welt: Ein Beitrag zu der Beziehung des Wortes Gottes auf die Societas in Dietrich Bonhoeffers theologischer Entwicklung* (Hamburg-Bergstedt: Herbert Reich Evang. Verlag, 1961).

2 *DB* (Munich, 1967).

3 *ThDB* (Munich, 1971).

4 This essay corresponds to part of my Ph.D. dissertation, entitled "Dietrich Bonhoeffers Kirchenverständnis: Ein Beitrag zur theologischen Prinzipienlehre" (Heidelberg, 1964; hereafter cited as BK). The title of this essay tries to take into account the justified criticism of Ernst Feil (see *ThDB* and his review of my dissertation in *Theologische Revue*, No. 1 [1968], 6). Since this essay was written

over ten years ago, it has been impossible to incorporate the significant recent discussion of Bonhoeffer.

5 This aspect of Bonhoeffer's theology has not been adequately dealt with by Feil.

6 *WEN*, p. 401.

7 Cf. Luther, *Bekennende Kirche*, pp. 28f. Bonhoeffer is able to juxtapose Christ and Luther (cf. *GS*, I, 77). In a discussion with Barth, it is sometimes sufficient for him to refer to Luther to lay Barth's argument to rest (cf. BK, p. 110, n. 1).

8 Holl, *Gesammelte Aufsätze*, I (1921), 35. Seeberg, *Dogmen Geschichte*, IV (Durmstadt: Wissenschaftliche Buchgesellschaft, 1959), 1, 175. Cf. Pannenberg, *Kerygma und Dogma* (Göttingen: Vandenhoeck and Ruprecht, 1961), p. 199, for a criticism of this interpretation. Holl knew that the interpretation of *actus purus* was not medieval, but he attributed it to Luther all the same.

9 *GS*, III, 47, 4th proposition.

10 Cf. *BK*, pp. 109-111.

11 *AS*, p. 10.

12 "Geist bei Luther," p. 2. Unpublished; the MS is in E. Bethge's possession.

13 *Ibid.*, p. 3.

14 *Ibid.*, p. 6.

15 *Ibid.*

16 *Ibid.*, p. 7.

17 *Ibid.*

18 *Ibid.*, p. 14.

19 *Ibid.*, p. 23.

20 *Ibid.*, p. 43.

21 Holl stresses God's majesty in this way (*op. cit.*, I, 17, 42, 47).

22 "Lässt sich eine historische und pneumatische Auslegung der Schrift unterscheiden und wie stellt sich der Dogmatik dazu?" (unpublished, in E. Bethge's possession). This paper, 20 typewritten pages, was read on July 31, 1925, when Bonhoeffer was 19 years old. It is perhaps interesting to note the grade given by Seeberg: satisfactory. As far as is known, this is the worst grade Bonhoeffer ever received for a paper as a student. He discusses Barth's hermeneutics explicitly and defends Barth's translation of "Israel" as "Church" in Romans 9ff.

23 *Ibid.*, p. 6.

24 *Ibid.*, p. 4.

25 *Ibid.*, p. 6.

26 *Ibid.*, p. 7.

27 *Ibid.*, p. 9.

28 *Ibid.*

29 "Aber *finitum incapax infiniti*, Gleiches wird nur durch Gleiches erkannt," in "Franks Anschauung vom Geist und von der Genade, dargestellt nach dem *System der christlichen Gewissheit*, 2. Aufl., und dem *System der christl. Wahrheit*, 2. Aufl.," a paper presented in a seminar under Seeberg, November 19, 1926, p. 6; and in a seminar paper under Karl Holl, "Luthers Anschauungen vom Hl. Geist nach den Disputionen von 1535-45, herausgegeben v. Drews," presented on February 22, 1926, p. 14 (unpublished, in E. Bethge's possession).

30 There is some criticism of Barth's concept of the canon, for example: "In this we are opposed to Calvin's Reformed principle of the Scriptures and its rejuvenation by Karl Barth" ("Hist. und pneumatische Auslegung der Schrift,"

p. 17). The criterion for understanding Scripture is Christ's work as recounted in Scripture itself.

31 "The new ego is, in Barth's words (*Römerbrief,* pp. 134ff.), indemonstrable, a divine double, Spirit in Luther" (*ibid.,* p. 18). "In Christ means: 'our partaking in the dissolution of the man Jesus by his self-revelation as the Christ, in which act his new humanity is established' (Barth)" (p. 3 of a paper on "Das 15. Cap. des Joh. Evgl. und Paulus" [*GS,* V, 98], which was probably read in a seminar under Deissman in the winter semester, 1925/26).

32 *AS,* p. 77: "Is the new ego to be considered as being one with the empirical total-ego, or does it remain its divine double? In this point Barth's concept of act is put to the test."

33 Cf. also on predestination, *GS,* III, 452.

34 It is significant that Bonhoeffer discussed this question on his first visit to Barth (*GS,* I, 20).

35 Cf. BK, p. 31.

36 Cf. *ibid.,* p. 36.

37 Cf. *SC,* pp. 80, 92, 137.

38 Cf. BK, pp. 73f.

39 *GS,* III, 47.

40 *AS,* p. 91, n. 39.

41 *GS,* III, 194ff.; *GS,* IV, 119ff., 183ff., 325ff.

42 "When Christ ascended into heaven, the kingdom of God descended closer to earth" (*GS,* IV, 186).

43 For Seeberg, cf. BK, pp. 28f. For Barth's concept of *actus purus,* cf. Pannenberg, p. 200. Holl also spoke of the existence of God beyond the revelation in Christ and was criticized for it by Gogarten. His reply to the criticism is contained in *Gesammelte Aufsätze,* III, 248ff.

44 BK, p. 12.

45 Cf. *ibid.,* p. 102.

46 *WEN,* p. 255 (*LPPE,* p. 376).

47 "Ritschl, on whose theology I was brought up in Berlin . . ." (*GS,* III, 118).

48 *GS,* III, 117f.

49 Cf. *GS,* IV, 119, 186. Perhaps Bonhoeffer expressed his own point of view most clearly in a sermon on Matthew 28:20 delivered in Barcelona on Low Sunday, April 15, 1928: "Behold, I am with you; . . . that is the Easter message. Not the God who is far distant but the God who is close at hand—that is Easter" (*GS,* V, 430; cf. *GS,* III, 406).

50 For instance, as early as 1927, in a lecture on the Catholic Church, he declared that one must agree with Luther in saying against the Catholic Church: "So much as thou believest, so much dost thou have" (unpublished, in E. Bethge's possession), p. 3; cf. *AS,* p. 96; *GS,* I, 91; *GS,* III, 180, 182, 187, 190, 209, 233, 316, 397. Barth had just been campaigning against this concept of faith (cf. Karl Barth, *Gesammelte Vorträge* [Munich: Christian Kaiser Verlag, 1924], p. 207).

51 *GS,* IV, 244, 285.

52 "God, too, is not a statically valid truth; he is an 'acting' truth. In other words, he is active in the process of human life. Otherwise he cannot 'be' at all. This expression, which is almost reminiscent of Luther's transcendentalism . . ." (*GS,* I, 91). The points that distinguish Luther from pragmatism have no bearing on the opinions expressed above (see the sentences following above quotation).

53 *WEN,* p. 401 (*LPPE,* p. 369).

54 *GS*, III, 76.

55 Moltmann, *MW*, III, 46. In connection with this, see Bethge, "The Challenge of Dietrich Bonhoeffer's Life and Theology," pp. 9-10, 37f.

56 *AS*, pp. 67f. Klaus Wilkens has also tried to stress this thought of Bonhoeffer's (cf. *Verkündigung und Forschung* [Munich: Christian Kaiser Verlag, 1960], pp. 170f.).

57 *AS*, pp. 61ff.

58 Cf. *GS*, III, 178.

59 "Jesus Christus und vom Wesen des Christentums," a lecture delivered on December 11, 1928 (*GS*, V, 134). Cf. also *GS*, III, 202: "Dogmatics is in need of the certainty of the historicity of Jesus Christ, i.e., the identity of the personage prophesied about with the historical personage."

60 Sermon on Romans 12:11, delivered on September 23, 1928, p. 2 (*GS*, V, 464).

61 *Ibid.*, 465.

62 *Ibid.*, 467.

63 *Ibid.*, 468; cf. also Bethge's preface to *GS*, III, 7.

64 Müller, p. 162. The essay on Christian ethics which Bonhoeffer wrote during his time in Barcelona is evidence of the importance of Nietzsche at that time (cf. *GS*, III, 5a).

65 *Op. cit.*, p. 197.

66 Cf. *GS*, III, 74ff., 160f., 163, 167ff.

67 "Ratio est, quia natura nostra vitio primi pecati tam profunda est in se ipsam incurva, ut non solum optima dona Dei sibi inflectat ipsisque fruatur (ut patet inivstiariis et hipocritis), immo et ipso Deo 'utatur' ad illa consequenda, verum etiam hoc ipsum ignoret, quod tam inique, curve et, prave omnia, etiam Deum, propter se ipsum querat, sicut propheta Hiere. 17: 'Pravum est cor hominis et inscrutabile, quid cognoscet illud?' i.e. ita curvum in se, ut nullus hominum, quantumlibet sanctus (seclusa tentationa) scire possit" (Martin Luther, *Vorlesung über den Römerbrief 1515-16* [Darmstadt: Wissenschaftliche Buchgesellschaft, 1960], pp. 326f.). In Bonhoeffer's writings the shortened version given above is to be found in *AS*, pp. 24, 36, 57, 66, 117; *GS*, III, 73ff., etc.

68 Cf. *GS*, I, 91: "Thought is understood in the main teleologically [i.e., in pragmatism], as purposive with regard to life. This we would not dispute, but we would question the possibility of revealing the nature of this purpose."

69 *Ek*, p. 135: "Having become conscious of good and evil through his separation from the Creator, man begins to reflect on his own nature. His life's task is to begin to understand himself, just as it was to know God at the creation. ... This remains the case even when man penetrates beyond the boundary of his own nature."

70 *AS*, pp. 9, 136ff.

71 *Ibid.*, p. 18.

72 *Ibid.*, pp. 13f.

73 *SC*, p. 20.

74 "Independent existence of the Spirit in the sense of idealist individualism is unchristian, because it implies the absolute value of human spirit, which can only be ascribed to the divine Spirit" (*SC*, p. 28).

75 *AS*, pp. 17ff.

76 *Ibid.*, p. 18.

77 *Ibid.*, p. 47; *GS*, III, 70ff.

78   *AS*, pp. 13ff.

79   *Ibid.*, p. 66.

80   *Ibid.*, p. 20.

81   *Ibid.*, p. 19 and p. 72 on "Knowing and Possessing."

82   *GS*, III, 112.

83   *Ibid.*, 102; cf. also 101 on the violation of reality by thought.

84   "Faith in the evangelical sense cannot be understood as belief in the truth." In a paper for a homiletics seminar in the summer semester of 1926 (unpublished, in E. Bethge's possession, p. 1), it is personal devotion to Jesus Christ in the synopsis of the second article of the Apostles' Creed.

85   The concept of potentiality has a place neither in theology nor, consequently, in theological anthropology" (*GS*, III, 38). Similarly: "One shudders to think of the consequences of *finitum capax infiniti*" (*GS*, II, 278).

86   Cf. *SC*, p. 23.

87   *GS*, III, 29.

88   *Ibid.*, 166ff.

89   *Ibid.*, 167. But Bonhoeffer sometimes also felt that the Word alone was inadequate for the reality of Christ. In *N*, p. 160, he expresses the idea that Christ, as the Word become flesh, is more than just God's Word. This explains why Bonhoeffer could say that the church might well have to do without the Word because it had become untrustworthy (*WEN*, p. 207).

90   A similar thought is to be found in Barth's writings when he says that theological thought is, above all, acknowledgment (*Church Dogmatics*, I/1, 213ff.). This idea, however, remains methodologically ineffective.

91   *GS*, III, 169.

92   *Ibid.*, 171ff.; cf. p. 108 above. Barth, too, had excluded the "what" question from Christology (cf. *Fides Quaerens Intellectum*, pp. 16f.), but he explicitly declared the "how" question admissible (pp. 25ff.).

93   *GS*, III, 170.

94   Cf. *ibid.*, 102.

95   *AS*, pp. 67f.

96   The criticism that Barth's theological approach contains the seeds of transcendentalism stems from this (*AS*, p. 60).

97   February-March, 1929, now in *Gesammelte Vorträge*, III, 54ff.

98   *Ibid.*

99   *Ibid.*

100   *Ibid.*, pp. 62ff.

101   *Ibid.*, pp. 72ff.

102   *Ibid.*

103   *Ibid.*

104   *Ibid.*

105   *Ibid.*, pp. 81f.

106   *Ibid.*, p. 84.

107   *Ibid.*, p. 85.

108   Heinrich Knittermeyer, "Review of *AS*," in *Zwischen den Zeiten*, Vol. XI.

109   Cf. *BK*, pp. 57f. Similarly, Pannenberg writes: "An understanding of revelation which sees it as something differing from natural cognition runs the risk of confusing historical revelation with Gnostic secret knowledge" (*Offenbarung als Geschichte* [Göttingen: Vandenhoeck and Ruprecht, 1961], pp. 98f.).

110   *AS*, p. 116.

111 *SC*, p. 249. Bonhoeffer criticized St. Augustine for using "false biological terms" for the human race (cf. *SC*, pp. 74f.).

112 *Ibid.*, p. 32.

113 *Ibid.*, p. 27.

114 See above, pp. 23ff.; also Ritschl, *Rechtfertigung und Versöhnung*, III (Göttingen, 1874), 320.

115 *SC*, p. 79: "Mankind is the community which includes all communities." Cf. Müller, p. 438, n. 91.

116 *SC*, pp. 77f.

117 *Ibid.*, p. 67.

118 *Ibid.*, p. 52.

119 *Ibid.*, p. 68, n. 2.

120 *Ibid.*, pp. 49ff.

121 See the statement on monads (BK, pp. 99f.).

122 *SC*, p. 247. "We are taking from St. Paul only the general idea that God imputes Adam's sin to the whole of mankind."

123 *Ibid.*, pp. 77f.

124 *Ibid.*, p. 80.

125 *Ibid.*, p. 79.

126 *Ibid.*, p. 102.

127 *Ibid.*, p. 94.

128 *Ibid.*, p. 98.

129 *Ibid.*

130 *Ibid.*, p. 99.

131 *Ibid.*, p. 109; cf. also pp. 112f. on the doctrine of predestination.

132 *Ibid.*, p. 95.

133 *AS*, p. 94.

134 Ritschl, *Rechtfertigung und Versöhnung*, III, 197ff.

135 *AS*, pp. 127ff.

136 Cf. Müller, pp. 36, 105.

137 *AS*, pp. 95, 106.

138 *SC*, p. 82; cf. p. 93.

139 *AS*, pp. 127ff.

140 Cf. Müller, pp. 36, 105.

141 *AS*, pp. 95, 106.

142 *SC*, p. 82; cf. p. 93.

143 Cf. BK, pp. 10ff.

144 Cf. *ibid.*, pp. 131ff.

145 *GS*, III, 49.

146 *Ibid.*, 53.

147 *Ibid.*, 180ff.

148 *Ibid.*, 178.

149 *Ibid.*, 180ff.

150 *Ibid.*, 194ff.

151 *Ibid.*, 181: "God in timeless eternity is not God, and Jesus in temporal bounds is not Jesus. Rather, God is God and the man Jesus." "Time and space are not only the human, they are also the divine destiny of the God-man." Both these sentences are immediately reminiscent of Ritschl. This connection can be seen particularly clearly in the statements on the sinlessness of Jesus (136ff.).

152 *Ibid.*, 170ff.

153   *Ibid.*, 173, 168f.

154   Transcendence is dealt with in connection with the term "form," and "worldliness" in connection with the term "place" (*ibid.*, 184ff., 194ff.).

155   Cf. *ibid.*, 178.

156   *Ibid.*, 195, 196, 199. It is strange that a sentence in the third part states that in the sacraments Christ is the mediator between nature and God. In the second part Christ is also described as the center between God and the state (195).

157   *Ibid.*, 195.

158   Cf. the discussion in *SF*, p. 70, about Eve as Adam's limit. In *N*, p. 71, Bonhoeffer also describes Christ as the mediator between the ego and reality.

159   BK, p. 116.

160   Cf. *MW*, I, 28, 82f., 90.

161   *GS*, III, 119.

162   *Ibid.*, 463ff.; *EK*, pp. 242ff.

163   That Nietzsche's concept of the living element in reality is important for Bonhoeffer's attitude toward reality can be seen in his seminar paper on the interpretation of Scripture. In that paper he contrasts the boundlessness of living being and dead being (p. 10). In this context I would also draw the reader's attention to the interest in pragmatism that Bonhoeffer acquired during his first visit to the United States (cf. *GS*, I, 90f.).

164   *GS*, III, 459: "The wish to see reality as existing without any divine action means living in an abstraction" (cf. *Ek*, pp. 231, 243).

165   Müller, p. 517, n. 877: "In Bonhoeffer's specific Christology, the separation of worldly reality from divine reality must be almost the same as a separation of God and man in Christ." Moltmann observes: "But in contrast, Bonhoeffer's unique conception of the incarnation as God's entrance into the reality of the world reveals much more clearly that Kierkegaard's category of the individual is deficient—and must be deficient—in representing the church's community in Christ" ("Herrschaft Christi und soziale Wirklichkeit nach Dietrich Bonhoeffer," in *Theologische Existenz heute*, LXXI [1959], 15). To distinguish this essay from Moltmann's lecture in Weissensee, I will refer to it as *Theol. Ex.*

166   *MW*, III, 42ff.

167   *Theol. Ex.*, p. 37.

168   *MW*, III, 45. Moltmann explains very clearly that Bonhoeffer's concept of revelation differs from Barth's in that it is not even primarily self-disclosure by God but rather a new existence for man.

169   *Ibid.*, 50ff. Worthy of attention in this connection is the Christology lecture, in which the epistemological assumptions behind this approach become clear. These assumptions are also fundamental to early parts of Bonhoeffer's ethics. Cf. *GS*, III, 166f., esp. 170f.; also *Ek*, p. 237: "The question 'What is life?' becomes the question 'Who is life?' (John 1:4)."

170   *Theol. Ex.*, pp. 11f.

171   *GS*, III, 464f.

172   *MW*, III, 9.

173   *Theol. Ex.*, p. 10.

174   *Ek*, pp. 288ff., 306ff.

175   *Church Dogmatics*, III/4, 21f.

176   *Theol. Ex.*, p. 10.

177   *MW*, III, 45. Presumably inhypostatization is meant, for it does not make sense to equate ahypostatization with formlessness.

178 *Ek*, p. 210: "The world has no reality independent of the revelation of God in Christ."

179 *AS*, p. 75.

180 *GS*, III, 101ff.

181 *Ibid.*, 458f.

182 *AS*, p. 64.

183 *Ibid.*, p. 89.

184 *SF*, p. 58.

185 The reader is reminded that Bonhoeffer was hardly able to conceive a purely forensic justification.

186 *Ek*, p. 242f.

187 *GS*, III, 270: "The only ones who can believe in the kingdom of God are . . . those who love the earth and God as one."

188 *N*, p. 84.

189 "The will of God is not only directed toward the re-creation of man but also toward the re-creation of the conditions" (*GS*, I, 156).

190 Seminar paper on "honor," perhaps dealing with Matthew 5:38ff., probably dating from 1926 (unpublished, in E. Bethge's possession), p. 15.

191 *GS*, I, 173.

192 BK, p. 84.

193 *Ibid.*, pp. 190, 193ff.

194 *GS*, III, 52f. Grace kills everything else (*GS*, I, 20). For that reason Bonhoeffer discarded orders of creation: "The solution to ethical problems in general, and in this case to ecumenical problems, should be sought solely in the revelation in Christ instead of in the order of creation" (*GS*, I, 129).

195 Similarly Müller, p. 489, n. 570.

196 *GS*, III, 53.

197 On freedom, see *Ek*, pp. 264ff., 277ff.

198 *Ek*, pp. 323ff. Cf. Bethge's preface to the sixth impression. Bonhoeffer disguises his own conclusion that *primus usus* is unbiblical in the form of a question (*Ek*, p. 248).

199 *GS*, I, 150: "The commandment cannot come from another place than where the promise and fulfillment come from—from Christ."

200 *GS*, I, 156.

201 *Ek*, pp. 61ff.

202 Bonhoeffer wanted to see the concept of the kingdom of God taken seriously: "It is right and biblical to take the kingdom of God as an earthly kingdom seriously, and this opinion is justified, in contrast to an atavistic position" (*GS*, I, 110; cf. the lecture "Dein Reich komme!" *GS*, III, 270ff.). In the lecture on Jesus Christ which he gave in Barcelona, he spoke of Jesus as the bringer of the kingdom of God (*GS*, V, 141; on the same subject, see *N*, p. 59). The end of the world means the coming of Christ on earth so that it can become the kingdom of God. "God will not abandon the earth."

203 Cf. *GS*, II, 384. In his critique, Frick obviously considered this title to be the most important (cf. *Monatschrift für Pastoraltheologie*, XXXIX [1950], 207f.).

204 "The kingdom of God cannot be built even with the most perfect morality" (*Kirche und Eschatologie*, p. 8). Seeberg said the following on this point: "But God is active in such morality!" The differences between teacher and pupil can be clearly seen at this juncture. See also the sermon on John 1:21ff., esp. p. 18.

205 Cf. *Ek*, pp. 130ff., 205ff., 291ff.; *GS*, III, 458ff.

206 *Ek*, p. 200; cf. also BK, pp. 115f.

207 *Ek*, p. 46.

208 *Ibid.*, p. 80: "Accepted by God, crucified and expiated—that is the reality of mankind" (cf. p. 231).

209 *Ibid.*, p. 73; cf. also p. 75.

210 *Ibid.*, p. 243.

211 *Ibid.*, p. 230.

212 *Ibid.*, p. 234.

213 *Ibid.*, pp. 136, 76.

214 *GS*, III, 467, 473f.

215 *Ibid.*, 455; *Ek*, pp. 68ff.

216 The section that begins on p. 11 of *Ethik* is particularly impressive. It occurs again in a similar form in *WEN* with the title "Nach Zehn Jahren" (pp. 11ff.).

217 *Ek*, p. 56. The same thing is meant when the discipleship is described as being without content (*N*, p. 29) and as pure dependence on Christ (*N*, p. 30).

218 *Ek*, p. 59. Strangely enough, it is this thought that Müller objects to (*op. cit.*, p. 280). He considers it to be a historical-theological idea serving a Christian organization of the lay middle-class opponents of Hitler.

219 *Ek*, pp. 59ff.

220 *Ibid.*, pp. 74ff., 131.

221 *Ibid.*, p. 40.

222 Cf. *GS*, I, 33f., 145-147.

223 *Ek*, p. 294: "God's commandment is God's word to man. Moreover, in its content as well as in its form, it is the concrete word to concrete mankind. God's commandment leaves man no scope for application. . . ."

224 *GS*, III, 461, 475; *Ek*, pp. 57f.

225 *GS*, III, 163. What he writes about this matter in *N* (p. 35) is almost a tautology: "Only he who believes is obedient, and only he who is obedient believes."

226 *GS*, I, 31, 34, 147. "Reality is the sacrament of the commandment."

227 *N*, p. 223, points to communion as the goal and perfection of the community in Christ.

228 *N*, pp. 207ff.; cf. p. 199. Müller is right in claiming that this thought ignored what Bonhoeffer had developed on the subject of the concept of reality in 1932 (*op. cit.*, p. 230; for his criticism, see p. 236; BK, p. 196).

229 Cf. the sigh of complaint: "The obscurity will finish us" (*GS*, I, 61).

230 *Ek*, pp. 24ff., 42f. Müller is correct in interpreting discipleship—contrary to Barth—as *passio passiva* (*op. cit.*, p. 481, n. 582).

231 *Ek*, p. 202.

232 *Ibid.*, p. 284: "als 'letztes' Wort."

233 Part of a letter expresses this in a characteristic manner: "For us it can only be a question of making room, giving ourselves space" (*GS*, III, 37).

234 *Ibid.*, 466ff.; *EK*, pp. 236ff.

235 *SC*, p. 106; cf. *GS*, III, 194: "Where does he exist? He exists *pro me*."

236 *SC*, p. 107, mentions deputyship as a theological concept, not an ethical concept. In certain respects, the idea that Christianity puts an end to ethics is also valid for Bonhoeffer's *Ethics*. It is not a question of man's actions but rather of Christ taking shape. The quotation above is from *Ek*, p. 238 (cf. also *N*, pp. 82ff.).

237 *GS*, III, 457.

238 *WEN,* p. 341.

239 *Ibid.,* p. 379, and esp. p. 395: "Being Christian means not to be religious in a special sense, i.e., to make something out of oneself according to given methods (a sinner, penitent, or even a saint), but it means to be a man. . . . Not the religious act makes a Christian but the participation in the suffering of God in this-worldly life."

240 *Ibid.,* pp. 415ff.

ADOLF VON HARNACK AND BONHOEFFER[1]

Carl-Jürgen Kaltenborn

MY INTEREST in Harnack's influence on Dietrich Bonhoeffer grew in retrospect. It developed when, upon close scrutiny, the discussion of theological problems which occupies many pages of Bonhoeffer's prison letters (published as *Letters and Papers from Prison*) proved to be a discussion with more than a few overtones of his bourgeois-liberal heritage. Thus we read in his accompanying letter to "Outline for a Book", the plan for publishing his months of reflection about the questions of a nonreligious interpretation:

> The church must come out of its stagnation. We must move out again into the open air of intellectual discussion with the world, and risk saying controversial things, if we are to get down to serious problems of life. I feel obliged to tackle these questions as one who, although a "modern" theologian, is still aware of the debt that he owes to liberal theology.[2]

The (sudden) appearance of theological liberalism at such a decisive juncture is an invitation to trace this influence. Because the biographical evidence demonstrates that Bonhoeffer's most intensive contact with liberalism had occurred in the person of his Berlin teacher Adolf von Harnack, our attention will focus on this man. As we examine the transformation of Harnack's thought in the theology of his most genuine pupil, we are guided by the larger question of the legitimate reception of theological liberalism.

I. Taking Seriously the Humanity of Jesus

In order to understand the theologian Harnack—and until the end of his life Adolf von Harnack understood himself primarily as a theologian—we must first of all take note of his Christology. We do justice to his Christology only when we keep in mind its pointed, antidocetic frontal attack. Against so-called positive Christianity, which identifies faith in Jesus Christ with the mere acceptance of a long tradition of dogmatic doctrines, Harnack wanted to place the humanity of Jesus in the foreground.

The real and final reason for maintaining his focus on the humanity of Jesus can be found in Harnack's ecclesiology. Harnack was interested in a church for people-come-of-age, in which people know what they believe. He opposed all patronizing clericalism that attempted to make the entire world a part of the church, or Christian. He did not want to pursue a phantom; for that reason he emphasized the "real historic [*geschichtlichen*] Christ."[3] Accordingly, his first lecture on the "Essence of Christianity" starts with the remark, refuting John Stuart Mill's claim concerning Socrates, that it is "still more important" than the remembrance of the Greek philosopher "to remind mankind again and again that a man by the name of Jesus Christ once stood in their midst."[4]

We cannot really speak of a true Christology in Harnack; rather the concept may better be termed a "Jesuology." For Harnack, Jesus is not divine, but the highest divine expression. According to him we cannot say that Jesus *is* the Messiah; the most we can claim is that Jesus *knows* himself as the Messiah—in the future. He is the designated Messiah, in which the concept of the Messiah—something metahistorical—signifies "the highpoint of what personality is and can be in history."

Harnack's Jesuology is embedded in the conception of a double gospel: Jesus' unique knowledge of God enables him to be the herald of the Father God (in this sense, stressing the prophetic office). At the same time, Jesus is the realization and power of the gospel, insofar as in his person, by virtue of a chain reaction in the feelings of man, faith is aroused. Thus the cross—merely a transitional point—becomes a code, meaning that the suffering of the righteous signifies salvation in history, whereas the resurrection signals that Jesus has turned into life, power, and majesty. As a matter of fact, Harnack thought of Jesus Christ without any reference to God and man. Jesus is distinct from the promise of God; his person and work are not a part of the divine "must." That is the reason that Harnack does not dare to use statements of fact. Thus the Jesus in himself becomes the Jesus for me—though Harnack's Christology does not change completely into soteriology.

Harnack's Jesuology, i.e., his accented highlighting of the humanity of Jesus, finds its modified continuation in the theology of Dietrich Bonhoeffer. Bonhoeffer demonstrates a Christology in the full sense of the word, at least insofar as his Christology reflects its particular orientation to the Chalcedonian Confession. But even within that concept of Christology that Bonhoeffer could not relinquish, ۔ Christ whose natures are without mixture and without separation, the emphasis nevertheless falls more on the humanity of Jesus Christ than on his divinity—evidence of Harnack's influence on him. We should therefore not simply speak (as we may in

Harnack's case) of the Bonhoefferian Jesuology, but rather—to use a term coined by H. Müller—of a "Jesuological determination of Christology," or of a Jesuology within Christology. Precisely in this way the influence of and the difference from his teacher Adolf von Harnack become clearly evident.

This Jesuological element which makes itself felt within Bonhoeffer's Christology is elaborated most fully in the last phase of Bonhoeffer's theology. After he received the report that the attempt on Hitler's life failed, Bonhoeffer wrote Bethge on July 21, 1944: "During the last year or so I've come to know and understand more and more the profound this-world-liness of Christianity. The Christian is not a *homo religiosus,* but simply a man, as Jesus was a man—in contrast, shall we say, to John the Baptist."[5] Bonhoeffer here exposes the Christological roots of his nonreligious interpretation. As Bonhoeffer contrasts Jesus' humanity with that of John the Baptist, and in this connection reveals his negative conception of the *homo religiosus,* his tendency to keep the humanity of Jesus free from any religionization becomes clear. It must appear "without mixture" with the divinity and not be "divinized" at all in the long run. The sharply accented Jesuology within Christology is for Bonhoeffer the counterpart of his theology of the cross, insofar as the obvious stress on the humanity of Jesus does not allow any scope, within theological reflection, for a *deus ex machina* able to play out the power of God in the world to the end. Bonhoeffer does not pass beyond the nettling paradox which requires, "You must point at this man and say: 'Here is God.' " It is from that point of view that his attempt to introduce a new Christological title of honor must be understood when he introduces the formula "the crucified one as 'the man for others' " (as distinct from "the man in himself").

II. The One and Undivided Reality

Harnack's world and life view posits *one* reality governed by the Spirit (i.e., the logos of God). Harnack could say in an academic sermon on March 4, 1917: "Reality is the hem of the garment of God; it is even more, for together with the world we live and move and have our being in God. He himself lives in this reality, . . . in the real world and its history."[6] From that perspective Harnack viewed the state, law, science, art, etc., as divine orders of creation. Thus he firmly opposed the attempt to make these independent realms "Christian." Whoever attempts to do so, in Harnack's opinion, makes the kingdom of God a corrosive "instead of a yeast."

How much he resisted a two-realm way of thinking is clarified most explicitly in the following sentences:

There is as little a Christian state [or a] Christian law, as there is a Christian war; and there is as little a Christian national economics or in general a Christian science *(Geisteswissenschaft)* as there is a Christian botany. What makes these realms Christian, insofar as they can be and must be Christianized, is given only in the fact that Christians are engaged and involved in them. By being involved in them, [Christians] pose, it is true, questions and present viewpoints that otherwise would have been absent . . . ; for a Christian who has found the living God is seeking for reality everywhere.

Harnack continues by asserting:

> The result of our labor, then, is that there is not and cannot as yet be a Christian science, a Christian view of the state, and a Christian law; though science, the state, and law are constructed in such a way that they correspond with reality—as it is and must be—and thereby with the salvation of humanity.

Harnack thus resists the common Christian view of the world as consisting of two parts. No wonder, then, that he rejected the separation between church history and profane history, since for him church history constitutes a part of general history.

What ethical consequences this emphatic rejection of a double interpretation of history and of the world produces may be evident in these few sentences from a speech given at the Evangelical-Social Congress in May 1894. Harnack is defending the opinion that a Christian, "who clearly recognizes that an economic condition has become an emergency situation for the neighbor," must search for help, "for he is the disciple of him who was a Savior. We truly help him who fell into the water by pulling him out of it. We can help him who remains in a locked home that is ablaze only, however, by changing the situation, by extinguishing the fire. The question whether it is a Christian-economical, or a purely Christian or a purely humanistic deed the disputant may answer. Love knows that she must give help—real help—everywhere."[7]

Harnack manifests here a pleasant consequence of his Jesuology which leaves him a free hand for concrete, earthly action free of a bad "Christian" conscience. It becomes clear what Adolf von Harnack finally strove to accomplish. But we must, it is true, simultaneously add that Harnack was unable with the means of his disposal—seen as a whole—effectively to ward off the Christian infiltration of the world. Jesus and the logos are opposites for him. The centralization and idealism of Jesus' humanity frequently cancel each other in their opposing tendencies; the world is thus being made religious. For Harnack religion turns out to be the uppermost concept: everything finally is subsumed under it. Even the man Jesus, in whose person universal religion finds its most condensed expression, is subject to it: "Every valuable occurrence in history" is "determined by a powerful urge to a higher elevation above natural planes . . . and by an evaluation of a mysterious 'whole' and 'part.' " And Harnack's more or less final word in this regard can therefore only be: "Humanity labors in history 'as if God exists.' "[8]

The opposite holds for Bonhoeffer. He agrees with his teacher on the rejection of two realms of history; he, too, holds to only *one* reality. But—and here we see the decisive difference between Harnack and Bonhoeffer—this reality is thought of from the point of view of Jesus Christ and not vice versa. Important for him is the *real man,* not reality.

Harnack's universal world view has found roots in the thinking of his pupil, but it has also been integrated—the jurisdiction of religion withdrawn—into a universalistic Christology. This fact alone could lead to a Christocratic domination of the world for Bonhoeffer. But something else accents even more clearly the difference between these two theologians: in the Christology of Dietrich Bonhoeffer, within the framework of his prison letters, Jesuology leads to a sharply accented theology of the cross. As a result, it produces such remarks as these, contradicting and opposing Harnack's "as if" (re the existence of God) quoted above:

> We cannot be honest unless we recognize that we have to live in the world *etsi deus non daretur.* And this is just what we do recognize— before God! God himself compels us to recognize it. . . . Before God and with God we live without God. God lets himself be pushed out of the world on to the cross. He is weak and powerless in the world, and that is precisely the way, the only way, in which he is with us and helps us.[9]

That Bonhoeffer's theology of the cross in no way corresponds to a pessimistic world view but rather leads to an optimistic view of life may again be traced to Harnack's influence on him. The universalism inherent in the Harnackian legacy, the consistent alignment with *one* reality, permits Bonhoeffer to think through a relation that would almost completely be thrust aside in evangelical theology—the relationship between Christ and, for instance, the good man.

In his interpretation of the Beatitude "Blessed are those who are persecuted for righteousness' sake," Bonhoeffer had already begun in his *Cost of Discipleship* to follow a train of thought which he completed in his *Ethics* with the theme "Christ and Good People" (or the Good).[10] In his ethics he argued against the Christian habit, induced by the point of view of the church, of seeing the good only as a splendid pagan vice or as a fruit of the Holy Spirit. Both in its general direction and even right down to his mentioning the splendid pagan vices, this objection parallels the thought, uttered by Harnack during his speech as rector in 1900 ("Socrates and the Early Church")[11] in which he thundered against the "clerical expressions" of Tertullian and negatively characterized Augustine's view as "a dreadful theory, as if all pagan virtues are only splendid vices."

Certainly for Bonhoeffer the occasion for such deliberations was the concrete situation under the Nazi regime. But viewed in this light it is very suggestive that in such a situation he sought to make fertile for theological reflection exactly those elements that were no doubt rooted in Harnack's way of thinking.

The problem of a Chrisitan ethics haunted Bonhoeffer during his entire life. He formulated his own question in extreme terms during the winter of 1942/43:

> A Christian ethic will have to begin by asking whether and to what extent it is possible at all to treat the "ethical" and the "Christian" as a theme. . . . We cannot, in fact, even set foot in the field of Christian ethics until we have first of all recognized how extremely questionable a course we are pursuing if we take the "ethical" and the "Christian" as a theme for our consideration.[12]

What Bonhoeffer formulated here as a groping question strikes us as a pointed affirmative proposition in his May 29, 1944, prison letter:

> In point of fact, people deal with these questions [about death, suffering, and guilt] without God . . . , and it is simply not true to say that only Christianity has the answers to them. As to the idea of "solving" problems, it may be that the Christian answers are just as unconvincing—or convincing—as any others. . . . In Christ there are no "Christian problems."[13]

Seen from this perspective, there can basically no longer be a Christian ethics. Harnack's initial proposition has been extended. The lack of all interest in "Christian" labels based on taking seriously the *one* reality makes its impact felt on Bonhoeffer's way of thinking.

III. Purposefully Acting on Behalf of the Whole

Harnack's factually oriented world view is best characterized by his definition of science.[14] He regarded science as a "knowledge of reality toward purposeful activity." We do history, according to Harnack's own utterance, "in order to intervene in the movement of history." For no labor is fitting for man "that does not enable him to act and to make deeds." It is important "to prepare prudently and purposefully the future," with "the direction for the maintenace and promotion of life" as the standard. Thus Harnack, especially in an Elmauer essay of 1928,[15] assumed "progress in history . . . as a given." An indomitable Harnackian optimism permits him to assert: "The achievement, the good that is really active, kills all costs. The sun is brighter than the darkness."

With what intensity the Harnackian heritage on this point is felt in Bonhoeffer's confrontation with Fascism, the following may demonstrate: "Although it is certainly not true that success justifies an evil deed . . . , it is impossible to regard success as something that is ethically quite neutral. . . . In the last resort success makes history. . . . The ultimate question for a responsible man is . . . how the coming generation is to live."[16]

Bonhoeffer adopted this kind of Jesuology from his teacher without its attachments to Harnack's idealism. In this way he is able to keep the theology of the cross alive while still being able to render fertile Harnack's optimistic, factually oriented world view. To a certain extent, however, he turned Harnack's ideas around. In his theological reflections, Bonhoeffer restored the profanization of the world, rescuing faith in Christ from its religiosity: "We are living in the penultimate but believe the ultimate."

In the pull of such a theological orientation, the Christian community is being granted the opportunity to win a new relationship to power. The attempt to win control over people in the interest of the church had been the mark of one attitude toward power. A complete renunciation of power (by falsely identifying power with evil) and the retreat to reservations of inwardness connected therewith, as, for instance, the flight from responsibility for our world into metaphysics—these mark the border in the other direction.

The concept of power is increasingly losing its "foreign" sound today for fully a third of the world by means of a conscious maintenance of the known laws of society and nature to the benefit of all. "Power" is recognized as being related to the concept of the "working, value-creating human being." To pose this question about power for the realm of ethics at precisely this moment in history shows itself to be as productive as it is urgent.

IV. Elaborations of Anti-Clericalism

From a theological point of view, Harnack's ecclesiology is basically controversial, and its forward looking vision is certainly so. He elaborates his Jesuology within his ecclesiology so thoroughly that he strongly refutes every kind of "church state." Harnack found the church state far worse than the state church, though he saw the disadvantages of the state church, too. He directs his polemic against the danger that the congregation remain perpetually immature. His greatest concern was "that our church" not be "a state, a school for perpetual minors, and a sacramental institution of assurance." At present "our churches are more mature than thirty years ago. For what reason do they have a mouth . . . , [if not] in order to testify in public concerning ethical questions . . . : 'that must be and that must not be'?"[17] The focus of Harnack's concern was the being-of-age of individual Christians vis-à-vis the church as institution; he sought the reassurance that every Christian must be able to express his faith. That concern was the reason for his "Answer to Cremer's Polemic Writing": "When we are now come of age—who will be spared the question: 'Do you know what you believe?' "[18] He rejected rigorously the "subjection to ecclesiasticism" called "implicit faith." But Harnack was also very actively engaged in the struggle concerning the Apostles' Creed. On the basis of his Jesuology he was able to take seriously both humanity and naturalness. At the same time he was trying to protect the center of the gospel against profanization by means of an appropriate operation of historical means. Behind this defense is Harnack's understanding of religion, which according to him is not related to the empirical ego but to its inner core. Thus the powers of the gospel are related to "the deepest layers of human nature. . . . Whoever is not able to go back to the roots of humanity . . . will try to render the gospel profane or will deplore its uselessness." Moreover, we cannot express "everything in religion; for it is life, and a great deal of it (our inner life) is a mystery to ourselves. We must enunciate only what promotes the well-being of another; the deepest aspects we must keep to ourselves."[19] While this is the case, Harnack felt "a sharp pain" nevertheless when he read "in the announcements in the press and public declarations" that "the most profound and exalted confessions of the Christian faith" were "angrily or callously articulated" because "they [were] being profaned."[20]

From this basic conviction Adolf von Harnack turned pointedly against apologetics, which was "not infrequently pursued in an undignified and obstrusive fashion," because apologetics praised religion "as though it were a job-lot at a sale, or a universal remedy for all social ills."[21]

Harnack's anti-clericalism is elaborated in a particular manner in the thinking of his pupil. Let us consider three key concepts: the world come of age, honesty in matters of confession, and a nonreligious interpretation with its accompanying secret discipline.

To grasp fully the concept of the world come of age in Bonhoeffer, we must remember that all the debates about coming of age and religion-lessness end in his "Outline for a Book" which is addressed to the church: "I hope it may be of some help for the church's future."[22] The church must be made capable for its task ("to be for others"). When he mentions the world come of age in this connection, it is clear that in the final analysis the judgment he calls for can not be made to depend on sociological, psychological, or political impositions. Rather, it is to be considered a theological judgment; the proclaiming congregation is told: Whether at present your analyses indicate a world come of age or not yet come of age, you must consider the world, to whom the message of Christ applies, as come of age in any case, for this is the message.

Next to maturity, honesty in questions of confession is a further consequence of Bonhoeffer's anti-clericalism. Here we may examine Harnack's influence on him in connection with the Apostles' Creed. Ever since his student days Bonhoeffer was haunted by his preoccupation with the problem of the Apostles' Creed. In the second chapter of his "Outline" he entered his concerns: "What do we really believe? I mean, believe in such a way that we stake our lives on it? The problem of the Apostles' Creed? 'What must I believe?' is the wrong question."[23] A few lines later the object of his comments becomes clear in his polemic against taking shelter "behind the faith of the church": "That is why the air is not quite fresh, even in the Confessing Church. To say that it is the church's business, not mine, may be a clerical evasion." Here the similarity to Harnack's sentences is nearly identical.

Finally, the complex subject of nonreligious interpretation can be summarized as follows: What may be proclaimed and how it is to be done is not to be determined any longer by some inner-worldly pre-understanding, but everything shall be understood from the point of view of "the gospel of Christ." Intertwined with this stance is the conviction that Christians can no longer understand themselves as privileged, but rather only as "belonging entirely to the world."

Basically Harnack strove after a Christianity that did not try to keep anyone spiritually immature and that discharged all of its tasks within the world. He realized that he could not realize that goal, because a religious infiltration had to come again in the long run. Bonhoeffer, however, brought the problem to a theologically legitimate solution.

We also come across Harnack's own writing in Bonhoeffer's secret discipline, which is the counterpart of his nonreligious interpretation. He gave this discipline the function of assurance: by means of it the "mysteries of the Christian faith must be protected against profanation." The secret discipline was to resist the attempt of the proclaiming congregation to ensure its existence. Such an attempt consisted of positing something alongside the gospel which permitted full realization—be it a law concerning faith, or a reference to the point of contact within human existence. In other words, the secret discipline is the renunciation of the point of contact and the law of faith. The secret discipline so understood betrays its point of departure, however, only through a formal similarity with Harnack's attempt to protect religious life from profanation—a complete change in its function has taken place.

Because religion for Harnack finds its own place in man's inner life, the assurance of this "legitimate inwardness" must collapse in constructing the external defenses of religion against profanation. For him the protest against the "impure and insensitive confessions" which penetrated the "mystery of personality" is in the final analysis a religious act. Bonhoeffer adopted this close fusion between religion and inwardness, but for him religion as well as this inwardness became more and more boring and irrelevant.

Whereas Harnack wanted to protect religion and its values from profanation, it was Bonhoeffer's aim (in precise reversal) to safeguard the profanation from religionization. Only in this manner did it seem certain to him that the proclamation of the church is the message of God's free grace directed to the world.

Notes

1   Cf. Carl-Jürgen Kaltenborn, *Adolf von Harnack als Lehrer Dietrich Bonhoeffers* (Berlin, 1973), for a more extensive treatment of the subject.
2   *LPPE*, p. 378
3   *Reden und Aufsätze* (Giessen, 1906), I, 290.
4   *What is Christianity?* (New York, 1957), p. 1.
5   *LPPE*, p. 369.
6   *Reden und Aufsätze*, Neue Folge IV (Giessen, 1923), 390.
7   *Reden und Aufsätze*, II, 32.
8   *Reden und Aufsätze*, NF IV, 191f.
9   *LPPE*, p. 360.
10   *Ethics* (London, 1955), pp. 181-84.
11   *Reden und Aufsätze*, I, 46.
12   *E*, p. 231.
13   *LPPE*, pp. 311f.
14   *Reden und Aufsätze*, NF V (Giessen, 1930), 202; IV, 7f.
15   "What is the cost of progress in history?" in Harnack's posthumous works; cf. Kaltenborn, *Adolf von Harnack*, pp. 104f.
16   *LPPE*, pp. 6f.
17   *Reden und Aufsätze*, II, 71.
18   *Ibid.*, I, 290.
19   *Ibid.*, I, 297f.
20   *Ibid.*, I, 295.
21   *What is Christianity?*, p. 7.
22   *LPPE*, p. 383.
23   *Ibid.*, p. 282.

TWO BONHOEFFERS ON PSYCHOANALYSIS

Clifford Green

DIETRICH BONHOEFFER'S polemics against psychotherapy, though hardly crucial to the theology of his *Letters*, are as well known as the more substantive ideas of those celebrated writings. Psychotherapy appeared to him as "secularized methodism," laying "pernicious eggs" in people's health and happiness. Along with existentialist philosophy he described psychotherapy as a "revolt of mistrust . . . revolt from below," spying out people's secret weaknesses and inner faults.[1] These colorful and cavalier phrases voice Bonhoeffer's impatient dismissal of psychotherapy from any partnership with Christian theology; his attitude is nothing short of contemptuous.

Precisely because these attacks—though brief and in passing—are so vivid and categorical, they call for explanation. Assuming that by "psychotherapy" Bonhoeffer in fact meant Freudian psychoanalysis,[2] many have concluded that his attitude derived from his father Karl Bonhoeffer, who was a leading psychiatrist in Berlin and certainly no Freudian. For example, John A. Phillips writes: "Dietrich's own mistrust of psycho-analysis may have had its roots in Professor Bonhoeffer's rejection of Freud and his followers, and may underlie his later unreceptiveness towards theologies which made use of existentialist philosophy."[3]

More authoritatively, Eberhard Bethge, after looking further into the matter than does Phillips, also concludes that "paternal influence" played a large part in the son's rejection of psychoanalysis. Karl Bonhoeffer, Bethge writes, "made Berlin into a bastion against the invasion of the psychoanalysis of Freud and Jung"; he also, Bethge implies, supported his colleagues when they "boycotted" Freud's contribution to a medical encyclopedia they were editing. Bethge concludes:

> In Dietrich Bonhoeffer's later work psycho-analysis—even when it was relevant to his own field of the cure of souls—either plays no part or is dismissed with contempt. Underlying this of course are theological prejudices on the lines of Karl Barth, but paternal influ-

ence in the matter cannot be denied. Though he possessed a copy of Jung's *Modern Man in Search of a Soul* (1931), as well as E. Spranger's *Psychologie des Jugendalters*, which he carefully studied, he can hardly have been said to have come to grips with Freud, Adler or Jung. Thus in this matter he remained completely within the limits imprinted on him by his father.[4]

When one adds to Bethge's view the opinion of Ernest Jones that Karl Bonhoeffer was "antagonistic to psychoanalysis,"[5] the case seems to be closed. Father and son had the same attitude, it seems, and the views of the latter derived in large part from the former.

Given this reading of the matter, it is little wonder that those interested in the relationship between theology and psychology have virtually ignored Bonhoeffer. For example, Peter Homans' *Theology after Freud* contains no discussion of Bonhoeffer.[6] Jung, in his letter to a Swiss pastor on "religionless Christianity," not only fails completely to understand Bonhoeffer's critical concept of religion and its psychological import; he doesn't even mention Bonhoeffer, being much more concerned to warn against Bultmann's demythologizing.[7] Thomas Oden is one of the very few who has found Bonhoeffer suggestive in the dialogue between theology and psychotherapy.[8] For Oden, Bonhoeffer's criticism in *Ethics* against "thinking in two spheres" is a mandate for this dialogue. Nevertheless, he admits that it is "a bit of a handicap that Bonhoeffer himself had such harsh and biting words against the forms of psychotherapy that he knew, and, in fact, said almost nothing encouraging or affirmative about these possibilities for dialogue."[9] Oden, who draws heavily on Carl Rogers, resolves the embarrassment by regarding Bonhoeffer's polemic as "altogether legitimate in an earlier behaviorist and Freudian setting but increasingly dated by the vigorous development of post-Freudian changes in psychotherapeutic practice."[10]

I agree with Oden about the psychological significance of Bonhoeffer's theology, though I believe we can best appreciate this by beginning somewhere else than with the rather formal, methodological principle which Oden takes from *Ethics*. I will take up this aspect in the third section of this essay. But first I wish to present some evidence that calls into question the common opinion about Karl Bonhoeffer's hostility to psychoanalysis. Then a new look at Dietrich Bonhoeffer's clearly hostile polemics will be in order.

I. Karl Bonhoeffer

Let us first examine Ernest Jones's statement that Karl Bonhoeffer was "antagonistic to psychoanalysis."[11] Jones records this judgment in relation to articles on hysteria and obsessional neurosis which Freud was invited to write in 1912 for a medical encyclopedia being edited by Professors Kraus and Brugsch, colleagues of Karl Bonhoeffer at the University of Berlin. Some months later Freud was annoyed to learn that Kutzinski, a Berlin neurologist and assistant to Karl Bonhoeffer, was also to contribute articles on the same subjects to the encyclopedia. Karl Abraham, Freud's protégé in Berlin, surmised that Kraus had issued the double invitations under the influence of Karl Bonhoeffer. But if, in fact, Karl Bonhoeffer influenced the decision to represent two schools of thought, this is not conclusive evidence of antagonism; it could just as easily be construed as a cautious attitude of open scientific inquiry and debate. Indeed, Jones refers to a letter from Brugsch to Freud explaining "that various theories of hysteria had to be represented, hence the choice of the two men."[12]

Eberhard Bethge, citing Jones as his source, writes that Karl Bonhoeffer's colleagues "boycotted" Freud's encyclopedia contribution.[13] But Jones does not say this. He continues the story as follows. After Freud's initial annoyance he negotiated a mutually acceptable arrangement with Brugsch: Kutzinski would write the two articles on the subjects first proposed, and Freud would write a major essay (over fifty pages) entitled "A Psychoanalytical Presentation of the Psychoneuroses"; in fact, this would amount to a comprehensive review of his life's work to that point, and he was quite aware of the opportunity the encyclopedia offered to gain an official place for psychoanalysis as a part of general medicine. Preoccupied with other matters, Freud did not begin writing until the summer of 1914. Then the outbreak of World War I delayed the encyclopedia project. Factors on both sides, then, led to postponement. After the war the editors renewed their invitation to Freud; they wanted the manuscript by 1920. But, since several years had elapsed from the initial agreement, Freud was now involved in a new stage of work. He proposed that Abraham write the essay, and the latter reluctantly agreed. Jones concludes the story by surmising "that the Editors decided it must be Freud or no one." And as for Freud's article, Jones feels "pretty sure that the essay never got written, or at least never got further than a first draft."[14]

There is no evidence here that Karl Bonhoeffer's colleagues, with his influence or approval, "boycotted" Freud's (probably unwritten) essay. On the contrary, the editors showed a determination that Freud write for them, and a persistence in renewing their invitation. (In addition, Jones writes that Professor Kraus's attitude toward psychoanalysis was friendly.) And why would the editors invite Freud in the first place, if they planned to boycott his essay? The most plausible interpretation of Karl Bonhoeffer's attitude in relation to this episode, then, is that he took the attitude of a conservative scientist if he influenced the editors to have the views of two schools of thought on hysteria and neurosis represented in the encyclopedia. This is in fact consistent with Bethge's own statement about Karl

Bonhoeffer: "Not that he had a closed mind to unorthodox theories, or denied on principle the validity of efforts to investigate unexplored areas of the mind; but he never came into personal contact with Freud."[15]

What, then, of Bethge's remark that Karl Bonhoeffer "made Berlin into a bastion against the invasion of the psychoanalysis of Freud and Jung"? If this conjures up the picture of Karl Bonhoeffer and his men manning the battlements of the city and driving away the heretic invaders, it hardly describes the situation in Berlin. In 1910, two years before Karl Bonhoeffer moved from Breslau to take up the appointment as professor of psychiatry and neurology at the University of Berlin, the Berlin Psychoanalytic Institute and Society was founded by Karl Abraham; indeed, that institute was even established a few months before its sister society in Vienna, in April 1910. While the psychoanalytic movement remained outside the university, as in Vienna, it flourished healthily. Many pioneers of psychoanalysis were trained there and were analyzed by Abraham. Indeed, so successful was the Berlin Institute that it "became the center of the international analytic movement and served as the model for institutes all over the world."[16]

During this development Karl Bonhoeffer adopted a cautious but tolerant "wait and see" attitude. Kate Friedländer, who came for training with the Berlin psychoanalysts about 1927, had a job as an assistant at Karl Bonhoeffer's university psychiatric clinic, The Charité. In her article on Friedländer, Barbara Lantos writes that "many of the young doctors working at the clinic were interested in psychoanalysis and were in training at the Berlin Psychoanalytic Society and Institute."[17] Karl Bonhoeffer, she continues, was "less openly antianalytic than many other leading psychiatrists, [and] tolerated the movement."[18]

Karl Bonhoeffer's attitude is stated fairly well by Martin Grotjahn: "Although Bonhoeffer was not totally antagonistic to psychoanalysis (as Jones had claimed), he was cautious and conservative and opposed the formation of a pocket-sized department within the university."[19] That this is a more correct assessment of Karl Bonhoeffer's attitude is confirmed by Robert Gaupp, who was professor of psychiatry at Heidelberg and a friend of Karl Bonhoeffer since their students days.

> It may perhaps seem a striking fact that a man who was a sensitive psychiatrist with a remarkable gift for empathy and who did outstanding work on the nature of hysterical symptom-formation *never*, so far as I know, *took up a specific and categorical position in the controversy about the theories of Freud, Adler, Jung, and other "psycho-analysts."* . . . In intuitive psychology and scrupulous observation Bonhoeffer had no superior. But he came from the school of Wernicke, which was solely concerned with the brain, and permitted no departure from thinking in terms of cerebral pathology. He practiced the psychology of empathy and understanding on the basis of his natural aptitudes

and gifts. Theoretical interpretation of unconscious activity taking place *behind* [italics in original] observed phenomena that might project into consciousness was foreign to his approach. Intuition was not alien to him, as his whole life's work shows. But he had no urge to advance into the realm of dark, undemonstrable, bold and imaginative interpretation, where so much has to be assumed and so little can be proved.

Bonhoeffer, who was by nature so acute and critical, but was cautious and modest in relation to philosophy, *remained within the borders of the empirical world that was accessible to him*. There are few scientific workers who at the age of eighty, after a career of more than half a century, have had to retract so little of what they once taught.[20]

Thus far our picture of Karl Bonhoeffer is of a psychiatrist, trained in the school of Carl Wernicke, whose orientation was medical and neurological. His attitude toward the psychoanalysts was cautious and judicious, yet tolerant and not dogmatic or obstructive.

Another important source of evidence is the correspondence between Freud and Karl Abraham for, while Freud and Karl Bonhoeffer had no direct dealings, Abraham was in Berlin and had personal contact with Karl Bonhoeffer and his colleagues. And since Jones reconstructed the encyclopedia episode chiefly from correspondence between Freud and Abraham, it is from Abraham that we are likely to get the most accurate impression of how Karl Bonhoeffer appeared to the pioneer psychoanalysts. While Freud was corresponding on and off with Kraus and Brugsch about the encyclopedia essay, Abraham was negotiating with Bonhoeffer and his colleagues about two plans: first, his own *Habilitation* so that he could lecture as a *Dozent* in the university and, later, a proposal to establish a professorship in psychoanalysis at the university.

Abraham repeatedly speaks well of Karl Bonhoeffer as a man: he is personally pleasant, has "a quite conciliatory nature," and "has kept apart from all attacks made against us."[21] Abraham himself enjoyed a good name even among the nonanalytic psychiatrists, as Freud reported to him after receiving a letter from Kraus. Kraus had informed Freud that he was not averse to Abraham's *Habilitation* plan, and that he "counted on the reasonableness of Bonhoeffer."[22] Kraus was virtually a sponsor of Abraham's *Habilitation*, and together they worked out a diplomatic solution: Abraham would write on a "harmless" subject. Bonhoeffer, Abraham writes to Freud, was not on principle opposed to his *Habilitation* so long as he wrote "eine gute Arbeit."[23]

Two reports of conversations between Abraham and Karl Bonhoeffer are quite significant. After a meeting with Bonhoeffer in December 1917, Abraham wrote: "We did not discuss *one* point which is nevertheless significant. Bonhoeffer is rather apprehensive that a partisan of an 'extreme' viewpoint would polemicize in his lectures against the prevailing school of thought" [in Berlin psychiatry].[24] This apprehension was apparently related to Bonhoeffer's opinion that by 1920 psychoanalysis had not yet established itself as a proven discipline. This comes out in a most illuminating paragraph which Abraham wrote after meeting with Bonhoeffer in June 1920 to discuss establishing a professorship of psychoanalysis. He tells Freud:

> Our memorandum is now with the Medical Faculty. A few days ago I had a long conversation with Bonhoeffer, the most influential person concerned. *Bonhoeffer is no friend of psychoanalysis, but nor is he an enemy in principle* [*kein prinzipieller Gegner*]; above all, he is not unfair. *He told me frankly that his objections* [to psychoanalysis] *were subjective, "completely unscientific"* [*gefühlsmässig, "durchaus unwissenschaftlich"*]! But he acknowledges a good deal. He has no substantive objections to establishing a professorship in psychoanalysis, only, after all, a technical consideration which needs discussing. There is a tendency in Berlin to convert all specialized professorships to "Ordinarius" status, with the result that the disciplines concerned become obligatory for students, and subjects in which they must be examined. He held that psychoanalysis was not yet mature enough for this. On the other hand he has no objection to a personal professorship for me. I replied that our position was that psychoanalysis would succeed in time, and that at present we definitely did not want recognition for psychoanalysis as an obligatory subject, but only as an option for those students who are interested and that they are numerous. To the latter he agreed. He promised to invite me again after perusing the proposal, which he did not have before him. I believe, then, that his verdict will not turn out completely unfavorable, especially because his attitude to me personally remains very friendly.[25]

To the now familiar points that Bonhoeffer was neither a friend nor an enemy of psychoanalysis, but wished to see how it developed before establishing it as a discipline in the university, Abraham here adds another. He quotes Bonhoeffer's objections as "subjective" and "unscientific." What does this mean? It cannot refer to the later mentioned "technical consideration" about psychoanalysis becoming a mandatory discipline for students, since this is not a "subjective" objection. In spite of its tantalizing brevity, the statement must refer to Bonhoeffer's own personal feelings, temperament, and taste.

It may be precisely here that we find common ground between Karl and Dietrich Bonhoeffer. By temperament and family training Dietrich Bonhoeffer was reserved about just those areas of the human psyche which psychoanalysis was probing. Respect for reticence was deeply embedded in his character. Inquisitive prying into people's inner life was repugnant to him, as was promiscuous self-disclosure. Uncovering everything that exists was not, he felt, truthfulness but cynicism. He was averse to "talking openly about sexual matters," and, after reading a "remarkably frank" French novel about marriage, he wrote that "the naturalistic, psychological novel is no longer adequate." He was also very wary of narcissistic people who took themselves too seriously. As his poem "Who am I?" shows, Bonhoeffer was something of a psychological agnostic. In connection with that poem he wrote: "I know less than ever about myself, and I'm no longer attaching any importance to it. I've had more than enough of psychology, and I'm less and less inclined to analyze the state of my soul. . . . There is something more at stake than self-knowledge."[26] It is highly likely that Dietrich Bonhoeffer shared such feelings with his father and family, and it is quite possible that Abraham's report refers to a very similar "subjective" attitude in Karl Bonhoeffer.

Finally, let us consider information from Dr. Paul Jossmann, who was from 1920 until 1936 first a student and then a colleague of Karl Bonhoeffer; Bethge mentions in the biography that he was also a friend of the family.[27] Replying to a letter of mine, he wrote:

> I should like to confirm your statement that [Karl] Bonhoeffer was not an "enemy" of psychoanalysis. His professional career was based on the empirical basis of psychiatry, which was *one* sector of medicine *not* an added addition *to* medicine. His whole attitude in psychiatry was based on observation, recording, experimentation, which means that hypothetical [theories] could be considered as explanations in psychiatry if there was observable data found to confirm the speculation. In his opinion, psychoanalysis had not reached this status during his professional career. On the other hand, it is remarkable that he never objected to any interest in psychoanalysis which was manifested by a large number of his assistants who were interested and took psychoanalysis as a training. [Given] his conservative and diplomatic attitude in professional activities, he never expressed objections against personal and professional interests of others. I also underline the fairly well-known lack of his interest in discussing psychoanalysis with his son.[28]

This account accords closely with that of Gaupp.

In an interview,[29] Jossmann elaborated on the points in his letter. Karl Bonhoeffer defined psychiatry strictly as a medical discipline, which required one always to look for the organic basis of psychic problems. Jossmann mentioned depression as an example of a psychic condition which could have many different organic bases, and stated that the psychiatrist's job was to diagnose and treat the organic condition, not to treat psychic symptoms apart from organic conditions. Jossmann agreed that there are psychic disorders which are not connected to an organic base, such as phobias, certain personality problems appearing in marital conflicts, and so forth. These problems, Jossmann said, belong to *psychotherapy*, which he distinguished sharply from the medical discipline of psychiatry. He described psychotherapy as discussion between the person and the therapist, in which problems would be examined, solutions considered, and probably some advice given by the therapist.[30] (This therapy deals primarily with conscious material and does not include the processes developed by psychoanalysis to uncover unconscious material—free association, dream analysis, transference, and so on; from Jossmann's description it was not clear how this approach would deal, for example, with a repressed childhood trauma underlying an adult phobia.) Previously Jossmann had written of Karl Bonhoeffer: "His psychotherapy did not follow any systematized, orthodox schemes as in psychoanalysis and its branches, but it was of the commonsense type."[31]

Jossmann believed that Karl Bonhoeffer read articles by Freud, Abraham, and other psychoanalysts. However, he did not discuss them in his lectures. If in conversation a student expressed interest in psychoanalytic theory, Bonhoeffer would neither argue about it nor condemn it. His typical response would be: Follow your interest if you like, but that approach lies outside psychiatry understood as a scientific-medical discipline.

Throughout our conversation Jossmann had spoken of psychotherapy, as defined above, quite positively. When I described Dietrich Bonhoeffer's polemics against psychotherapy he was surprised and puzzled; he had not previously read the remarks in the *Letters*. He could not explain Dietrich Bonhoeffer's attitude in terms of the way psychotherapy was practiced in Germany during the 1920s and 1930s. On one point, however, he was most definite: Dietrich's categorical condemnation was in no way characteristic of his father, and Jossmann insisted that he could not have adopted this attitude from his father.

A rather consistent account of Karl Bonhoeffer emerges from the foregoing evidence. The public record does not show him hostile or contemptuous toward psychoanalysis. Of course, since Dietrich's views were initially expressed in the privacy of personal letters, one might ask whether Karl Bonhoeffer privately spoke quite differently than he did in public. It is hard to believe there could be such a discrepancy between his public and private views (certainly there was not between Dietrich's letters and his previously published writings—he just spoke more baldly in his letters); in any case, only those privy to conversations of the family circle can speak to this question. Unless contrary evidence appears, we must proceed on the basis of the record.

We may now examine Dietrich Bonhoeffer's writings, from the perspective that we are dealing with his own personal opinions and not the inherited, professional judgment of his father.

II. Dietrich Bonhoeffer

One does not come to the *Letters* unprepared for the polemics against psychotherapy. In 1927 Bonhoeffer had argued the essentially Barthian thesis that "faith . . . rests not on psychic experiences but on itself."[32] "Psychological interpretation is unable to conceive of the reality of grace at all," he wrote in another early paper.[33] His report on William James' *The Varieties of Religious Experience* is hardly enthusiastic.[34] In *Life Together* he states that "the most experienced psychologist . . . knows infinitely less of the human heart than the simplest Christian who lives beneath the cross of Jesus," and so knows sin and forgiveness, whereas "the psychiatrist views me as if there were no God."[35] Later he writes in a similar vein: "Psychology . . . will never be able to discover the simplicity, the freedom and the deed of which Jesus speaks; behind the supposed simplicity, freedom and absence of reflexion it will always find a final reflexion, a final lack of freedom, a final disunion."[36] The points Bonhoeffer makes in these statements cannot be dismissed as if only prejudice and not substantive issues are involved. Nevertheless, the statements show a consistent disinterest in exploring any insights which theology might gain from psychology.

When we turn to the *Letters* and examine closely Bonhoeffer's remarks about *Psychotherapie* and *Psychotherapeuten*, three points are quickly apparent. First, his comments are offhand, not studied. His prison reading included a good deal of literature, history, and theology, and some science. We know that some of this reading, especially in Dilthey, was quite influential for his thinking about the autonomy of modern people, his critique of religion, and his "religionless Christianity" proposal. By contrast, his comments about psychotherapy do not derive from extensive reading and reflection. They are casual opinions, not studied conclusions.

Next, these comments are clearly ancillary to his central themes; they are not decisive for the argument. In the letter of June 8, 1944, Bonhoeffer gives an historical sketch of the development of human autonomy and the defensive reaction of Christian apologetics. He then, in passing, fires a broadside against

> the secularized offshoots of Christian theology, namely existentialist philosophy and the psychotherapists, who demonstrate to secure, contented and happy mankind that it is really unhappy and desperate and simply unwilling to admit that it is in a predicament about which it knows nothing, and from which only they can rescue it.[37]

After this aside, he returns to his critique of modern Christian apologetics and his assessment of contemporary theology in light of his historical sketch. The argument does not depend on the aside; indeed, any force in the comments about existential philosophy and psychotherapists derives from the historical-theological argument.

Three weeks and three letters later, on June 30, 1944, he briefly reviews the historical sketch and again includes a short reference to "existentialist philosophy and psychotherapy" as undermining human strengths and happiness. The next and final reference (in the following letter, July 8, 1944) again yokes "psychotherapy and existentialist philosophy" and repeats the same criticism: they parallel Christian apologetics by trying to undermine human strengths and autonomy. In each of these three references, Bonhoeffer is making one basic point: that psychotherapy and existentialist philosophy are "secularized offshoots" of modern Christian apologetics, engaged in the same dubious enterprise of undermining relative human well-being. The remarks about psychotherapists have the same point as those about Christian apologists; indeed, the former seem designed to reinforce the latter. It is as if Bonhoeffer is saying to various theologians and churchmen who are looking for problem areas in human personality to get a beachhead for their views: "Look what bad company you are in!" In any case, it is clear that the remarks about psychotherapy are subordinate to—and indeed, a variant of—the criticism against Christian apologetics.

Third, these remarks have a repetitious, *formula* character. In each case psychotherapy is mentioned in the same breath with existentialist philosophy. Further, this is a catchall phrase, without any discrimination between different types of existentialist philosophy (Camus and Bonhoeffer could easily be allies, though not Heidegger and Bonhoeffer), or between different psychoanalytic theories and therapies.

There is a degree of invective in the letters which is not found in Bonhoeffer's earlier criticism of psychology. Perhaps some allowance should be made for the fact that he is here writing letters; but this is hardly enough. In light of the foregoing observations, it is likely that the invective largely derives from the parallel he draws between "religion" and its secular counterparts, existentialism and psychotherapy. (The critique of religion, of course, is not new in the letters, though it, too, is sharpened and intensified there.) For Bonhoeffer, the experiential base of religion is human weakness, fear, anxiety, ignorance. He attacks Christian apologetics for a strategy that attempts to spy out areas of weakness and vulnerability underneath human strengths, achievement, and happiness. Precisely the same criticism is made of "existentialist philosophy and psychotherapy": "Wherever there is health, strength, security, simplicity, they scent luscious fruit to gnaw at or to lay their pernicious eggs in. They set themselves to drive people to inward despair, and then the game is in their hands."[38] Given the exact parallel Bonhoeffer draws between religion, existentialism, and psychotherapy, it is difficult to avoid the conclusion that "religion" serves as a model for his sketch of "psychotherapy." This would help explain why Bonhoeffer's description of psychotherapy has frequently been criticized as a caricature.[39]

Could Bonhoeffer's views have been formed in response to various psychologists he had studied? In the winter semester of 1924-1925 he took a course in Berlin with Max Wertheimer on psychology, and another on *Gestalttheorie* with Wolfgang Köhler.[40] At Union Seminary he studied James' *The Varieties of Religious Experience*. As we have seen, he owned and studied Jung's *Modern Man in Search of a Soul* and Edward Spranger's *Psychologie des Jugendalters* (he had taken Spranger's "Kulturphilosophie" course in the winter semester of 1926-1927). In prison he read Ludwig Klages' *Handschrift und Charakter*, renewing an interest he had held from student days.[41] And in *Ethics* he makes one approving reference to a general statement of Fritz Künkel, in a way that suggests he had read several of his "characterological books."[42] This rather short and diverse list hardly qualified Bonhoeffer as an expert on psychotherapy, though research in these works may shed light on his attitude.

Of these, perhaps Fritz Künkel is worth special investigation, not only because Bonhoeffer had apparently read several of his books, but also because he sought to relate psychoanalysis and religion. He saw his psychology as a synthesis of Freud, Adler, and Jung (with a strong leaning to the last), and he mentioned Reinhold Niebuhr, John Macmurray, and Gerald Heard as those who had significantly influenced his religious thought.[43] At least seven of his books were translated into English, chiefly in the 1930s, and that suggests he was popular in Germany as well.

A quick look at Künkel indicates that his social approach to psychology (he called it *Wir-psychologie*) may have had some appeal for Bonhoeffer, as well as his criticism of Freud's "pansexualism." Bonhoeffer may also have been attracted by his interest in the transition from narcissism to accepting one's life with others and one's responsibility to serve the common human cause.[44] However, one can see Bonhoeffer wincing at statements like "man must find God or remain diseased" in speaking of neurotic compulsion.[45] Again, Christianity has a "great chance" when "the inner crisis begins";[46] God is the answer to the ultimate loneliness of the human person.[47] Above all, Bonhoeffer would be horrified when Künkel speaks of "the psychologist's capacity to dig out every root of darkness (he is the expert of sin and therefore in our days the very best father confessor)."[48] If Künkel was popular in Germany, he might have provided Bonhoeffer with a model of the psychotherapist he attacks in the *Letters*; the statements above lie directly in the sights of his guns.

Further research on Künkel, and other popular approaches to psychotherapy in Germany between the wars, may prove conclusive rather than suggestive.[49] At least it seems clear that we need to find another reason for Bonhoeffer's animus than merely his father's influence. We can, however, be fairly confident about two factors that informed his attitude toward psychotherapy: first, personal temperament, which placed a high value on reticence and respect for privacy, and was averse to too much introspection; and second, a theological orientation, influenced by Barth, which regarded psychology as reductionist compared with a Christian anthropology based on the judgment, grace, and calling of Christ.

III. The *Letters* and the Psychological Infrastructure of Theology

What follows is virtually independent of the two previous sections. While we need to understand the historical record as accurately as possible with regard to Karl Bonhoeffer, and while we need to understand Dietrich Bonhoeffer's polemics against psychotherapy as best we can, neither was interested in psychological dimensions of theology or the theological insights to be gained from psychology. Dietrich Bonhoeffer, who initially sought an interdisciplinary engagement between theology and sociology,[50] never had the same attitude toward any branch of psychology. In this he shared the limitations of his older theological contemporaries. (Barth's theology, whatever its psychological implications, proceeded by a methodological asceticism which expressly forbade such interdisciplinary liaisons. Tillich, in spite of his theology of culture, his method of correlation, and his references to psychoanalysis, never really achieved more than a typological integration of psychoanalysis into his ontology and *Geistgeschichte*. Bultmann, for all the prominence he gave to theological anthropology, drew on the implicit psychologies of neo-Kantianism and Heidegger's existentialism without reference to any explicit psychological models.) Nevertheless, Bonhoeffer's *Letters* are an uncommonly suggestive source for exploring the relationship of theology and psychology. In this concluding section I wish to indicate briefly several points meriting further work.

No one who comes to the *Letters* with a knowledge of Freud can overlook the many similarities between Bonhoeffer's theological critique of religion and Freud's psychoanalytic critique, though there is no historical influence of one on the other. For Freud religion was rooted in anxiety, which induced regression to an infantile state of dependency that generated the wish ("illusion") for the powerful father God, who is both protector and moral authority.[51] Bonhoeffer's description of the psychic posture of religion focuses on the same pattern of infantile dependency and the powerful God, the *deus ex machina*. Freud goes on to point out that religion as a defense mechanism exacts the price of keeping one in perpetual dependence on the father God, thus reinforcing the infantile attitude from which it arose; and furthermore, the moral authority of the cosmic father often generates excessive moral scrupulosity and neurotic guilt, which increases the natural anxiety at the root of regression.

Without suggesting that Freud's diagnosis holds good for all types of religion, one must say that it is certainly an impressive analysis of the sort of religion Bonhoeffer described. And it obliges us to consider the psychosocial infrastructure which produced that religiosity: structures and relationships in family and church; child-rearing patterns; forms of authority; the psychological impact of liturgy with its imagery and actions, and so forth. Had Bonhoeffer been familiar with the Freudian analysis, he would have realized that more was involved in his religionless Christianity than a nonreligious interpretation of biblical and theological *concepts*, as necessary as that is; a psychic posture must be dealt with on the psychological level as well as the conceptual. Here the psychoanalyst can be seen as tutor to the theologian.

On another point, the theologian and psychoanalyst become allies. Viewed theologically, what Freud was describing was *spurious transcendence*. His psychological critique assailed religion as a cyclical and self-perpetuating pattern of behavior. God, rather than enabling people to grow out of infantile dependence and develop mature independence, responsibility, and skills with which to deal effectively with "reality," kept people in a state of perpetual childhood, anxiety, and guilt. Such a God did not introduce new and transforming dynamics into the human psyche; such religion basically reflects and replicates the human condition from which it was born. Central to Bonhoeffer's critique of religion, of course, is his charge that it offers no authentic transcendence and is an idolatrous extension of human needs and wishes. Freud provides psychological documentation of Bonhoeffer's charge, and Bonhoeffer provides a theological critique of the psychically dysfunctional religiosity Freud described.

This alliance extends to a further point. It is an intriguing coincidence that Bonhoeffer chose the metaphor *Mündigkeit* to describe the new psychic posture which his religionless Christianity was to engage. For this metaphor points to just those adult qualities of independence, autonomy, responsibility, and acceptance of reality which Freud sought to promote, and which he saw religion inhibiting. Of course, Bonhoeffer might be challenged in his view that this new psychic posture is virtually universal in the contemporary West. However, it is clear that his theology of religionless Christianity seeks to enhance and promote strengths of the ego and vigorously opposes any efforts to undermine them. I believe that this perspective sheds significant light on the centrality of the weak and suffering Christ in the *Letters*, a type of *theologia crucis* which has often puzzled commentators and produced unwarranted speculation about how the prisoner's suffering influenced his theology. Seen from a psychological perspective, the "weak" Christ removes at a stroke the powerful God wished for by weak egos. The cosmic screen on which the religious person projects fantasies of compensatory power is chopped down. In its place stand the cross and the Christ who frees religious people from infantile dependence, sending them back to find God in their strengths, knowledge, responsibility, and happiness.

Bonhoeffer is here describing an authentic and transforming transcendence.

At the same time, the "weak" Christ who demythologizes the power God of religion guarantees and supports human *Mündigkeit* and autonomy. One is no longer threatened and inhibited by the absolute divine power standing over against him, sapping him of his own strength, independence, and creativity—an accusation leveled against Christianity by all its nine—teenth-century critics. Yet it is not as if Bonhoeffer was concerned only to provide a theological justification for a new psychic posture. Such ego strengths as modern, secular people possess can be used in either humane or demonic ways, as Bonhoeffer well knew. The Christ who supports the strengths of secular psyches also enlists them in a life of co-humanity and pro-humanity. The paradigm of Christ's "being-there-for-others" checks demonic power and transforms all human power, humanizing it in genuine service of others.

Once again an authentic transcendence is disclosed. By now we have reached the point where the theologian has become tutor to the psycho-analyst; at least we can be sure that a debate between Bonhoeffer and Freud on social ethics would be lively and fruitful.[52]

I have briefly brought Freud and Bonhoeffer together because the similarity of their attitudes toward religion demanded further exploration. One could perhaps even more fruitfully consider Bonhoeffer and Erikson together, since Erikson focuses on the process of developing ego strengths which was Bonhoeffer's point of departure in the *Letters*. But that cannot be pursued here. However, in light of the preceding comparison, brief though it is, I believe we can confidently conclude that further work on the interaction of the psychoanalytic tradition and Bonhoeffer's theology would be fruitful, in spite of Bonhoeffer's invective, which has heretofore confused the issues.

Notes

1   Cf. *LPPE* (New York, 1972), pp. 326, 344ff. See also the less well-known comment in Bonhoeffer's *Dramenfragment*: "We hold mistrust to be common and low. We look for the frank word and deed of the other man and we want to accept it without suspicion. Nothing is more destructive of social life than to suspect a person's spontaneity and to be suspicious of his motives. The psychologizing and analyzing of people which has now become fashionable means the destruction of all trust, the public calumniation of all that is decent, the revolt of all that is common

against what is free and true. Men are not in a position to look into the depths of each other's heart ... but they should encounter each other and accept the other as he is, simply, candidly, in confident trust" (*GS,* III, 492; *True Patriotism*, p. 212; now also published in Bonhoeffer, *Fragmente aus Tegel* [Munich: Chr. Kaiser, 1978], pp. 61f.—see also another draft of this dialogue, *Fragmente,* p. 223). (This essay expands an appendix, "Preliminary Note on Karl Bonhoeffer's Attitude to Psychoanalysis," in my doctoral dissertation; the latter is now published, without the appendix, as *Bonhoeffer: The Sociality of Christ and Humanity* [Missoula, Montana: Scholars Press, 1975].)

2 The grounds for this assumption are presumably Bonhoeffer's references to sexuality, the scrutiny of the inner life, and the unveiling of unconscious or hidden roots of behavior; cf. *LPPE*, pp. 326, 344ff.

3 Phillips, *Christ for Us in the Theology of Dietrich Bonhoeffer* (New York: Harper, 1967), pp. 13f. Here Phillips refers to the encyclopedia incident, discussed below, mentioned in Ernest Jones's life of Freud, and uncritically appropriates Jones's belief that Karl Bonhoeffer "rejected" Freud.

4 Bethge, *DBET* (New York: Harper, 1970), pp. 11f. (*DB*, p. 44).

5 *The Life and Work of Sigmund Freud* (New York: Basic Books, 1955), II, 248ff.

6 Indianapolis: Bobbs-Merrill, 1970.

7 Jung's letter, originally written in 1959 and published in the Swiss *Kirchenblatt*, No. 125 (May 29, 1969), pp. 164ff., was translated by Mrs. Stephen Benko and published in the *Journal of the American Academy of Religion*, XXXIX, 1 (March 1971), 43-47.

8 In addition to Oden, see also the doctoral dissertations of William J. Peck, "Interpersonal Simplicity in Theology and Psychiatry: a comparison of Dietrich Bonhoeffer and Harry Stack Sullivan" (Harvard Divinity School, 1962), and Graeme M. Griffin, "The Self and Jesus Christ . . . ," on Bonhoeffer and Jung (Princeton Theological Seminary, 1965).

9 Oden, *Contemporary Theology and Psychotherapy* (Philadelphia: Westminster, 1967), pp. 32f.; see also Oden's "Theology and Therapy: A New Look at Bonhoeffer," *Dialog*, V, 2 (Spring 1966), 98-111. Oden's inference (*op. cit.*, p. 15) that Bonhoeffer, in view of his family setting, was "thoroughly familiar with Freudian psychoanalysis and the psychotherapies of the 1920's" is highly dubious. James Woelfel, *Bonhoeffer's Theology: Classical and Revolutionary* (Nashville: Abingdon, 1970), p. 48, makes a similar assertion. There is no sign of this awareness in Bonhoeffer's writings; his library and reading did not include, so far as I have been able to determine, any Freud. Bethge, as we have seen, certainly states that Bonhoeffer did not "come to grips with Freud, Adler or Jung."

10 Oden, p. 33.

11 Jones, II, 248ff.

12 *Ibid.*

13 *DB*, p. 44.

14 Jones, II, 248ff.

15 *DBET,* p. 11.

16 Martin Grotjahn, "Karl Abraham: The First German Psychoanalyst," in Franz Alexander, Samuel Eisenstein and Martin Grotjahn (eds.), *Psychoanalytic Pioneers* (New York: Basic Books, 1966), p. 9; cf. pp. 2ff.

17 *Ibid*, p. 510.

18 *Ibid.* Professor J. Zutt, Director of the Neuroclinic, University of

Frankfurt/Main, sometime colleague of Karl Bonhoeffer and co-editor of the *Festschrift* (see below, note 30), has recently added some new information on Karl Bonhoeffer's attitude. Though Zutt himself came to adopt a critical position on psychoanalysis, he underwent a training analysis in Berlin with Abraham in 1921 on Freud's advice and participated for two years in the activities of the Berlin Psychoanalytic Association. Abraham suggested he try to get a position with Bonhoeffer in the psychiatric clinic. "Bonhoeffer welcomed my arrival," Zutt writes, "since he had previously written to Freud inquiring whether he could send an *Assistent* to Vienna to become familiar with his method. Freud declined on the grounds that one could learn everything from his writings." (Letter of Zutt to E. Bethge, April 21, 1976.) I have not located the texts of these letters, but Zutt's report seems at the very least to show an attitude of professional curiosity on Karl Bonhoeffer's part—certainly not hostility or a closed mind. (For further comment by Zutt, see note 30 below.)

19 *Ibid.*, p. 2.

20 Cited in *DBET*, p. 11 (italics mine). We must note here a curious contradiction in Bethge's picture of Karl Bonhoeffer in relation to psychoanalysis. On the one hand he speaks of his turning Berlin into a "bastion" against it, and being connected with a "boycott" of Freud's encyclopedia articles. On the other hand he describes him as not a dogmatic thinker with a mind closed to unorthodox theories; and he quotes Gaupp's statement that Karl Bonhoeffer "never . . . took up a specific and categorical position in the controversy about the theories of . . . [the] 'psycho-analysts'." It seems impossible to reconcile these two sets of statements, or to verify the very negative statements on the basis of the public record.

21 *Briefe, 1907-1926. Sigmund Freud, Karl Abraham*, Hilda C. Abraham and Ernst L. Freud, eds. (Frankfurt/Main: S. Fischer, 1965), pp. 129, 150. English translation: *A Psycho-analytic Dialogue: The Letters of Sigmund Freud and Karl Abraham, 1907-1926*, trans. Bernard Marsh and Hilda C. Abraham (New York: Basic Books, 1965). In both these texts Karl Bonhoeffer is mistakenly referred to as "Professor W. Bonhoeffer" in an editors' note.

22 *Briefe*, p. 131.

23 *Ibid.*, pp. 134f.

24 *Ibid.*, p. 250.

25 *Ibid.*, pp. 289ff. (italics mine). The sentence "But he acknowledges a good deal" ("Er erkenne aber vieles an") is somewhat opaque. (The published translation, "but that he accepts much of it" [*A Psycho-analytic Dialogue*, p. 310], is perhaps an overstated translation.) The statement suggests a certain reluctant acknowledgment of psychoanalysis, despite subjective objections. Probably the sense is: but he concedes there might be something in psychoanalysis. That would certainly be consistent with Bonhoeffer's "wait and see" approach. In the later sentence, "To the latter he agreed," the word "latter" refers to the interest of numerous students and perhaps also to Bonhoeffer's awareness of the limited nature of the proposal; it does not imply Bonhoeffer's agreement with Abraham's statement that psychoanalysis would succeed in time. (The plan, incidentally, did not work out. The editors report that members of the faculty were too hostile. When the question came up again it was intimated that the possibility of a *Dozent*'s position would exist were Abraham to be baptized! He declined.)

26 *LPPE*, pp. 162f.; cf. pp. 158ff., 190, 212f., 233f., 347f. Similar remarks are found in earlier writings where, as here, the theological notion "that in *statu*

corruptionis many things in human life ought to remain covered" (p. 158) is also invoked.

27 *DBET*, p. 10.

28 Letter to me from Jossmann, October 31, 1973. Dr. Jossmann (who died in 1978) was for many years Chief of the Neuro-Psychiatric Service, Veterans Administration, Boston, and sometime Professor of Neurology and Psychiatry, Boston University. He published an article on Karl Bonhoeffer in the *Monatschrift für Psychiatrie und Neurologie* (1948), but I have not had a chance to see it.

29 July 26, 1974, in Boston.

30 In a brief summary such as this it is hardly possible to do justice to Karl Bonhoeffer's own approach to psychiatry and psychotherapy. Even a layman can get a much richer impression from his memoirs; see "Lebenserinnerungen von Karl Bonhoeffer Geschrieben für die Familie," in *Karl Bonhoeffer zum Hundertsten Geburtstag am 31 März 1968*, J. Zutt, H. Straus, H. Scheller, eds. (Berlin: Springer Verlag, 1969), pp. 8-107; the volume also contains a bibliography of Karl Bonhoeffer's writings. There is no mention of Freud, Abraham, psychoanalysis, etc., in the memoirs. Professor Zutt has recently interpreted this fact with a somewhat different emphasis from Robert Gaupp's stress on Karl Bonhoeffer's preoccupation with neurology. He writes: "Certainly the fact that Bonhoeffer disliked polemics played a role. But what is much more important is that he was a master of silence as a mode of communication. That he passed over psychoanalysis in silence was a sovereign value judgment. He wanted to correct even at that time the extravagant and modish exaggeration of its importance" (letter to E. Bethge, April 21, 1976).

31 Letter to Graeme Griffin, quoted on p. 65 of his dissertation (cited above). Griffin himself states in the same paragraph: "It can be said with some assurance that Professor Karl Bonhoeffer influenced his son's views on psychoanalysis and psychotherapy." But he does not quote anything from Jossmann to support this; in my discussion with him, Jossmann vigorously contested the sort of similarity of attitude which Griffin implies.

32 *GS*, III, 47. In remarks at the 1974 Bonhoeffer Consultation, Geffrey Kelly felt that a strong case could be made for a Barthian source underpinning Bonhoeffer's polemics. Noting, following Bethge's biography and Benktson's *Christus und die Religion* (Stuttgart: Calwer Verlag, 1967), that Barth's *The Word of God and the Word of Man* (London: Hodder & Stoughton, 1928) was influential for the young Bonhoeffer, he pointed to Barth's remarks on psychology both in this text and in the *Römerbrief*, observing that Barth's critique of religion is found in both books. I would respond by saying: 1) the passages cited in Barth have none of the contemptuous disdain typical of Bonhoeffer's polemics; 2) while Barth puts the response of faith to the Word beyond psychological explanation, he seems more concerned to *relativize* psychology than to *reject* it out of hand; 3) Bonhoeffer's view and critique of religion is more distinctly his own than borrowed from Barth, even though he saw an influence (and legitimation!) in Barth's approach; 4) the link proposed by Benktson between Bonhoeffer's youthful reading of the early Barth and his *Letters* is too academic and tenuous, in my view, to explain Bonhoeffer's originality and passion in his prison writings.

33 "The Religious Experience of Grace and the Ethical Life," *GS*, III, 95f.

34 *GS*, III, 127-29.

35 *LT*, pp. 118f.

36 *E*, p. 37. Griffin, pp. 69ff., 125, gives a fairly detailed review of the

various references to psychology prior to the *Letters*, and the way Bonhoeffer typically dissociates revelation, faith, and theology from psychology.

37 *LPPE*, p. 316; cf. pp. 341, 344ff.

38 *Ibid.*, p. 326.

39 See, for example, John Godsey, *The Theology of Dietrich Bonhoeffer* (Philadelphia: Westminster Press, 1960), p. 275; Griffin, p. 271.

40 *DB*, p. 101.

41 *LPPE*, p. 245.

42 *E*, p. 148.

43 Künkel, *In Search of Maturity: an Inquiry into Psychology, Religion and Self-education* (New York: Scribner, 1944), p. ix.

44 See Künkel's chapter on "Society and Religion" in *Conquer Yourself* (New York: Ives Washburn, 1936).

45 *Ibid.*, p. 282.

46 *In Search of Maturity*, p. 18.

47 *Ibid.*, p. 28.

48 *Ibid.*, p. 10.

49 William J. Peck has made the valuable suggestion that a study of Nazi psychologists, being part of a movement Bonhoeffer disdained as a "revolt from below," might shed further light on his attitude.

50 See his *Sanctorum Communio* (London: Collins, 1963), printed in the United States as *The Communion of Saints* (New York: Harper, 1963).

51 See, particularly, *The Future of an Illusion* (Garden City, New York: Doubleday, 1964).

52 The previous paragraphs draw on ideas discussed in more detail in my book on Bonhoeffer cited above, pp. 309ff., 341ff. Some of this, in summary form, was contributed to the Introduction of *Critical Issues in Modern Religion* (Englewood Cliffs, N.J.: Prentice-Hall, Inc., 1973), Roger Johnson, Ernest Wallwork, Clifford Green, *et al.*, eds. The three chapters on Freud, Bonhoeffer, and Erikson are most germane to the present discussion.

BONHOEFFER AND THE POSSIBILITY OF JUDAIZING CHRISTIANITY

Douglas C. Bowman

HARVEY COX has identified four areas in which the theological world has yet to appropriate, much less move beyond, the deep richness of Bonhoeffer's thinking:[1] 1) the enlargement of the ecumenical perimeter; 2) the tactics for determining concrete and specific political involvement of the churches; 3) the exploration of new structures and forms for church life; and 4) the delineation of a nonreligious hermeneutic commensurate both with tradition and modern life.

To be sure, these four broad areas do constitute what could be called the Bonhoeffer legacy, and the contents of this commemorative volume add weight to Cox's contention that we have yet to move beyond Bonhoeffer. Recognizing also that there was considerable movement in Bonhoeffer's thought, Cox concludes his essay in a fashion typical of many Bonhoeffer studies by recording his perception of the *direction* in which Bonhoeffer was finally heading, along the lines of the four topics enumerated.[2] What results—and this also is quite typical, I think—is a fourfold challenge to dare "on the border of unbelief" to do and to think and to believe what is needful for "the health and renewal of the world" on the basis of certain "hints" found in the last letters.

Now one may speculate (as Cox does) concerning Bonhoeffer's last direction of thought—claiming all manner of support for new possibilities—or one may warn against such speculation on the grounds that such procedure does violence to the substantive main body of Bonhoeffer's more obvious contribution and runs the great risk of obviating his "true intentions," which we all have yet to discover. Two observations may be made at this point. First, since we shall never know precisely where the later Bonhoeffer would have come out, we are ill-advised to chastise one another for honest and prudent speculation, provided that such speculation is recognized for what it is—a high and ephemeral art—thereby keeping discussion free and open, and provided that those so engaged are informed by careful analysis of the Bonhoeffer literature. Much fertile and imaginative thinking has been prompted already in theological and lay circles by Bonhoeffer's last fragments. Who would wish to call a halt to this movement and scrap obvious gains made, which rightly or wrongly claim Bonhoeffer as inspiration and authority? Let it be recognized that Bonhoeffer's legacy does, after all, include just such a dimension of theological work.

Second, it is abundantly clear that during those last eventful days Bonhoeffer was developing questions which grew out of and enlarged portions of his finished works, and that he intended to set down in book form his statement as to the nature of those questions. Accordingly, it should come as no surprise to find scholars engaged in the fruitful enterprise of attempting to develop further those same questions judiciously, inventively, and—most appropriately where Bonhoeffer is concerned—courageously.[3] Since Eberhard Bethge has provided us with these fragments, we should use them in the manner indicated and not count it violence or degradation to match Bonhoeffer's efforts.

In the spirit of these observations, I set down what follows, which is at once a report to fellow students and an invitation to speculative discussion concerning certain questions that have come to me during several years of sorting through the progress of Bonhoeffer's thought. The burden of what is on my mind may be stated by asking: *Would it not be possible to conclude that an outcome appropriate to the trend of Bonhoeffer's thinking would be a process of Judaizing Christianity?* I am not alone in making this suggestion. Nor (as I shall attempt to prove) am I indulging in unfounded speculation or perpetrating a notion antithetical to serious Christian faith (as someone more competent than I has already argued convincingly[4]). The implications of this could prove very interesting and render considerable advantage both to Bonhoeffer studies and more general theological and ecclesiastical endeavor.

What might the Judaizing of Christianity involve? No doubt one formidable adjustment required, especially of the Protestant traditions, would concern notions of man—his nature, possibilities, and capacities. To put the matter historically, there would have to be a complete reversal of the Augustinian development, which, as Martin Buber viewed it, "was not . . . adapted to further that especial connection of the ethical with the religious that true theonomy seeks to realize through the faithful autonomy of man."[5] In point of fact, what Buber calls the "Israelite mystery of man as an independent partner of God" would have to gain preeminence in Christian thinking, thus utterly transforming notions of law and grace, sin and salvation. The formal *theological* correlate to this anthropological shift would be the rethinking of the omnipotence and supremacy of God's grace—God's sole and exclusive prerogatives respecting the future of his autonomous partner, who no longer need rely upon the church as the touchstone of salvation.

A second theological factor in Judaizing Christianity would have to be the diminution of the importance of theology itself, thereby bringing reason to bear on concerns more typically Jewish.[6] Judaism, after all, has always been content to live with as little data as possible respecting formal theology—a trait which accords with the intent of the first commandment.

Central, of course, to the entire program would be a radical Christological translation. Indeed, it would be appropriate to ask with Bonhoeffer, "What *is* Christ for us today?"[7] As we shall indicate, a recent study shows that an altered Christology can be found that is at once congenial to Christianity and to Judaism. In point of fact, a *Jewish* Christology was likely the most potent one advanced in earliest Christian circles.

Finally, Judaizing Christianity would mean the appropriation of the whole ethical tenor—the *pan-halakic* character—of the Jewish tradition, which, as Abraham Heschel describes it, celebrates the "wonder of doing" and the "divinity of deeds."[8] Hence the drive is from theology to ethics. Not that ethics has had little place in Christian thought in the past. Rather, an altered anthropology and Christology place man's doing at the top of the modern agenda, and demand that it be given utter priority in Christian circles. Thus from theology to ethics, the Judaizing of Christianity means the total revision of a tradition and the complete change of its course of development.

At this point, we cannot avoid the question: Why all of this? Obviously, a massive internal collapse of the basic structure of Christian thought, the cessation of its historical development, and the impingement on it of inordinate external pressures would constitute the conditions necessary for seriously acknowledging the demand for change and revision. Moreover, these factors coupled with convincing evidence concerning the Jewish nature of Christian origins—evidence such that nothing short of reassessment of the course of progress from those origins is called for—could lend the weight needed to drive thought to the initiation of the project of making the Christian religion Jewish once again and not so gradually sloughing off structures, doctrines, and casts of mind acquired from non-Jewish orientations that serve only to stifle the life of the church in the present age.

Once these elements are enumerated and appreciated, it is clear how enormous and far-reaching the implications of the project become for a tradition that has run so completely counter to all that is being suggested. One cannot minimize the revolutionary consequences involved. Now it is remarkable how these very ingredients begin to emerge in the final prison letters. The letter dated 30 April 1944 presents the initial challenge respecting the total collapse of Christian theology and religion:

Our whole nineteen-hundred-year-old Christian preaching and theology rests upon the "religious premise" of man. What we call Christianity has always been a pattern—perhaps a true pattern—of religion. But if one day it becomes apparent that this *a priori* "premise" simply does not exist, but was an historical and temporary form of human self-expression, i.e. if we reach the stage of being radically without religion—and I think this is more or less the case already . . . what does it mean for "Christianity"?

It means that the linchpin is removed from the whole structure of Christianity to date. . . .[9]

One can hardly miss the stark import of these words, which cannot be made to indicate anything short of the complete demise of the traditional Christian development in the West. What is more, the point is equally clear that the foundation of theology (the "religious premise of man") was false and is now shattered. There is little point in seeking to restructure the Christian religion on the old foundation. The linchpin is gone. The whole has collapsed. Accordingly, a nonreligious hermeneutic cannot mean, in Bonhoeffer's subsequent letters, the restructuring of given developments. Something radical and different is demanded by these challenging words *along all lines*, and especially along the lines of Christology—the question that pervades the final letters.

One need not mention, at this late date in Bonhoeffer studies, how the important and much-explored theme *"die mündige Welt,"* found throughout the letters, delineates Bonhoeffer's assessment of those historical forces and pressures that succeed in calling forth a complete stock-taking (*Bestandsaufnahme*) of Christianity as well as the eventual revision of its substance.[10] How, now, can Christians have recourse to "Christ" in the matured world without recourse to previous casts of thought? And who can help but notice that arranged alongside these progressing themes is an unmistakable quickening of interest in the Old Testament, together with attempts at sketching a hermeneutic that links the church to its ancient origin? Observe the following:

To resume our reflections on the Old Testament. Unlike the other oriental religions the faith of the Old Testament is not a religion of salvation. Christianity, it is true, has always been regarded as a religion of salvation. But isn't this a cardinal error, which divorces Christ from the Old Testament and interprets him in the light of the myths of salvation? . . . It is said that the distinctive feature of Christianity is its proclamation of the resurrection hope, and that this means the establishment of a genuine religion of salvation, in the sense of release from this world. The emphasis falls upon the boundary drawn by death. But this seems to me to be just the mistake and the danger. Salvation means salvation from cares and need, from fears and longing, from sin and death into a better world beyond the grave. But is this really the distinctive feature of Christianity as proclaimed by the Gospels and St. Paul? I am sure it is not. The difference between the Christian hope of resurrection and a mythological hope is that the Christian hope sends a man back into his life on earth in a wholly new way which is even more sharply defined than it is in the Old Testament.[11]

Thus Bonhoeffer had noted the collapse of Christian theology and religion since the high Middle Ages, and had sharply criticized attempts to adjust to the new situation emerging for the churches, which, because the new situation itself can be viewed in a positive light, demanded an end of adjustment-making.[12] He allowed the fulness of the historical forces to bear upon his thinking (i.e., the analyses productive of *"die mündige Welt"*), and he returned to the Old Testament for directive regarding the formulation of a totally new hermeneutic, which he would call the "non-religious interpretation" of the Bible, and which would demand Christological reassessment.[13] The ground was prepared thereby for the emergence of Judaizing tendencies in his thinking more specifically. It remains for us now to take especial notice of these tendencies.

Embedded in Cox's account of Bonhoeffer's last directions is a significant and far-reaching observation about man that is in no sense incidental to the direction Cox believes Bonhoeffer was heading. "Bonhoeffer," Cox insists, "wanted us to believe in man and his possibilities, and he did not feel that this should weaken our faith in God."[14] Bonhoeffer's emphasis on the strong and healthy capacities of man (e.g., seeking to address him honestly at the center of his powers and life[15]); the emphasis he gave to "human example" that "has its origin in the humanity of Jesus";[16] his serious injunctions to learn to live in the mature world as a Christian *etsi deus non daretur*;[17] his excoriations of certain existentialists and psychotherapists and religious apologists (he could well have included all those theologians of Augustinian persuasion) who demean and call into question the goodness and power of man[18]—all of these elements provide evidence for the bold assertion Cox makes.

Naturally, therefore, Bonhoeffer's thoughts turned to questions concerning sin and salvation, law and grace, for what was now at stake was the radical reassessment of the "Christian" man under grace. Could one describe what it means to be "Christian" man in this age, given what such an age demands ethically of all men (Bonhoeffer's own life is the best case in point), and given the collapse of tradition and the coming-of-age of humanity? Notable is the fact that Bonhoeffer could not, conclusively, since all previous ways of describing Christian men in tradition were no longer open to him and since those ways rested on the demeaning tendencies and religious premises he was taking pains to avoid. Accordingly, the "Christian man" became, for him, the "man pure and simple,"[19] who knew and enjoyed the full powers of modern man, who did not have religion and sin put upon him. All of this is commensurate with "the ability of traditional Judaism to articulate a theory of human nature, both realistic yet more hopeful than the doctrine of man's innate corruption."[20] Bonhoeffer's arresting remarks about the sin of man match exactly the distinctions observed by a modern rabbi:

> At the risk of oversimplification, the difference between the Christian and the Jewish attitude toward the nature of man may be put as follows: for traditional Christianity, man sins because he is a sinner; for traditional Judaism, man is a sinner because he sins. But to this observer, at least, it seems clear that in increasing measure Christians are approximating the outlook traditional in Judaism.[21]

Thus there are grounds for the assertion Cox makes about Bonhoeffer's emphasis on man, as there are also for the assertion that Bonhoeffer's anthropology and ethics became increasingly humanistic in the final letters, or—dare we say forthrightly?—more Jewish in orientation.

Striking above all else is Bonhoeffer's following out the correlate to the new emphasis on man, namely the radical changes respecting a nonreligious view of God, and the relationship between man and God:

> What do we mean by *God*? Not in the first place an abstract belief in his omnipotence, etc.[22]

> God is teaching us that we must live as men who can get along very well without him.[23]

Imagine such resonant proclamations sounded in the name of Augustinian theology! Moreover, the only hint Bonhoeffer eventually gives regarding his developing theology is the concept of "*der Mensch für Andere*," which is to serve as the appropriate analogy of "God in human form"[24] and which is to provide considerable resource for ethical reflection. This amounts to nothing short of the typical rabbinic displacement of theology by ethics. Need I point out that "theological" reflection subsequent to Bonhoeffer's impact, which moves out of his influence, bears clear testimony to this Judaizing tendency in Protestant circles?

Thus in anthropology and theology especially we see Bonhoeffer's thought take on the characteristics of the Judaizing process. What of the important area of Christology? Here *the* problematic as well as enigma of the final letters presents itself. Jesus as the "man-for-others," who bids men "suffer with him at the hands of a godless world" and who is the prototype of the "worldly" man in the modern age, hardly resembles the complex figure described and developed by the massive pronouncements of tradition. Obviously, something radically new in orientation is called for in

Christology, which, as we noted earlier, must be related to Old Testament origins. There is just not enough substance of a Christological nature in the final letters to warrant meaningful speculation. Thus the enigma of Christology must stand, and we are driven back to Bonhoeffer's own question, "What *is* Christ for us today?" in the full recognition that this question was central to all that he wished to work through. The relationship of Christology to the modern world is, indeed, the question.

One must take Bonhoeffer's "Outline for a Book" as the serious indicator of the final directions of the thought implicit in all of the last letters. When this is done, one final element presents itself, namely the burden of his remarks contained in the section to be entitled "Consequences."[25] The thrust is ethics. The problematic is *human example*, described as "something we have well-nigh forgotten," and from the long list of moral verities Bonhoeffer enumerates, it is clear that major moral reform is what he is after. In point of fact, everything from general church teaching to apologetics to creeds to ministerial training and clerical life is to be touched by his struggles with the question of human example. What resources will he have? The outline suggests the teachings of Paul and the "humanity of Jesus." Surely nothing here could contradict the idea that the Judaizing of Christianity emerges as a lively possibility of the future. The moral tenor of Jewish thought could intrude quite naturally into the flow of discussion of the verities enumerated without doing violence to the resources he suggests.

I invite the reader to reflect on the enormous consequences of the points advanced in this essay. The conditions for and the characteristics of the Judaizing of Christianity have been outlined, and we have seen how the final letters lend themselves to the interpretation advanced, making it feasible to assess the Bonhoeffer legacy in a totally new light. Not only does this assessment prove helpful with respect to the Bonhoeffer fragments, but it also serves to account for post-Bonhoeffer developments, which have sometimes seemed so confusing. The illustrative passages and citations in this essay by no means exhaust the possibilities for continued study with regard to Bonhoeffer himself, nor concerning the range of post-Bonhoeffer developments.

Where might this trend eventually lead?[26] I recommend an inventive study by Professor Neill Q. Hamilton in the field of New Testament interpretation, which he has entitled *Jesus for a No-God World*.[27] To be sure, this particular study does not overtly set out to Judaize the Christian faith, but it fits the pattern most admirably. Indeed, it succeeds in meeting the conditions of Bonhoeffer's own program respecting hermeneutics, theology, anthropology, ethics, and especially Christology. One of the book's summary statements indicates the basic direction it takes:

It is one of the great ironies of history that the Western, Hellenistic wing of the church eventually suppressed the Jewish wing that gave it birth and permitted it to develop.

    We have reviewed the tragic story that produced this sad turn of events. It would appear to be absurdly irrelevant to perpetuate the subapostolic prejudice against Jewish Christianity, once the historic factors are known.[28]

Accordingly, Professor Hamilton sets about the arduous task of getting at those "historic factors" concerning the earliest of Christian origins including the recovery of the historical Jesus. It is his intention to revive for our time a way of thinking about Jesus that is peculiar to Jewish Christianity,[29] thereby uncovering a Christology—most likely the earliest initiated within the church—smothered by unfortunate political considerations in the Hellenistic world of the first century. It is Hamilton's conviction that he discovers a Jesus "who not only was more firmly at home in this world but also one whose culture is more in tune with the modern world than the traditional figure apparently alienated from his own people."[30] A Jewish Jesus emerges from the sources unencumbered by interpretations and claims that would preclude the serious attention of modern men. Moreover,

> there is hope that a form of Christianity may emerge from this foundation that will not feel compelled to break with Judaism. The fact that Jesus was a Jew and not the first Christian could recall contemporary Christians to the original situation of the church when it was possible to be both Jew and Christian at the same time.[31]

The Jesus of this treatment is the eschatological prophet of Jewish culture, who stands in bold contrast to the ontological God-man of tradition. Precisely because of this definition, this Jesus arising out of the sources provides substance both in terms of his person and teachings for translation into modern idioms of anthropology and ethics. He is a "non-religious" Jesus, in Bonhoeffer's terms, who is thoroughly one with Old Testament roots and first-century culture.

    Since Hamilton is able to discover the method whereby the early church translated the importance of Jesus for its own time on the basis of secular forms and constructs, the cultural relativity of traditional Christology is laid bare with new force relative to our earliest known sources. Therefore, ways of viewing Jesus that are at odds with the modern "convictional structure"[32] need not be repeated, but Jesus' pertinence for our times may be explored freely on the bases of new forms and constructs drawn from secular culture. This Professor Hamilton carries out with considerable ingenuity. Outstanding is the fact that what results in translation for modern Christianity is 1) a view of Jesus as prototypical man; 2) a diminution respecting theology proper;[33] 3) an elevation of the place of man as the independent partner of God;[34] and 4) a vigorous ethic which outstrips the confines of the New Testament with its quite limited social perspective.[35]

It remains for students of the New Testament to discuss the more refined aspects of Hamilton's theses. However, if the serious consequences of what this essay has outlined are appreciated, it behooves theologians to welcome his study and to engage his translations seriously and critically—not inappropriately, I would venture, in the name of Dietrich Bonhoeffer, whom we honor with this volume. Bonhoeffer may or may not have viewed his own last efforts as indicative of the form of Judaizing Christianity I have attempted to demonstrate and which I believe is implicit in the illustrations cited from works subsequent to his own. Nevertheless, he would have been hard pressed, I think, to show that his questions did not in fact make possible the process outlined above. It is my conjecture that the new world opened up by the idea of the Judaizing process would have been a congenial one for him. Indeed, that world, I maintain, is a very real part of his own legacy.

Notes

1   Harvey Cox, "Beyond Bonhoeffer? The Future of Religionless Christianity," *The Secular City Debate*, Daniel Callahan, ed. (Macmillan, 1966), pp. 205f.

2   *Ibid.*, pp. 212-214.

3   See, for example, the recent treatment by Benjamin A. Reist, *The Promise of Bonhoeffer* (Lippincott, 1969). Based on the acquisition of the Bethge biography, Reist is able to remark: "Therefore we can proceed to the task of second guessing his ideas. For the only point to thinking his thoughts after him is to think these thoughts beyond him" (p. 116).

4   See what follows respecting theses advanced by Neill Q. Hamilton.

5   Martin Buber, *The Eclipse of God* (Harper Torchbook, 1957), p. 107.

6   Robert Gordis, "Re-Judaizing Christianity," *The Center Magazine*, I, 6 (Sept. 1968), 7f. "The entire thrust of Jewish tradition has always been to minimize concern with God and to maximize concern with man. . . . Jewish theologians [feel] no need for 'theology' " (p. 7).

7   *WE*, p. 178: "Was mich unablässig bewegt, ist die Frage, was das Christentum oder auch wer Christus heute für uns eigentlich ist" (*LPPE*, p. 279).

8   As cited in W. D. Davies, "Torah and Dogma: A Comment," *Harvard Theological Review*, I, 2 (April 1968), 98, n.11.

9   *WE*, pp. 178f.: "Unsere gesamte 1900jährige christliche Verkündigung und Theologie baut auf dem 'religiösen Apriori' der Menschen auf. 'Christentum' ist immer eine Form (vielleicht die wahre Form) der 'Religion' gewesen. Wenn nun aber eines Tages deutlich wird, dass dieses 'Apriori' gar nicht existiert, sondern dass es eine geschichtlich bedingte und vergängliche Ausdrucksform des Menschen ge-

wesen ist, wenn also die Menschen wirklich radikal religionslos werden—und ich glaube, dass das mehr oder weniger bereits der Fall ist . . . was bedeutet das dann für das 'Christentum'? Unserem ganzen bisherigen 'Christentum' wird das Fundament entzogen . . ." (*LPPE*, p. 280).

10   See as the final assessment the book outline, *WE*, pp. 257f., "Entwurf einer Arbeit."

11   *WE*, pp. 225f.: "Noch etwas zu unseren Gedanken über das Alte Testament. Im Unterschied zu den anderen orientalischen Religionen ist der Glaube des Alten Testaments keine Erlösungsreligion. Nun wird doch aber das Christentum immer als Erlösungsreligion bezeichnet. Liegt darin nicht ein kardinaler Fehler, durch den Christus vom Alte Testament getrennt und von den Erlösungsmythen her interpretiert wird? . . . Nun sagt man, das Entscheidende sei, dass im Christentum die auferstehungshoffnung verkündigt würde, und dass also damit eine echte Erlösungsreligion entstanden sei. Das Schwergewicht fällt nun auf das Jenseits der Todesgrenze. Und eben hierin sehe ich den Fehler und die Gefahr. Erlösung heisst nun Erlösung aus Sorgen, Nöten, Ängsten und Sehnsüchten, aus Sünde und Tod in einem besseren Jenseits. Sollte dieses aber wirklich das Wesentliche der Christusverkündigung der Evangelien und des Paulus sein? Ich bestreite das. Die christliche Auferstehungshoffnung unterscheidet sich von der mythologischen darin, dass sie den Menschen in ganz neuer und gegenüber dem Alten Testament noch verschärfter Weise an sein Leben auf der Erde verweist" (*LPPE*, p. 336).

12   See especially the letter of 8 June 1944, *WE*, pp. 215-221; *LPPE*, pp. 324-329.

13   Gordis, p. 9: "The thesis may be set forth simply as follows: From its inception until our day, Christianity, which arose within the Jewish community, underwent a process of de-Judaization. Today the opposite tendency is making itself felt—a far-flung process of re-Judaization, taking on a variety of forms." My own attempt in this essay is simply to substantiate Gordis' thesis respecting one root cause, i.e., the thought of Bonhoeffer and its profound influence on subsequent thought. Gordis adds this interesting note: "When Bonhoeffer asked, 'How can we speak of God without religion' he had only to look to the Hebrew Scriptures for his answer. There is no word for 'religion' in the Hebrew Bible" (p. 7).

14   Cox, p. 212.

15   *WE*, p. 211; *LPPE*, p. 312.

16   *LPPE*, p. 383; *WE*, p. 262.

17   *LPPE*, p. 360; *WE*, p. 241; see also the analysis in Reist, pp. 80-94 and *passim*.

18   *LPPE*, pp. 158-160; *WE*, pp. 233-237.

19   *LPPE*, p. 369; *WE*, pp. 247f.

20   Gordis, p. 9.

21   *Ibid.*, p. 12. Cf. Bonhoeffer, *LPPE*, pp. 341f.: "When Jesus blessed sinners, they were real sinners, but Jesus did not make every man a sinner first. He called them out of their sin, not into their sin. . . . Never did Jesus question a man's health, vigour or fortune, regarded in themselves, or look upon them as evil fruits."

22   *WE*, p. 259: "Wer ist Gott? Nicht zuerst ein allgemeiner Gottesglaube an Gottes Allmacht etc" (*LPPE*, p. 381).

23   *WE*, p. 241: "Gott gibt uns zu wissen, dass wir leben müssen als solche, die mit dem Leben ohne Gott fertig werden" (*LPPE*, p. 360).

24   *LPPE*, p. 381; *WE*, p. 259.

25   *LPPE*, pp. 382f.; *WE*, pp. 261f.

26   A rather conservative estimation is provided by Davies, p. 105: "The dogmatic development of Christianity, in short, remains as the barrier to reducing

the relation between the two faiths to a mere schism. It is part of wisdom to recognize this. . . . At least the time is long overdue for Christians to recognize that the attempt to overcome Torah by Dogma is long past: its almost total ignominious failure is evident. This already points toward the emergence of a new era or at least new possibilities for Christian-Jewish relations." Note, however, the more daring challenge sounded by Professor Willard Oxtoby of Yale in his article entitled "The Post-Ecumenical Age," *Theology Today*, XXIII, 3 (Oct. 1966), 380: "But an openness to Judaism, important though it may be, will not be enough for the future of Protestant theology. To achieve a formula for Jewish participation in the National Council of Churches or to hammer out a common biblical theology would be to work within the American or at best the western cultural tradition, and within the spiritual heritage of part—if not all—of the Bible. The elements of faith shared by Christians and Jews, if not central, are at least numerous. If Jews are not members of our family, they have been historically our closest neighbors. But the true ecumenism called for in the next three decades will have to be much broader still."

    27   Neill Q. Hamilton, *Jesus for a No-God World* (Westminster, 1969).

    28   *Ibid.*, p. 140.

    29   *Ibid.*, p. 87.

    30   *Ibid.*, p. 122.

    31   *Ibid.*, p. 137.

    32   *Ibid.*, pp. 173-177. This category Hamilton develops along lines set forth by Willem Zurdeeg, *An Analytic Philosophy of Religion* (Abingdon, 1958).

    33   *Ibid.*, p. 179: "To bring the doctrine of God into conformity with modern convictions requires that God be related to the world by suasion rather than by a direct exercise of power. The power will have to reside where the convictional structure specifies: in the forces of nature and in the agency of man. God's role is to persuade man to use his agency in history in the way that he indicated in the career of Jesus of Nazareth. That, I submit, would be the beginning of an analogous equivalent to the traditional Christian doctrine of God in the convictional structure of our illustration." Also p. 201: "If we shift the model from king to father, we are in a better position to understand the self-effacing side of the Biblical tradition about God. . . . It will not be surprising if a world come of age produces men who, for a time, need to forget their heavenly father to reach fuller maturity as his children."

    34   *Ibid.*, p. 190: "But secular Christianity grounds its hope upon the new possibilities available to man rather than upon the arbitrary, irresistible intervention of God."

    35   *Ibid.*, pp. 188f., 196-198. P. 196: "The ethic thus devised would be a religious ethic because of the common conviction that constituted the group. Jesus provides the supreme declaration of what human life ought to be. The ethic would not be a simple repetition of Jesus' teaching. Much of Jesus' ethic would be directly usable, but since his ethic was not designed to inform a program of social change, the new ethic will need to incorporate elements that never occurred to Jesus."

III.
HISTORY

BONHOEFFER'S THEOLOGY OF HISTORY AND REVELATION

Geffrey B. Kelly

DIETRICH BONHOEFFER had an extraordinary sense of the future implications for both church and society of those historical events which unrolled in the period of his active life as minister, teacher, and conspirator within Nazi Germany. At times his perceptiveness seemed to mark him among his contemporaries as a pesky, no-compromise agitator, stirring up trouble when people hankered after nothing more than security. He was, in many respects, a prophet of doom and hope, a pace ahead of his colleagues and with a cause few embraced and still fewer were willing to die for. His reading of history was often clear—his own actions, after some initial wavering, decisive. His theological justification of those actions which led him inevitably to the conspiracy, however, was at once as tortuous and inspiring as it was deeply undergirded by his Christocentric faith. In this essay I will attempt to develop Bonhoeffer's theological understanding of history and revelation as these concepts shaped his own attitude toward both church and state. In a final section I will draw from his later writings some theological implications for a more universal concept of revelation based on a closer link between historical events and God's self-manifestation.

In the eleventh theological thesis for his doctoral examination, Bonhoeffer contended that "there is no Christian teaching of history."[1] He had jotted the following note on his personal copy of these theses: "A Christian philosophy of history exists, and so do historically edifying lessons. The purpose of the teaching of history is to present the most likely facts in as objective a way as possible, with the relation which links these facts, so that a correct historical assessment may be made. We cannot see the heart, but the person; we are not judges of the world. Thus basically everything in history evades a Christian evaluation."[2] This was a thesis Bonhoeffer could have defended with increased vigor some sixteen years later, when the trauma of becoming personally involved in a political conspiracy and being subsequently imprisoned caused him to wonder just what meaning

89

the tragedy of Germany and his own personal suffering could have. Had
there been a specific "Christian teaching" on history, the ethical decisions
of the conspirators might have been facilitated. Instead, they had to cope
with uncertainty and ethical isolation, forcing them to adopt modes of
action which, in conscience and in other circumstances, they would have
repudiated.[3] As a student, Bonhoeffer was arguing simply against the
superimposition of a Christian teaching of history on history itself; the
events of history evade a "Christian" interpretation.

For the same reason, he also rejected a specifically "Christian ethic,"
warning against easy solutions to problems based on unalterable principles
and laws.[4] The distinction between Christian principles and human, secular
knowledge he branded as misleading. Being Christian was not something
more than human. Although the Christian must himself be imbued with a
certain "earthly wisdom" in order to act as a Christian, this could hardly
establish a split between faith and human history.[5] Bonhoeffer's conviction
that the two must somehow be seen as one impelled him to search for a
more primordial unity which could overcome the traditional split between
revelation and science, the Christian and the human. This unity he would
center in the "heart" of the world, the hidden presence of Christ in human
history. His resulting theology of history will seem, in a way, an implicit
denial of the very thesis he had defended as a student, since he will argue
for a Christian interpretation of history in which a Christian can see himself
or herself addressed by the Word spoken in those concrete events which
demand responsible decision to follow Christ whatever the consequence
for one's personal safety. Keeping in view his own caution that this is not
something that compels acceptance by any empirical evidence, we turn now
to an examination of how Bonhoeffer links history and revelation in a
Christocentric understanding of all reality.

I. Bonhoeffer's Concept of History

Bonhoeffer generally uses the term "history" as a qualifier to designate
God's actions in time or the events that give a certain concreteness to
revelation. Ultimately, history for him is the period between the creation
and the end-time. God's plan for the world unfolds in the events and social
relationships of history. Only faith, however, can ever see the connection.
According to Bonhoeffer, history begins with the fall and terminates with
God's final judgment of the world. "History lives between promise and
fulfillment";[6] otherwise, history has no clearly discernible order.[7] Bonhoeffer recognized that history is ambiguous and does not always yield an
answer to the nagging problems which seem to defy a solution, nor does
it always reveal the designs of God which a person of faith can acclaim.
Hence he reminded his students in Berlin that "it is impossible to argue

directly from history to God."[8] In his homiletics lectures to his seminarians at Finkenwalde he noted that "the so-called concrete historical situation is ambiguous. Both God and the devil are at work in it. It cannot become the source of our understanding and proclamation of the Word of God."[9] He pointed out in an analysis of Harnack's *Das Wesen des Christentums* that history is not to be understood by dragging in dogmatic or rationalistic viewpoints but solely from history itself and, therefore, the "essence" of Christendom is dependent on its present historical shape. To this he added a remark on the presence of ideals or universal concepts under which particular events are often understood and judged. To determine the "essence" of something, one must, according to Bonhoeffer, shape that essence. To understand history will similarly demand that one personally decide history through historical deeds. If nothing else, Bonhoeffer attempts to demonstrate how relative so-called historical knowledge was and how difficult it was to arrive at an "objective" perception of history, past or present.[10]

Bonhoeffer himself opts for an openness to what the facts of history might mean in one's individual and social life but always in relationship to what he in faith has constantly affirmed, namely, the ordering of all events toward their Christic fulfillment at the end of history. In this sense, Bonhoeffer could call Christ the center and the consummation of history even while affirming that this was not demonstrable in scientific terms.[11] His assertion that Christ is the center of human existence and of history does not refer to a predictable and demonstrable structure in human personality as such but to the human person as he stands before God.

Bonhoeffer raised the question of Christ's place in the world and in history in the context of his Christology lectures at the University of Berlin.[12] To say that Christ is the center and the boundary of one's existence is, according to Bonhoeffer, to restate in spatial and temporal terms the only authentic Christological question: "Who is Jesus Christ?"[13] As mediator of the revelatory relationship between God and his creatures, Christ exists for persons at the center of life. He has fulfilled the Law, that symbol of the human sinful condition and of the human capacity for failure, and in this way he points to a new existence in transcendent union with him. Just as people are confronted by their inability to fulfill the Law, so they cannot of themselves achieve the promise of messianic fulfillment. This depends on God's own promise in Christ.

II. History and Revelation

Bonhoeffer sees history moving, therefore, in expectation of that fulfillment when Christ will be revealed as the hidden center of history. Such had already been proclaimed in the prophetic hope of Israel. It was accomplished, but in a veiled manner, by God's entering history. Bonhoeffer contends that the meaning of history is mediated at its hidden center by the crucified and risen Christ.[14] In his lectures on Genesis, Bonhoeffer would use this Christic structure to contrast human existence in Adam with human existence in Christ.

> Our history is history through Christ. . . . Our imagination cannot help us to know about the beginning. We can only know about it from the new middle, from Christ, as those who are freed in faith from the knowledge of good and evil and from death, and who can make Adam's picture their own only in faith.[15]

If God makes known the hidden center of history in Christ, history itself is—because of Christ—the theater of God's self-revelation. God as absolutely free personality is beyond any sphere of ideas which human reason can conjure up. The "onceness" or uniqueness of God's free personality is accessible only indirectly through the events made possible by his own free entrance into human history. Developing this point in his article "Concerning the Christian Idea of God," Bonhoeffer writes that "God spoke his Word in history, yet not only as a doctrine but as the personal revelation of himself. Thus Christ becomes not the teacher of mankind, the example of religious and moral life for all time, but the personal revelation, the personal presence of God in the world."[16] This statement contains two elements that are capital to Bonhoeffer's understanding of revelation, namely, God as person-in-relationship and as presence-in-history. For Bonhoeffer, it is important to emphasize that Jesus does not reveal God to man, but *God reveals himself to man in the historical person of Jesus Christ.* Assuming this nuance, he then declares that God is accessible only in Christ. Bonhoeffer does not thereby intend to deny the possibility of God's presence elsewhere than in the history of Christ. He is speaking rather of the "once for all" character of God's entry into history in Christ and therefore of a certain fullness to his revelation in time. Christ cannot be bypassed in human efforts to grasp and understand God because God's entering history in Christ is indissolubly linked to his historical self-revelation.[17] In his *Ethics,* Bonhoeffer qualifies the Christic-historical form of God's manifestation as limited by its very temporality. Christ had taken form only in a special moment of human history. Hence Bonhoeffer wanted to limit the application of his own ethical conclusions to the so-called Christian West.[18]

Bonhoeffer's insistence on God's becoming accessible in the history of Jesus leads him further to refuse the distinction between the kerygmatic or present-historical *(geschichtliche)* Christ and the historical *(historische)* Jesus of Nazareth. This was the distinction of liberal theology which Bonhoeffer says simplified the dogmatic problem to the point of falsification. He agreed, therefore, with Martin Kähler that, because the historical Christ was the same as the preached Christ, the whole quest for the historical Jesus had operated on a wrong presupposition.[19] Both dogmatics and preaching would falter if such a differentiation were valid.[20] We see his pastoral concern on this point rather clearly in his lectures on preaching. Speaking on "the proclaimed word" to his seminarians, he insisted:

> As little as the incarnation is the outward shape of God, just so little does the proclaimed word present the outward form of reality; rather, it is the thing itself. The preached Christ is both the Historical One and the Present One. . . . He is the access to the historical Jesus. Therefore the proclaimed word is not a medium of expression for something else, something which lies behind it, but rather it is the Christ himself walking through his congregation as the Word.[21]

Of course, Bonhoeffer's attitude toward the "quest for the historical Jesus" begs the question of Jesus' historicity. If the historicity of the life and death of Jesus is of absolute significance for the church, how can the church be sure of the historical foundations of its dogmatic and homiletic assertions? Bonhoeffer's solution to this problem is based on his assumption that, in this instance, historical investigation and methodology are transcended. Jesus himself eludes both absolute affirmation or absolute denial of his historicity. What is constitutive of the church, on the other hand, is the faith in Christ's resurrection whereby the historical past becomes present and what had been hidden becomes revealed. Bonhoeffer refuses to recognize the *absolute* grounding of faith in history. Only through the witness of the risen Christ and through his presence in the community can it be said that the Christ preached in the community or congregation is the historical Jesus.

Bonhoeffer would thus turn around the premises of the "historical quest" so that the historical investigation itself would become irrelevant in the face of Christ's present self-attestation. The faith created by the risen-historical Christ would then give a "direct" but Christ-oriented access to history. In Bonhoeffer's opinion, this attitude removes the difficulty in preaching a specific word attributed to Jesus but whose authenticity had been either questioned or denied by historical investigation. To excise the word because of its historical inauthenticity, Bonhoeffer argues, would be to deny the presence of the resurrected Christ and to exaggerate history instead of interpreting history in the light of faith. Bonhoeffer claims he is not advocating that theology be indifferent to history. History should rather strengthen faith, even as it attempts to uncover the hiddenness of Christ. This hiddenness is part of Christ's continued humiliation. However, Bonhoeffer insists that the questions of Jesus' historicity and continued presence in the world must be integrated into the present faith of the community.[22]

This qualification should be kept in mind in analyzing why Bonhoeffer criticizes liberal theology for its "latent docetism" or for attributing only an apparent reality to the manhood and historicity of Christ. Ancient docetism had proceeded from an abstract idea in which God as absolute, suprahistorical idea was known apart from any real embodiment or incarnation. The result was a doctrine of God fundamentally unrelated to man and his history. Christ had taken on the essence of man but not his individuality, the external form of man but not his true corporeality. His divinity was his substance, his manhood a mere appearance or fantasm of that substance. Bonhoeffer thought he detected this tendency of docetism lurking behind liberal theology's interest in separating the historical Jesus from the preached Jesus. Those engaged in the effort were simply substituting a speculative concept of history for the docetist abstraction from the physical reality of Christ. History was the support and manifestation of liberal theology's particular "supra-historical ideas." The incarnation would, then, become the means to an end, and the man Jesus would become only the manifestation of those values attributed to him by the community. In the last analysis Bonhoeffer believed that liberal theology failed to take Christ's humanity seriously, despite its declared intention to probe after that humanity. Inevitably it either passed over his manhood or used it as a support for a particular idea of God. The real man Jesus was thus confused with the "ideal" man.[23]

Bonhoeffer sought to emphasize the empirical character of the incarnation by attacking the concept of history favored in idealist philosophy. His stand against idealism is also seen in his Barcelona Conference, "Jesus Christus und vom Wesen des Christentums." In this conference he reviews the options for understanding history and declares that there are basically only two hermeneutical procedures. The first is that influenced by idealist philosophy. This attempts to fit history into a ready-made scheme beginning from certain universally recognized truths or ideas. History itself would then be subordinated to these truths and ideas. In principle, no absolute meaning could be claimed for history as such; it could neither say anything ideationally new nor make any urgent demands on people. History would be relativized. Against this, Bonhoeffer countered that, if history is so relativized, then in practice one would never reach beyond the ideational criteria in judging the historical data.

Bonhoeffer proposed, rather, a second possibility for interpreting history, namely, that which drew a concrete meaning from history without imposing any preformed ideas, categories, or systems of values. In short, he advocated an understanding of history in which history not only speaks and makes claims on people but also acts as a test and judgment for all ideas, since "history is more than an idea." The proper attitude toward history, according to Bonhoeffer, would be to face up to the demands of an integral life by making those practical, ethical decisions which shape not only history itself but one's existence in society as well.[24]

Bonhoeffer himself does not concede any absoluteness to history independent of God's control. Theologically speaking, history for him is always history structured by the incarnation. Bonhoeffer argues here mainly against efforts to declare Jesus of Nazareth a personage in whom the mythical and the kerygmatic crowd out the historical. This, he felt, undermined God's historical manifestation in the man Jesus by attempting to reduce the facts of Jesus' life to nonmythical and eternal truths, ideals, or values. Such, he objected, was an attitude toward history that substituted preformed ideas for the empirical and, as a consequence, evaded the challenge of the facts themselves. If history can be said to have any absoluteness for Bonhoeffer, it would lie in Christ's having entered history to initiate its process toward fulfillment and in the significance of each event as touched by God's presence.

Bonhoeffer extends his reproach of liberal theology for having relativized history through the abstract categories of Hegel and Hegelian idealism. While Bonhoeffer would agree with Hegel that "only as the one who is historical is God God," he nonetheless disputes Hegel's making this a *necessary* manifestation of God in history. He argues that Hegel would reduce the incarnation to an abstract principle, whereas in principle the incarnation was "inconceivable." God became a real man, not an idea of man. The incarnation cannot be deduced from divine necessity; it remains rather God's free decision to achieve the incomprehensible. The danger of idealism, Bonhoeffer concludes, is that it "removes the first principle of all theology, that God really became man of his own free grace."[25] Bonhoeffer's reaction both to docetism and to the docetic tendencies he imputes to liberal theology provides an insight into his theological understanding of history. It is clear that he wanted a concept of history that took Christ's manhood seriously but would, in turn, be subordinated to an aprioristic idea of God's freedom. God's free entrance into history involved a full incarnation but was in no way dictated by any compulsion inherent to his *nature*. His revelatory action is still *extra nos*. History constitutes the tangibleness of this manifestation but only in an indirect manner, and thus the notion of God's simultaneous hiddenness in history must also be maintained. Each of these terms must be seen in relationship.

a) History and the Concreteness of Revelation

The historical category was used by Bonhoeffer principally as a critical gauge of genuine talk either about God's manifestation to his creatures or about responsible Christian living. Bonhoeffer refused any theory that dipped into abstractions to explain God's nature. This attitude on his part would later dictate his rejection of the abstract images of God which he accused metaphysics of having fashioned into a lifeless idol. Moreover, one of his frequent complaints against theological systems was that they failed to take history seriously.[26]

Yet it can be said that Bonhoeffer himself had no fully developed theory of history. Often enough, his own concept of the "historical" became a synonym for the visible, material, and situational whereby God manifested himself. The concrete historical situation was for him the material forum in which a human person was addressed by God's Word.[27] The historical was, likewise, the locus of ethical decision.[28] The concreteness of Christian preaching depended for Bonhoeffer more on God's acting in his Word in specific situations than on history itself as a source of that preaching. In his essay on interpreting the New Testament, Bonhoeffer insists that the tangibleness of the Christian message was not a human act but the work of God himself.[29] Having once entered history, God had become available to people and could no longer be spoken of in the abstract. God had to be completely other than the so-called eternal truths conjured up by one's own imagination and desires.[30] Nor could God be said to retreat into some invisible realm.[31] In this regard, Bonhoeffer's fear was that, without a grounding in the biblical life-relatedness of God's manifestation and specifically in the historicity of Christ's person, descriptions of God would be nothing more than projections of the self. This explains his eagerness to speak of the God of the Bible rather than the God of the "gaps." The biblical emphasis was on historical encounter and concrete forms. As Bonhoeffer explained it to his brother-in-law, Rüdiger Schleicher, in order to find out what God was saying he turned naturally to the Bible. He did this because of the uncertainty of everything else and through fear of otherwise stumbling into a mere "divine counterpart" of himself.[32] For Bonhoeffer, history is a tangible characteristic of mankind's existence in which *God* has acted and in which *God* reveals himself.

As a consequence, Bonhoeffer praised critical Christology for having protected this historical-experiential grounding of revelation. On the negative side, it had excluded those objective thought forms which had constructed a theology from some kind of prior knowledge of the isolated substances of God and man; on the positive side, it had worked from the historical fact of the God-man. This approach accorded more with Bonhoeffer's own approach to revelational Christology, which held that "only in the light of the fact itself can one know who God is."[33] For the same reason, Bonhoeffer had earlier opposed Max Scheler's *Wertethik,* or an ethic founded on prior acceptance of a system of values. In Scheler's system, the highest place had been accorded aprioristically to the religious value of the "Holy," which was then supposed to act as a unifying thread binding persons together into one community. Bonhoeffer objected to this on the basis that Scheler's argument seemed to proceed from a metaphysical understanding of the "Holy," which, because of its absoluteness, was inaccessible to man. According to Bonhoeffer, it would have been more attuned to reality had Scheler begun with "the historically positive revelation of the Holy in Christ, the 'material bearer of the value.' "[34] This critique depends, of course, on Bonhoeffer's treatment of Christ's role in human existence and salvation. Briefly, Bonhoeffer affirms that in his salvific death Christ had reconciled all peoples with God and reestablished the revelatory communion that brings a person to a new life. Christ's presence in the church would then be the continuation of his *historical* existence as the man living totally for others.[35] In no way can it be a question of separating his person from his works, the whole Christ from the so-called historical Christ.[36] Through the incarnation God had entered into a perceptible revelational relationship with humans. This act not only affirms the world and mankind, but it summons believers to a new responsibility vis-à-vis their particular situation.

Even though Bonhoeffer insists that God manifested himself in history, he acknowledges that God remains at the same time the hidden God. Hence "revelation in history means revelation in hiddenness."[37] In asserting this paradox, Bonhoeffer seeks to preserve a sense of God's transcendence. The God revealed is also the "wholly other," beyond the grasp of religion, ethics, or metaphysical knowledge, but somehow present where sin and death grapple with faith in the depths of a human person and in the life-death rhythms of human society. Bonhoeffer admitted to Rüdiger Schleicher that it was quite possible to construct an image of God according to one's own specifications and expectations, but this would ignore Christ's suffering and death. The cross was a totally unexpected and disagreeable mode of God's interrelationship with his creatures; yet this was the one place where he most clearly showed his paradoxical nature. Neither God's methods nor his thoughts were those of man.[38]

Why this should be so Bonhoeffer explains in terms of the free and contingent nature of God's having bound himself to humans in the incarnation. So entirely did God enter history in Jesus that the divine manifestation, recognized in faith, would have to be concurrently a veiling of his glory.[39] The same Jesus in whom God made himself known to his people was simultaneously the incarnate and the crucified, the humiliated and the exalted. None of his divine attributes was visible in his death. Bonhoeffer traces Christ's "humiliation" to the situation of a sinful world which necessitated that he become a beggar, an outcast, a victim, even—in the words of Luther—a "sinner among the sinners." If Christ was exalted in the resurrection, he was also the one who bore human guilt on the cross. And, although only faith could penetrate the incognito of the resurrection to discern the God manifest in the man Jesus, even this faith could only bring people to the limits of their own vision.[40] This was the boundary where in

Christ God's works achieve a certain transparency. Nevertheless, the work of salvation and its disclosure remain God's hidden activity. The cross which had become comprehensible only in the resurrection was still conceivable only by faith in the "hidden ways" of God.[41]

b) History and Eschatology

The hidden nature of God's historical revelation in Christ likewise accentuates Bonhoeffer's sense of the relationship between history and eschatology and of the eschatological nature of revelation. History, in fact, takes its meaning for him from its poles of creation and eschatology. Bonhoeffer's doctrine of the "orders of preservation"[42] represented his effort during the church crisis to describe God's action in the "fallen world," reconciling people in his son, and in him working to achieve the "new creation" at time's end. In this sense, Bonhoeffer could speak of mankind's continued waiting for the second coming of Christ.[43] Consequently, eschatology would determine the preaching of the cross and resurrection in such a way that the past was raised to the present and beyond that to the future. The net effect was that Christian revelation could not be interpreted as a totally past occurrence but would have to qualify, on the contrary—because people live in the community of the present—as both a present and a future event. Revelation is never something that has already "definitively" happened.

Bonhoeffer's attempt to integrate the past, present, and future of revelation within a present community of believers is somewhat clarified by an examination of his seminar paper, "Kirche und Eschatologie," and the last section of *Sanctorum Communio.* These constitute his only detailed attempt to relate the church to eschatology.[44] Bonhoeffer distinguishes in his seminar paper between the church and the kingdom of God. The kingdom of God is an eschatological or supratemporal concept for Bonhoeffer. But insofar as the kingdom of God does exist in time, it must become visible in history. He sees this happening in the empirical church whose word of preaching becomes the temporal expression of God's judgment.[45] Through the visible community's mission the members of the church are brought into the kingdom of God, and thus the historical community formed by God becomes identical in purpose with the kingdom of God. Both depend ultimately on the elective decision of God and on the Spirit which binds the members of each community into a relationship of love. One major difference between them, aside from the "spiritual nature" of the kingdom of God, is what Bonhoeffer observes to be the limitation of the church to a section of history whereas the kingdom of God includes the whole development of world history.[46] Nonetheless, the empirical church is the forerunner and sign of the future kingdom. The ultimacy of the kingdom of God, however, only accentuates for Bonhoeffer the additional significance of the empirical church. The kingdom of God must begin in time if it will ever become a future reality. And so Bonhoeffer concludes that "at every moment judgment through the word of God takes place in history. Each epoch is directed immediately to God. . . . Each moment is the end of history and yet not the end since the end will first exist when 'death is swallowed up in victory.' "[47]

Bonhoeffer's understanding of the church's relation to the eschatological future brings out more clearly his entire attitude toward history as such. In his dissertation, for example, he adopts Ranke's view that history itself can provide no adequate solution to the problem of eschatology.[48] Only faith, which can choose the *Sanctorum Communio* over the "Antichrist," can discern God's judgment on each succeeding moment in the community's history. Bonhoeffer sees two aspects to the church's eschatology: judgment and communion. With the dawning of Christian eschatology, the isolation of the individual, which had been partially overcome by the human and Christian communities, is finally banished as the members of the community enter into the relationship of a "full" revelation. This condition had already been anticipated through the eschatological signs within the Christian community. The final reality, then, is pictured by Bonhoeffer as the communion of wills of those for whom the full revelation of God's love will have turned into vision.[49]

This eschatological perspective, which was somewhat stressed by Bonhoeffer during the prewar church struggle, was very evident in *The Cost of Discipleship*. In this book he tries to point up the challenge of Christianity for a church under pressure from authorities, both secular and ecclesiastical, to compromise the gospel. Bonhoeffer's answer is to call to mind the radical obedience demanded by the Sermon on the Mount. Christ did not preach the "cheap grace" of a once-for-all justification without works but a faith characterized by radical obedience to the gospel. In the confusion and turmoil of taking a decisive stand either for or against Christ, Bonhoeffer recalls that this was a life or death struggle. He portrays the church in a situation similar to the hostility faced by Jesus and his first disciples. For this reason Bonhoeffer reminds the church of its belief that Christ's imminent return is always a possibility. It is, in fact, "more certain than that we shall be able to finish our work in his service, more certain than our own death."[50] He characterizes the crisis as a time in which the church would at last have the opportunity to become identical with Christ in all things.[51]

In his *Ethics,* Bonhoeffer describes the present-future nature of revelation as a dialectical tension between the penultimate *(die vorletzten Dinge)* and the ultimate *(die letzten Dinge)*. Bonhoeffer pictures all life as "held in tension between the two poles of eternity."[52] The "ultimate" in this time span fluctuates in meaning between the temporal moment of God's justifying gift of faith[53] and the beginning of a timeless eternity.[54] Faith begins a new life for the sinner, determining his subsequent attitudes and actions, but it also conditions the final moment of life when all penultimate action is fused into eternity. Ultimate and penultimate are not intended here to be mutually exclusive concepts.[55] The ultimate validates the penultimate; but this penultimate must lead necessarily to the ultimate. Although the world has been reconciled in Christ, and in Christ God has spoken his word of justification, this reality has not yet attained the fullness of the end-time when Christ will be revealed as God's final reconciliation of all creation. The final word has been pronounced in the cross of Jesus, but insofar as the Christian lives between penultimate and ultimate, he must experience the tension between his present faith in God's grace and the eschatological future. "Already in the midst of the old world, resurrection has dawned as a last sign of its end and of its future, and at the same time as a living reality."[56] This life "between the times" must mirror the unity and diversity of Christ's incarnation, crucifixion, and resurrection. In other words, for Bonhoeffer, Christian life is necessarily a participation in the life of Christ and in the rhythms of his death and resurrection. In this way it also becomes a real encounter with the world because "in Christ the reality of God meets the reality of the world."[57]

This perspective changes in the prison letters to an emphasis on a "this-worldly" Christianity. Here he berates his fellow churchmen for preaching a flight from the immediate problems of radical service and advocates involvement in the secular to the point of active resistance to the war then being waged. Part of the reason for the apathy and noninvolvement of the churches, he felt, came from interpreting Christianity in terms of a "salvation myth" preoccupied with deliverance from the world or an escape into a better world beyond.[58] This for Bonhoeffer was to miss the essential character of the gospel, which, in the hope of the resurrection, "sends a man back to his life on earth in a wholly new way which is even more sharply defined than it is in the Old Testament."[59] The Christian is called not to an escape into the eternal but to a concern for human betterment in the secular world. Bonhoeffer is pinpointing here the "decisive factor" of Christianity, namely, that Christ's death and resurrection have redeemed the whole of history. In consequence, the possibility of living as Christ has become a historical possibility, and the church has been mandated to proclaim by its own totally other-centered existence the revelation personified by Christ.

If eschatology is not in the foreground of the prison letters, the eschatological perspective is not, for that matter, altogether absent. Bonhoeffer would set a Christic other-oriented attitude as one pole of the church's dialectic with the world opened up by Christ's resurrection. The new life of Christians in union with the death and resurrection of Christ necessarily involved a recommitment to secular tasks. Bonhoeffer was as opposed to a pure other-worldly or despairing apocalyptic attitude as he was to making Christianity depend on politics or worldly laws. His balanced attitude in this regard is brought out in reflections on William Paton's book *The Church and the New Order*, attributed to him and circulated by W. A. Visser 't Hooft in 1941. On the postwar problems, we read the following:

> The insecurity of life and the tremendous upheavals have made Continental Christians acutely conscious of the fact that the future is in God's hands and that no human planning, however intelligent and however well intentioned, can make men masters of their own fate. There is, therefore, in Continental Churches today a strongly apocalyptic trend. This trend may lead to an attitude of pure other-worldliness, but it may also have the more salutary effect of making us realize that the Kingdom of God has its own history which does not depend upon political events, and that the life of the Church has its own God-given laws which are different from those which govern the life of the world.[60]

What Christianity would be like in the postwar era would depend on Christians becoming once again the "salt of the earth" by an ever-increasing dedication to the human, this-worldly existence with more than a passing glance at God's judgment on the world in the cross of Christ.

III. Christ the Structure of Historical Reality

Despite the tension inherent in living between the existential present of faith and the eschatological future, Bonhoeffer attempted to portray the Christian life and reality itself as forming a paradoxical unity. This unity he derived from his Christocentric view of all reality, structuring not only the life of faith but the meaning underlying the entire historical process. From the unique person of Jesus Christ, Bonhoeffer traced the intelligibility behind all events in human history. In terms of this theological structure Bonhoeffer likewise attempted to collate all the penultimate realities of life and to dislodge Christianity from its traditional "thinking in two spheres."

Bonhoeffer's earliest formulation of the convergence of human history in Christ describes Christ as having transformed the "man of Adam," the creation under sin, into his own mankind or body. Christ's life, then, became a model of the inner movement of all mankind toward the new creation. "Because the whole of the new mankind is really established in Jesus Christ, he represents the whole history of mankind in his historical life."[61] The frame of reference here is reminiscent of the Pauline language of universal reconciliation and the Hegelian notion of the collective person on which Bonhoeffer based his early ecclesiology. In *Ethics* the centrality of Christ's representative nature and reconciling action on behalf of all peoples is extended in an even more cosmic and universal direction. If in his doctoral dissertation Bonhoeffer spoke of the history of mankind as being established in Christ, he widened this scope in his later writings to merge Christ and the world into a dialectical unity. His aim was to take all the traditional opposites—natural-supernatural, profane-sacred, rational-revelational—and show that these concepts have an original unity in Christ.

Bonhoeffer argued against separating these concepts, as he also opposed sacred or profane systems that would unite them by force. In the latter case the result would be little more than a static antagonism between the various spheres in which the Christian must move. According to Bonhoeffer, this would also sidestep the New Testament view that all of reality, whether it be considered specifically sacred or profane, has been taken up by God in Christ from the beginning of creation. To split off the profane from the sacred, the natural from the supernatural, or the rational from the revelational, and to assign them an autonomous sphere apart from God would miss the point that these so-called spheres have their reality only in the reality of God. Where the spheres have been set in competitive isolation, the decisive problem of history becomes essentially the juggling of the frontiers between sacred and profane. Against this, Bonhoeffer advocates a shift in perspective: "The whole reality of the world is already drawn into Christ and bound together in him, and the movement of history consists solely in divergence and convergence in relation to this center."[62] The unity of reality would, then, derive from Christ and—on the part of human attitudes—from faith in this ultimate reality.

The brunt of Bonhoeffer's criticism of those who would separate the world reality from the Christ reality is directed against the effects of maintaining such a perpetual conflict, a hyphenated Christianity unresponsive to the world's needs. A unity was needed, yet not a unity which should simply identify the worldly with the Christian. The Christian and secular elements of life share reality and are united in the reality of Christ, so that neither can assume a static independence in relation to the other. They stand in a polemical unity. Christianity can never withdraw from the world but neither can the world isolate itself from the fellowship revealed in Jesus Christ.[63] Bonhoeffer declares further that Christ constitutes the origin, the essence, and the goal of all reality.[64]

Bonhoeffer promotes in his *Ethics* an incarnationalism in which knowledge of Christ is linked to knowledge of reality itself. He claims that this is possible not only from the revelation of the Christic structure of reality but also from a consideration of the human, historical situation as experienced by Christ. Christ was not "alien" to reality; on the contrary, "it is he who alone has borne and experienced the essence of the real in his own body, who has spoken from the standpoint of reality as no man on earth can do, who alone has fallen victim to no ideology, and fulfilled the essence of history, and in whom the law of the life of history is embodied."[65] This Christocentric perspective is determinative of the Christian orientation toward life that would make a Christian ethic possible. Taking Christ as a point of departure for a specific Christian commitment steers clear of abstract principles and pious generalities unrelated to the lived reality. History, as fulfilled in Christ, thus becomes for Bonhoeffer the area where the community and the individual exercise freedom for responsible action.

IV. The Church, Concrete Locus of Historical Revelation

Since nearly every aspect of Bonhoeffer's ecclesiology unfolds into a Christology, it can be expected that his explanation of the historical aspects of revelation in Christ should likewise extend to the church. In picturing Christ as continuing his resurrected presence in and through the community, he had very early equated church with "Christ existing as community."[66] Later he would chide this church for not having followed the example of Christ by a total, selfless, and risk-defying life for others.[67] If Christ is God's revelation in history, so too "the reality of the church is a reality of revelation."[68]

In his early ecclesiology Bonhoeffer is insistent that this church be recognized and acknowledged in its actual, empirical form. It is not surprising, then, that he vigorously opposes an idea current in theological circles which would mentally distinguish a visible from an invisible church: one church the gathering of sinners and the other its heavenly, sinless and, therefore, more authentic double. For Bonhoeffer the distinction was meaningless, even when, following Luther's theology, it meant nothing more than the relationship similar to that of body to soul in a church conceived ultimately as one. The danger, as Bonhoeffer indicates in *Sanctorum Communio*, is that the terms are misleading, as if the task of faith were simply to make the invisible church visible.[69] Often enough, it had led to a splintering of the visible church in the mistaken belief that only the invisible church mattered. Bonhoeffer's attitude toward this was in keeping with his driving interest to relate revelation and faith to the practical details of life. In raising the question, "What does 'believing in the church' mean?" he replied that it made no sense to profess belief in some kind of invisible church. Only the visible, empirical church warranted faith. He declared, therefore, that "we do not believe in an invisible church, nor in the kingdom of God existing in the church as *coetus electorum;* but we believe that God has made the actual empirical church. . . . We believe in the church as the church of God and as the communion of saints . . . but within the historical form of the empirical church."[70] At the root of this endorsement of the visible, empirical church over a supposed invisible church is Bonhoeffer's association of revelation with the real and historical. For this reason he also advocated beginning dogmatics not with the doctrine of God but with the more tangible doctrine of the church, a procedure he himself followed in his theological writings. Again, it was a question of the inner connection between the reality of revelation and that of the church. According to Bonhoeffer, the church in all its concrete religious forms is, like Christ, the visible point of contact between God's self-revelation and human religious experience.[71]

In developing the sociality of Christ's presence in time as church,[72] Bonhoeffer also wanted to avoid two extremes: the *historicizing* extreme, which confuses the church with the religious community, and the *religious* extreme, which identifies the church *simpliciter* with the kingdom of God. The first of these blurs the revelational reality of the church into the empirical community whose upbuilding, even through good motives of faith, pushes the more fundamental relationship with God to the background. Such an attitude can cause a congregation to lose its identity with Christ in a rush to engage in missionary or conversion activity. The second, the "religious" extreme, fails to take history seriously when it either glorifies historicity as an object or shrugs it off as merely accidental to the church.[73] This perspective would see only the communion of *saints* and would avoid God's revelation of his will in Christ, albeit concealed "in the guise of historical events." This "will" is the judgment of Christ on the sinfulness of any church, reminding the church to be constantly engaged in a process of internal reform. Bonhoeffer maintains that the reality of the church must include both a sense of its own historicity and an acknowledgment of its dependence on God's actions in Christ.[74]

Bonhoeffer opts for an understanding of the church from *within* its claim to be the church of God, "not as historically comprehensible, but as having its basis in the reality of God and his revelation."[75] At this juncture he declares that the church is a revelational reality requiring faith as the only adequate criterion for judging its claims. This faith is a premise, not for empirical analysis but for that positive theological knowledge which presupposes its own basis, the revelation in Christ. Bonhoeffer's point of departure for ecclesiology is, then, the reality of the revelation which in turn yields the concept of community relationships.[76] All understanding of the phenomenon of community would bend back upon the prior question of revelation. "The Christian concept of the church is reached only by way of the concept of revelation."[77]

For revelation to reach the human person, there is a need not only for the tangibility of history in which God acts but also for the specific locus of Christ's presence in history, the congregation of believers gathered in his name. Believers derive their very faith from their solidarity in this fellowship. "Revelation," Bonhoeffer insists, "happens within the community."[78] He adds that "the being of revelation 'is' the being of the community of persons, constituted and embraced by the person of Christ."[79] Later, in his lectures on the nature of the church, he would assert even more strongly—if idealistically—that God's revelation in the community constitutes "the whole revelation."[80]

Bonhoeffer makes this assertion from his Christocentric understanding of the church. He envisions the church as a collective person: "Christ existing as community." Bonhoeffer's early theology depicts Christ as the representative of mankind who restores people to revelational communion with God and establishes the church as revelational reality, making possible a renewed relationship with God and the new social relationships of the Christian community. Here the *pro nobis* being of God in Christ becomes the a priori condition of possibility of the "new humanity" living in a faith fellowship. Christ's death and resurrection have revealed God's incarnate love at the root of all community life and have overcome the two great obstacles to human communion with God—sin and death. Broken relationships are thus healed in Christ, who, as the collective person of the community, reconciles people to one another and to their common Father.

The church is also the historical locus for Bonhoeffer's synthesis of the act-being aspects of revelation. Is revelation a past, present, or future event? It is, Bonhoeffer would answer, all three: it is the past brought into the present and the future, although revelation is never interpreted as "having happened" or reified into static propositions, be they dogmatic or biblical. The cross and resurrection, as eschatological events and core of the Christian revelation, are unique because they draw revelation into a "yet to come" model while guaranteeing at the same time that revelation be a "present" happening by reason of Christ's presence in the church. This is so because revelation pulsates "within the Church, for the Church is the Christ of the present, 'Christ existing as community.' "[81]

With Bonhoeffer's statement of the personal identity of Christ and his church, there results in his theology an interdependence of proclamation *(Verkündigung)* and community *(Gemeinde)* in which Christ as the corporate person is the common subject. His highly personalized concept of church influences his entire theology of revelation. "God reveals himself as a person in the Church. The Christian community is God's final revelation."[82] God's self-giving in Christ to the faith community establishes the locus of revelation because Christ is active in both preaching and believing the Word. Since God's freedom is bound to his people in this way, revelation is seen as somehow occurring within the church. As each member of the community becomes a "Christ" to the other in living and proclaiming the gospel, the divine revelation occurs and is extended. As a consequence, Bonhoeffer thinks of revelation in terms of God's personal relationship to the community. This view enables Bonhoeffer to search out a middle path between Barth's actualistic transcendentalism and the effort of the "being theologies" to encase revelation within doctrine, psychic experience, or institution. Revelation is neither a nonobjective, occasional impingement on existence nor a unique past occurrence at man's disposal, in no way connected to his personal existence. Its being " 'is' the being of the community of persons, constituted and embraced by the person of Christ, wherein the individual finds himself to be already in his new existence."[83]

This idealistic description of the church in his early theological writings did not altogether disappear when Bonhoeffer began his teaching career and became involved in the church crisis within Nazi Germany and later in the conspiracy against Hitler. It soon became clear to Bonhoeffer that he had to move away from his idealistic structures for understanding civil and ecclesiastical reality in order to arrive at clearer, more compelling arguments that would promote free and responsible decisions to oppose the Nazi state and even his own church. His portrayal of the state as a collective person, for example, could easily absorb enough mythology to stack any debate over resistance in favor of patience, patriotism, and cautious inactivity. Bonhoeffer could be patient, patriotic, and cautious, but he was hardly inactive in the work of resistance to what he believed to be an insidious attack on the Christian gospel itself. The turmoil in the church in Germany, together with his teaching, pastoral ministry, and ecumenical activity, catalyzed his conviction that effective work in the church and the future of Christianity itself demanded his total commitment to renew the church in its self-sacrificing service to others, particularly the oppressed, and to challenge it to relevance even at the risk of its suppression by the civil authorities. For Bonhoeffer the main issues in the church struggle of the 1930s were those of freedom for the proclamation of the gospel and a sense of responsibility for decisive action against evils threatening both civil and ecclesiastical life. At the heart of the problem of adopting a course of action that would be ethically sound and convincing to others was Bonhoeffer's own theological and philosophical heritage, his tendency to personalize the state in his earlier writings and to accept the traditional separation of church and state in Lutheran theology.

Even as Bonhoeffer was himself stymied in his theoretical working out of a Christian *ratio operandi* in the church crisis by the Lutheran doctrine of the two realms, which appeared to justify noninvolvement, his holistic Hegelianism pushed him to overcome the traditional dichotomy of the divine and the human, the sacred and the profane. Something better than peaceful coexistence between state and church, based on a mutual stand-off, was needed if the church was to be true to the gospel call to responsible discipleship. For Bonhoeffer the underpinning of any plan of action or critique directed against the state or schismatic church was to be, like his entire theology, thoroughly Christocentric.[84]

In his Christology lectures Bonhoeffer claimed that, because of Christ's presence, the church was "the center of history."[85] Such a statement, he admitted, might imply that the church is also the center of the state or that which gives both meaning and promise to the actions of the state. Bonhoeffer cautions against this conclusion. Where the church had jockeyed for such a central place in the state or permitted itself to be incorporated into the state, there usually followed some infidelity to the gospel or compromise of principle. Bonhoeffer proceeds, therefore, to speak of the church as a *hidden* center of the state, operable whether the state is aware of it or not. For that very reason he adds that his assertion is indemonstrable. Nonetheless, he affirms that the church is both center and boundary of the state, pronouncing judgment on the actions of the state and announcing that the state's ultimate purpose had already been proclaimed and fulfilled by the cross of Christ. The church's centrality to history is mediated by Christ, who is likewise the form of the church.[86]

One significant application of proclaiming the church the "hidden center" of the state is the corrective and the judgment which the cross of Christ pronounces against the pretensions of the state. Bonhoeffer confronts political history's messianic aspirations: states, he notes, tend to promise ultimate fulfillment as if salvation can be achieved in history apart from the penetration of God's kingdom into that history. If history has any lesson, Bonhoeffer believes it would be a word of caution against the succession of self-dubbed messiahs whose pretensions, along with the human selfishness that makes political messianism possible, have corrupted the promise of history. History, therefore, has been and will continue to be unfulfilled until it recognizes its true messiah at its hidden center. This messiah has upset all the claims of history by his paradoxical triumph over death. In the "secret depths" of Jesus' crucifixion lies the true meaning of history. According to Bonhoeffer, this is a fulfillment in secret in the person of Jesus, who is the very center of history and the mediator between singular events and the presence of God in those events.[87]

Furthermore, Jesus' presence as church establishes for Bonhoeffer the basis for a church-state dialectic in which faith can play the dominant role. Bonhoeffer sees the state both judged and upheld by the cross of Christ or, as Luther put it, the state is God's rule "with his left hand."[88] Without its hidden center (the church) and the uplifting force of Christ's saving death and continued resurrection presence, the state would overstep its bounds, attempt to usurp the messianic role of Christ, and thus perish in the destruction of its own order.

The mission of the church to the world is, then, to indicate the limit of human possibilities while proclaiming that this limit has been penetrated by Jesus Christ. Christ, as the simultaneity of word and revelation, can straddle the boundary between institutions that make up the structures and laws of the world and those that point to a final dissolution of this order. Hence the church can limit the state, and can itself—as a human institution—be limited in turn. But in no way can state politics prevent the church from exercising its function as a critical reminder of the limitations of all human authority. Here the word of revelation in the church stands opposed to any church-world anthithesis. "The church proves itself to be the church of God in the world simply by a right ordering of the message of the Gospel, by a right preaching of grace and commandment. Thus the church is concerned with giving the word of God to the world; with testifying to the penetration of the world and its laws in the revelation of the seriousness and the goodness of God in Jesus Christ."[89]

The state is also a reminder to the church that it must not retreat to an "otherworldly escapism." Relating to the world is sewn into the church's call to be a community mediating Christ's revelational presence and urging its members to greater responsibility in their earthly service to others. Bonhoeffer sharply denounces the pious fraud of the religious otherworldly. This is brought out very clearly in his 1932 essay "Thy Kingdom Come." In this essay the Nietzschean influence in the form of a love of the earth leads Bonhoeffer to assert that escape into the "eternal beyond" by being religious "at the expense of the earth" is the refuge only of the weak and dispirited. "However, Christ does not will or intend this weakness; instead, he makes man strong. He does not lead man in a religious flight from this world to other worlds beyond; rather, he gives him back to the earth as its loyal son."[90] On the other hand, an uncritical secularity, which Bonhoeffer defines as "the Christian renunciation of God as the Lord of the earth,"[91] is a foolish failure to recognize or pay allegiance to God's dominion and, consequently, is of a piece with otherworldliness, since both lead away from God and his world. One cannot love God as Lord of the earth without thereby loving the earth.

Obedience to God's word exacts an evaluation of the earthly existence in which God operates and in which the Christian mediates God's love to his fellow man and woman. "The kingdom of God is not to be found in some other world beyond, but in the midst of this world. . . . God wants us to honor him on earth; he wants us to honor him in our fellow man—and nowhere else."[92] Bonhoeffer would visualize the church's role in this biblically realistic picture of God's kingdom as an opportunity to mediate the Word by being bound to the earth and standing necessarily in solidarity with all mankind simultaneously under the curse and the promise. The way will thus be set for Bonhoeffer later to urge the church to say "Yes" to the "world-come-of-age," because this is the world God has loved and reconciled in Christ.

For the church to challenge both itself and a self-contained nation-state, however, there was a need for a renewed understanding of the church's nature and mission in the world. This Bonhoeffer proposed in his address to the Youth Peace Conference in 1932. In effect, he was offering a theological basis for the ecumenical movement then budding. He stated in his opening remarks: "Theology is the church's self-understanding of its own nature on the basis of its understanding of the revelation of God in Christ, and this self-understanding of necessity always begins where there is a new trend in the church's understanding of itself."[93] Without this theological anchoring to God's revelation, the ecumenical movement would drift along without power to relate the gospel to the world. The church had to address itself to specific situations and thus be attentive to the concreteness and contemporaneity of the message and the command, avoiding the feeble generalizations of the past that led to the incongruity of war among Christians and the fracturing of fellowship. Bonhoeffer saw two sources for the concrete command: the Sermon on the Mount and what had been called the "orders of creation." This latter designation of state, church, marriage, and family Bonhoeffer now wished to avoid. The danger, as Bonhoeffer saw it, in the notion that these "orders" were evident in creation itself and thus to be considered normative was the human tendency to forget the fact of sin and to justify war, class struggle, economic exploitation of the poor, and racism as belonging to a necessary condition of life—and hence unavoidable. Bonhoeffer pointed out that "it was impossible to single out some features of the world above others as orders of creation and base a course of Christian moral action upon them."[94] Christian moral action had to be grounded in the revelation in Christ and in the fellowship of love between Christians which that revelation makes possible.

To designate structures of society more congruent with this revelation, Bonhoeffer coined the expression "orders of preservation."

> It is not as though we now knew all at once from Jesus Christ what features we should regard as orders of creation and what not, but that we know that *all* the orders of the world only exist in that they are directed toward Christ; they *all* stand under the preservation of God as long as they are still open for Christ, they are *orders of preservation,* not orders of creation. They obtain their value wholly from outside themselves, from Christ, from the new creation.[95]

The theological designation of the state as an order of preservation is significant because it subordinates the state and church to God's revelation in Christ, who alone mediates the meaning of these orders. Further, as Bonhoeffer pointed out—even before the Barmen Declaration—when any order hinders the gospel proclamation "it may be . . . dissolved."[96] This had immediate application to the crucial problem of the day in Germany and the world, the issue of war and peace. In the light of revelation, war could never be justified through appeal to the order of preservation; it was simply too destructive of life and brotherhood. Church and state would represent in these structures the two forms of God's presence preserving the "fallen world." The state's function is solely to *preserve* life and order, protecting communities, such as marriage, family, and nation, from the chaotic whim of individuals.[97]

While the new terminology was significant for the impending church struggle against Nazism, it too could be co-opted by the Nazi regime, which saw itself as the sole hope for the rule of right order in the world. Hence the concept of "orders of preservation" would give way in Bonhoeffer's *Ethics* to the notion of "mandates." His efforts to relate church to state through the concept of the mandates is an outgrowth of earlier descriptions of Christ as the corporate person of the community and as the center of both community and state. All of life comes under the divine mandate, because all of life is included in the reality of Christ. "The divine mandates are dependent solely on the *one* commandment of God as it is revealed in Jesus Christ. They are introduced into the world from above as orders or 'institutions' of the reality of Christ, that is to say, of the reality of the love of God for the world and for men which is revealed in Jesus Christ."[98] The worldliness and law of the state have their original foundation in Christ.

This is, of course, a holistic understanding of the state which Bonhoeffer felt to be fully in accord with true Reformation theology. The church, in this schema, has the calling to proclaim God's revelation in Christ to the world. No longer does he call the church the center of history, but he does relate the church's mandate to the world with its inner purpose to mediate the historical presence of Christ to all mankind. Bonhoeffer perceives a dynamic unity between church and world in which the secular and the Christian prevent each other from assuming any static independence apart from their mutual relationship in Christ. "Whoever professes to believe in the reality of Jesus Christ as the revelation of God must in the same breath profess his faith in both the reality of God and the reality of the world; for in Christ he finds God and the world reconciled."[99] Church and world are related to each other in the manner of ethical persons: each limits the other, but each must respect the freedom of the other. Responsibility and mutual service will also keynote this relationship. In such a perspective the church would stand "at the point at which the whole world ought to be standing; to this extent it serves as deputy for the world and exists for the sake of the world."[100]

If the terminology on church-state relations has undergone a change from his early writings to the composition of *Ethics,* there is still a remarkable unity between his earliest thoughts on politics and the state and the understanding of these realities developed in *Ethics.* Historian Ruth Zerner has observed that the altered nomenclature is merely a new label for Bonhoeffer's previous, essentially unchanged descriptions of the political sphere of society. Even though he rejected "the extreme forms of nineteenth- and twentieth-century German state-worship," he "still uses the Teutonic categories of organic thought, emphasizing the responsibilities of abstract entities like government and church."[101] Fundamentally, Bonhoeffer's *Staatsidee* is an amalgam of the Lutheran concept of church and state, the nineteenth-century organic view of the state, and the post-World War I academic stress on wholeness, synthesis, and community (versus individualism).[102] It is questionable whether Bonhoeffer surmounted—as he would have liked—his tendency toward two-realm thinking in his efforts to formulate an ethic of resistance to the unjust state, particularly when the practical action called for meant going counter to one's entire upbringing and ethical sensitivity.[103] On the other hand, Bonhoeffer's development of the concept of the mandates, in particular his desire to subsume the arts, education, friendship, and joy under church as the protector of beauty, joy, and freedom and as the community of reconciliation, signaled an important step beyond two-realm thinking. Later he would use the figure of the polyphonic fugue as an alternative to images of duality, and under this figure affirm the unity of life in which the point-counterpoints of eros and agape, faith and reason, action and reflection could be seen in the deeper unity of one's faith in Christ.[104]

In practice, Bonhoeffer's own actions during the church crisis were courageously close to the theory he was then enunciating. At the various ecumenical conferences he grappled with the salient issue of international brotherhood and peace in the world. He attacked not only nationalism but the vague and cowardly placebos issued by the church on major issues affecting the relationship between nations and between the churches themselves. More and more he became the interpreter of the church situation in Germany to the leaders of the various national groups as he continued to prod the World Alliance to take up the challenge of really becoming one church. Despite his efforts, however, it soon became clear that nationalistic interests were playing too great a role in the life of the churches. Not only were the churches speechless before the rising militarism in Nazi Germany and the hatred and mistrust existing among so-called Christian nations, but often enough they were willing to overlook patent abuses of basic human rights in order to maintain their privileges and avoid being suppressed should they protest too loudly. The church, Bonhoeffer insisted, could not just condemn wars in general; it had to condemn *this war*.[105]

Bonhoeffer's work in the 1930s as one of the leaders of the Confessing Church, as director of the illegal seminary at Finkenwalde, and finally as member of the conspiracy to overthrow Hitler are part of history. Finally, in 1943 he was arrested and brought to Tegel Prison in Berlin. It was from this prison that he posed his most disquieting questions on the church's future and engaged in a radical reappraisal of all religious structures and religious language and their relationship to the deeper meaning of Christianity. He criticized not only the traditional images of God but especially the weak attitude of a church so pietistically wrapped up in the world beyond that it had compromised its relevance and integrity. The church had in effect failed to take history seriously. For Bonhoeffer this meant acting freely and responsibly on behalf of human rights and in the name of the gospel.

V. Taking History Seriously: Freedom and Responsibility

The shape of Bonhoeffer's life and consequently his theology was forged in the kiln of Nazi political and ecclesiastical policy. His thoughts on the history of his time and on the proper reaction of a Christian community to the vulgar, if not downright brutal, attempts of the Nazi regime to manipulate the churches was hasty and more the reaction of a committed believer than a systematic analyst of the historical situation. If theologian and pastor Bonhoeffer could hardly be called a political analyst, he nonetheless had remarkably cogent views on how a state should comport itself with regard to freedom for both individuals and community. His reading of the importance of specific events in the context of their far greater ramifications was accurate to the point of being creative, especially regarding the Jewish question, Hitler's threat to basic human rights, the issue of war and peace, and the nature of the ecumenical movement.

Bonhoeffer's correct diagnosis of the importance of the Jewish question to the Christian churches, for example, was in advance of the more lumbering pace of his fellow pastors and theologians, who tended to compromise and wait until they could see the issues more clearly. Karl Barth acknowledged this in a letter to Eberhard Bethge in 1967:

> It was new to me above all else that Bonhoeffer was the first, yes indeed almost the only theologian who in the years after 1933 concentrated energetically on the question of the Jews and dealt with it equally energetically. For a long time now I have considered myself guilty of not having raised it with equal emphasis during the church struggle (for example in the two Barmen Declarations I composed in 1934).[106]

This is not to deny that Bonhoeffer's initial written reaction to the Aryan clause being foisted on both civil and church government was cautious, weakened by two-realm thinking and, regarding theological assessments of the Jewish people, highly problematical.[107] What Bonhoeffer did achieve was to reveal his concern for his "Jewish brethren"[108] and to provide a practical and humanitarian basis for actions by individuals against the state policy even if his Lutheran separation of church and state impeded him from linking the church more closely with humanitarian aims and causes. He says in this essay, for example, that the church cannot "exert direct political action, for the church does not pretend to have any knowledge of the necessary course of history."[109] Responsibility for effecting any change even in the face of such blatantly unjust laws would fall to individuals and humanitarian associations. Bonhoeffer is not yet at the point where the church can "jam the spokes" of the political wheel itself. He did see, however, the need for a responsible attitude on the part of individual Christians, who could thus freely oppose the impersonal and heartless bureaucracy behind unjust laws.[110] This essay, together with his actions on behalf of Jews in the 1930s, does show Bonhoeffer's courage and willingness to speak out on sensitive and dangerous issues even as he stood in a twilight zone of decision, where nothing was clear or precise.

This decisiveness on his part is in keeping with his own sense of the importance of accepting responsibility. History itself, he would declare, "arises through the recognition of responsibility for others."[111] This is, moreover, the challenge of Jesus in the Sermon on the Mount, a challenge which becomes operative only in the reality of history, not in the formulation of an abstract ethic. At times the decision to become involved would mean, as Bonhoeffer observed in his *Ethics,* to enter—following the example of Jesus—"into the fellowship of the guilt of men and to take the burden of their guilt" upon oneself.[112] Not to accept this "guilt," which could arise from engaging in violent actions against the unjust state, threatening life, freedom, and the gospel, would lead only to worsening the evil and to a greater guilt. Bonhoeffer deplored the results of such Christian apathy in his confession of guilt on behalf of the church. "The church," he wrote, "confesses that it has witnessed the lawless application of brutal force, the physical and spiritual suffering of countless innocent people, oppression, hatred and murder, and that it has not raised its voice on behalf of the victims and has not found ways to hasten to their aid. It is guilty of the deaths of the weakest and most defenseless brothers of Jesus Christ."[113] Apathy in the name of a desire to preserve one's innocence or in the name of obedience to "law" would, in Bonhoeffer's opinion, be an irresponsibility, even an inexcusable complicity in the evil being perpetrated.[114]

In *The Cost of Discipleship,* Bonhoeffer had stressed obedience to the state except where the state interferes with faith in Christ, and he had emphasized that Christians should never go counter to the "divine law," which forbids killing. Now, in his *Ethics,* even this limit would give way to the freedom to act responsibly, given circumstances in which the divine law must be violated in the name of freedom, in order—paradoxically—to make the divine law more effective in the future.[115] Freedom in the cadre of resistance to evil thus takes precedence over obedience to a lawfully constituted state. The final referent of resistance in the name of freedom is Jesus Christ. Jesus is likewise the model after whom all resistance to established authority can be patterned.[116] This is so because Bonhoeffer was convinced that Jesus himself possessed a personal freedom allowing him to cut through the dehumanizing structures of the organized religion and politics of his day. Christ's words and actions reflected a wholeness and integrity that were also the hallmarks of a mature outlook on life. This was a freedom for responsible action in the world capable of recognizing human obligation and genuine human values.[117] Far from blocking the world's efforts to exert its autonomy, Jesus Christ encouraged this growth in its amplest sense.

Bonhoeffer also recognized that the ideal of imitating Jesus Christ in the important matter of freedom and responsibility was not without its own difficulty, especially amidst the yeasty confusion of the Hitler era. He was sensitive to historical complexity in the political sphere. Hence he wanted to avoid decisions derived from some historical *a priori* larded with metaphysical and historico-apocalyptic presuppositions. He decried the uselessness of basing judgments for action on a general theory of history rather than on the evidence of facts themselves. Yet he realized that even the "factual evidence" could be ignored. The events that made the Hitler era possible should have alerted people to the evil growing in their midst and dictated a course of action for the church. However, the impact of the facts, though obvious to Bonhoeffer and a few others, was so blunted by the prevailing attitudes of opportunism, fear, and obtuseness that a paralysis of responsibility and dullness toward the suffering of others set in. The Christian church in Germany had, in Bonhoeffer's opinion, reached the situation of *ultima ratio* or *necessità,* in which "the exact observance of the formal law of a state . . . suddenly finds itself in violent conflict with the ineluctable necessities of the lives of men."[118] Law and principle are of little help in such a conflict. Nor can guilt be avoided, because the Christian must engage in action equally violent and forceful as the evil he is trying to destroy in order to restore the inner freedom needed to enable people to think clearly and to act responsibly. These are actions he would hardly call Christian; nonetheless, given the historical situation, they are actions no responsible Christian would shirk.[119]

In this perspective, freedom to act had to be linked with an increased awareness of one's autonomy. Bonhoeffer describes in his letters the progression of history, with its rhythms of scientific advancement and spasms of insurrection, war, and the dissolution of social order, to argue for acknowledging that the world had come of age and that man had reached adulthood in that world.[120] He asserts, therefore, that the world has reached a certain scientific, technological, and societal maturity which has liberated it from the primitive religious or superstitious solutions to its problems. Religion, he says, is an "historically conditioned and transient form of human self-expression." In this case, Christ can no longer be viewed as "an object of religion" if he is to be acknowledged as the Lord of history.[121] People are also caught up in the signs of this progress toward maturity. They have outgrown the tutelage of religion and the attitude of using God as a stopgap solution to the seemingly insoluble or as a ready-made excuse to avoid responsibility for shaping the progress of history.

Bonhoeffer declares that the emergence of human autonomy is a phenomenon with all the force of historical progress behind it. The self-defeating, rear-guard action of the church against the assertion of this autonomy over against the controls of religion Bonhoeffer labels as pointless, ignoble, and unchristian.[122] The new power that comes to the autonomous person, however, can be as ambiguous as the events of history itself. Here it is important to differentiate the "worship of power," which Bonhoeffer had condemned in both church and state as efforts to dominate and exploit people, from the need for self-affirmation and fulfillment. He praises the achievement of the latter as a strength leading the human person in a rational, courageous, and effective manner to undertake solutions to the problems of life formerly thought to be in the domain of religious ritual.[123]

The exercise of one's autonomy in responsible service to others is, in the final analysis, what Bonhoeffer means by taking history seriously.[124] He was supported by his faith and his family in his own decisions to accept the "guilt" of the conspiratorial actions against the state, as well as by his own sense of responsibility to his fellow man. He was also helped by his theological reflections during his involvement in the resistance movement, reflections which later would become his *Ethics*. His decision to become involved in Germany's fate[125] was fired, too, by his reading of history and historical analysis, which encouraged attitudes of nobility and chivalry in opposing any nation-state's arrogant claims to omnipotence and unaccountability before God or man. Ruth Zerner has pointed out the importance of Friedrich Meinecke's *Die Idee der Staatsräson* for those sections of *Ethics* that deal with the state and politics as well as for the ethical rationale behind his own participation in the plot against Hitler. One significant passage from Meinecke, which Bonhoeffer had marked in the margins of his text, points to at least a partial resolution of the moral dilemma to assume the personal shame of "treachery." Meinecke had written: "It is not always possible to win the approval of one's contemporaries or of posterity, or to convince world opinion; *but the hero must as least justify his action to himself*."[126]

An even stronger motive for Bonhoeffer's decision to exercise his freedom and responsibility in actions against his own government was the example of Jesus, who also risked the loss of honor in order to carry out his father's will. The text of Mark 15:34, "'My God, my God, why hast thou forsaken me?'" is presented by Bonhoeffer not only as the touchstone of faith which has a strong this-worldly dimension, but also as a vital aspect of Christ's historical situation. This cry of abandonment signified to Bonhoeffer that Jesus chose to participate fully in the human condition even to the death exacted for such a total involvement. Not even Jesus could avoid the human consequences of living completely and responsibly for others, immersed in one's duties, sharing both earthly blessings and sufferings. "Like Christ himself ('My God, why hast thou forsaken me?') he must drink the earthly cup to the dregs, and only in his doing so is the crucified and risen Lord with him, and he crucified and risen with Christ."[127] Bonhoeffer's point here is that Christ was not like a *deus ex machina* who could come to earth from on high, remain supremely aloof except to intervene at certain moments with opportune miracles, and then depart virtually untouched by the world's inexorable laws. Christ experienced the absence of God at the very moment when he humanly ached for deliverance. Christ was completely human and thereby able not only to reconcile people to God but also to reveal something of what it means to live as a person before God. Christ, as Bonhoeffer describes him in his *Ethics,* did not love a theory of good, but he loved real human persons. Conformation to Jesus Christ is, then, to enter into the full throes of history, to become a "new man before God."[128]

Conclusion: Bonhoeffer's Theory of History and Openness to Historical Revelation

It should be clear from the foregoing that Bonhoeffer's view of revelation in history is that of a hidden salvation history in which a person in faith comes to understand the revelation that occurs in Jesus Christ. This revelation is God's self-disclosure in the history of Jesus Christ. Because there is a special decisiveness to this event, Bonheffer considers it incorrect either to speak of many revelations or to equate the revelation in Christ with the revelation which may occur through other events of history or through the interaction of persons on each other. All revelation becomes Christic revelation. Consequently, when Bonhoeffer speaks of revelation in history, he is really speaking of revelation in Christ, who structures all history from creation to the end-time. History should then be interpreted theologically as a movement of either divergence from or convergence toward its hidden center, Jesus Christ.

The church's role in history is to witness to this hidden center. As the empirical continuation of Christ's historical presence, the church stands as the visible point of contact between God's revelation and human experience. The church proclaims God's revelation and serves the human community. For this reason the church is the sign of Christ's other-centered dedication to mankind and of the final reconciliation of all peoples. Through his faith and responsible action on behalf of others, the believer becomes open in full freedom to the Christic meaning behind all human reality and thus conformed to the incarnate Christ, the Lord of all history.

Bonhoeffer's affirmation of the lordship of Christ over all reality derived from an understanding of history in which, theologically, the function of history itself is to lend a temporal, somatic concreteness to Christian revelation and faith. If this be so, one may legitimately ask whether Bonhoeffer has taken empirical history seriously enough. Hans Schmidt, for one, raises this question when he accuses Bonhoeffer of negating history by teaching that "God's historical revelation happened . . . in this world, but in the end was not related to this world." Schmidt concludes that "Bonhoeffer merely sanctioned the status quo of an abstractly conceived reality of creation for the time between the Fall and the Last Judgment as the end of reality of this world."[129] Against this extreme critique of Schmidt it can be posited that Bonhoeffer's writings exhibit a veritable passion for basing ethical judgments and specific decisions on a correct appraisal of the historical data, albeit seen ultimately in a Christic context. Further, the uncanny precocity of so many of his assessments of the catastrophic implications for Germany of the historical decisions of the 1930s can be seen in any number of postwar histories of the Third Reich. Bonhoeffer's moral posture on the question of resistance and conspiracy, even without the support of his church or of the masses, was finally and fully appreciated only as the horrors of the Nazi regime were documented for the world at large.[130] He saw his actions as an expression of responsibility for the shaping of history to benefit the coming generation.[131]

On the basis of this sense of responsibility, Bonhoeffer did in fact move close to a break with the strong German tradition of unquestioning obedience to civil authority. Hence he would complain in his essay "After Ten Years" that Germans

> did not realize that . . . submissiveness and self-sacrifice could be exploited for evil ends. What then happened, the exercise of the calling itself became questionable, and all the moral principles of the Germans were bound to totter. The fact could not be escaped that the German still lacked something fundamental: he could not see the need for free and responsible action, even in opposition to his task and his calling; in its place there appeared on the one hand an irresponsible lack of scruple, and on the other a self-tormenting punctiliousness that never led to action.[132]

Historian Ruth Zerner sees in these Bonhoeffer insights talents similar to those of Alexis de Tocqueville, who a century earlier had analyzed the problems of power and obedience in the corrupt state. Bonhoeffer, she says, displays a sensitivity "to the realities of his time and place."[133]

Because Bonhoeffer's *theology* of history colors his reading of empirical history, Schmidt says he is not interested in the phenomenon of history. It would be more accurate to view Bonhoeffer's theology—or, more exactly, his faith in Jesus Christ—rather as the *Vorgriff* of his interpretation of events in relationship to the more complex context of a lifetime or of the future of church and society. All human knowledge, in fact, demands a certain "fiduciary rootedness," especially if one is to commit himself to a course of action grounded in an unresolved hypothesis of history.[134] In interpreting historical experience itself or the documents of this experience, we tend to project a wholeness of meaning based on clues drawn from past experience and the whole matrix of one's present relationship with particular people or groups. There is, in effect, a *tacit* dimension to the act of judging historical perceptions, especially as these tend toward heuristic acts of understanding the broader meaning of what has happened in one's life. This is what Plato has called an "intimation of the unknown." While it is true that the historian must strive for a certain objectivity, this itself would be impossible unless the historian operated from a certain horizon or background of meaning, culture, tradition, and language toward the articulation of a new horizon of historical significance. It would seem that, for Bonhoeffer, this tacit dimension is at once his faith in the hidden presence of Christ in the concrete events and decisions of history and his trust that God's judgment on the world will continue to be spoken in the new forms that that presence will assume.

Bonhoeffer's overall approach to historical understanding is strikingly similar to the model of history and of historical interpretation espoused by Wilhelm Dilthey.[135] We find that Dilthey uses the concept of universal history to illuminate the meaning of individual moments in that history. Meaning would then depend on the interrelationship of parts to whole in which the individual's experiences are comprehended in the total context of an entire lifetime. The individual, in turn, is himself or herself a part of the nexus of meaning transcending his individualized existence. Beyond a particular existence or moment lies the totality of historical life that encompasses all peoples and all forms of society. Dilthey says that ascertaining this meaning of life can elude both present reflection and acts of retrospection. It may, in fact, have to wait for the end of life in order—somewhat after the manner of Bonhoeffer's prison reflections—to retrace the sense of that life now seen as a whole. In terms of universal history, "one would have to wait for the end of history to have all the material necessary to determine its meaning."[136] All meanings preliminary to the end of history, therefore, would at best be partial and provisional, even though the interpretation of the "whole of history" itself depends for its comprehensibility on insights gleaned from individual interrelated moments. We see this aspect of Dilthey's hermeneutic in Bonhoeffer's description of the tension between penultimate and ultimate and in his insistence that history finds fulfillment only in Christ's incarnation and the final reconciliation of the world in God.[137] Or as he expresses it in his poem "Stations on the Road to Freedom":

> Come now, thou greatest of feasts on the journey to freedom
>   eternal;
> death, cast aside all the burdensome chains, and demolish
> the walls of our temporal body, the walls of our souls that are
>   blinded,
> so that at last we may see that which here remains hidden.
> Freedom, how long we have sought thee in discipline, action, and
>   suffering;
> dying, we now may behold thee revealed in the Lord.[138]

In addition to this Diltheyan view of history as a structural unity whose meaning is determined contextually, Bonhoeffer's theology of history also exhibits a dependence on the power of particular episodes in history to anticipate and signify the meaning of universal history. Such would be the historical "event" of Jesus Christ who, in Bonhoeffer's theology, is transcendent to history and so present in every past and future that history as a whole is summed up in his person, and all developments in world history are contracted into the significance of his incarnation and redemptive death. We see this model of historical inquiry in Bonhoeffer's insistence that "the whole reality of the world is already drawn in into Christ and bound together in Him, and the movement of history consists solely in divergence and convergence in relation to this centre."[139] This interpretation of history is related to Bonhoeffer's theology of revelation in that Jesus is for him the transparency through whom God makes himself known and challenges believers to involvement in a life of discipleship on behalf of a better human community.

Moreover, when Bonhoeffer speaks of taking history seriously through one's free and responsible decisions to act for others, particularly those who are suffering and oppressed, his understanding of history follows this second, complementary model. One's ethical decisions do, in fact, shape history and have an existential impact on the total context of historical meaning. An active faith, in such a perspective, is more than a hermeneutic principle for understanding. It is that which establishes a more meaningful life for each succeeding generation, or, as Bonhoeffer puts it, determines "how the coming generation is to live."[140]

In sum, while we do not see in Bonhoeffer's theology the fully developed skills of an historian, his interest in historical analysis, in basing his judgments on historical inquiry, and in grounding his theology of revelation in the concretion of history is evident. In fact, his personal and social history is determinative of many of his theological conclusions, despite his earlier disclaimer of such a procedure. Whether his understanding of history could move his theology toward a more universal understanding of revelation is another question.

Bonhoeffer's theology of revelation is definitely a *Christian* theology. His interest lay in determining the *Christic* foundation of all revelation. Revelation was revelation in Christ, which continued in the living faith of a Christian community. Given the culture in which he lived and the particular circumstance of his own theological training in a strongly Lutheran tradition, this limitation to his concept of revelation is to be expected. Yet there is undeniable evidence in his writings that the horizons of his theology were open to the possibility of a more universal understanding of revelation. One indication of this is found in his sympathetic treatment of the "natural" in *Ethics*.[141] Another is his decision to limit his ethical considerations to the Christian West even though he realized that Christ's structuring of reality was far more universal than this particularization in history.[142] In prison he wrote of an "unconscious Christianity."[143] But even more significant is his lifelong interest in visiting India and his conviction that in the non-Western religious culture of India lay the possible alternative to the decadent "religious" form Christianity had assumed in the West. He wished to discover Christ in an entirely new form in "non-Christian" India.[144] These are, of course, only indications of the direction Bonhoeffer's theology of revelation might have taken had he lived to complete his reflections and perhaps even to take that long-desired trip to India.

One can surmise that Bonhoeffer would have come to recognize that revelation itself is a far broader concept than its particularization within the Christian religious experience. To say this is not to lose the Christian point of reference; the two concepts are not incompatible. All peoples, because of their spiritual openness to the transcendent manifest in their personal history, can enter into communion with God in a revelation-faith relationship. People are led to God through their faith, their moral decisions, and their struggles to go beyond themselves in their love for others. In affirming the man Jesus, God affirms the totality of human experience. The universal revelation of God as the power over all history is already present by anticipation in the death and resurrection of Jesus Christ. This is why Bonhoeffer would call Jesus the Lord of history. All of history belongs to this revelation: its ultimate significance is to reveal God's essence. Often enough, Christian contact with non-Christian religions has provoked astonishment at the richness of the religious experience and the nobility of the ideals to be found in these religions. Robert Schlette has gone so far as to suggest that non-Christian religions are the normal or ordinary way of salvation, the Christian religion an *extraordinary* way.[145] Regarding the uniqueness of Christianity, such a position would not be too far from what Bonhoeffer says in his *Ethics:* "The Church bears the form which is in truth the proper form of all humanity. The image in which it is formed is the image of man. What takes place in it takes place as an example and substitute for all men.

... The church is nothing but a section of humanity in which Christ has really taken form."[146]

During his involvement in the German resistance and during the days of his imprisonment, Bonhoeffer was drawn to consider more intensely the correlation of the human with the divine in the revelatory process and to state more forcefully the need for reshaping the Christian church. He himself took history seriously in the moment of the German church's greatest crisis of this century. His own personal freedom to act courageously and responsibly on behalf of suffering humanity and from unselfish motives of faith may be the most attractive feature of his theology of history and revelation because it brings that theology, as he wished, into the concrete sphere of life itself.

Notes

1   NRS, p. 33 (GS, III, 47).

2   DBET, p. 68; DB, p. 128.

3   How this uncertainty and ethical scrupulousness contributed to the tactical failure of the resistance movement has been thoroughly documented and analyzed by Larry Rasmussen in his impressive study of Bonhoeffer's ethics. See Dietrich Bonhoeffer: Reality and Resistance (Nashville, 1972), especially pp. 149ff.

4   NRS, pp. 41-46 (GS, III, 50-56).

5   See "Gibt es eine christliche Ethik?" GS, V, 293; "Die systematische Theologie des 20. Jahrhunderts," GS, V, 213.

6   CC, p. 63 (GS, III, 196).

7   See CS, p. 61 (SC, pp. 240-241), where Bonhoeffer writes: "As history by its nature finds its telos at the boundary of history (regarded as the end of time and beyond time), that is, in God, so community is founded in God, and willed by him. History has no rationally perceptible purpose, it comes from God and goes to God, it has meaning and value as such, however broken its origin and its destiny may be."

8   CC, p. 39 (GS, III, 177).

9   WP, p. 141 (GS, IV, 254).

10   GS, V, 199-200.

11   CC, p. 63 (GS, III, 196).

12   CC, pp. 61ff. (GS, III, 194ff.).

13   CC, pp. 32-33 (GS, III, 171-172).

14   CC, p. 64 (GS, III, 197). See also CFT, p. 88 (SF, p. 105).

15   CFT, p. 57 (SF, p. 66). See also GS, I, 110.

16   GS, III, 104.

17   GS, III, 105.

18   E, p. 67 (Ek, p. 93).

19   CC, pp. 72-73 (GS, III, 202). Bonhoeffer refers to Kähler's book, Der sogennante historische Jesus und der geschichtliche biblische Christus (1892).

20   *CC*, p. 73 (*GS*, III, 202). Bonhoeffer does not, however, deny the value of historical research for theology. Hence in his Berlin lectures, "Die Geschichte der systematischen Theologie des 20. Jahrhunderts," he cautions against sweeping the historical aside. The theologian, he insists, must attend to the historical foundation of faith. See *GS*, V, 203-206.

21   *WP*, p. 126 (*GS*, IV, 240).

22   *CC*, pp. 71-77 (*GS*, III, 200-205).

23   *CC*, pp. 78-84 (*GS*, III, 207-212).

24   Conference held in Barcelona, December 11, 1928 (*GS*, V, 139-140).

25   *CC*, p. 85 (*GS*, III, 212).

26   See, for example, *CS*, pp. 145-146 (*SC*, p. 155); *AB*, p. 102 (*AS*, p. 77); *GS*, III, 106; *CC*, p. 84 (*GS*, III, 211-212); *E*, p. 186 (*Ek*, p. 228).

27   *WP*, pp. 140-142 (*GS*, IV, 253-254).

28   *NRS*, p. 46 (*GS*, III, 56); *E*, pp. 185ff. (*Ek*, pp. 227ff.).

29   *NRS*, p. 311 (*GS*, III, 307); see also *NRS*, p. 316 (*GS*, III, 111).

30   Letter of April 8, 1936 (*GS*, III, 28). One can gain a deeper understanding of what Bonhoeffer means by history and concrete reality by a glance at the concepts which are opposed to this historicity or concreteness. Such include: principles, norms, law, ideal, ideology, general principles, everlasting truth, etc. For a listing of these *Gegenbegriffe*, see Ernst Feil, *Die Theologie Dietrich Bonhoeffers* (Munich-Mainz, 1971), p. 98.

31   Hence in his letter to Rossler he had written: "What is your opinion on the imperishability of Christianity as regards the world situation and our own style of life? . . . The invisibility is killing us ("Die Unsichtbarkeit macht uns kaput"). If we cannot perceive the presence of Christ in our personal life, then we would like to find it at least in India, but this continuing absurdity of being thrown back upon the invisible God himself—nobody can stand it any longer." Letter of October 18, 1931 (*GS*, I, 61).

32   *GS*, III, 29. This statement is close to the reservations expressed in *Act and Being* vis-à-vis Barth's theology. In this work Bonhoeffer describes Barth's presentation of the new "I" in supratemporal terms as seeming to reduce the new "I" to the "heavenly double" of the empirical "I." See *AB*, p. 102 (*AS*, p. 77).

33   *CC*, p. 106 (*GS*, III, 231).

34   *CS*, p. 91 (*SC*, pp. 87-88). In this section Bonhoeffer calls Christ's revelation "historical" and "positive." In the next sentence he adds that this is a "concrete revelation." In *Act and Being* the revelation is also called "contingent"; see *AB*, p. 15 (*AS*, p. 12). Bonhoeffer does, in fact, develop revelation in terms of "act" philosophies under the subtitle "The Contingency of Revelation"; see *AB*, p. 79 (*AS*, p. 58). He uses the concept of revelation in this section to defend his thesis that human existence can only be given in a manner contingent to the real life situation of man, which for him is man living in community. Feil is, therefore, correct in his judgment that *Act and Being* accentuates far more than *Sanctorum Communio* the historicity of revelation. See *ThDB*, pp. 50, 103.

35   *CS*, pp. 97ff. (*SC*, pp. 91ff.) and *passim*.

36   *CC*, pp. 38-39 (*GS*, III, 176-178).

37   *GS*, III, 105. See also *CS*, p. 153 (*SC*, p. 165). Bonhoeffer seems to be in agreement with Karl Barth on this point. This is evident from his Berlin lectures on the "Jüngste Theologie" during the winter semester of 1932/33. See *GS*, V, 303-307. However, Bonhoeffer links the concept of the historical far more closely

to revelation than does Barth, as is clear from his criticism of the actualism and supratemporality of Barth's theology. See *AB*, pp. 90-91 (*AS*, p. 68).

38 *GS*, III, 28.

39 For an explanation of the Lutheran basis of this "revelation in hiddenness," see my article "Revelation in Christ. A Study of Bonhoeffer's Theology of Revelation," *Ephemerides Theologicae Lovanienses*, L, 1 (May 1974), 60-65.

40 *CC*, pp. 110-116 (*GS*, III, 235-240).

41 *GS*, III, 108-109.

42 For a discussion of the reasons behind this choice of terminology, see *NRS*, pp. 166-167 (*GS*, I, 150-151), and below, under the section "The Church, Concrete Locus of Historical Revelation."

43 "Konfirmanden-Unterrichtsplan (Zweiter Katechismus Versuch)," *GS*, III, 351.

44 Bonhoeffer wrote the paper "Kirche und Eschatologie (oder: Kirche und Reich Gottes)" for Reinhold Seeberg's dogmatics seminar. It is as yet unpublished but is available through the English language secretariate of the International Bonhoeffer Society for Archive and Research, La Salle College, Philadelphia, Pa.

45 "Kirche und Eschatologie," pp. 4-5.

46 *Ibid.*, pp. 6-7.

47 *Ibid.*, p. 14.

48 *CS*, p. 198 (*SC*, p. 212). Bonhoeffer's intention in adopting this thought of the historian Leopold von Ranke is to indicate clearly that history itself cannot decide the problem of salvation, which must remain an eschatological concept. Eschatology is the end of history; it is not to be identified with history. On the other hand, time and eternity stand in dialectical relationship with each other in Bonhoeffer's theology. One must seize the present moment to commit himself or herself to Christ. Hence Bonhoeffer agrees with Ranke that "every age is in direct relationship with God." He wishes to deny any possibility of a continuum in history whereby history itself would mediate one's relationship with God. He returns to this notion in prison in the context of a further attack on the notion of continuum in history which would have the whole course of history culminating in modern times. This notion he traces to Hegel through Ranke and Delbrück, even though he admits that Ranke's notion, that "every moment of history is 'immediate to God,'" might have served as a corrective to the continuum theory but failed to do so. See *LPP*, p. 230 (*WE*, p. 258). On Bonhoeffer's idea of the "immediacy to God" enjoyed by each age in history, see *ThDB*, pp. 244-245.

49 *CS*, pp. 202-204 (*SC*, pp. 216-219).

50 *CD*, p. 192 (*N*, p. 188).

51 *CD*, p. 193 (*N*, p. 188).

52 *E*, p. 98 (*Ek*, p. 128).

53 *E*, pp. 100-102 (*Ek*, pp. 131-132).

54 *E*, p. 102 (*Ek*, p. 132). The ambiguity in Bonhoeffer's use of the term "ultimate" is heightened in this section when he calls Luther's leaving the monastery and Paul's conversion from his bigoted zeal for the Law a "final time" in which they heard the "last word." Here his concept of ultimate approaches what Tillich has called "ultimate concern." The choices made by Luther and Paul under God's grace were decisions undertaken in the face of an ultimate meaning of life disclosed to them in their religious experiences.

55 *E*, p. 105 (*Ek*, p. 136).

56 *E*, p. 109 (*Ek*, p. 141).

57 *E*, p. 110 (*Ek*, p. 141).

58   *LPPE*, p. 336 (*WEN*, p. 369).

59   *LPPE*, p. 337 (*WEN*, p. 369).

60   *GS*, I, 362. See *GS*, I, 356-360, for a reconstructed, incomplete version of Bonhoeffer's original manuscript, parts of which have not been recovered.

61   *CS*, p. 107 (*SC*, p. 99).

62   *E*, p. 170 (*Ek*, p. 211).

63   *E*, pp. 171-172 (*Ek*, pp. 211-213).

64   *E*, p. 199 (*Ek*, p. 244). Bonhoeffer's Christocentric theology here is close to that of Teilhard de Chardin, as has been already noted by two studies of Bonhoeffer's theology. See Charles M. Hegarty, "Bonhoeffer and Teilhard: Christian Prophets of Secular Sanctity," *The Catholic World*, April 1968, pp. 31-34; and Heinrich Ott, *Reality and Faith* (Philadelphia, 1971), esp. chapter ten, "The Future for Christology," pp. 374-387. Both Bonhoeffer and Teilhard affirmed strongly that Jesus Christ is the center of the Christian life as he is the center of all reality. For Teilhard, the world is the divine milieu in which people are confronted by both God and the world and, through their faith-inspirited contacts with the world, become progressively "Christified." This joins Bonhoeffer's conviction that since the world has no reality outside of the revelation of God in Jesus Christ, the Christian becomes an *alter Christus* through his living as Christ wholeheartedly in the world. Both rejected the undialectical separation of secular from sacred, the temporal from the eternal and the double life—living as citizens of both the city of God and the city of man—led by so many Christians. Bonhoeffer's description of the unity of reality in Jesus Christ as similar to a polyphony held together by a *cantus firmus* seemed to echo Teilhard's Christogenesis. If Bonhoeffer could state that belonging to Christ meant belonging wholly to the world, Teilhard could also pray that "there be revealed to us the possibility of believing at the same time and wholly in God and the world, the one through the other" (see Hegarty, p. 34). In addition to the above points of convergence, Ott likewise emphasizes the *mystical* aspect of Christ's taking form within the community and in the universe. He notes, too, that the fundamental motif is similar to both Bonhoeffer and Teilhard, namely, God's concrete availability *(Greifbarkeit Gottes)*. See Ott, pp. 374-380. This is, of course, not to ignore their notable divergences. Teilhard's vision of man's becoming Christ (Christogenesis) as a part of the universal process of the cosmos is a far more extensive concept than Bonhoeffer's description of Christ as the center of the community, history, and nature. Finally, Bonhoeffer's statement of the positive benefits of experiencing the "absence of God" in order not to use God to fill in the gaps of human experience becomes in Teilhard's writings an invitation for man through his faith to seek the divine presence behind the veil of events. See Hegarty, pp. 32-33.

65   *E*, p. 199 (*Ek*, p. 244).

66   *CS*, p. 101 (*SC*, p. 266); *AB*, p. 120 (*AS*, p. 90).

67   *LPPE*, pp. 382-383 (*WEN*, pp. 415-416).

68   *CS*, p. 89 (*SC*, pp. 84-85); see also *AB*, p. 121 (*AS*, p. 91).

69   *CS*, p. 237 (*SC*, p. 164). This represents a development of his thought from the distinctions he drew in the paper "Kirche und Eschatologie" (see note 44). In that paper he spoke of the *invisible* kingdom of God and a *visible*, empirical church. He likewise called the empirical church the "door and landmark to the 'beyond' land of the invisible church" ("in das jenseitige Land der unsichtbaren Kirche"). See p. 8 and *passim*.

70   *CS*, p. 197 (*SC*, p. 210); see also *CS*, pp. 106-116 (*SC*, pp. 96-111). In his Berlin lectures, "Das Wesen der Kirche," Bonhoeffer explicitly states that the church is not identical with the kingdom of God ("Kirche ist nicht identisch mit dem Reich Gottes"). See *GS*, V, 273.

71   See, for example, *CS*, pp. 96-97 (*SC*, p. 90). Bonhoeffer, in his Christology lectures, describes Christ's presence as word, sacrament, and community, as a presence in the very center of human existence, of history, and of nature. These anthropological categories—existence, history, and nature—represent for Bonhoeffer the dimensions of human existence mediated by Christ. In this perspective, personal existence is always inserted into one's social history, and nature would link bodily existence to sacramental signs of the presence of Christ who thus stands for all creatures before God. The social and historical are linked here by the word calling believers to responsible decisions which must occur within and have an impact on life in society. This word is also addressed to the state, which has the responsibility to preserve order. On the interrelationship between Bonhoeffer's three fundamental anthropological categories, one should note Clifford Green's perceptive comments: "While Bonhoeffer delineates the Gestalt of Christ in these anthropological categories, it is imperative to notice the movement of the correlation. The order is Word-Existenz, sacrament-Natur, Gemeinde-state (political history), not the reverse. The method is Christological; but the form of the Christology is anthropological. The reason for this correlation and for its order is Bonhoeffer's fundamental Christological premise: in Christ *God* becomes *man* for men; it is *God* who becomes man, but he truly becomes *man*. Methodologically, this means that the movement is from the particular to the general, from revelation to reason, from church to state. This movement is built into the structure of the lectures, the first section of Part One dealing with the Gestalt of Christ, the second section treating Christ as Mediator of man's historical existence, of his political life, and of nature." Clifford Green, *Bonhoeffer: The Sociality of Christ and Humanity* (Scholars Press, 1975), p. 265 (emphasis Green's).

72   At the very beginning of his doctoral disseration Bonhoeffer had declared that theological "ideas such as 'person', 'primal state', 'sin' and 'revelation' are fully understandable only in relation to sociality." *CS*, p. 13 (*SC*, p. 7).

73   *CS*, pp. 87-88 (*SC*, pp. 83-84).

74   *CS*, pp. 87-88 (*SC*, pp. 83-84).

75   *CS*, p. 89 (*SC*, p. 84).

76   *CS*, pp. 90-93 (*SC*, pp. 86-89).

77   *CS*, p. 97 (*SC*, p. 90).

78   *AB*, p. 122 (*AS*, p. 92). Translation slightly altered from "communion" to "community."

79   *AB*, p. 123 (*AS*, p. 92).

80   *GS*, V, 267.

81   *AB*, p. 120 (*AS*, p. 90).

82   *AB*, p. 121 (*AS*, p. 91).

83   *AB*, p. 123 (*AS*, p. 92).

84   See *E*, p. 177 (*Ek*, pp. 218-219).

85   *CC*, p. 65 (*GS*, III, p. 197).

86   *CC*, pp. 65-66 (*GS*, III, 197-198).

87   *CC*, pp. 63-65 (*GS*, III, 196-198).

88   *CC*, p. 66 (*GS*, III, 198).

89 "What is the Church?" *NRS*, p. 155 ("Was ist Kirche?" *GS*, III, 288). The church is described by Bonhoeffer in this essay as being at once worldly and holy, a social institution and God's judgment on society, a religious organization and the communion of saints.

90 "Thy Kingdom Come," in John Godsey, *Preface to Bonhoeffer* (Philadelphia, 1965), p. 29 ("Dein Reich komme," *GS*, III, 271).

91 *Ibid.*, p. 30 (*GS*, III, 271).

92 *Ibid.*, p. 45 (*GS*, III, 283).

93 "A Theological Basis of the World Alliance," *NRS*, p. 157 ("Zur theologischen Begründung der Weltbundarbeit," *GS*, I, 140).

94 "Berlin Youth Conference, April 1932," *NRS*, p. 179 ("Theologische Konferenz der Mittelstelle für ökumenische Jugendarbeit am 29.-30. April 1932 in Berlin," *GS*, I, 128).

95 *NRS*, pp. 166-167 (*GS*, I, 150-151)—emphasis Bonhoeffer's. See also the distinction Bonhoeffer wrote in a memorandum which he presented to Dr. Willem A. Visser 't Hooft in Geneva in 1941 and which is cited by J. Glenthøj in "Bonhoeffer und die Ökumene," *MW*, II, 133. Bonhoeffer continued to insist on the theological expression "orders of preservation" in his lectures on Genesis in the fall term of 1933. See *CF*, pp. 88ff. (*SF*, pp. 104ff.).

96 See *NRS*, p. 167 (*GS*, I, 151); also *NRS*, pp. 179-180 (*GS*, I, 128-129); *CFT*, p. 88 (*SF*, pp. 104-105).

97 "Thy Kingdom Come," *Preface to Bonhoeffer*, pp. 42-43 ("Dein Reich komme," *GS*, III, 279-280). See also Ruth Zerner, "Dietrich Bonhoeffer's Views on the State and History," p. 131 below. This was a paper presented during the Bonhoeffer sessions of the annual convention of the American Academy of Religion, Washington, D.C., 1974. Dr. Zerner notes that "in describing the specific functions of the state, however, Bonhoeffer displayed a loose and confusing use of terminology. . . . He continues, insisting that the state does not create new communities but rather upholds the existing communities. Thus he uses the term 'communities' for those societal categories other than the church and the state (which are orders of preservation). Throughout the essay he seems to provide a special position for both church and state, distinctive from and—one could imply—superior to the other groupings in society. The inconsistent use of terms like 'communities' and 'orders of preservation' may merely indicate that during these years Bonhoeffer was still experimenting tentatively with various linguistic vehicles for expressing his thought. Sometimes all of the major groupings in society are called orders of preservation, and other times only the church and the state. . . ."

98 *E*, p. 254 (*Ek*, pp. 305-306). Bonhoeffer lists these mandates here as church, marriage and the family, culture, and government. Earlier he had labeled these four mandates as labor, marriage, government, and the church (*E*, p. 179 [*Ek*, p. 220]). He describes the difficulty of naming the mandates in a letter dated January 23, 1944: "Marriage, work, state and church all have their definite, divine mandate; but what about culture and education? I don't think they can just be classified under work, however tempting that might be in many ways. They belong, not to the sphere of obedience, but to the broad area of freedom, which surrounds all spheres of the divine mandates" (*LPP*, pp. 192-193 [*WE*, p. 216]).

99 *E*, p. 173 (*Ek*, pp. 213-214).

100 *E*, p. 266 (*Ek*, p. 318); see also *E*, p. 64 (*Ek*, p. 88).

101 Ruth Zerner, p. 147 below.

102 *Ibid.*, p. 138.

103   See, for example, the tortuous reasoning in the sections of *Ethics,* where Bonhoeffer describes the ecclesiastical responsibility of government and the political responsibility of the church (*E,* pp. 312-315 [*Ek,* pp. 370-373]). See also the section on "The Measuring of Tyrannicide," in Larry Rasmussen, pp. 127ff.

104   *LPPE,* pp. 303-305 (*WEN,* pp. 331-334).

105   "A Theological Basis for the World Alliance," *NRS,* p. 163 ("Zur theologischen Begründung der Weltbundarbeit," *GS,* I, 146).

106   Eberhard Bethge, *Bonhoeffer: Exile and Martyr* (New York, 1975), p. 65.

107   See "The Church and the Jewish Question," *NRS,* pp. 221-240 ("Die Kirche vor der Judenfrage," *GS,* II, 44-53). On the question of Bonhoeffer's attitude toward the Jews and the Jewish question in Nazi Germany, see Ruth Zerner's well-detailed and perceptive essay, "Dietrich Bonhoeffer and the Jews: Thoughts and Actions, 1933-1945," *Jewish Social Studies,* XXXVII, 3-4 (Summer/Fall 1975), 235-250. See also William Jay Peck, "From Cain to the Death Camps: An Essay on Bonhoeffer and Judaism," *Union Seminary Quarterly Review,* XXVIII, 2 (1973), 158-176; and Bethge, *Bonhoeffer: Exile and Martyr,* pp. 65-72.

108   Hence Ruth Zerner writes: "While Bonhoeffer's public statements in 1933 revealed the caution and restraint of a church leader conscious of his role in this community, his personal actions and private comments steadily revealed his concern for the plight of Jews in general. His personal letters show the depth of his concern for the 'sensible' people in the Church who 'completely lost their heads and their Bibles' in dealing with the Jewish question. The testimony of Bonhoeffer's Jewish-Christian friend, Franz Hildebrandt, is clear and unequivocal in relation to Bonhoeffer's support of Jewish-Christian clergy: Bonhoeffer 'reasoned, in view of the so-called "Aryanization" of the clergy under the nazi laws, that he could not be in a ministry which had become a racial privilege. I cannot recall or imagine any other man to have taken this line of solidarity with those of us who had to resign their pastorates under that legislation'" ("Dietrich Bonhoeffer and the Jews," pp. 244-245).

109   *NRS,* p. 223 (*GS,* II, 46).

110   *NRS,* pp. 225-226 (*GS,* II, 48-49). Ruth Zerner suggests that Bonhoeffer may have been influenced here by Emil Brunner's statement on the importance of free, autonomous groups in society to counteract the bureaucracy and totalitarian tendencies of the state. Zerner notes that Bonhoeffer's copy of Brunner's *Das Gebot und die Ordnungen* is heavily marked at an important passage pertinent to this point. See pp. 143, 155 n. 65 below.

111   "Die Geschichte und das Gute," *GS,* III, 470.

112   *E,* pp. 209-210 (*Ek,* p. 255).

113   *E,* p. 93 (*Ek,* pp. 121-122).

114   *E,* pp. 93-95 (*Ek,* pp. 121-123). See also the essay "After Ten Years," *LPPE,* pp. 4-6 (*WEN,* pp. 12-15).

115   *E,* p. 229 (*Ek,* pp. 277-278).

116   *E,* pp. 209-210 (*Ek,* pp. 255-256). See also Larry Rasmussen, pp. 50ff.

117   *E,* pp. 192-194, 226 (*Ek,* pp. 236-237, 274-275).

118   *E,* p. 207 (*Ek,* p. 253).

119   See *E,* pp. 207-210 (*Ek,* pp. 253-256), but especially the whole argument of Bonhoeffer's essay "After Ten Years," *LPPE,* pp. 3ff. (*WEN,* pp. 11ff.).

120   *LPPE,* pp. 229-230, 325-327 (*WEN,* pp. 257-259, 356-359).

121   *LPPE,* p. 280 (*WEN,* p. 305).

122   *LPPE,* p. 327 (*WEN,* p. 358).

123   See Clifford Green, pp. 307-309. Dr. Green notes that Bonhoeffer makes a clear distinction between strength and power, criticizing power because authorities wielded it to manipulate and dominate people, yet affirming strength as a capacity needed for self-fulfillment. The strengths he associates with autonomy and maturity are ego strengths, enabling the individual to exert leadership and responsibility. From this Dr. Green sketches an important biographical context of Bonhoeffer's prison theology: "Bonhoeffer, as a Christian, had now truly found freedom from the ambitiousness of self, and the competitiveness it entailed. This was true freedom because it no longer had to take the form of submission, renunciation and self-denial; it now had the form of serving and self-giving. In the resistance movement he entered into an authentic freedom for others. This fulfilled freedom then allowed him to affirm his own strengths, now with the confident knowledge that they were no longer self-serving; the suppression of the ego strength and autonomy advocated in *Nachfolge* was no longer necessary" (p. 309).

124   *GS*, III, 456-458; *E*, pp. 69, 194-199 (*Ek*, pp. 94, 238-244); *LPPE*, pp. 6-7, 381 (*WEN*, pp. 14-16, 414).

125   Letter of December 22, 1943, *LPPE*, p. 174 (*WEN*, pp. 195-196).

126   Zerner, p. 148 below. Dr. Zerner also suggests the possible influence of Emil Brunner's *Das Gebot und die Ordnungen*, particularly in those sections which opposed state absolutism and the "unknightliness" of modern warfare. Bonhoeffer was, however, critical of Brunner's listing the national state as among the "orders which God wishes to maintain."

127   *LPPE*, p. 337 (*WEN*, p. 369).

128   *E*, p. 62 (*Ek*, p. 86).

129   Hans Schmidt, "The Cross of Reality," *WCOA*, pp. 228, 233. Schmidt's position, which differentiates the concepts of reality and history in Bonhoeffer's theology, draws heavily from Bonhoeffer's early works, in particular *Sanctorum Communio* and *Creation and Fall*. According to Schmidt, Bonhoeffer protested in *SC* against social movements which had only contempt for the world's historicity. But in reality Bonhoeffer himself conceived of the world only as remaining a world of sin and death. To this he fitted an historical schema of creation, historical temporality, last judgment, and final establishment of the kingdom. The flaw in Bonhoeffer's argument was that he was speaking of a dualistic historical process in which Christ was present in history "analogous to an eternal presence of a timeless order; which . . . reveals itself, but is not itself history" (p. 224). Then, in an effort to lay claim to the "religionless" world for God's kingdom, Bonhoeffer interpreted reality similarly to the nonredemptive Jewish wisdom literature. Bonhoeffer thus looked for the secret God had planted in the world, but without any corresponding interest in the phenomenon of history (pp. 242ff.). As a result, Schmidt declares that Bonhoeffer was incapable of answering the question of how one could exercise a free responsibility in the face of an open future of the world (p. 246). This critique of Schmidt has been answered at length by Martin Kuske in his doctoral dissertation, published as *Das Alte Testament als Buch von Christus. Dietrich Bonhoeffers Wertung und Auslegung des Alten Testaments* (Göttingen, 1971), pp. 119-130. As evidence that Schmidt's critique of Bonhoeffer's concept of history is fundamentally false, Kuske cites sections of Bonhoeffer's *Ethics,* particularly "Inheritance and Decay" and "History and Good." Kuske concedes that at times Bonhoeffer stands in a very old tradition, such as in his teaching on the mandates. He also grants the Hegelian influence discerned by Schmidt but refuses to associate this with any anti-historical attitude on the part of Bonhoeffer. Kuske's principal *caveat* against Schmidt, however, is his objection that Schmidt uses the late wisdom literature of Israel to explain

Bonhoeffer's conclusions on the world come of age. If the Old Testament must be used to explain Bonhoeffer's statements, then, according to Kuske, it must be in the way in which Bonhoeffer himself used the Old Testament. Kuske sees this as much more after the manner of the Old Testament concept of prophetic judgment rather than that of the wisdom literature. This prophetic judgment is neither metaphysical nor individualistic, two conditions Bonhoeffer sets for a nonreligious interpretation of biblical concepts. The judgment was, rather, in terms of historical events and so could be used by Bonhoeffer as concrete evidence to justify his plea for the renewal of Christianity. Bonhoeffer's letters are seen by Kuske in connection with the "Inheritance and Decay" section of *Ethics*, where Bonhoeffer tries to understand the history of Europe and America in a positive way. According to Kuske, this was a stage on Bonhoeffer's way toward a positive affirmation of Christ's presence in the world and to a discovery of the development of the world under God's direction *in* history and not *despite* that history.

130   This is not to assert that the ethical reasoning behind Bonhoeffer's involvement in the plot was always coherent or adequate. See Larry Rasmussen's detailed critique of Bonhoeffer's ethics in this regard, pp. 149ff.

131   *LPPE*, p. 7 (*WEN*, p. 16).

132   *LPPE*, p. 6 (*WEN*, p. 15).

133   Zerner, p. 151 below.

134   My remarks in this concluding section are based on what I perceive to be the compatibility of the cognitional theory of Michael Polanyi to Bonhoeffer's theology of history. See especially Polanyi's *Personal Knowledge: Towards a Post-Critical Philosophy* (Harper Torchbook, 1964), *The Tacit Dimension* (New York, 1966), and *The Study of Man* (Chicago, 1964).

135   The influence of Wilhelm Dilthey's thought on Bonhoeffer's concepts of autonomy, worldliness, and maturity, through three of Dilthey's books which Bonhoeffer read in prison, has been well documented by Ernst Feil in *ThDB*, pp. 355ff. My own remarks here bear more on Dilthey's theory of universal history and its congruence with Bonhoeffer's theology of universal history structured by both Christology and eschatology. I refer for this principally to H.P. Rickman, ed., *Meaning in History: W. Dilthey's Thoughts on History and Society* (London, 1961). This highly schematic presentation of models of historical interpretation which are evident in Bonhoeffer's theology of history and revelation should not imply that Bonhoeffer was consciously developing his insights from a universal theory of history. Such a theory to praxis mode of operation is exactly the reverse of Bonhoeffer's desire to integrate judgment on historical facts and the attitude of faith toward these facts, an attitude to be translated into responsible action in service of people in need, especially suffering humanity.

136   *Meaning in History*, p. 106.

137   *E*, pp. 98-119, 162-163, 199 (*Ek*, pp. 128-152, 202-203, 243-244). See also *GS*, III, 470.

138.   *LPPE*, p. 371 (*WEN*, p. 403).

139   *E*, p. 170 (*Ek*, p. 211).

140   *LPPE*, p. 7 (*WEN*, p. 16).

141   *E*, pp. 120ff. (*Ek*, pp. 152ff.).

142   *E*, p. 67 (*Ek*, p. 93).

143   *LPPE*, p. 373 (*WEN*, p. 405).

144   On the significance of India to Bonhoeffer's theology, see especially Feil, *ThDB*, pp. 387ff., and William Jay Peck, "The Significance of Bonhoeffer's Interest in India," *Harvard Theological Review*, LXI (July 1968), 431-450, and above, note 31.

145   Cited by Peter Schreiner, "Roman Catholic Theology and Non-Christian Religions," *Journal of Ecumenical Studies*, VI, 3 (Summer 1969), 388. It is not my intention here to identify revelation with salvation. However, it should be obvious from this study that revelation is an essential condition or moment in God's achieving the salvation of an individual.

146   *E*, p. 64 (*Ek*, p. 88).

DIETRICH BONHOEFFER'S VIEWS ON
THE STATE AND HISTORY

Ruth Zerner

JESUS CHRIST, the world, the church, and the Word of God—Dietrich Bonhoeffer orchestrated much of his theology around these leitmotifs. Most of his scholarly interpreters agree that Christology is central to his thought. In his Nazi prison cell Bonhoeffer crystallized this continuing concern of his life with these words: "What is bothering me incessantly is the question what Christianity really is, or indeed who Christ really is, for us today."[1] Two of the leading scholarly studies of the "worldly" aspects of Bonhoeffer's theology both stress this Christological framework. In America Larry L. Rasmussen has suggested that the anti-Nazi conspiratorial activity of Bonhoeffer, "the gentle resister," was "his Christology enacted with utter seriousness."[2] On the other side of the Atlantic, the German Roman Catholic scholar Ernst Feil, focusing his microscope on Bonhoeffer's theology of "the world," has asserted that "Bonhoeffer's understanding of the world" can be legitimately explained only "when developed within the 'brackets' of Christology."[3]

This essay will focus on some political-historical corners of Bonhoeffer's writings on the world. Just as it is impossible to separate Bonhoeffer's worldview from his Christology, so one should avoid any artificial attempt to separate Bonhoeffer's political attitudes from his faith—despite the shadow of the German Lutheran "two spheres" tradition. Bonhoeffer was not in any strict sense a political theorist. His writings about the state and about the historical background shaping modern life and politics were primarily the responses of a concerned Christian thinker to the crisis choreography of Nazi politics and war. Undoubtedly, some of these works were rapidly improvised reactions to Nazi initiatives. For example, within the week following the Nazi promulgation of the Aryan clause on April 7, 1933, Bonhoeffer completed his urgent essay on "The Church and the Jewish Question."[4] This document, which contains several crucial passages on the state, was hastily shaped in the crucible of political crisis and can hardly be considered a systematic, long-pondered proposal. Yet one should not forget that some of Bonhoeffer's most challenging, seminal theological statements have been fragmentary, partial insights rather than components of a well-ordered, systematized totality. Perhaps Bonhoeffer was at his best when responding under pressure to the concrete, pressing problems of the world.

Although Bonhoeffer's ecumenical colleague Willem Adolf Visser 't Hooft has perceptively proposed that "hunger and thirst for reality, for becoming incarnate, for *living* the Christian life and not merely *talking* about it" provide "the real key to Bonhoeffer's message,"[5] this essay will limit itself to the political and historical ideas Bonhoeffer talked and wrote about (and also underscored in his personal library books). The focus will not be on the acts he lived out. Eberhard Bethge's monumental biography documents in detail Bonhoeffer's tense and treacherous political path of anti-Nazi conspiratorial activity.[6] This essay will emphasize Bonhoeffer's *Staatsgedanke,* sketching his historical views only as a framework or setting for the evolution of his political attitudes. The rich variety of Bonhoeffer's historical comments, speculations, and interests will not be fully explored in this essay. Our interest will center on Bonhoeffer's historical perspectives and interpretations primarily as they related to his ideas on the state.

In addition to organizing the widely scattered, fragmentary references to the state in Bonhoeffer's writings, this study will attempt to place Bonhoeffer's views on the state in the wider historical context of the German academic community. To what extent did Bonhoeffer share attitudes toward the state common to other German intellectuals? To what extent did he diverge from typical post-World War I German academic opinions about the state? Which thinkers influenced the development of his political-historical ideas? Before answering these queries, we must recognize that distinctive Teutonic ambiance which nourished Bonhoeffer's life and thought: the world of German university professors, which included his father, a famous Berlin psychiatrist, as well as the parents of many of Bonhoeffer's playmates and friends. This privileged, sheltered circle of professional and academic contacts stretched from Bonhoeffer's Berlin-Dahlem childhood experiences through his doctoral studies and teaching responsibilities at the University of Berlin.

According to Fritz K. Ringer's indispensable historical research, the German academics—or in his terminology "mandarins"—formed during the years 1890 to 1933 "a highly integrated and relatively homogeneous intellectual community."[7] Pressed by anxieties about their threatened position in a new machine and mass-culture age, these scholars, says Ringer, "made war upon individualism, naturalism, mechanism, and the like."[8] Ringer's study suggests a startlingly long enemies list of "and the likes" that were loathed by the orthodox German intellectual mandarins, among whom an outspoken leader was Dietrich Bonhoeffer's doctoral professor, Reinhold Seeberg.[9] Anti-Enlightenment, antimaterialism, antipositivism, antiegalitarianism, antiparliamentarianism, antiutilitarianism, antiempiricism—all resounded as parts of a polyphony of antimodernism, which underscored the divergence between western European (Anglo-French) thought and unique German traditions. Epithets hurled against Western political theories included: the "whole mathematical-mechanistic West European scientific spirit" and "the barren abstraction of a universal and equal humanity."[10]

While acknowledging the achievements of disciplined, consistent respect for abstract thinking, which was a hallmark of early twentieth-century Teutonic university life, one perceives with Ringer the problem of German historical-political traditions, which tended "to treat cultures, states, and epochs as personalized 'wholes,' " emphasizing that "each of these totalities embodies its own unique spirit."[11] German academics saw the whole as greater than its parts. Using organic analogies (popular since the nineteenth century), German thinkers conceived of states or communities as having lives of their own, more significant than any individual's "egoistic" (a favorite invective adjective among Teutonic theologians) concern. The German concept of community, argued Ernst Troeltsch in 1923 at the Berlin Hochschule für Politik, was distinctive:

> The state and society are not created from the individual by way of contract and pragmatic construction, but from the suprapersonal spiritual forces which emanate from the most important and creative individuals, the volk spirit or the religious aesthetic idea. A quite different idea of humanity also results: not the ultimate union of fundamentally equal human beings in a rationally organized total humanity, but the fullness of contending national spirits, which unfold their highest spiritual powers in this contest.[12]

According to the *Brockhaus* definition, a community consisted of "a group of human beings who feel united in being and in action through common thinking, feeling, and willing. . . . The community is considered naturally and organically grown."[13]

The search for such "community"—for holism and synthesis—was the compelling concern of post-World War I German university professors in all disciplines. Too often, however, slogans about the supremacy of "the whole" and battles against mythical "isms" led to "crude stereotypes . . . caricatures . . . and fruitless name-calling."[14] Such judgments and criticisms may be convincingly leveled against the verbose pretensions of Reinhold Seeberg during the Weimar era. Seeberg, a staunch nationalist inclined toward a kind of idealistic Christian socialism, called for a union of Christianity and idealism in the battle against materialism, egoism, and lack of faith.[15] Seeberg's fears and rhetoric reveal in microcosm the sense of tension, instability, and European cultural crisis which prompts Ringer to conclude that "the German university professors felt themselves involved in a genuine tragedy."[16]

Seeberg, an admirer of Adolf Stoecker, Houston Stuart Chamberlain, and Richard Wagner, exhorted native-born German Christians to conquer the corrupting influence of Judaism, "which has served as the yeast of a national, religious and moral disintegration of our people." He abjured the use of brute force or of crude racial anti-Semitism in such a battle against the materialist influences of Judaism. Rather he recommended weapons of faith for the faithful in overcoming Judaism: "strengthening of the spirituality, historical sense and piety of the German people."[17] Critical of capitalism, social democracy, individualism, and internationalism, Seeberg appears to be a paradigm of Ringer's "orthodox" antimodernist German professor.

Yet a close examination of some of Seeberg's writings on the state reveals that Ringer may have overlooked "accommodationist" strands in Seeberg's thought. Although stressing the difference between German Lutheran and Anglo-Saxon Calvinist ideas of the state, Seeberg acknowledged the problem of the German church imprisoned in a conservatism rooted in the dependence of the church on the state. "To maintain such a position in light of recent developments would be suicide. The church should not recommend a specific political course, but she should demand that her members participate in politics as a form of obligation."[18]

Despite Seeberg's almost hysterical attacks on modern materialism, he displayed a robust realism concerning the "orders" or "communities" of society: industry, commerce, politics, state. "These communities, resting on natural foundations, follow inherent laws." An alteration of these immanent laws would destroy their functioning:

> A state which renounces power and law crumbles. Commerce and industry, politics and government are not in themselves moral or immoral, but rather they are practical or impractical, wise or foolish.[19]

According to Seeberg, individuals as individuals may be won to moral causes, but since such moral individuals "are at the same time members of human communities, it is their responsibility to influence the orders and laws in a Christian sense." Thus the communities should be shaped in keeping with "the social will," not egoism. The aim is to establish each order (such as industry or the state) "as a useful organ of the social will." This becomes the responsibility of moral persons.[20] Seeberg's ideas on community, orders, and responsibility probably played a role in the evolution of Bonhoeffer's own concepts of communities, orders, and finally, mandates.

Reinhold Seeberg, Adolf von Harnack, and Karl Holl ranked as the most influential professors in Bonhoeffer's Berlin theological studies. In

September 1925, when the young doctoral candidate decided to write his dissertation under Seeberg, he had taken only two courses with Seeberg, whereas he had taken four courses with Holl and two courses with Harnack. Bonhoeffer had wavered between the options of church history (the specialty of Harnack and Holl) and systematic theology (or a combination of dogmatics and history) under Seeberg.[21] According to Ringer's two basic categories of antimodernist professors and modernist, accommodationist academics, Reinhold Seeberg looms as Ringer's most resistant and recalcitrant antimodernist theologian; Harnack, on the other hand, stands out as one of the courageous accommodationist academics.[22] In light of Bonhoeffer's latter-day fame as a herald of Christian "this-worldly" encounter with the forces of the modern age, it is intriguing to note that he chose to write his dissertation under a leading orthodox, antimodernist theologian rather than under the modernist Harnack. The evidence of family letters indicates, however, that the choice was apparently motivated less by the quality or trend of Seeberg's thought than by Seeberg's personal benevolence and willingness to allow Bonhoeffer freedom in his research project. Seeberg, a genial *Doktorvater,* had already conferred with Bonhoeffer's father and indicated that he had long been waiting for a student to suggest a study of "religious community."[23]

In Bonhoeffer's dissertation description of the state (essentially incidental to his analysis of the church) one discerns a cogent weaving of three threads of European intellectual history: Reformation (Lutheran) conceptions of the state, nineteenth-century organic interpretations of the state, as well as the post-World War I academic search for holism and emphasis on community (accompanied by strands of anti-individualism). Bonhoeffer succinctly shapes a two-page mini-history of state and society as viewed by the patristic fathers and Aquinas.[24] Such historical sensitivity, despite the obvious selectivity and superficiality of the survey, adds dimensions of continuity and authority to Bonhoeffer's work. This characteristic concern for historical roots continues into Bonhoeffer's prison papers. Indeed, the amalgamation of specific Reformation, organic, and community-oriented conceptions of the state also lingers in the background of Bonhoeffer's later, expanded explications of the state.

Thus the skeleton of Bonhoeffer's *Staatsidee* is already present in *Sanctorum Communio,* only to be fleshed out—not radically altered—in *Ethics.* Acknowledging this essential unity in Bonhoeffer's view of the nature and character of the state does not mean one overlooks his increasingly intense focus on Christ, "the center," the convergence of all human groupings, including the state. But this accelerated Christological concentration as related to the nature of the state is more a matter of tone or shading than fundamental reorientation. One does discern, through the 1930s and 1940s, changes in emphasis or relationships (i.e., Bonhoeffer's repositioning of the state in terms of other societal groupings) or changes in terminology (from "orders" to "mandates"). Yet in his various commentaries on the character and role of the state, the similarities are more fundamental than the differences.

Such an emphasis on continuity of thought does not imply that Bonhoeffer's intellectual life was rigid or static. On the contrary, a stretching and expanding of this central core continued until the end. Flexibility and fluidity were especially evident in his ability to rephrase, reevaluate, or reexamine complexities and contradictions. But certain themes remained constant. In the early 1940s Bonhoeffer spoke in a telling way of the danger of refusing to accept "a historical inheritance" (on the part of the church or the European world).[25] It is clear that Bonhoeffer, as early as 1927, understood the importance of accepting the historical legacy of the German Reformed trend and of several leading German intellectuals. This did not mean that he sacrificed his right to criticize, update, or synthesize. The Continental scholars Heinrich Ott and Ernst Feil have both educed what Ott calls "the astonishing unity in the progress of his thought."[26] Feil, in his typically thorough and meticulous fashion, has catalogued references to themes of unity and continuity in Bonhoeffer's theology, which are found in the majority of works about Bonhoeffer.[27]

From 1927 through the 1940s, Bonhoeffer continued to link the state with the watchwords of his Weimar academic elders and peers: community, order, law—as opposed to egoism, individualism, natural law, and anarchy. In his dissertation, *Sanctorum Communio,* Bonhoeffer's sense of the state was neither startling nor innovative. His comments do, however, reveal a talent for sophisticated, succinct synthesis, unusual for a twenty-one-year-old. The core of this analysis of the state stood the test of time, reemerging in his extended discussions on the state in *Ethics* more than a decade later.

Like his mentor Seeberg, Bonhoeffer emphasized the role of "will" in his initial explanation of the state. In the first place, the state (apparently used interchangeably with "the nation") is a "community" alongside other communities, such as family, race, marriage, friendship, and the religious community.[28] According to Bonhoeffer's definition, "Community is community of will, built upon the separateness and the difference between persons, constituted by reciprocal acts of will, with its unity in what is willed, and counting among its basic laws the inner conflict of individual wills."[29] Secondly, Bonhoeffer placed the nation in a special position in relation to other communities, because it had not "grown" but had been "willed, moreover as an end in itself, having its own value."[30] Admittedly, Bonhoeffer's assumptions disclose a familiar Teutonic penchant for personalizing abstractions. Unlike liberal western European political theories, the German view of the state (assimilated by Bonhoeffer) made the state or nation "an end in itself," rather than a means to an end. Many Anglo-French theorists have maintained that the state is merely a means to protect the rights and freedom of the individual. In Western liberal thought the individual's welfare is the common denominator that could be termed "an end in itself"—not the mental configuration known as "the state" or "nation."

Self-consciously, Bonhoeffer accepted the organic view of the state (and of the church), positing the existence of the "collective person" (Gesamtheit). Using the example of Israel, Bonhoeffer asserts that "it was the people, and not the individuals, who had sinned. . . . There is a will of God for the people, just as there is for the individual. . . . It is not only individual Germans and individual Christians who are guilty; Germany and the church are guilty too. . . . The community which is from God to God . . . this community stands in God's sight, and does not dissolve into the fate of the many. . . . The center of action lies in the collective person."[31] One's willingness to support Bonhoeffer's conception of social reality as organicism is severely strained when he proposes that "the collective human person has a heart. . . . The collective person's heart beats at the point where the individual recognizes himself both as the individual and as the race, and bows to God's demand."[32] Such warmed-over "sociological Hegelianism" and "theological imperialism" (to borrow Peter Berger's caustic tags)[33] are less than conclusive for the contemporary Western social and political thinker. One must grant, however, that Bonhoeffer did attempt to establish an equilibrium of tensions between the individual and the community:

> God does not desire a history of individual men, but the history of the community of men. Nor does he desire a community which absorbs the individual into itself, but a community of men. In his sight the community and the individual are present at the same moment, and rest in one another.[34]

Yet, can one agree with his assumption that "the structures of the individual and the collective unit are the same"?[35]

Peter Berger has challenged Bonhoeffer's contention that "collective persons" can command ethical responsibility on the part of individuals. One cannot help finding Berger's critique compelling in the post-Holocaust age:

> It is one thing to speak of the independent being of collectives as an exploratory device for a better understanding of society. . . . It is quite another thing when these entities (such as "the family," "the nation," "the state") take on the quality of mythological beings that make moral demands over against the imperatives of personal morality.[36]

Essentially, Bonhoeffer's ethical observations rest on what Berger aptly characterizes as "pre-Marxian use of Hegelianism" within "a long tradition of German conservative ideology."[37]

Thus in *Sanctorum Communio* the elements of nineteenth-century German organic views of the state merged with Weimar strivings for community and holism. Although Bonhoeffer attempts to leave a place for the individual in his speculative system, there is no doubt that the scales are tipped in favor of the community. In keeping with traditional Lutheran conceptions, the state comes from God. To put it in Bonhoeffer's language: ". . . genuine community, in marriage, the family, the nation, is from God to God."[38]

A convenient capsule summary of the Reformation *Staatsidee* appears in the footnotes to Emil Brunner's *Das Gebot und die Ordnungen* (1932); more than once Bonhoeffer praises these reliable, thorough, and thoughtful footnotes.[39] Unlike the Catholics, the Protestant Reformers, claims Brunner, had no Christian "philosophy" of the state. For the Reformers the state was "a worldly order" existing alongside the church:

> Indeed the Reformers do have a very definite teaching (necessarily following from their confessions of faith) of the sharp division between state and church, of the independence of the state over against the church, of the relationship of the Christian to the state. Emphasis on the worldliness of the order of the state does not mean, as Catholic theologians always assume, that the state has nothing to do with God, and that the relationship of the Christian to the state has nothing to do with the faith; instead it means that God has assigned the state a different function from that of the church, and the will of God applicable to the state is not to be derived from the scriptures nor from a natural law and not from the faith; instead it must be sought also by believing statesmen looking at reality. . . . The Reformers' conception of the state limits itself to the simple thoughts which are based on Romans 13. The state is a divine order, established as a power to exert force because of sin; the state's purpose is the creation of order and the establishment of external justice. Therefore the Christian owes obedience to the state, even the bad state and the unjust law, except in the event that the state attempts to force the Christian to disobey God. Even in the issue usually considered a specifically Calvinist approach, one finds both [Luther and Calvin] in agreement: there is a right of resistance by the estates against the monarch (although accented differently by each [of the two Reformers]).[40]

Although Bonhoeffer's personal copy of this volume by Brunner does not show underlinings or marginal comments in the section quoted above, it would appear from the internal evidence in Bonhoeffer's writings in 1932 and later that he accepted Brunner's interpretation of sixteenth-century Reformation political ideas. In 1932, the year that this Brunner volume was first published, Bonhoeffer read it eagerly, still commenting years later on the "very wise things" Brunner said in his footnotes.[41] Nevertheless,

Bonhoeffer criticized Brunner's tendency toward dogmatic individualism and his failure to focus on "the possibility of proclaiming the concrete command through the church." Indeed, Brunner's message for the church was so meager, in Bonhoeffer's opinion, that it actually represented "a real threat to its [the church's] substance."[42]

Such concern for the role and message of the church, coupled with a Christological emphasis, increasingly preoccupied Bonhoeffer during 1932 and 1933. Undoubtedly the focus on the person of Jesus Christ was related to his hidden experience of 1931/32, resulting in a change which his biographer describes as a move from "theologian" to "Christian."[43] Concern for the Christian church in Germany was already apparent in Bonhoeffer's prophetic warnings at an international youth conference in July 1932:

> Responsible theological work, supported by the ecumenical world, faces the task of strengthening that segment of Germans and of Christians in Germany who are fighting against Hitler. The victory of Hitler's party would have unforeseen consequences, not only for the development of the German people, but also for the whole world. Christians must unite in battle against those forces which seduce peoples into a false nationalism, which encourage militarism, and which threaten the world with a disturbance, out of which a war could arise.[44]

Bonhoeffer's foresight and political realism in assessing Germany's future were impressive. A week after Hitler came to power, Bonhoeffer predicted "a dreadful cultural barbarization," which might result, he told Reinhold Niebuhr, in the need to establish in Germany a Civil Liberties Union.[45] Bonhoeffer was obviously not unprepared for the political significance and dangers of the Nazi seizure of power.

Bonhoeffer's writings on the state during 1932 and 1933 reflect this concern for clarifying the position of the church and, more importantly, the relationship of Christ to the state. A change occurred in the terminology used in Bonhoeffer's taxonomy for society. State and church (along with marriage, family, Volk, and even international peace) are classified as "orders of preservation" rather than simply "communities" (as in his dissertation).[46] Although the labels changed, the substance of these categories remained essentially the same (except for the occasional addition of international peace as an "order of preservation"), with a more pronounced emphasis on the roles and relationships of church and state. By using the term "orders of preservation" rather than the traditional theological phrase "orders of creation," Bonhoeffer accented the possible disruption of these orders of preservation "if they no longer allow the revelation through Christ."[47] Here he was surely responding to a sense of looming national and international crisis—of impending destruction. His schema, however, projected a distinctive role for the church of Christ, which was to "render judgments about the orders of the world. And from this perspective she [the church] must hear the command of God. . . . Solely from Christ, not from any established law, nor from any eternal order, does the church hear the command, and she perceives it in the orders of preservation."[48]

In the November 1932 address "Dein Reich komme!" Bonhoeffer provided some of his clearest definitions and clarifications of state-church relations:

> The form in which the kingdom of God attests itself as wonder, we call—the church; the form in which the kingdom of God attests itself as order, we call—the state. The kingdom of God in our world is nothing other than the two-fold form of church and state. Both are of necessity related to each other. Neither is solely for itself. Every attempt of the one to seize possession of the other disregards that relationship of the kingdom of God to the earth. . . . The church limits the state, just as the state limits the church.[49]

A mutual recognition of limits and a continuing balance of tensions characterized Bonhoeffer's vision of church-state relations, which should never evolve into a penetration of one by the other. Authority, force, and the preservation of order all belonged in the realm of the state. In describing the specific functions of the state, however, Bonhoeffer displayed a loose and confusing use of terminology. In this November 1932 address he speaks of the state's role in the "preservation of the orders of the communities, marriage, family, *Volk*. . . ."[50] He continues, insisting that the state does not create new communities but rather upholds the existing communities. Thus he uses the term "communities" for those societal categories other than the church and the state (which are orders of preservation). Throughout the essay he seems to provide a special position for both church and state, distinctive from and—one could imply—superior to the other groupings in society. The inconsistent use of terms like "communities" and "orders of preservation" may merely indicate that during these years Bonhoeffer was still experimenting tentatively with various linguistic vehicles for expressing his thought. Sometimes all of the major groupings in society are called orders of preservation, and at other times only the church and the state are thus designated.

Despite this ambiguity of expression, Bonhoeffer's ideas in these 1932/33 essays and lectures are clearly in keeping with Brunner's footnote interpretation of the Reformation teaching on church and state.[51] Just like the reformers, Bonhoeffer called for obedience and emphasis on the reality of this world: "Obedience to God in the church and in the state. The kingdom of God is not in some hidden world, it is in our midst. . . ."[52]

Alert to the political realities represented by the Nazi movement and to its seductive appeal to the Youth Movement generation of the 1920s, Bonhoeffer prepared a radio message on "The Leader and the Individual in the Younger Generation," which he delivered on February 1, 1933 (only in part due to Nazi censorship), two days after Hitler's accession to power. While acknowledging the postwar search for escape "from solitude to community, from isolation to association, from lack of authority to a new authority," he warned against the dangers of the *Führer* concept, "entangled in a widely stretched extended new individualism."[53] Bonhoeffer perceived the psychological pattern of transference, whereby "the individual abdicates for the sake of the *Führer*," turning the desire for community, for "collectivism" into "intensified individualism." The balance between order and responsibility, crucial to Bonhoeffer's view of society and specifically the state, was dissolved, leaving "the free individual, who is a law unto himself." Condemning the contemporary "political messianic concept of the leader," Bonhoeffer called for the true leader, who "must lead his followers away from the authority of his person to the recognition of the real authority of the orders and of the offices. The leader must lead his followers towards a responsibility to the orders of life, to father, teacher, judge, state."[54] As in his previous writings, the emphasis was on responsibility toward existing "orders," with the need for a political leader to recognize that in commitment to his followers he is "in fact quite simply a servant."[55] All the now familiar motifs of Bonhoeffer's political and social statements are present: historical perspective, community, orders, order, authority, responsibility, opposition to extreme individualism, service to others, with special emphasis on the ultimate authority of God.

In the concluding paragraph (which was never aired), Bonhoeffer echoes Martin Luther and St. Paul in the call for an individual free before God but committed to others: "Alone before God, man becomes what he is, free and committed in responsibility at the same time. . . ."[56] This final note somewhat modifies Bonhoeffer's tendency toward anti-individualistic statements. On the other hand, it is in keeping with German intellectual and spiritual traditions of "inner freedom" for the individual, which may actually accompany external conditions of subservience and servitude. This Teutonic tendency to combine spiritual independence and secular submission to an authoritarian state has been thoughtfully traced in Leonard Krieger's *The German Idea of Freedom.* In analyzing the ideas of German philosophers and political theoreticians through several centuries, Krieger shows how Germans came to view the authoritarian, monarchical state as the agency of freedom as well as of order. According to the German thinkers selected by Krieger, "the individual would find his freedom increasingly in conformity rather than in resistance to the power of the state."[57] Bonhoeffer's writings channel such German thoughts from the sixteenth century, and especially from the nineteenth-century highpoint of organic political and social theories of the state, combining them with secularized interpretations of the Pauline-Lutheran legacy of "inner freedom."

However, in the decade following 1933, Bonhoeffer restored a Christian content to such secularized terms as "freedom" and "responsibility." For example, in battling against the Nazi state's attempt to prevent baptized Jews from serving as Christian ministers, Bonhoeffer argued that "the true service and loyalty of the church in relationship to the state never lies in blind imitation of the state's methods, but rather solely in the freedom of the church's proclamation and development of its own unique *Gestalt* as the church."[58]

Unfortunately, however, Bonhoeffer's first response to the Nazi Aryan clause sounded equivocal and conservative, less inclined to focus on the church's freedom. In "The Church and the Jewish Question," completed on April 15, 1933, he characterizes the church as the "most loyal servant" of the state. The church of the Reformation, he maintains, has no right to tell the state how to act in specifically political matters, no right "to praise or to censure the laws of the state."[59] He grants that the state could legislate concerning "the Jewish question":

> Without doubt the Jewish question is one of the historical problems with which our state must deal, and without doubt the state is justified in adopting new methods here. . . . The church cannot in the first place exert direct political action, for the church does not pretend to have any knowledge of the necessary course of history. Thus even today, in the Jewish question, it cannot address the state directly and demand of it some definite action of a different nature.[60]

Bonhoeffer reserved to individuals and to "humanitarian associations" the right to accuse the state of offenses against morality; the church, however, did not fit into this grouping of humanitarian associations. Bonhoeffer sketched the multiple alternatives open to the church in relation to the new laws of the state; the third—and last—drastic step involved "not just bandaging the victims under the wheel," but jamming the spokes of the wheel itself. Such direct political action by the church was conceivable only as a result of a decision by a church council and only if the church perceived that the state refused to maintain law and order.[61]

Ironically, the interpretation of Luther's church-state legacy by Bonhoeffer's conservative, anti-Semitic teacher, Reinhold Seeberg, provides for a more dynamic interaction between the two spheres:

> The so-called "pure separation" between state and church, which makes both powers indifferent to each other, is not in accordance with Luther's conception. He had too great a sense of reality to sink into such abstractions. The ethical task of the state is the bridge on which the church's judgments and Christian concepts of ethics move into the state's ordinance of law *(Rechtsordnung)*.[62]

Seeberg stressed the need for the state to consider the suggestions of the church in ethical and social issues, and "so far as its [the state's] purpose and methods allow—turn them into laws."[63] Although Bonhoeffer did not consider it the church's role to challenge the morality of the state's laws, he did sense the need for such challenge by humanitarian groups and "knowledgeable Christian men. . . . Every strong state needs such associations and such individual personalities" and will cultivate and care for their continued existence.[64] These comments in his essay on the Jewish question do not allow one to write off Bonhoeffer as an ultraconservative supporter of an authoritarian state concept. While he did not seem to follow Seeberg's more flexible concept of Luther's church-state heritage, Bonhoeffer's marginal notes in the text indicate that he may have been influenced by Brunner's footnotes on the importance of free, autonomous groupings in society.[65] In addition, Bonhoeffer's emphasis on the importance of such free groups (as earlier stressed in Max Weber's writings) probably grew out of conversations with the legal experts in his family, especially his brothers-in-law, Hans von Dohnanyi and Gerhard Leibholz.

With his 1933 lectures on Christology, Bonhoeffer moved into a period in which his writing is permeated with the person of Jesus Christ, as the center of human existence, of history, and of nature. Although the thoughts of this period contain some of the most profound personal religious insights, it is difficult to discern in the 1930s a systematic, logical structure or theory revising his ideas on the state. Instead, his previous positions appear to be undergirded and reinforced, although they are now all linked to Christ. The church is still the boundary of the state, but now in a special, semimystical way the church is also "the hidden centre of the sphere of the state." Bonhoeffer's historical interpretation of the state includes a new element: the cross, which has resulted in a new relationship between church and state. The historian has difficulty accepting Bonhoeffer's claim that "there has been a state in the proper sense only as long as there has been a church. The state has its origin since and with the cross (like the church), in so far as this cross destroys and fulfills and affirms its order."[66]

Previously Bonhoeffer spoke of church and state as the twofold form of the kingdom of God. Now Christ enters into the characterization: "Christ is present to us in a double form, as church and as state." The messianic claim "secretly" infuses the state's role in creating law and order. Bonhoeffer's old watchwords for the state are still present, with the addition of Christ and the cross.[67]

In a 1934 London sermon, the Christian theme of weakness (seen as perfect and holy "in the eyes of Christ") caused Bonhoeffer to challenge the political predilections of Christendom. He admits a truth too many Germans discovered too late:

Christianity stands or falls with its revolutionary protest against violence, arbitrariness and pride of power and with its plea for the weak. I feel that Christians are doing too little to make these points clear rather than too much. Christendom has adjusted itself far too easily to the worship of power. Christians should give more offence, shock the world far more, than they are now doing.[68]

In *The Cost of Discipleship,* published in Germany in 1937, this call to protest the pride of power seems to be submerged in Bonhoeffer's emphasis on the Christian who obeys power "not for material profit, but 'for conscience' sake.' " In his explication of Romans 13, Bonhoeffer's call is to obedience: "The Church must obey the will of God, whether the State be bad or good. . . . The Christian should receive praise from authority." If, however, he suffers at the hands of the state, he is strengthened by St. Paul's admonition not to be overcome by evil, but to overcome evil with good. Once again the theme of Christian inner freedom is sounded: "The Christian is still free and has nothing to fear, and he can still pay the State its due by suffering innocently." Sovereign power remains with God. In this passage Bonhoeffer adds to his description of the state the new image of "only" the "minister" of God.[69]

Honored by such a relationship to God, the state, for Bonhoeffer, maintains the dignity derived from Reformation teaching. In his 1939 comparison of American and European church-state attitudes, he comments critically upon the secularization that resulted from American failure to clearly delineate and separate the spheres and offices of church and state. The "limitless" claims of the church upon the state, as well as "the continuous impact" of the American church upon the state, undermine and belie for Bonhoeffer the American "dogma" concerning the separation of church and state. Americans, he claims, should learn from the Reformation, in order to stem the tide of secularization. At the same time, Bonhoeffer emphasizes the need for an updating, "a new testing and correcting" of the Reformation teaching of the two spheres. Clearly challenging the validity of American claims in this area, Bonhoeffer concludes that both European Reformation churches and American churches (without the Reformation) can learn in dialogue with each other.[70]

Still clinging to the framework of Reformation church-state teachings in 1939, Bonhoeffer's concern for updating the Reformation legacy was to be fulfilled in his magnum opus, *Ethics,* which he was writing in the early forties. Although never completed, this work contains the most thorough and systematic survey of Bonhoeffer's political ideas. Though expanded, refined, and with new tags, Bonhoeffer's description of the political sphere represents basically the same amalgamation seen in his prior works: the synthesizing of German Reformation, nineteenth-century, and Weimar legacies.

In this culminating manuscript Bonhoeffer makes a self-conscious effort to employ new terminology in order to avoid misinterpretations or assumptions and connotations that have become encrusted around the old terms. Hoping to dodge the pitfalls of "romantic conservatism" (which assumes divine sanctions "for all existing orders and institutions in general"), Bonhoeffer chooses to clarify the concept he originally called "community" or "order" by suggesting a new expression, "mandate"—in order "to renew and restore the old notion of the institution, the estate [a Reformation concept] and office."[71] But he sharply limits the application of this title "mandate" to four (and occasionally five) groupings: marriage and the family, labor, government, church, and—at least once—culture (including "aesthetic existence"—art, friendship, and play).[72]

Significantly, Bonhoeffer also chooses to distinguish between "state" and "government." For his purposes, "government" now becomes the more useful "New Testament" concept, replacing his previous reliance on the expression "state." Although Bonhoeffer delves briefly into the distinctions separating one caption from another, one cannot help noting that the content and characteristics listed under the label "government" are essentially the same as his earlier explanations of "state."[73] To indicate the artificial and forced character of this nomenclature, one need only note that Bonhoeffer himself reverts to the term "state" in the prison years following his work on Ethics (which was shaped between 1940 and 1943). In a January 23, 1944 letter to the Bethges, Bonhoeffer, despite insistence in Ethics on the term "government," mentions "state" as one of the four mandates.[74]

According to Bonhoeffer's definition in Ethics, "government" is "a power which comes down from above, no matter whether it discharges its office well or badly"; it refers only to the rulers, not to the ruled. Only government, not state, can have a theological application. Hence Bonhoeffer's mandates include government rather than state, because the mandates refer to "a divinely imposed task," each mandate in its own way "through Christ, directed towards Christ, and in Christ." Government's role is to preserve, maintaining order by "law and the force of the sword." Everyone, insists Bonhoeffer, "owes obedience to this governing authority—for Christ's sake," until government openly denies its divine commission, by compelling the Christian to "offend against the divine commandment."[75] Bonhoeffer's new distinction between "government" and "state" could possibly provide an intellectual justification for opposition action by a person of Christian conscience. One might argue that an individual could reject a particular government while still being loyal to the nation-state.

This discussion of political resistance by the Christian individual is more explicit than Bonhoeffer's commentary on the church's opposition to the government. He vaguely suggests that if the government opposes the church, "there may come a time when the church no longer wastes her words. . . ." The church may warn the government, but if that word is not received, the only recourse Bonhoeffer clearly recommends is: "establishing and maintaining, at least among her own members, the order of outward justice which is no longer to be found in the *polis,* for by so doing she serves government in her own way."[76] Thus the individual in Bonhoeffer's *Weltanschauung* is allowed more latitude for action than the church. Such thinking has led Franklin Littell to propose that Bonhoeffer's "inadequate understanding of the nature of the church was the most tragic element in his eventual martyrdom."[77] Many contemporary Western political and social thinkers would add "inadequate understanding of the state" to this judgment.

But in fairness to Bonhoeffer, one should try to evaluate him in his own terms, in terms of the historical legacy which he used and revised. It is clear from his new definition of the state that he was attempting to shake off the extreme aspects of nineteenth-century German thought, in which a state became "the real God" (Hegel). Whereas government comes from above, the state comes from below; the state is "the supreme consummation of the rational character of men, a product of human nature."[78] Bonhoeffer sees Catholic political theory based on this view of the state, yet he acknowledges that in both main branches of Christendom, "the question of the form of the state is always treated as a secondary problem." Recommending no special form, Bonhoeffer sketches briefly some propositions for a state (one obviously *not* found in Nazi Germany):

—evidence that the government is from God

—power secured by outward justice, rights of family and labor, and by proclamation of the Gospel of Jesus Christ

—mutual confidence towards subjects, by just action and truthful speech.[79]

Although Bonhoeffer provides new skins (or titles), the old wine is still present in the political parts of *Ethics.* The key phrases have been heard before: law, order, obedience, authority, responsibility, preservation, divinely ordained. The concentration on Jesus Christ, already evident in 1933, provides a special focus for the political ideas in *Ethics.* All assertions about secular institutions must now be "founded upon Jesus Christ." Since everything must be related to "the dominion of Christ," Bonhoeffer rejects the "conception of the state as a self-contained entity, a conception which fails to take account of the relation of the state to Jesus Christ." He sees the value of the Reformation idea of a state "ordained from above," as an institution of God, not essentially a culture-state or nation-state "from below."[80] Although rejecting the extreme forms of nineteenth- and twentieth-century German state-worship, Bonhoeffer still uses the Teutonic categories of organic thought, emphasizing the responsibilities of abstract entities like government and church. The post-World War I search for wholeness led Bonhoeffer to "the dominion of Christ," meaning emancipation of secular institutions for "true worldliness, for the state to be a state." The worldly order was not to be made godly or subordinated to the church, but "set free for true worldliness."[81] Thus in *Ethics* Bonhoeffer displays a continuity with his earlier writings on the state, combining Reformation, nineteenth-century organic, and Weimar holistic streams of thought. Expansion, revision, and clarification of terminology, with the new emphasis on the "free life under the dominion of Christ"—none of these destroys the unity which links the political thought in *Ethics* with *Sanctorum Communio*.

This unity is in part related to Bonhoeffer's lifelong respect for history. He relates modern disregard for historical legacies to the acceleration of secularization:

> What the west is doing is to refuse to accept its historical inheritance for what it is. The west is becoming hostile towards Christ. . . . Amid the disruption of the whole established order of things there stand the Christian churches as guardians of the heritage of the Middle Ages and of the Reformation. . . . The church, as the bearer of a historical inheritance, is bound by an obligation to the historical future.[82]

Bonhoeffer also tied his concepts of community, responsibility, and power to history, which finds its "final reality" in Christ. History, he asserts, "arises through the recognition of responsibility for other men, specifically for whole communities and groups of communities."[83] Bonhoeffer's 1940s emphasis on "free and responsible action"[84] carried forward his earlier maxim that "being free means 'being free for the other.' "[85]

All of Bonhoeffer's political concepts, as I have suggested throughout this essay, were influenced by his particular perception of historical traditions. His entire theological structure was rooted in an interpretation of Western history, expounded in considerable detail in the portion of *Ethics* entitled "Inheritance and Decay," with its claim that "the historical Jesus Christ is the continuity of our history."[86] In this work, as well as in his prison letters, Bonhoeffer shows a sensitivity to the complexity of historical motivation and causation, especially as related to political events. The Reformation led to consequences exactly opposite to Luther's intent: "gradual dissolution of all real cohesion and order in society."[87] Bonhoeffer's vivid sketch of the process of secularization ends with the Western world at "the brink of the void."[88] In *Ethics,* as in the earlier works, Bonhoeffer "uses" historical developments as a framework or support for his ideas on the state or theology; his historical sense remains in dynamic interaction with his conception of Christ.

Although aware of the variety of schools of historical interpretation, Bonhoeffer claimed that he did not want to base his views on some abstract philosophy of history, "but solely on *facts* and *achievements*."[89] His prison letters, such as that of June 8, 1944, reveal a decided flair for intellectual history. Bonhoeffer discerns a movement from the thirteenth century onward toward "the autonomy of man," a "world come of age."[90] The contemporary popularity of these phrases, derived from Bonhoeffer's historical insights and explorations, tends to confirm Harnack's opinion that Bonhoeffer might have successfully specialized in church history.[91] One could devote an entire study to Bonhoeffer's historical insights and interpretations, but that is neither appropriate nor possible in the context of this essay. Indeed, two recent scholarly studies have shown how Bonhoeffer's historical ideas were significantly shaped by Adolf von Harnack and Wilhelm Dilthey.[92]

A less recognized influence is that of Friedrich Meinecke, considered by many the dean of twentieth-century German historians. Bonhoeffer's personal copy of Meinecke's *Die Idee der Staatsräson*, available in the Bonhoeffer archives, contains numerous marginal markings and a handwritten phrase (identified by Bethge as Bonhoeffer's handwriting). The internal evidence of marked passages indicates that Bonhoeffer most likely read and marked this book in the period before or during his conspiratorial activities (probably between 1939 and 1943, perhaps while he was working on *Ethics*).[93] Undoubtedly, this work by Meinecke influenced some of the political passages in *Ethics;* the section on the techniques of statecraft and the necessity of state (based on Machiavelli's *necessità*) can be linked to Meinecke's initial chapter on Machiavelli.[94] Also the section on Ranke indicates Bonhoeffer's interest in necessity of state, with the marking of sentences such as: "It was 'not free choice, but rather the necessity of things' that was dominant in the activity of states."[95] But Bonhoeffer's most vivid interest lay in the realm of individual decision concerning such necessity, as revealed in his markings, exclamation point, and written comment near the end of Meinecke's Machiavelli chapter. "Cynicism and Responsibility" penciled across the top of this page indicates Bonhoeffer's response to the following sentences, marked in the margin:

> And ultimately he [Machiavelli] was even capable of rising to the highest ethical feeling which is possible for action prompted by *raison d'état;* this sacrifice consists in taking on oneself personal disgrace and shame, if one can thereby save the Fatherland. . . . "When it is a question of saving the Fatherland, one should not stop for a moment to consider whether something is lawful or unlawful, gentle or cruel, laudable or shameful; but, putting aside every other consideration,

one ought to follow out to the end whatever resolve will save the life of the state and preserve its freedom."[96]

Many other marked passages concern the conflict between power and morality in the life of the state, as well as the historical tragedy and guilt associated with the tension between the demands of personal and public morality. Obviously, Meinecke's work influenced Bonhoeffer's personal decisions and conspiratorial activities, as well as his abstract ruminations on the state.

"Cynicism and responsibility"—both concepts characterize Bonhoeffer's political attitudes in the late thirties and after. "Responsibility" is familiar from previous writings, but "free responsibility" became a favorite new phrase of the forties.[97] One can speculate about whether Bonhoeffer applied "cynicism" to himself. If so, it was not a perverse, sterile type but a robust, sinewy version, related to the deceptions of political conspiracy and to the Lutheran sense of sin. Perhaps Bonhoeffer's interpretation of Luther's "Sin boldly . . ." applies here.[98]

Another probable source of Bonhoeffer's political understanding and conceptions was Brunner's *Das Gebot und die Ordnungen*. Bonhoeffer's underlinings and marginal markings are prevalent in passages emphasizing the following themes: opposition to state centralization and absolutism, opposition to the suicidal, "unknightly" character of modern warfare, discussion of pacifism and nonresistance.[99] Bonhoeffer questioned Brunner's assertion that the "national state belongs to the orders which God wishes to maintain."[100] Thus it follows that in *Ethics* Bonhoeffer criticizes and demotes the nation-state, holding that it comes from below, not from above.[101]

The political attitudes and watchwords evident throughout this analysis of Bonhoeffer's writings are most effectively encapsuled in a 1941 book review, composed as part of his conspiratorial activity. This critical commentary on William Paton's *The Church and the New Order* is a paradigm of Bonhoeffer's political thinking. "Freedom" for the Germans and for Bonhoeffer is distinct from the Anglo-Saxon concept, which emphasizes free press, free assembly, and specific liberties. Freedom is "not in the first instance an individual right, but rather a responsibility." Freedom means "living within the limited authorities and bonds ordered by God's Word." The battle against state-omnipotence aims at restoring genuine community bonds, such as family, friendship, and authority. Bonhoeffer admits that this Teutonic emphasis on the state's order and authority may not lead to a democracy in Germany after the Nazi era.[102] The more cosmopolitan Bonhoeffer became (through American and European ecumenical travels), the more he seemed to acknowledge his German national roots. This did not mean a narrow nationalism or state messianism, but it did mean a recognition and affirmation of a uniquely German historical-political heritage. From the start one perceives in Bonhoeffer an almost sponge-like memory, apparently absorbing and retaining all he read. The impressive fact remains, however, that he did not allow his inherited ideas of the state and history to prevent him from taking part in a political conspiracy to overthrow the government.

Despite changes in terminology, one can discern throughout his works compelling continuities in his political concepts of the state (or government). Although Bonhoeffer's distinction between "government" and "state" in *Ethics* is not insignificant, striking, imaginative new breakthroughs are not apparent in his teachings on the state. In this realm he remains a synthesizer, not an innovator. While criticizing and refocusing, Bonhoeffer integrates three historical strands—from the Reformation, the nineteenth century, and the Weimar era. First, he salvages for the state (and later the government) the dignity accorded it by the Reformers; he also updates the sixteenth-century Reformation legacy. Then he incorporates the tradition of German organic political theories, eventually discarding extreme nineteenth-century versions of state autonomy and glorification. Finally, he reflects the striving for community, wholeness, and synthesis so characteristic of his own generation.

Although Bonhoeffer's balanced synthesis avoids the extremes of German statism, he is still caught in the contradiction between a group-oriented, community approach and the individualism which could be necessary to overcome the corruption of and by groups. In the final crisis, "free, responsible" individuals remained, acting outside the communities of the church and the state. In Bonhoeffer's case, family and friendship lingered as sustaining "mandates"; but due to historical circumstances, ultimately the individual, not the group, was left to act against immoral abuse of political power. The organistic theories of state did not prove creative or life-supporting for the opposition in the Nazi era. Thus, despite Bonhoeffer's criticism of excessive individualism, including the Western emphasis on the freedom of the individual, one wonders whether Bonhoeffer's final acts did not reveal the possible strength of an individualistic emphasis in political life.

With a liberating experience of faith in Christ, Bonhoeffer's creative energies were released in the mid-1930s for a strident Christological breakthrough in his theology. The effects of this Christological liberation were not creative or intellectually compelling when applied to his discussions of the state. The friendship and correspondence with Eberhard Bethge during the prison years did, however, lead to the kind of spontaneous, unguarded theological commentaries which are truly creative.[103] Moreover, in at least one instance Bonhoeffer's writings reveal a dramatic break with the legacy of political obedience found in certain German and Christian traditions:

Civil Courage?

What lies behind the complaint about the dearth of civil courage? . . . In a long history, we Germans have had to learn the need for and the strength of obedience. In the subordination of all personal wishes and ideas to the tasks to which we have been called, we have seen the meaning and greatness of our lives. We have looked upwards, not in servile fear, but in free trust, seeing in our tasks a call, and in our call a vocation. This readiness to follow a command from "above" rather than our own private opinion and wishes was a sign of legitimate self-distrust. Who would deny that in obedience, in their task and calling, the Germans have again and again shown the utmost bravery and self-sacrifice? But the German has kept his freedom—and what nation has talked more passionately of freedom than the Germans, from Luther to the idealist philosophers?—by seeking deliverance from self-will through service to the community. Calling and freedom were to him two sides of the same thing. But in this he misjudged the world; he did not realize that his submissiveness and self-sacrifice could be exploited for evil ends. What then happened, the exercise of the calling itself became questionable, and all the moral principles of the Germans were bound to totter. The fact could not be escaped that the German still lacked something fundamental: he could not see the need for free and responsible action, even in opposition to his task and his calling; in its place there appeared on the one hand an irresponsible lack of scruple, and on the other a self-tormenting punctiliousness that never led to action. Civil courage, in fact, can only grow out of the free responsibility of free men. Only now are we Germans beginning to discover the meaning of free responsibility. It depends on a God who demands responsible action in a bold venture of faith, and who promises forgiveness and consolation to the man who becomes a sinner in that venture.[104]

In this passage Bonhoeffer displays the insights and departure from the past that make his theological thoughts, if not his political concepts, so seminal and challenging. Here one glimpses the talents that make it appropriate to call him a theological de Tocqueville—perceptive, prophetic, aristocratic in temperament, suspicious of the masses, and sensitive to the realities of his time and place. A century earlier, Alexis de Tocqueville had also deftly diagnosed the problem of power and obedience, later to be exposed in the Third Reich:

Men are not corrupted by the exercise of power or debased by the habit of obedience, but by the exercise of a power which they believe to be illegitimate, and by obedience to a rule which they consider to be usurped and oppressive.[105]

Would the Bonhoeffer of "Civil Courage" have affirmed and supported de Tocqueville's observation? Probably. But the most eloquent and startling comments on political power, freedom, and the state lie in Dietrich Bonhoeffer's life, not his writings.

Notes

1   *LPPE* (New York: The Macmillan Company, 1967, 1971), p. 279.

2   Larry L. Rasmussen, *Dietrich Bonhoeffer: Reality and Resistance* (Nashville: Abingdon Press, 1972), pp. 11, 15.

3   Ernst Feil, *Die Theologie Dietrich Bonhoeffers: Hermeneutik, Christologie, Weltverständnis* (Munich: Christian Kaiser Verlag, 1971), p. 18. While Feil has focused on the continuity of themes throughout Bonhoeffer's theological writings, another German Catholic scholar, Tiemo Rainer Peters, has more recently analyzed the complexities of continuity in Bonhoeffer's political theology. Sketching the development and tensions in Bonhoeffer's understanding of church and state, Peters, in contrast to Feil, suggests change and a new direction in the "late" Bonhoeffer's "Tegel theology." Peters suggests that in prison Bonhoeffer, as a "post-liberal," "post-dialectical," "modern" theologian, endeavored to overcome the "deadly dualism between society and church, science and theology, worldview *(Weltanschauung)* and revelation." Tiemo Rainer Peters, *Die Präsenz des Politischen in der Theologie Dietrich Bonhoeffers* (Munich: Christian Kaiser Verlag, 1976), pp. 12, 90, 198.

4   Dietrich Bonhoeffer, "Die Kirche vor der Judenfrage" (Vortrag, April 1933), *GS*, II, 44-53. For the English translation, see *NRS*, pp. 221-229.

5   Willem Adolf Visser 't Hooft, "Foreword" to J. Martin Bailey and Douglas Gilbert, *The Steps of Bonhoeffer: A Pictorial Album* (New York: The Macmillan Company, 1969), pp. v-vi.

6   Eberhard Bethge, *DB; DBET*.

7   Fritz K. Ringer, *The Decline of the German Mandarins: The German Academic Community, 1890-1933* (Cambridge: Harvard University Press, 1969), p. 3. Ringer defines "mandarins" as "a social and cultural elite which owes its status primarily to educational qualifications, rather than to hereditary rights or wealth," including "doctors, lawyers, ministers, government officials, secondary school teachers, and university professors, all of them men with advanced academic degrees based on the completion of a certain minimum curriculum and the passing of a conventional group of examinations" (pp. 5-6). Ringer's study focuses on the German academic humanists and social scientists; these nonscientist university professors constitute Ringer's "mandarin intellectuals."

8   *Ibid.*, p. 387. For a thorough, perceptive critique of Ringer's book, see Kenneth D. Barkin, "Fritz K. Ringer's *The Decline of the Mandarins,*" *Journal of Modern History*, XLIII, 2 (June 1971), 276-286. While faulting Ringer for his "ill-concealed animus" against the German mandarins, Barkin contends: "It is inconceivable to me that scholars concerned with any aspect of the German professoriat

will be able to proceed in the future without first coming to terms with Ringer's iconoclastic theory" (pp. 279-280).

9   Ringer, pp. 225-226. Ringer quotes from a "secular sermon" given by Seeberg at Berlin University in 1925. Seeberg extolled the strong state which transcends individual interests, linking the positive trends of idealism and patriotism. Idealism and religion were to do battle against individualism, materialism, and the Enlightenment.

10   *Ibid.*, p. 100. Ringer here quotes from Ernst Troeltsch, *Naturrecht und Humanität in der Weltpolitik: Vortrag bei der zweiten Jahresfeier der Deutschen Hochschule für Politik* (Berlin, 1923), pp. 13-14.

11   Ringer, p. 102.

12   Troeltsch quoted in Ringer, pp. 100-101.

13   Definition quoted in Ringer, p. 243.

14   *Ibid.*, pp. 232-233.

15   Reinhold Seeberg, *Christentum und Idealismus: Gedanken über die Zukunft der Kirche und der Theologie* (Berlin Lichterfelde: Verlag von Edwin Runge, 1921), especially pp. 75-77.

16   Ringer, p. 244.

17   Reinhold Seeberg, *Zum Verständnis der gegewärtigen Krisis in der europäischen Geisteskultur* (Erlangen and Leipzig: A. Deichertsche Verlagsbuchhandlung Dr. Werner Scholl, 1923), pp. 35, 134-136. In 1906, Seeberg dedicated a collection of his essays to the famed anti-Semite Adolf Stoecker on Stoecker's seventieth birthday: Reinhold Seeberg, *Aus Religion und Geschichte* (Leipzig: A. Deichertsche Verlagsbuchhandlung Nachf., 1906), Vol. I. A few years later, Seeberg edited a collection of Stoecker's essays: Reinhold Seeberg, ed., *Reden und Aufsätze von Adolf Stoecker* (Leipzig: A. Deichertsche Verlagsbuchhandlung, 1913).

18   Seeberg, *Christentum und Idealismus,* pp. 71-74.

19   *Ibid.*, p. 72.

20   *Ibid.*, pp. 71-73.

21   Bonhoeffer, *GS,* VI, 23-24, 96-97.

22   Ringer, pp. 133, 190-191, 202.

23   Bonhoeffer, *GS,* VI, 96-97. In a letter to his parents on September 21, 1925, Bonhoeffer explained that it really didn't matter much whether he went to Holl, Harnack, or Seeberg with his topic in the dogmatic-historical field. He anticipated no opposition from Seeberg on a dissertation in this area.

24   *CS,* pp. 64-65.

25   Bonhoeffer, *E* (New York: The Macmillan Company, 1955), pp. 108-109.

26   Heinrich Ott, *Reality and Faith: The Theological Legacy of Dietrich Bonhoeffer* (London: Lutterworth Press, 1971), p. 220. See also pp. 193-194.

27   Feil, *ThDB,* pp. 128-129, especially footnote 6. See also pp. 133 and 311 for emphasis on the essential unity and consistency of Bonhoeffer's thought.

28   Bonhoeffer, *CS,* pp. 53-61.

29   *Ibid.*, p. 55.

30   *Ibid.*, p. 57.

31   *Ibid.*, p. 83.

32   *Ibid.*, p. 84.

33   Peter Berger, "Sociology and Ecclesiology," in *The Place of Bonhoeffer,* Martin E. Marty, ed. (New York: Association Press, 1962), pp. 60, 63, 77.

34   Bonhoeffer, *CS,* p. 52.

35   *Ibid.*

36 Berger, p. 62.

37 *Ibid.*, p. 64. Berger's thesis in this case can be supported by Bonhoeffer's obvious appropriation of nineteenth-century idealistic and Hegelian concepts of organism, conflict, and synthesis. Bonhoeffer sees "divine grace" as responsible for the continuance of the historically rooted German national church, despite the national church's tendency toward conservatism. In his particular Christian interpretation of history, Bonhoeffer identifies the concept of organism as "the sociological expression of the progressive element in the church." For Bonhoeffer, the "law of life for every community" is fulfilled in a fighting movement, resulting in "a quickening mingling of proper conservatism and proper progress in the church" (Hegelianism alive and well in Bonhoeffer's thought!) (*CS*, pp. 188-189). It is significant and prophetic that Bonhoeffer glimpses the possibility that the national church may head toward complete degeneration: "moving into complete petrification and emptiness in the use of its forms, with evil effects on the living members as well" (*CS*, p. 190).

38 Bonhoeffer, *CS*, p. 61.

39 Bonhoeffer, *GS*, III, 34; V, 335. See also Bethge, *DB*, p. 1087. In the lecture notes given in the last two citations, Bonhoeffer spoke of the footnotes in the appendix as "the most valuable" portion of Brunner's book.

40 Emil Brunner, *Das Gebot und die Ordnungen: Entwurf einer protestantisch-theologischen Ethik* (Tübingen: Verlag von J. C. B. Mohr, 1932), pp. 647-650. The author of this article is responsible for the English translation.

41 Bonhoeffer, *GS*, III, 34. This comment appeared in a letter of March 7, 1940 to the Leibholz family.

42 *Ibid.*, I, 33-34; V, 338-339. *DB*, p. 1089.

43 *DB*, pp. 246-250.

44 *GS*, VI, 244. The author of this article is responsible for the English translation.

45 *Ibid.*, p. 260.

46 *Ibid.*, I, 129, 150-153, 160; III, 278-282. See also the dissertation of Clifford James Green, "The Sociality of Christ and Humanity: Dietrich Bonhoeffer's Early Theology, 1927-1933" (Th.D. dissertation, Union Theological Seminary, 1971), especially pp. 366-368, for additional references to "orders of preservation" as well as a discussion of the circumstances surrounding the introduction of this term. This dissertation has been published, without appendices and bibliography, as No. 6 in the Dissertations Series of Scholars Press for the American Academy of Religion (Missoula, 1972). See pp. 247-249 for "orders of preservation."

47 *GS*, I, 151; *DB*, pp. 1074-1075.

48 *GS*, I, 151. In his 1932/33 Berlin University lectures, Bonhoeffer emphatically insisted on Christ as the center of all societal structures: "All the orders of our fallen world are God's orders of preservation on the way to Christ. They are not orders of creation but of preservation. They have no value in themselves. They are accomplished and have purpose only through Christ." Bonhoeffer, *CFT* (New York: The Macmillan Company, 1959), p. 88.

49 *GS*, III, 279.

50 *Ibid.*, p. 280. This overlapping, imprecise use of terms reveals the ever-present danger in the Teutonic tendency to personify abstractions. Each new "organic" abstraction should be clearly defined and clarified.

51 See above, footnote 40.

52 *GS*, III, 283.

53 Bonhoeffer, *GS*, II, 27, 30. For the English translation of this address, see *NRS*, pp. 186-200.

54 *GS*, II, 30, 32, 33, 35-36.

55 *Ibid.*, p. 36.

56 *Ibid.*, p. 37.

57 Leonard Krieger, *The German Idea of Freedom: History of a Political Tradition* (Boston: Beacon Press, 1957), pp. 65, 80.

58 Bonhoeffer, "Der Arierparagraph in der Kirche" (Flugblatt, August 1933), *GS*, II, 67-68.

59 *GS*, II, 45, 49. A discussion of this essay in the context of Bonhoeffer's attitudes toward the Jews appears in an essay this writer delivered in March 1974 at the Conference on the Church Struggle and the Holocaust: Ruth Zerner, "Dietrich Bonhoeffer and the Jews: Thoughts and Actions, 1933-1945," *Jewish Social Studies*, XXXVII, 3-4 (Summer/Fall 1975), 235-250.

60 *GS*, II, 45-46.

61 *Ibid.*, pp. 45, 48-49.

62 Seeberg, *Aus Religion und Geschichte*, p. 269. A similarly pragmatic and convincing interpretation of Luther's political thought may be found in J. W. Allen, *A History of Political Thought in the Sixteenth Century* (London: Methuen & Co., 1928, 1951), pp. 15-30.

63 Seeberg, *Aus Religion und Geschichte*, p. 270.

64 Bonhoeffer, *GS*, II, 45.

65 Bonhoeffer's copy of Brunner, *Das Gebot und die Ordnungen*, p. 659, shows heavy pencil lines marking the following passage:

For the sake of its own health, the state must insist on the delegation of as much authority as possible to free corporations [corporative groupings]; because the bureaucracy (which is the necessary result of the centralizing state that seeks to rule all things) is death for all free life. . . . It is deadly to life, when a state, with its centralized administrative apparatus, faces nothing but a mass of unorganized individuals. The wise state places between itself and the individual as many autonomous and legitimately competing entities (which are close to life) as possible.

The author of this essay is responsible for the English translation.

66 Bonhoeffer, *Christology* (London: Collins, 1966), pp. 65-67.

67 *Ibid.*, pp. 65f. See above, p. 140, footnote 49.

68 Bonhoeffer, *GS*, IV, 180-181.

69 Bonhoeffer, *CD* (New York: The Macmillan Company, 1959), pp. 294-296.

70 Bonhoeffer, "Protestantismus ohne Reformation," August 1939, *GS*, I, 340-343, 354.

71 *E*, p. 288.

72 *Ibid.*, pp. 207, 286, footnotes on pp. 286-287, 329; *LPPE*, pp. 192-193.

73 *E*, pp. 332-333.

74 *LPPE*, p. 192.

75 *E*, pp. 207, 210-211, 332, 338, 342-343.

76 *Ibid.*, pp. 348, 350-351. "According to Holy Scripture, there is no right to revolution; but there is a responsibility of every individual for preserving the purity of his office and mission in the *polis*" (p. 351).

77 Franklin H. Littell, "The Churches and the Body Politic," *Daedalus*, XCVI, 1 (Winter 1967), 23.

78 *E*, pp. 333-334.

79   *Ibid.*, pp. 352-353.
80   *Ibid.*, pp. 327, 335-336.
81   *Ibid.*, pp. 328-329.
82   *Ibid.*, pp. 108-109.
83   Bonhoeffer, "Die Geschichte und das Gute," *GS*, III, 456, 470, 477.
84   *LPPE*, p. 6.
85   *CFT*, p. 37.
86   *E*, p. 89.
87   *LPPE*, p. 123. See also *GS*, III, 502-506. In this segment of an unfinished novel, Bonhoeffer speaks of the ambiguous legacy of great movements and great men in history. One of the characters calls for a history of failures, the history "of the victims of success," as well as a history of average men (pp. 505-506).
88   *E*, p. 105.
89   *LPPE*, p. 230. This realistic approach to history was also evident in his 1931 essay "Concerning the Christian Idea of God": "The true attitude of man toward history is not interpretative, but that of refusing or acknowledging, that is to say, deciding. History is the place of decision, nothing else" (*GS*, III, 106).
90   *LPPE*, pp. 324-329.
91   *Ibid.*, p. 126.
92   Carl-Jürgen Kaltenborn, *Adolf Harnack als Lehrer Dietrich Bonhoeffers* (Berlin, G.D.R.: Evangelische Verlagsanstalt, 1973). Ernst Feil, "Der Einfluss Wilhelm Diltheys auf Dietrich Bonhoeffers *Widerstand und Ergebung*," *Evangelische Theologie*, XXIX (1969), 662-674. See also Kaltenborn's essay above, pp. 48ff.
93   Friedrich Meinecke, *Die Idee der Staatsräson in der neueren Geschichte* (Munich and Berlin: Druck und Verlag von R. Oldenbourg, 1929, 3. durchgesehene Auflage). That Bonhoeffer read this work while contemplating the moral dilemmas of his conspiratorial activities is evident from marginal markings of the following quotation in three separate places in the text:
> It is not always possible to win the approval of one's contemporaries or of posterity, or to convince world opinion; *but the hero must at least justify his action to himself* (italics printed in the text) (pp. 481, 492, 535).

The English translation of this work by Meinecke is entitled *Machiavellianism: The Doctrine of Raison d'État and Its Place in Modern History* (New Haven: Yale University Press, 1957).
94   *E*, pp. 237-240; Meinecke, *Die Idee der Staatsräson*, pp. 31ff. Although Meinecke taught at the University of Berlin during Bonhoeffer's student days, Bonhoeffer never took a course with him, and there is no evidence that he read *Die Idee der Staatsräson* during the 1920s. Bonhoeffer's personal copy was the 1929 edition (original publication date was 1924).
95   Meinecke, p. 483.
96   *Ibid.*, pp. 55-57.
97   *E*, p. 240. Bonhoeffer even found the concept of "free responsibility" applicable to Bismarck:
> The greatness of British statesmen . . . for example, of Gladstone, is that they acknowledge the law as the ultimate authority; and the greatness of German statesmen—I am thinking now of Bismarck—is that they come before God in free responsibility.

See Rasmussen, *Dietrich Bonhoeffer: Reality and Resistance*, pp. 49-51, commenting on the evolution of Bonhoeffer's ideas on freedom and responsibility.
98   Bonhoeffer, *CD*, pp. 55-57.
99   Brunner, *Das Gebot und die Ordnungen*, pp. 448, 450, 456-458, 618,

659. Marked with a special marginal star are these sentences: "Life is to be rescued from oppression by the state." "The teaching of the basic ethical and religious neutrality of the state is a product of an abstract rationalism and overlooks the foundations on which the authority of the state itself rests" (pp. 448, 450).

100   *Ibid.*, p. 442. Bonhoeffer penciled a question mark alongside this sentence.

101   *E*, pp. 333-335.

102   *GS*, I, 359-360.

103   See above, p. 152, fn. 3. For Tiemo Rainer Peters, Bonhoeffer's prison letters reveal an anti-idealistic ethics of responsibility, moving increasingly towards an ethics of freedom, with new criticisms of authority and obedience. In these "Tegel theses" Peters perceives that for Bonhoeffer church and world are no longer so sharply separated, but are more closely linked in mutual, dialectical tension. Peters, pp. 89-90, 194-195.

104   "After Ten Years: A Reckoning made at New Year 1943," *LPPE*, pp. 5-6.

105   Alexis de Tocqueville, *Democracy in America* (New York: Vintage Books, 1958), I, 9.

IV.
CHRISTOLOGY AND DISCIPLESHIP

THE LEGACY OF DIETRICH BONHOEFFER

John D. Godsey

THE YEAR 1980 marks the thirty-fifth anniversary of that diabolical act that snuffed out the life of Dietrich Bonhoeffer. As the dawn broke on April 9, 1945, the thirty-nine-year-old German pastor-theologian was hanged by the Gestapo at their extermination camp at Flossenbürg, the victim of Adolf Hitler's order to liquidate all those conspirators who were connected with the abortive attempt on his life on July 20, 1944. Thus Bonhoeffer became part of the Holocaust, not, to be sure, in the same sense as did the six million innocent Jews, but as one who shared their fate because he resisted their oppressors and did so with the awareness that no non-Jew in Germany could dissociate himself from the guilt of the Nazi terror.

After such an ignominious end, it is astounding that today the name of Bonhoeffer should be so well known around the world. It is altogether unlikely that he would have arisen from the ashes of obscurity had it not been for the painstaking and prodigious efforts of his friend Eberhard Bethge, the collector and editor of all of Bonhoeffer's posthumously published writings. Bethge is "the friend" to whom the famous uncensored letters and papers from prison were written, and he is the author of the definitive biography of Bonhoeffer's life.

With all due respect to Bethge's instrumental role, however, it is Bonhoeffer himself who, by his words and deeds, has fired the imagination and sparked the obedience of the church since his death. I think it is safe to say that during the last two decades there has been no more potent influence on the thinking and acting of Christians than that of Dietrich Bonhoeffer. His thought has been seminal, providing stimulus in some measure to almost every significant theological trend—whether conservative or liberal, hermeneutical or radical. Indeed, Bonhoeffer has helped Christians go beyond such labels to a reconsideration of the basic relationship between theology and reality.

161

How is Bonhoeffer's contribution to be characterized? What are the most important elements of his legacy? It is obviously impossible to do justice to the richness of our Bonhoeffer inheritance in a brief essay, but I will endeavor nevertheless to indicate three emphases in his thought which I think are fundamental and which continue to challenge and provoke those who live after him.

The first of these is the *Christ-centeredness of Christian thinking.* This may seem self-evident to a Christian theologian, but the fact is that few Christians have allowed their thought to be shaped by Christ as consistently as did Dietrich Bonhoeffer. For him Jesus Christ formed the center around which all thought of God, humankind, and the world must revolve. To deal with human existence, history, or even nature apart from Christ, he insisted, is to miss the heart of reality. Why? Because the purpose and meaning of existence is revealed in Christ's life, death, and resurrection. A human being is created to exist freely and vicariously for others. Self-abandoning love is the purpose of God; and Bonhoeffer believed that in the man Jesus, God concretized his love for humankind. While men and women in their sinful self-love want to become as gods, God becomes man. In Jesus he assumed our flesh and lived his love among us, identifying himself with us, bearing our sin and guilt, reconciling us to himself, and calling us to a new life of free and vicarious living for others.

In thinking about Jesus Christ, Bonhoeffer tended to emphasize Christ's humility. For him the really incomparable miracle was not the incarnation as such but the Incarnate One's identification with sinners. Like Luther, Bonhoeffer inclined toward a theology of the cross. The note that God's power is shown forth in weakness is struck throughout Bonhoeffer's writings, but nowhere more forcefully than in two letters. In the first, written to Theodor Litt in January 1939, he says:

> Solely because God became a poor, suffering, unknown, successless man, and because from now on God allows himself to be found only in this poverty, in the cross, we cannot disengage ourselves from man and from the world. For this reason we love the brethren. Because in the Christian faith it is thus understood that, indeed, out of the sovereign freedom of grace, the "unconditioned" has enclosed itself in the "conditioned," the "otherworldly" has entered into the "this-worldly," the believer is not torn asunder but finds God and man united at this one place in the world, and from now on love of God and love of the brother are indissolubly united with one another.[1]

The second letter was written to Eberhard Bethge on July 16, 1944, when Bonhoeffer was in prison. Here he writes:

> God lets himself be pushed out of the world on to the cross. He is weak and powerless in the world, and that is precisely the way, the

only way, in which he is with us and helps us. Matt. 8:17 makes it quite clear that Christ helps us, not by virtue of his omnipotence, but by virtue of his weakness and suffering.[2]

Although the cross of Christ is a dominant element in Bonhoeffer's thought, he insisted that it would be a mistake to establish a separate theology of the incarnation or of the cross or of the resurrection, for these three go together to form a whole. "In Jesus Christ," he explains, "we have faith in the incarnate, crucified, and risen God. In the incarnation we learn of the love of God for His creation; in the crucifixion we learn of the judgment of God on all flesh; and in the resurrection we learn of God's will for a new world."[3]

With such a dynamic view of Christ as the person in whom God and humankind are inextricably related, it is little wonder that Bonhoeffer's thinking was Christocentric. The ramifications of this reached into every Christian doctrine. Man, for example, is not to be understood in individualistic isolation from his brothers and sisters, but only in relationship to God and his fellow humans. This is because he is created in the image of God, and God revealed himself in Christ to be, not in and for himself, but in a loving relationship to others. The analogy between God and humankind, Bonhoeffer says, is not an analogy of being but an analogy of relationship.[4] Because of Christ we can never think of man-in-himself or of God-in-himself, but only of their being related to each other.

Sin for Bonhoeffer is humankind's refusal to accept the grace of God revealed in Christ, the breaking of the relationship with the Creator. Salvation is to hear and to live in accordance with the Word of God spoken to humans in and through Jesus Christ. The church is "Christ existing as a community," the fellowship of persons constituted by the person of Jesus and held together by a life of vicarious love, the community where Christ himself takes form among men and women. Ethics has to do with how humans can achieve participation in the reality of the fulfilled will of God as this is manifested in Christ. Even creation is to be understood only in terms of Christ, for in harmony with the New Testament, Bonhoeffer claimed that everything was created by, through, and for Christ. All worldly reality is related to Christ.

While the emphases and foci of Bonhoeffer's thought changed from time to time during his life, his thought nevertheless remained consistently Christ-centered. During the early years he saw Jesus Christ as the revelational reality of the church; then during the years of the German church struggle he emphasized that Jesus Christ is the Lord who calls the church to discipleship; and finally in the last period of his life he concentrated attention on Jesus Christ as Lord not only in and over the church but of the whole world.[5]

A second characteristic emphasis that we inherit from Bonhoeffer is that of the *costliness of Christian discipleship*. Already in his earliest books he stressed the visibility of the church as the fellowship of those called to the life of vicarious love or deputyship. But it was during the church struggle that the theme of the cost of discipleship surged to the fore. It then continued during the war years in his challenge to Christians to participate in the sufferings of God in the midst of a godless world and in his belief that the church might have to maintain a secret discipline of worship and devotion in a world come of age.

In his book *The Cost of Discipleship* (in the original German edition entitled simply *Discipleship*), Bonhoeffer engaged in a strong polemic against what he called "cheap grace." His chief target was his own Lutheran Church, which had prided itself on its proclamation of Luther's doctrine of justification by faith alone—or, to be more exact, not by works but by grace through faith alone. What distressed Bonhoeffer was that many of his fellow Christians seemed to be using this battle cry of the Reformation to justify their doing no "good works" at all, or at least doing as little as they deemed possible. They were making "salvation by grace" into an initial datum by which to calculate the cheapest way to live the Christian life. Bonhoeffer pointed out that this was not a datum with which Luther began; it was rather a confession that Luther made after many years of struggling to follow Christ and to live a life of obedience. Bonhoeffer put the question of discipleship squarely before the church in Nazi Germany, and he still puts it before us and before the church of all times.

"Cheap grace," says Bonhoeffer, "means grace as a doctrine, a principle, a system . . . the justification of sin without the justification of the sinner." It is "the preaching of forgiveness without requiring repentance, baptism without church discipline, Communion without confession, absolution without personal confession . . . grace without discipleship, grace without the cross, grace without Jesus Christ, living and incarnate."[6] Such grace, insists Bonhoeffer, is the deadly enemy of the church, and so we must fight for costly grace, which involves hearing Christ's call, leaving our nets, and following him. "Costly grace," writes Bonhoeffer, "is the gospel which must be *sought* again and again, the gift which must be *asked* for, the door at which a man must *knock*. Such grace is *costly* because it calls us to follow, and it is *grace* because it calls us to follow *Jesus Christ*. It is costly because it costs a man his life, and it is grace because it gives a man the only true life. It is costly because it condemns sin, and grace because it justifies the sinner."[7]

Without doubt we all recognize the problem that Bonhoeffer was attacking, for none of us is immune to the scourge of cheap grace. Bonhoeffer reminded Christians that they should not expect grace to be cheap when it was so costly for God himself, and he further pointed out that faith and discipleship go together. This conviction he sums up in the succinct formula: "Only he who believes is obedient, and only he who is obedient believes."[8] Both propositions, he emphasized, are equally true and must be held together. Faith is real only where there is obedience, even though it is faith alone that justifies. This means that faith and obedience may be logically but not chronologically separated. To the person who says, "I find it difficult to believe," Bonhoeffer could answer, "Then obey, and you may learn to believe." The biblical warrant for this Bonhoeffer found in the Gospels, where the call of Jesus and the response of the disciples *precede* faith. The disciples found out who Jesus was only by following him.

Much later in his life, when he was in prison, Bonhoeffer wrote to Bethge that he could see the danger in what he had written in his book on discipleship. I believe that the danger he referred to was not one of "works righteousness," that is, that we would try to justify ourselves before God by doing good works. Rather, it was that our efforts to lead a holy life of discipleship might lead us to be more interested in ourselves than in others. We might want to make something out of ourselves rather than "being there for others."

Of permanent value is a third emphasis bequeathed to us in Bonhoeffer's theology, namely, the *worldliness of Christian faith*. This theme is especially strong during the last period of his life, in his *Ethics* and his *Letters and Papers from Prison,* although it is by no means to be found exclusively there. As early as 1932, in an address entitled "Thy Kingdom Come!" Bonhoeffer warned the church against an otherworldliness that encourages men and women to become disloyal sons and daughters of this earth, which is our home and the place where God wishes his kingdom to be established.[9] In his *Ethics* Bonhoeffer argued that, because in Jesus Christ God has concretely entered our world and has reconciled it to himself, humans can no longer have the world without God or God without the world. In Jesus, God and the world are joined in what Bonhoeffer termed a "polemical unity," so that the sacred can no longer be separated from the secular or the Christian from the worldly. Indeed, he emphasized, now the sacred can be found only in the secular, the Christian only in the worldly, the supernatural only in the natural, the revelational only in the rational. Thus Bonhoeffer called on Christians to cease thinking of reality as divided into two spheres, the sacred and the secular, and to think, rather, of one reality in which humankind finds certain divinely imposed, universally applicable mandates, the chief of which are marriage and family, labor (including culture), government, and church. These mandates regarding human life on earth are equally "divine," with the result that the man or woman who is called by God to responsible service in the church is likewise called to be a responsible family member, worker, and citizen.

As Bonhoeffer was writing his *Ethics,* he was at the same time becoming ever more involved in the resistance movement against Hitler, in which he met many people who would not call themselves Christians but who rather thought of themselves as wholly "secular." He was impressed by the elements of goodness and humanness he found in them, their willingness to give of themselves unstintingly for a just cause that would benefit their fellow humans. Bonhoeffer came to believe that it would be better not to attempt immediately to convert them, but instead to claim their goodness and humanness for Christ and then gradually to lead them to see that Christ is also their Lord, the true source of all they hold dear. Theirs seemed to be a hopeful godlessness; and later, when he was in prison, Bonhoeffer conjectured that they were perhaps closer to God than many of those in the churches who confessed belief in God with their lips but not with their lives. As Luther once said, God may prefer the curses of the ungodly to the alleluias of the falsely pious. Or as Bonhoeffer himself said, only those who cried out for the Jews in Germany should be allowed to sing Gregorian chants!

In any case, Bonhoeffer came to understand that "the more exclusively we acknowledge and confess Christ as our Lord, the more fully the wide range of his dominion will be disclosed to us."[10] Christ is indeed Lord of the world. God in Christ loved the real world and real people without any veneer of religiosity, and Christians should not try to be more pious than God. Bonhoeffer came to the conviction that it is only when we live fully in the world, taking in stride all its problems and involvements, its joys and its sorrows, that we come to believe. Faith in God immerses us in the life of the world. Faith is to be lived in this world; it is not a holding action for the next. Christ came not to found a new religion but to call us to real life. In our modern world, concluded Bonhoeffer, Christianity should not even ally itself with religion as this is commonly understood, for religion has become so suspect or irrelevant for many people that it no longer provides an advantageous point of contact for Christian faith.

Such thoughts, which came to the fore while Bonhoeffer was in prison, led him to ask who Christ really is in our twentieth-century world. How is his lordship to be understood in a world that can no longer be religious in the old way? Bonhoeffer became convinced that the church must develop a nonreligious interpretation of Christian concepts for a world that is fast coming of age, that is, is learning how to answer its questions and to solve its problems without recourse to "God" as a working hypothesis. It is time for a religionless or worldly Christianity which views Christ not as an object of religion but as Lord of the world.

Bonhoeffer was obviously breaking new ground in his writings from prison, and his ideas have generated tremendous excitement in the theological community. Unfortunately, he did not live long enough to develop a nonreligious interpretation, and many interpreters have taken his ideas in directions that would undoubtedly have been uncongenial to him. Nevertheless, he did not leave us without clues to what he had in mind. On the positive side, it involved his whole conception of Jesus Christ as the one in and through whom God created and reconciled and renewed the world; on the negative, it involved his interpretation of religion.

When Bonhoeffer defined religion, he most often identified it with individualism or metaphysics, but he also connected it with thinking of God as a *deus ex machina* who can be called upon to solve our unsolved problems or to fill the gaps in our knowledge, with the practice of segregating some sacred human province from the secular world, and with the elevation of Christians to some privileged position vis-à-vis others. By individualism Bonhoeffer meant the cultivation of an inward personal piety in order to save one's soul for the next world, meanwhile leaving this world to its own devices. But this kind of individualistic sainthood at the expense of the world is nothing short of religious self-centeredness. It caters to oriental myths of salvation rather than viewing the New Testament in the light of the Old, where everything focuses on righteousness and the kingdom of God on earth. Metaphysical interpretations of Christianity are religious because they turn God into an idea, an object of thought which provides the necessary completion for an understanding of the world. But today humans are able to explain much of the world without calling on the concept "God." When secularity, dominated by science and technology, makes "God" superfluous, religion tries to find a place for God on the borders of human existence, in crisis situations such as sickness, guilt, and death. This leads to the attempt of clerics to convince men and women that they need God as the answer to the "ultimate questions" of life, and it even encourages Christians to think of existentialism and psychotherapy as precursors of the divine. But, objected Bonhoeffer, the Word of God is much too aristocratic to align itself with this sort of revolt from below, this suspicious attitude that plays on our so-called existential despair. The ordinary person who has a job and family and hobbies just does not have time to be troubled by such things.

In the end, religious interpretation in all its forms succeeds in placing God at humankind's disposal. According to their own self-interest, religious people use God, and at the same time they abandon or violate this world that God loves. Neither the God who is metaphysically beyond the world nor the God who is piously confined to the inner life is, in Bonhoeffer's view, the God of the Bible. The biblical God is found in the midst of worldly life, and for this reason the Christian cannot write off the world prematurely but must drink the cup of life to the lees. God is the "beyond" in the center of life. He suffers at the hands of the godless, and Christians are challenged to suffer there with him.

In summary, Bonhoeffer conceived of religion as concern of the individual for otherworldly salvation, metaphysical interpretations that wrongly separate God and the world and turn God into a cognitive object who is necessary for the completion of our total view of the universe, the tendency to look on Christians as specially favored over others, the misuse of "God" as a *deus ex machina,* and the assigning of God to a circumscribed place in the world. If these are the characteristic marks of a religious interpretation of Christianity, then a nonreligious interpretation would be one in which the concern is not for oneself but for one's neighbors in their worldly context, the refusal to separate God from the world or to divide reality into two opposing spheres, the belief that God is personal and as close to us as the nearest neighbor at hand, the alignment of ourselves in solidarity with all humankind, the assumption of responsibility for answering our problems and questions ourselves, and the conviction that because God is the Lord of life he is present at its center and not merely on the boundaries.

Bonhoeffer obviously had some model in mind as he thought of Christian faith expressed in a nonreligious mode, and at first glance that model appears to be the mature man or woman. The world has come, or at least is coming, of age, just as a child grows up and enters adulthood. At the age of twenty-one he/she is capable of receiving an inheritance, and thereafter he/she is held responsible for it. In the eyes of society he/she can never return to those childhood days of dependence on others. Bonhoeffer seems to be saying that the gradual process of secularization has brought the world to adulthood. That is, humans are learning to cope with life in the world without God, at least without attempting to use God in such a way as to forego their own responsibility for the affairs of the world. Furthermore, it is Bonhoeffer's belief that this accords with God's intention. God wants mature sons and daughters who will accept the world as their inheritance and who will look after it as if it were their own.

But at a different level Bonhoeffer seems to be using a different model, the example of Jesus Christ himself. Jesus is the mature man, the man come of age. He lived his life not for himself but for others; he made this world the concern of God; he refused to lord it over others and became servant of all; he accepted the fact that God would not miraculously save him from suffering and the cross; and he recognized God's presence in the midst of life. In the end, I think it is the figure of Jesus that stands behind Bonhoeffer's thought about the nonreligious interpretation of biblical concepts for a world come of age. God through his self-revelation in Jesus has set in motion a movement from religion to life, from otherworldliness to this-worldliness, from using him as a working hypothesis to living before him as if he were not there.

To live before God without God—that is the strange-sounding dialectic of modern Christian existence; to live without God but not before

God—that is atheistic existence. The God of the Bible, who has revealed his inmost self in the life and death of Jesus, does not overcome humankind by a display of omnipotent power but by the weakness of self-giving, suffering love. Thus in his brief "Outline for a Book," which he sketched in prison, Bonhoeffer explained the nature of our relationship to God:

> Our relation to God is not a "religious" relationship to the highest, most powerful, and best Being imaginable—that is not authentic transcendence—but our relation to God is a new life in "existence for others", through participation in the being of Jesus . . . "the man for others."[11]

To be a Christian, then, is to be in communion with the Crucified, to share in the sufferings of God at the hands of a godless world.

Bonhoeffer might have said and written all of these deep thoughts and still have made little impact on the church and the world had he not practiced what he preached. In the "Conclusions" to his "Outline for a Book" we find this striking statement: "It [the church] must not underestimate the importance of human example (which has its origin in the humanity of Jesus and is so important in Paul's teaching); it is not abstract argument, but example, that gives its word emphasis and power."[12] Bonhoeffer's witness has been powerful because his own life exemplified his teaching. More and more, he became a man for others, taking in his stride life's duties and problems, successes and failures, experiences and complexities, throwing himself completely into the arms of God, taking seriously not his own sufferings but those of God in the world.

Bonhoeffer's life supplies the hermeneutical clue to his thought. He provides an example of Christ-centered thinking, costly discipleship, and worldly faith. Thus he leaves us a goodly heritage.

Notes

1 *GS,* III, 32 (author's translation).
2 *LPPE,* pp. 360f.
3 *E,* pp. 130f.
4 *CFT,* p. 38.
5 John D. Godsey, *The Theology of Dietrich Bonhoeffer* (Philadelphia: The Westminster Press, 1960), p. 266.
6 *CD,* pp. 45ff.
7 *CD,* pp. 47f.
8 *CD,* p. 69.
9 John D. Godsey, *Preface to Bonhoeffer: The Man and Two of His Shorter Writings* (Philadelphia: Fortress Press, 1965), pp. 31f.
10 *E,* p. 58.
11 *LPPE,* pp. 381f.
12 *LPPE,* p. 383.

DIETRICH BONHOEFFER'S WAY BETWEEN RESISTANCE AND SUBMISSION

Jørgen Glenthøj

DIETRICH BONHOEFFER belongs not only to Germany and the German Evangelical Church but also to the church as a whole.

My interest in Dietrich Bonhoeffer was initially stimulated almost symbolically as a result of a meeting with German theological students in Woudschoten, the Netherlands, following the 1948 World Council of Churches Conference in Amsterdam. A group of Scandinavian theological students realized that the walls around Germany had to be broken from the outside. As a consequence, we decided at that meeting to invite the German students to Scandinavia the following year. At this conference, in Liselund, Denmark, every participant reported on a significant book recently written in his own country. The German student Eduard Haller discussed Bonhoeffer's *Life Together* with us. He mailed me a copy of that book as well as the first commemorative volume containing the 1945 memorial services held in London and Berlin. From that time on I have been captivated by Bonhoeffer. Later, I was able to reflect on my own participation in the Danish resistance movement, my reflection aided by the German theologian of the Confessing Church who himself was a member of the German resistance movement. Most of all I have been touched by Bonhoeffer's thinking about "deputyship." No other contemporary theologian has spoken as powerfully about that subject as Bonhoeffer.

Thus, I can only begin this essay[1] with a word of gratitude. It is indeed striking that in Denmark we can no longer remember the act of violence against Norway and Denmark on April 9, 1940, without remembering the act of violence in Flossenbürg on April 9, 1945. But God has effected an act of reconciliation and of blessing from the latter act of violence. This essay examines the reconciliation and blessing wrought from the death in Flossenbürg.

My subject is "Dietrich Bonhoeffer's Way Between Resistance and Submission." But can Bonhoeffer's entire life and work be summed up by this single subject? Can all his responsibilities and testimonies as a theologian and Christian, as an interpreter and preacher of the Word, as a disciple and trailblazer, as a conspirator and martyr, be subsumed under this description? As he himself commented regarding his decision of June 20, 1939, to return from the United States to Germany: "Ultimately one acts from a plane that remains hidden. Therefore one can but pray that God will judge and forgive us."[2] The meaning of living and acting from this (hidden) plane is the leitmotif of Bonhoeffer's entire work. He did not feel free to make his final decision in the United States; on July 2, 1939—still in New York—he writes in his diary: "The Americans speak too much in their sermons about freedom. The Church's possession of freedom is a dubious matter. Freedom must be gained under the pressure of 'necessity.' The Church's freedom comes from the 'necessity' of the Word of God. Otherwise it develops into arbitrariness and results in many new restrictions."[3] In pursuing "resistance and submission" in the life and work of Dietrich Bonhoeffer, we may observe that it was this very decision to return from the United States to Germany which led him to the seemingly secular key words "resistance" and "submission." But we may also observe that these simple words testify to living simultaneously under that "necessity" of God's Word and acting from that hidden plane. In this way, the subject "resistance and submission" leads us ultimately to the depths of Bonhoeffer's theology.

The reality of "resistance and submission" led Bonhoeffer from the academic profession of a theologian to the existential life of a Christian long before the specific words were coined. On January 21, 1934, he himself described this inner process in a striking sermon on Jer. 20:7 ("O Lord, thou hast deceived me, and I was deceived; thou art stronger than I, and thou hast prevailed"):

> The Word that intercepts, grips, captivates, and binds man does not come from the depths of our soul. Rather, it is the strange, unknown, unexpected, mighty, overpowering Word of the Lord, who calls into his service whomever he wants, whenever he wants. Resistance is of no avail. . . . A lasso has been thrown over man's head, and now he cannot get away. Should he try to resist, he experiences how impossible it is, for the lasso becomes ever tighter and more painful, and reminds him that he is a prisoner. He is a prisoner who must follow. His path has been prescribed. . . .
>
> His path leads to the utmost weakness. [He becomes] the fool, ridiculed, despised, declared insane, but the more dangerous for quietness and peace among men—the fool, whom they smite, imprison, torture, and put to death the sooner the better. . . . He [Jeremiah] has been called dreamer, crank, disturber of the peace, traitor; by these names have all been called throughout history to whom God became too strong.[4]

And again, with the authority of an only partly hidden autobiographical cover, which reveals the most crucial decisions of a young man who saw himself bound to renounce his most tender happiness on earth:

> God, you began with me. You went after me, confronted me suddenly and continuously in my path, tempted and deluded me, made my heart indulgent and willing; you spoke to me about your longing and everlasting love, about your faithfulness and strength. When I sought strength, you strengthened me; when I sought footing, you steadied me; when I sought forgiveness, you forgave my guilt. I did not want it, but you overcame my will, my resistance, my heart; God, you tempted me irresistibly, so that I surrendered. You laid your hands on me as on one unsuspecting, and now I cannot escape any more. Now you pull me like your booty, bind me to your victory chariot, and drag me along so that, maltreated and tortured, I "participate" in your triumphal procession. How could I know that your love is so painful and that your grace is so pitiless? You became stronger than I and prevailed. When my thoughts about you grew strong, I grew weak. When you defeated me, I was lost. Then my will was broken, my strength diminished, my path the way of suffering with no return, the decision about my life made. I did not decide; you did. You bound me to you, in fortune and misfortune. God, why are you so terribly near to us?[5]

and

> But the moment one believes that he can no longer go the way with God because it is too difficult, . . . then God's nearness, his faithfulness, and his strength become a comfort and a help; only then do we fully recognize God and the meaning of our Christian life.[6]

Bonhoeffer called the plane from which this Christian life-commitment is enacted "the majestic hiddenness." In his sermon on Col. 3:3, delivered in Berlin on June 19, 1932, he explained:

> Here is one [Christ] who had transcended the border which separates us from the Creator and from true life, has broken into our death sphere, has tasted the very depth of our life and death, through death has gone to the eternal Father and to life eternal, and now is seated at the right hand of God. He has raised the entire world with him to life and light, has swallowed up death in victory, has captured our entire prison, and has brought us liberty, the glorious liberty of the children of God.[7]

He continues:

> Our visible life with its joy and success, with its grief, sorrow, and disobedience stands holy, without blemish, and perfect for Christ's sake in that hidden world of God before the eyes of the Almighty today, tomorrow, and for ever.[8]

We have given the young theologian and Christian Dietrich Bonhoeffer such an extensive hearing as an interpreter and preacher of the Word because the hidden plane, the ground of his most crucial decisions, is so apparent in these sermons. Hearing his interpretation and preaching, we come to realize that in all his crucial decisions he sought God's decision for himself. The "extremely great hesitation" he sometimes felt becomes just as evident as his certainty that he was no longer able to undo a decision. For example, "we cannot undo Barmen and Dahlem, not because they are historical facts of our church to which we must pay homage, but because we cannot undo the Word of God."[9] To inquire after the hidden plane of such a decision implies not only the sin of the pious question of the Serpent ("Did God say . . . ?") but also conscious separation from salvation (i.e., the presumption of knowing the hidden plane behind God's decision).

With such an understanding of the submission demanded by God's Word, it is clear why throughout his life Bonhoeffer brought every "pious godlessness," i.e., everything that was called "religion," under the saving judgment of the Word of God, and why he fought all attempts to save the world through principles, programs, and resolutions. He saw in these a perversion of the original relation between the Creator and the creature, and the source of Christendom's own paralyzing influence on such ethical questions as unemployment, rearmament, peace, race, minority rights, and the church. For "when man proceeds against the concrete Word of God with the weapon of a principle, with an idea of God, he is in the right from the first, he becomes God's master, he has left the path of obedience, he has withdrawn from God's addressing him."[10]

For a long time Bonhoeffer found himself in the condition of a man jumping from ice floe to ice floe, without solid footing, because he had not found the concrete Word of God. Finally he found support in the realization that to be a Christian means to be a disciple. His entire literary output, as well as his most crucial personal decisions during the thirties, are to be understood only through that hallmark.

The force of this conviction was used to bolster a paralysed and faltering Lutheranism, which had abandoned and forgotten the unity between law and gospel, between obedience and faith. The content of the gospel is no cheap comfort for the soul but fullness of life from God in imitation of Jesus. Imitation or discipleship is joy in the empirical, visible, confessing church, for she is the place for the fullness and reality of life.[11]

Discipleship is also a part of the divine "necessity" which the Christian must taste. "The cross is not the terrible end to an otherwise god-fearing and happy life, but it meets us at the beginning of our communion with Christ."[12] And again:

Suffering means being cut off from God. . . . [Jesus] takes upon himself the suffering of the whole world, and in doing so proves victorious over it. . . . While it is still true that suffering means being cut off from God, yet within the fellowship of Christ's suffering, suffering is overcome by suffering, and becomes the way to communion with God.[13]

Discipleship, then, means to be a Christian while tempted by the divine necessity. This divine necessity, however, is not some pedagogical means of strengthening man in his weakness, but the experience of being forsaken by God:

Who are we to speak of temptation being bound to come? Are we in God's counsel? And if—by virtue of a divine [necessity] which is incomprehensible to us—temptation is bound to come, then Christ, the most tempted of all, summons us to pray against the divine [necessity]—not to yield in Stoic resignation to temptation, but to flee from that dark [necessity] in which God lets the devil do his will, and call to the open divine freedom in which God tramples the devil under foot. "Lead us not into temptation."[14]

But the term "discipleship" still does not fully describe what it means to be a Christian. Near the end of the thirties it became more and more clear to Bonhoeffer that being a Christian also meant being a trailblazer. His *Ethics* and his *Letters and Papers from Prison* testify how the disciple became the trailblazer. Trailblazing implies extending discipleship to all of life. It is not the same as emigration, either outwardly or inwardly, as he noted in the diary of his American journey on June 28, 1939: "I cannot believe it to be God's will that in case of war I must remain here without a special task."[15] A few days earlier he had mentioned that he could not be separated from his destiny, especially not at that time, and he had deplored displaced persons. Germany and the brethren had become his country and his destiny, i.e., his divinely imposed necessity:

There is a necessity of sharing in the assuming and carrying of the guilt of a father or a brother. There is no glory in standing amid the ruins of one's native town in the consciousness that at least one has not oneself incurred any guilt. That is rather the self-glorification of the moral legalist in the face of history.[16]

The task awaiting him after his return from the United States was to lay the foundation for a new beginning after the war holocaust. From passively sharing he turned to actively preparing, to being a conspirator. Bonhoeffer felt pressured by an unwelcome choice—to be responsible either for the blood of millions or for the blood of a single tyrant. Thus, he reached the ethical point at which the sword of the magistrate had to be used against the tyrant by the deputy power of right and order, in order to stop the spread of the tyrant's guilt.

Here trailblazing simultaneously became political resistance. But for Bonhoeffer it really did not mean any new task. His role in the conspiracy was not primarily in preparing the attempts on Hitler's life, but in taking care of the church's province, including its ecumenical relations.

From his conversations with Bishop Bell in Sweden during May 1942, Bonhoeffer returned home with two mandates. First, knowledgeable Christians were to prepare guidelines for the reconstruction of Europe from the German point of view as well. In this way a common ecumenical goal was to be set and implemented in order to exert influence on the peace treaties. Some Freiburg professors carried out this mandate. Second, together with Otto Dibelius, Bishop Wurm, and Martin Niemöller, Bonhoeffer was to participate in a small confidential conference on Sweden's neutral soil immediately after the cease fire—invited as a personal guest of Archbishop Eidem. Twenty to thirty church leaders from the combatant nations, who had earlier become acquainted through their ecumenical activities, were to find a common basis of confidence and reconciliation, so that ecumenical activity and Europe's atmosphere in general should not remain poisoned for ten years by the question of guilt, as it had after World War I. This conference did not take place. A similar conference, however, was held in Stuttgart during October 1945, when the new leaders of the German Evangelical Church met with delegates from the Ecumene, and pronounced the so-called Stuttgart Declaration on guilt.

A third task for Bonhoeffer was added to these ecumenical mandates. Friedrich Justus Perels, the lawyer of the Confessing Church, whom we also commemorate today,[17] had drafted a new provisional constitution for the German Evangelical Church after the overthrow (early fall, 1942). In this draft, which Bonhoeffer personally had corrected, Bonhoeffer and Hans Lilje are designated the leaders of the office of foreign affairs in the German Evangelical Church.

There cannot be any doubt that Bonhoeffer's letters from prison, including his controversial ones, were written to fulfill these concrete mandates. This is unmistakably clear in the following extracts, when after months of increasing hopes the conspirator had to prepare himself for martyrdom:

> I've often wondered here where we are to draw the line between necessary resistance to "fate", and equally necessary submission [without being either a Don Quixote or a Sancho Pansa]. . . . I think we must rise to the great demands that are made on us personally, and yet at the same time fulfill the commonplace and the necessary tasks of daily life. We must confront fate . . . as resolutely as we submit to it at the right time. One can speak of "guidance" only on the other side of that twofold process, with God meeting us no longer as "Thou,"

but also "disguised" in the "It"; so in the last resort my question is how we are to find the "Thou" in this "It" (i.e., fate), or in other words, how does "fate" really become "guidance"? It is therefore impossible to define the boundary between resistance and submission in abstract principles; but both of them must exist, and both must be practiced [resolutely]. Faith demands this elasticity of behavior. Only so can we stand our ground in each situation as it arises, and turn it to gain.[18]

At first he saw his task as standing his ground in the boundary situation. Thus the time of his imprisonment assumed the meaning of a time of significant preparation for a future task—"a *status intermedius.*"[19] "I sometimes feel that I'm living, just as long as I have something great to work for";[20] "this Easter may be one of our last chances to prepare ourselves for our great task of the future";[21] "if I were to end my life here in these conditions, that would have a meaning that I think I could understand; on the other hand, everything might be a thorough preparation for a new start and a new task when peace comes";[22] "as I see it, I'm here for some purpose, and I only hope I may fulfill it."[23] After the Normandy invasion he writes: "Let us face the coming weeks in faith and in great assurance about the general future, and [confidently] commit your way and all our ways to God. Χάρις καὶ εἰρήνη!";[24] "The next feast is sure to be ours; I've no doubt about that now";[25] and a month later, "I think that we shall meet again soon."[26]

Later, after the failure of the plot on July 20, 1944, he writes: "How can success make us arrogant, or failure lead us astray, when we share in God's suffering through a life of this kind? . . . I am glad to have been able to learn this, and I know I've been able to do so only along the road that I've travelled."[27] In the same letter he enclosed the poem, "Stations on the Road to Freedom," which included the stanzas "Discipline," "Action," "Suffering," and "Death." Not only action, but also suffering "is a way to freedom. In suffering, the deliverance consists in our being allowed to put the matter out of our own hands into God's hands. In this sense death is the crowning of human freedom. Whether the human deed is a matter of faith or not depends on whether we understand our suffering as an extension of our action and a completion of freedom. I think that it is very important and very comforting."[28] And finally: "I am so sure of God's guiding hand that I hope I shall always be kept in that certainty."[29]

So it was. His certainty rested in the majestic hiddenness with Christ in God and in the freedom that came with the pressure of the divine "necessity," both earned in resistance and submission. Even in Dietrich Bonhoeffer's last words, shortly before his execution in Flossenburg, this *cantus firmus* is still clear. Through an English fellow prisoner he sent this message to Bishop Bell: "Tell him that for me this is the end but also the beginning—with him I believe in the principle of our universal Christian brotherhood which rises above all national interests, and that our victory is certain. Tell him also that I have never forgotten his words at our last meeting."[30]

Notes

1 This essay is an adaptation of an address delivered in Berlin April 16, 1970, commemorating the twenty-fifth anniversary of the death of the Berlin victims of the Confessing Church.

2 *GS*, I, 304.

3 *Ibid.*, I, 312.

4 *Ibid.*, V, 505f. (the sermon was given Jan. 24, 1934, in London).

5 *Ibid.*, V, 507.

6 *Ibid.*, V. 508f.

7 *Ibid.*, IV, 76f.

8 *Ibid.*, IV, 78.

9 *Ibid.*, II, 231.

10 *CFT*, p. 68.

11 Rainer Mayer, *Christuswirklichkeit: Grundlagen, Entwicklung und Konsequenzen der Theologie Dietrich Bonhoeffers* (Stuttgart, 1969), p. 157.

12 *Cost of Discipleship* (London, 1959), p. 79.

13 *Ibid.*, p. 81.

14 *CFT*, p. 100.

15 *GS*, I, 310.

16 *Ethics* (London, 1955), p. 304.

17 See note 1 above.

18 *LPPE*, p. 217f. (*WEN*, 150f.).

19 *Ibid.*, p. 229 (*WEN*, 155).

20 *Ibid.*, p. 223 (*WEN*, 163).

21 *Ibid.*, p. 241 (*WEN*, 169).

22 *Ibid.*, p. 272 (*WEN*, 173).

23 *Ibid.*, p. 289 (*WEN*, 188).

24 *Ibid.*, p. 323 (*WEN*, 214).

25 *Ibid.*, p. 324 (*WEN*, 215).

26 *Ibid.*, p. 347 (*WEN*, 237).

27 *Ibid.*, p. 370 (*WEN*, 249).

28 *Ibid.*, p. 375 (*WEN*, 254).

29 *Ibid.*, p. 393 (*WEN*, 267).

30 *GS*, I, 412.

CHRISTOLOGY: THE GENUINE FORM
OF TRANSCENDENCE

Rainer Mayer

I. The Crisis of a Metaphysical Understanding of Transcendence

IT HAS BECOME difficult, even in theology, to speak of transcendence if we use the term to mean a divine reality beyond natural, social, and cultural realities. Our scientific and technological civilization seems to leave no room for transcendence; everything not accessible to empirical examination is being eliminated. There is a self-restraint expressed within the decision to stay within the bounds of the immanent, but this decision must also be understood to reflect the deliberate expansion of human possibilities. The world, now freed of religious taboos, is open to unhindered control by human reason. By excluding transcendence we now have free access to immanence.

This concentration on the immanent has influenced the mind of modern man. Man creates his environment, but since he is a being open to his world, he is at the same time a product of his environment. At first metaphysics was excluded deliberately and by choice, but now its exclusion is a matter of habit. Modern man, unlike his forebears, has no experience of the beyond, even if he wishes he did.

The history of Western culture has acknowledged this devastating loss and sensed its meaning. When Nietzsche proclaimed the death of God, he was both frightened and overwhelmed by the senselessness of life. Quantity has been converted into a new quality. The methodological application of the working hypothesis of God's nonexistence ("etsi deus non daretur"— Hugo Grotius) in science and technology has created a scientific-technological culture as the new reality. The experience common to this culture is the experience of God's nonexistence. The experience of the death of God is a theological phenomenon as well as a cultural phenomenon. In a theological discussion of transcendence, the cultural context out of which the discussion arises must be taken into account.

The traditional concept of God's transcendence has been influenced by the Aristotelian and Thomistic metaphysics of being and by the mythology of classical antiquity. The *metaphysics of being* depicts God as the supreme being; his qualities are the values and qualities of mankind projected into the infinite. Human being is then divine being in miniature form. In *mythology* God appears in human form. A general, eternal religious truth is cast in narrative form, and in the process God is conceived of in anthropomorphic terms.[1] The world we live in and the "world beyond" are then understood as separate spaces.

Today both mythology and the metaphysics of being are losing their relevance. A metaphysical God is only relevant when mankind cannot control his own situation by his own abilities but has to look somewhere for help. Such a God acts from the "beyond," where human wisdom and ability are at a loss. But his space is shrinking fast: the world-come-of-age declares him an idol. He dies by degrees whenever people "by their own strength push these boundaries somewhat further out, so that God becomes superfluous as a *Deus ex machina.*"[2]

In his inaugural dissertation, entitled *Act and Being,* Bonhoeffer had studied the metaphysical understanding of transcedence as it relates to the presuppositions in the theory of knowledge. He came to the conclusion that this way of thinking interprets revelation in terms of being, as a kind of ontologism.[3] Relying on the terminology of Karl Barth, he called this ontologism "religion." Bonhoeffer conceives of the religious man as follows:

> Religious people speak of God when human knowledge (perhaps simply because they are too lazy to think) has come to an end, or when human resources fail—in fact it is always the *deus ex machina* that they bring on to the scene, either for the apparent solution of insoluble problems, or as strength in human failure—always, that is to say, exploiting human weakness or human boundaries.[4]

Christian faith differs from religion in that it recognizes God as sovereign Lord over man, claiming all of life as his domain. God is not a figure who is relevant only at the limits of human knowledge and possibilities. Bonhoeffer stresses:

> Here again, God is no stop-gap; he must be recognized at the centre of life, not when we are at the end of our resources; it is his will to be recognized in life, and not only when death comes; in health and vigour, and not only in suffering; in our activities, and not only in sin.[5]

The Christian's relationship to God is nonreligious and corresponds to a nonmetaphysical conception of God which is defined by negation. "Our relation to God is not a 'religious' relationship to the highest, most powerful and best Being imaginable—that is not authentic transcendence."[6] "God's 'beyond' is not the beyond of our cognitive faculties. The transcendence of epistemological theory has nothing to do with the transcendence of God."[7] Parallel to his distinction between faith and religion, Bonhoeffer makes a distinction between *true and false transcendence.* He rules out the idea of a spatial beyond (mythology) as well as transcendence in the theory of knowledge (metaphysics), declaring them to be religious and false.

This gives us the context in which the experience of the death of God must be understood. It is an experience of the religious man who is confronted with the failings of mythology and metaphysics. But the Christian faith, because it is nonreligious in nature, should remain undisturbed by the loss of mythology and metaphysics. Nevertheless, Christian proclamation is drawn into the crisis of the metaphysical understanding of transcendence. How is this possible? Bonhoeffer declares: " 'Christianity' has always been a form—perhaps the true form—of religion."[8] In the nineteen hundred years of proclamation and theology, God's transcendence has in fact been conceived of often in terms of the transcendence of the theory of knowledge, and his "beyond" has regularly been conceived of as a spatial beyond. In short, faith took the shape of religion.[9] Bonhoeffer does not question the religious past of Christianity; he is convinced that religion is no longer a force on the scene. A world without religion, a world that has come of age, requires a *nonreligious proclamation of the gospel.* What he questions is not the Christian faith as such but the traditional religious form of Christianity. Bonhoeffer is struggling toward a "nonreligious interpretation of the gospel" and looks forward to a renewed "nonreligious Christianity."

This leads us to an important limit that we must recognize: contemporary Christian theologians who proclaim the death of the biblical God cannot gain any support from Bonhoeffer. Bonhoeffer distinguishes between true transcendence and metaphysics, between faith and religion. The fading away of the reality of a supreme being in a world beyond does not affect the reality of the biblical God! Unlike some of the hasty commentators on his thinking, Bonhoeffer draws very careful distinctions here and does not confuse God's transcendence with metaphysics or the Christian faith with religion. He emphasizes: "God is the supramundane reality transcending consciousness, the lord and creator. This postulate is an unconditional requirement of Christian theology."[10] We should add immediately that he is equally insistent on the condescension of God. Only when the transcendence and immanence of God can be thought of simultaneously is a positive explication of transcendence possible. But first let us explore some unsuccessful attempts to achieve a new understanding of transcendence.

II. Unsuccessful Attempts at a New Understanding of Transcendence

The first important attempt to achieve a new understanding of transcendence was undertaken by *dialectical theology*. Since transcendence was no longer experienced in the modern world, dialectical theologians retreated from human existence and intelligence to the absolute freedom of God, who discloses himself in his freedom. God is not bound to anything; he is free to give himself at will and to retreat again. He is never at man's disposal, and he is not bound to any conditions by which everything else is conditioned. Revelation is not a doctrine, nor is it an institution, nor is it human psychic experience. Revelation occurs as a pure act—whenever and wherever God wills. When, where, and how he will give himself to man remains entirely his free choice. He is always giving himself in a timely way and is never at anyone's disposal. Even the act of revelation, actually, is not to be conceived of in terms of time; otherwise revelation would become comprehensible in human terms. No, God remains free; he never becomes object for us but remains pure act. No moment in history is capable of infinity—able to comprehend eternity. In *Act and Being,* his inaugural thesis, Bonhoeffer studied the presuppositions of this starting point in terms of the theory of knowledge. The conclusion he came to was that dialectical theologians interpret revelation in terms of act concepts, which becomes a kind of transcendentalism.[11]

Bonhoeffer criticizes one-sided interpretations of revelation in terms of act concepts or actualism, especially Barth's actualistic understanding of transcendence:

> In revelation it is a question less of God's freedom on the far side of us, that is, his eternal isolation and aseity, than of his forth-proceeding, his *given* Word, his bond in which he has bound himself, of his freedom as it is most strongly attested in his having freely bound himself to historical man, having placed himself at man's disposal. God is not free of man but *for* man.[12]

When revelation is interpreted in terms of act concepts, two difficulties manifest themselves. The first arises in attaining knowledge of revelation. If we proceed in a theocentric way (for example, via Karl Barth) and conceive of God as pure act, it is difficult to "descend" from his theocentric position to real human beings living in concrete historical situations. However, if we proceed in anthropocentric fashion (for example, via Rudolf Bultmann) and assume that we can only talk about God when we talk about man, we locate the "being" of God in human self-understanding and have trouble "ascending" from an anthropocentric subjectivism to God as absolute subject.

The second difficulty arises in connection with the continuity between empirical and justified existence, and also in connection with the continuity within the new self. Again, Barth and Bultmann offer contrasting approaches. It is either possible to "preserve the continuity of the new existence at the expense of that of the total I" (Barth) or to "assert the continuity of the total I at the expense of that of the new existence" (Bultmann).[13]

Transcendentalism understands God's freedom and contingency in purely structural terms. The loss of the experience of transcendence in our scientific and technological society is replaced by an intellectual artifice: God is claimed to be independent of man in principle, which means that revelation cannot be part of human experience.[14] This opens the possibility of speaking of God and his revelation in a world without God. But if one agrees with Bonhoeffer's claim that the visible, tangible, true reality of God must be manifested through a "nonreligious interpretation of the gospel" since God is not free *of* man but *for* man,[15] we must turn away from any understanding of revelation in terms of acts and turn to ontological language instead. The basic problem then remains unsolved, and we are left asking: How can transcendence convincingly be interpreted in categories other than those of actualism and ontologism?

We see another attempt to gain a new understanding of transcendence in the limitation of transcendence to a strictly *this-worldly transcendence.* Rudolf Bultmann affirms this position when he says: "Theologians such as Tillich, Bonhoeffer, Ebeling, Vahanian, R. G. Smith, and Robinson agree . . . that transcendence should not be sought for, and cannot be found above or beyond this world, but *in the midst of the this-worldly.*"[16] We are not yet in a position to decide whether Bultmann can legitimately claim Bonhoeffer's support in this affirmation. First we must elucidate the understanding of transcendence found in R. G. Smith and John A. T. Robinson, both interpreters of Bonhoeffer.

These two theologians agree with Bonhoeffer in his criticism of the metaphysical idea of God and of transcendence conceived in terms of the theory of knowledge. But it remains problematic how we are to conceive of and understand true transcendence. Claiming support from Bonhoeffer, R. G. Smith says: "The transcendent is met in the solicitude for others as given to us in the life and way of Jesus."[17] And Robinson concurs when he says: "This 'life for others, through participation in the Being of God,' *is* transcendence."[18] Human pro-existence is seen as opening up a kind of this-worldly transcendence. John A. T. Robinson argues for this position in a wider context. In his opinion, the notion of a God as a being above and beyond our world who is endowed with personal qualities defies actual conception. However, to state that God is "personal" means that 'reality at its very deepest level is personal,' that personality is of *ultimate* significance in the constitution of the universe, that in personal relationships we touch the final meaning of existence as nowhere else. 'To predicate personality for God,' says Feuerbach, 'is nothing else than to declare personality as the absolute essence.'[19]

In "a tremendous act of faith,"[20] Robinson identifies personality, the ground of being, and love. He uses the symbol "God" to speak of this unity. In order to reach transcendence, one has to penetrate through "the mathematical regularities and through the functional values"[21] of our technological world to the personal relationship as the ground and depth of being.[22] Understanding the reality of the world in terms of personal categories is already a theological understanding of the world, for it is *"ipso facto* making an affirmation about the *ultimacy* of personal relationships: it is saying that *God,* the final truth and reality 'deep down things,' is *love."*[23]

Following the terminology of Tillich, Robinson does not conceive of God as above and beyond; he conceives of him rather as in the depths of being. In the final analysis he has not enriched the discussion of transcendence but has only led it into a new blind alley. In Aristotelian thinking man has to lift himself up to God as the ultimate being. According to Robinson's thinking, however, man has to penetrate to the primordial foundation of the world in order to meet transcendence in the depth of being. This is *ontologism*, metaphysics of being with completely reserved promises. Eternal values are attached to the essence of a this-worldly reality.

The existing conditions are not seriously questioned. Instead, they are metaphysically justified through this-worldly metaphysics, through the attempt to find truth in a cosmic dimension of depth. "Securing of that which is, by sacralization,"[24] however, is the primal function of religion.

A comparison of two passages, one by R. G. Smith and one by Bonhoeffer, will show how much Bonhoeffer differs from this type of religious interpretation of the gospel. Smith says: "The eternal is *in* time, heaven is *through* earth, the supernatural is *not other* than the natural, the spiritual is *not more* than the wholly human."[25] Bonhoeffer, on the other hand, struggles against this identity-thinking of the "shallow this-worldliness of the enlightened."[26] He says:

> Just as in Christ the reality of God entered into the reality of the world, so, too, is that which is Christian to be found only in that which is of the world, the "supernatural" only in the natural, the holy only in the profane, and the revelational only in the rational.

But he adds immediately:

> And yet what is Christian is not identical with what is of the world, the natural not identical with supernatural, or the revelational with the rational. But between the two there is in each case a unity which

derives solely from the reality of Christ, that is to say solely from faith in this ultimate reality.[27]

The crucial point is not simply to identify immanence and transcendence in human pro-existence but to recognize the dynamic and polemical union between the reality of God and the reality of the world in the reality of Christ.[28] This unity in duality has been the concern of Bonhoeffer's theology from his book *The Communion of Saints* to his *Letters and Papers from Prison*.

III. Christ's Reality: Transcendence Without Metaphysics

There is general agreement between Bonhoeffer and his interpreters, including some of the "God-is-dead theologians," that the metaphysical idea of God is to be rejected and that transcendence is not to be understood in terms of theory of knowledge. I pointed out earlier that a new and valid understanding of transcendence can be based on neither an interpretation of revelation in terms of actualism, as attempted by dialectical theology in its transcendentalist endeavors, nor an interpretation of revelation in terms of ontology, as usually undertaken in the ontological-metaphysical system of a theology of human pro-existence.

According to Bonhoeffer, a valid concept of transcendence requires that human existence must be met (immanence). Moreover, such a concept requires that transcedence be conceived of in continuity as something encountered by man, as crisis and limitation, as something not at man's disposal and in principle free of being known by man (transcendence).[29] In other words, we are to think of a kind of reality that neither treats revelation wholly as an entity nor volatilizes revelation into nonentity. This reality must rather be thought of as enjoying a mode of being that embraces both entity and nonentity, while at the same time "suspending" within itself man's awareness of it—faith.[30]

According to Bonhoeffer, these conditions are met in "revelation's mode of being within the church."[31] The Protestant concept of the church is to be understood as the concept of a person; that is to say, "God reveals himself as a person in the church." The Christian communion is God's final revelation—God as "Christ existing as community."[32] Bonhoeffer identifies the reality of the church with the presence of Christ. The person of Christ embraces all whom he has obtained for his own.

> The "Church" therefore has not the meaning of a human community to which Christ is or is not self-superadded, nor of a union among such as individually seek or think to have Christ and wish to cultivate this common "possession"; no, it is a communion created by Christ and founded upon him, one in which Christ reveals himself as . . . the new man—or rather as the new humanity itself.[33]

This concept of "Christ existing as community," as a corporate person, makes it possible for Bonhoeffer to overcome individualism and to find true transcendence. The corporate person of the community is not at my disposal. (This is the continuity and the "beyond" of transcendence.) Rather, she is the absolute thou, challenging and limiting my I. (This is the ethical and social dimension of transcendence.) At the same time, I, as a Christian, am a member of this community and part of Christ. (This is the relationship of transcendence to existence and this world.)

> This is where the question of explaining revelation in terms of act or being assumes an entirely new aspect. God gives himself in Christ to his communion, and to each individual member of that communion. This he does in such a way that the active subject in the communion, of both the preaching and the believing of the Word, is Christ. It is in the personal communion, and only there, that the gospel can truly be declared and believed. There, it follows, revelation is in some way secured or possessed. God's freedom has bound itself, woven itself into the personal communion, and it is precisely that which proves it is God's freedom—that he should bind himself to men. The communion genuinely has at its disposal the Word of forgiveness; in the communion may not only be said existentially "I have been forgiven," but also—by the Christian Church as such, in preaching and sacrament—"thou art forgiven"; furthermore, every member of the Church may and should "become a Christ" to every other in so proclaiming the gospel.[34]

Bonhoeffer has posed the question of transcendence as a question of existence, that is, as a question concerning the being of a person—the being of the Christ-person. In his lectures on Christology[35] he demonstrates that we can adequately ask for transcendence only in asking, "Who are you?" Yet the "how" question, which is aimed at determining how transcendence is thinkable, Bonhoeffer rejects as the question of immanence, the "godless question . . . the serpent's question."[36] The Chalcedonian Confession, which is also influenced by the "how" question, demonstrates in its logical contradictions and its strictly negative form that an answer to the "how" question cannot be found because the question is inadequate to the Christ-person. The Chalcedonian Confession is limited by its speculation about natures and its thinking in terms of substances, but the terms are used in a contradictory and paradoxical way, with the result that they cancel each other out. The greatest achievement of Chalcedon is: "From now on it will no longer be permissible to say anything about the *substance* of Christ."[37] By rejecting the "how" question and seeing validity only in the "who" question, Bonhoeffer has replaced the transcendence of a theory of knowledge with an *ethical and personal transcendence* of the Christ-person. The Christ-person becomes real in the community, and the community becomes real in the other person. Transcendence is removed from metaphysical speculation and related to a concrete reality.

But how can a transcendence that binds itself to historical man and is incarnate in empirical reality be kept from being misunderstood as a "shallow this-worldliness" and being identified with actuality, with that which exists? Bonhoeffer wants to get away from understanding transcendence as something that is at man's disposal. Therefore we must try once more to define the "who" question and distinguish it from the "how" question. The latter question endeavors to investigate how the "fact" of revelation can be conceived.

> This question is tantamount to going behind Christ's claim and providing an independent vindication of it. Here the human Logos presumes to be the beginning and Father of Jesus Christ. With this inordinate claim human Logos pretends to trinitarian form.[38]

The early church speculated on the "how" question. "Modern theology since the Enlightenment and Schleiermacher has foundered on the question of the 'fact' of revelation. The New Testament, Paul and Luther have taken the middle course."[39] The question of the "fact" is the "how" question in stronger form. To doubt it is to test the possibility of revelation, for that leaves the "how" question unanswered. It is a decisive insight for Bonhoeffer that the natural man can never extricate himself from the "how" question. Even if he formulates the question correctly—asking, "Who are you?"—all the natural man really means is: "How can I deal with you?"[40] He has no desire to leave his own sphere of existence, and he is unable to really reach his fellow man.[41] Acquired insight cannot be divorced from the existence in which it was gained.[42] The question of transcendence can only be posed scientifically in the context of the church.[43]

> It can only be put where the basic presupposition, Christ's claim to be the Logos of God, has been accepted. It can only be put where God is sought because men already know him. . . . Here a man can only seek what has already been found.[44]

This is the fundamental contradiction that must be overcome:

> Human reason is strained to the limit by the question "Who?" What happens when the Anti-logos raises his claim? Man annihilates the "Who?" with whom he is confronted. "Who are you?" asks Pilate. Jesus is silent. . . . The Logos cannot endure the Anti-logos. It knows that one of them must die.[45]

> In the end there are only two possibilities of encountering Jesus: either man must die, or he kills Jesus.[46] Because the human Logos does not want to die, the Logos of God, who would be the death of it, must die so that it can live on with its unanswered questions of existence and transcendence.[47]

But as soon as the crucified one shows himself as the risen, the "Who are you?" question is reversed and is addressed again to the human logos.

> "Who are you to ask thus?" "Are you truly there to ask thus?" "Who are you, who can still only inquire after me when I restore you, justify you and give you my grace?" The christological question "Who?" is finally formulated only where this reversed question is also heard.[48]

To sum up: Bonhoeffer has bound transcendence to the *sociological reality of the community and the other,* but he has by no means identified transcendence with an empirical human reality. Community and fellow man must be understood in the light of Christ. Christ is more than both; he entered both, but is not absorbed in them. Bonhoeffer maintains the *extra nos* aspect and the continuity of revelation by the Christ-person, who is "the absolute extrinsicality for my existence."[49] This extrinsicality "is essentially transcendent of existence, yet it 'is' in its action on human existence."[50]

> If the I as person suffers the impact of the person of Christ in judgment or in the process of incorporation into the communion, it cannot conceive that this having-to-suffer derives from itself but must recognise that it comes from outside. Herein lies the peculiarity of the theo-sociological category.[51]

These statements provide the context for correctly understanding Bonhoeffer's notes on transcendence in his *Letters and Papers from Prison,* where he says:

> Jesus' . . . "being there for others" is the experience of transcendence. It is only this "being there for others," maintained till death, that is the ground of his omnipotence, omniscience, and omnipresence. Faith is participation in this being of Jesus (incarnation, cross, and resurrection). Our relation to God is not a "religious" relationship to the highest, most powerful, and best Being imaginable—that is not authentic transcendence—but our relation to God is a new life in "existence for others," through participation in the being of Jesus. The transcendental is not infinite and unattainable tasks, but the neighbour who is within reach in any given situation. God in human form—not, as in oriental religions, in animal form, monstrous, chaotic, remote, and terrifying, nor in the conceptual forms of the absolute, metaphysical, infinite, etc., nor yet in the Greek divine human form of "man in himself," but "the man for others," and therefore the Crucified, the man who lives out of the transcendent.[52]

Even in this passage Bonhoeffer very clearly binds ethical and personal transcendence to the person of the living Christ, thereby giving priority to Christology in favor of empirical reality. Bonhoeffer asserts: "From God to reality, not from reality to God, goes the path of theology."[53] The experience of transcendence is to be sought not simply in being-for-others but in *Jesus'* being-for-others. Not our fellow man as such but our fellow man seen with the eyes of Christ is transcendence.

> We think that, because this or that person is living, it makes sense for us to live too. But the truth is that if this earth was good enough for the man Jesus Christ, if such a man as Jesus lived, then, and only then, has life a meaning for us. If Jesus had not lived, then our life would be meaningless, in spite of all the other people whom we know and honour and love.[54]

One could argue that Bonhoeffer did not really get rid of speculative thinking since he so clearly gave priority to the Christ-reality over empirical reality. The question of transcendence here reaches a final formulation: Is it metaphysics to speak of the reality of the incarnate, crucified, and risen Christ?

The decisive point to grasp is that Bonhoeffer does not depict the Christ-reality as an end in itself but presents it in the reality of the world— as related to man and in its structure of the *pro me*.[55] His "speculation"— if indeed we can use this term here—serves only to answer the non-speculative question of who Christ really is for us today,[56] simultaneously in his *extra nos* and *pro me*. An insight, however, cannot be separated from the existence in which it has been gained,[57] and for Bonhoeffer "the question of transcendence is the question of existence and the question of existence is the question of transcendence."[58] The nonspeculative way of understanding transcendence, therefore, is only possible in the act of obedient faith—that is to say, in discipleship. That is the reason Bonhoeffer held works in such high esteem. Works are never speculative, but obedient works constitute the first step to faith[59]—the faith that man does not acquire on his own but receives from God as a free gift.[60] Faith again urges man to act, to intercede courageously for others. *Faith is the experience of transcendence, the experience of transcendence is the recognition of Christ, the recognition of Christ is freedom, and freedom is obedient action out of faith.*[61] This completes the cycle of "believing understanding"[62] for the new man who participates in the being of Christ. This new existence does not permit an investigation of an underlying ultimate reason. It is new existence. Existence is not metaphysical, nor is it accessible to logical inquiries. It is not a possibility but a reality.[63]

Only when it is put to the test can existence be gained or lost. Bonhoeffer's final answer to the question of transcendence is given not just in his theology but in his example.[64] His life is an example of what it means to follow Christ, to "exist for others," to live "a life based on the transcendent."

Notes

1   In contradistinction to the revelation of God in Jesus Christ, the ἐφ' ἅπαζ of the historical dimension is neglected here.

2   Bonhoeffer, *LPP* (New York, 1966), p. 165 (*LPPE*, p. 282).

3   For an epistemological criticism of ontologism, see *AB* (London, 1962), pp. 112f.

4   *LPP*, p. 165 (*LPPE*, pp. 281-282).

5   *LPP*, p. 191 (*LPPE*, p. 312).

6   *LPP*, pp. 237f. (*LPPE*, p. 381).

7   *LPP*, p. 166 (*LPPE*, p. 282).

8   *LPP*, p. 162 (*LPPE*, p. 280).

9   Initially Bonhoeffer himself was convinced that religion and faith belong together. Cf. *CS* (New York, 1964), p. 112: "And yet there is a necessary connection between revelation and religion, as there is between religious community and the church. Nowadays that connection is often overlooked."

10   *AB*, pp. 45f. Cf. *GS*, III, 107: "It is just here that the personalities of God and of man come in contact with each other. Here God himself transcends his transcendence, giving himself to man as Holy Spirit. Yet, being personality, he remains in absolute transcendence. . . ."

11   *AB*, pp. 79-91.

12   *Ibid.*, p. 90.

13   *Ibid.*, p. 101.

14   *Ibid.*, p. 146: "In the final analysis, it is only because dialectical theology thinks individualistically, i.e. in constant abstractions, that it takes its own method more seriously than is consonant with its own premises."

15   This is the concern of the "nonreligious interpretation of Biblical concepts." Since this point cannot be dealt with more extensively here, see Rainer Mayer, *Christuswirklichkeit; Grundlagen, Entwicklung und Konsequenzen der Theologie Dietrich Bonhoeffers* (Stuttgart: Calwer Verlag, 1969), esp. pp. 248ff.

16   Rudolf Bultmann, "Der Gottesgedanke und der moderne Mensch," *Glauben und Verstehen*, IV (Tübingen: J.C.B. Mohr, 1965), p. 121 (my translation).

17   Ronald Gregor Smith, *The New Man: Christianity and Man's Coming of Age* (New York: Harper, 1956), p. 98.

18   John A.T. Robinson, *Honest to God* (Philadelphia: Westminster, 1963), p. 76.

19   *Ibid.*, pp. 48f.

20   *Ibid.*, p. 49.

21   Robinson, *The New Reformation?* (London: SCM Press, 1965), p. 117.

22   *Ibid.*, pp. 116f.

23   Robinson, *Honest to God*, p. 49.

24   Hans Schulze, *Gottesoffenbarung und Gesellschaftsordnung* (Munich: Christian Kaiser, 1968), p. 60; cf. Kurt Goldammer, *Die Formenwelt des Religiösen; Grundriss der systematischen Religionswissenschaft* (Stuttgart, 1960), p. 29.

25   Smith, *New Man*, pp. 111f. (italics by the author).

26   Bonhoeffer, *LPP*, pp. 225f. (*LPPE*, p. 369).

27   *E* (New York, 1965), pp. 198f. It is important that R.G. Smith writes, "the supernatural is *not other* than the natural," whereas Bonhoeffer claims, "the 'supernatural' is only *in* the natural." According to Bonhoeffer, the supernatural has entered the natural, though it remains different from it. Not equality, but unity is the concern of Bonhoeffer.

28 *Ibid.*, p. 199: "This unity is seen in the way in which the secular and the Christian elements prevent one another from assuming any kind of static independence in their mutual relations. They adopt a polemical attitude towards each other and bear witness precisely in this to their shared reality and to their unity in the reality which is in Christ."

29 *AB*, pp. 113f.

30 *Ibid.*, pp. 112f.

31 *Ibid.*, p. 119.

32 *Ibid.*, p. 121. In his early writings Bonhoeffer coined this phrase in modification of Hegel's claim: "God existing as community."

33 *Ibid.*, p. 121.

34 *Ibid.*, pp. 121f.

35 Summer semester, 1933; published as *Christ the Center*, introd. by E.H. Robertson, trans. J. Bowden (New York: Harper & Row, 1966).

36 *CC*, p. 31.

37 *Ibid.*, p. 92.

38 *Ibid.*, p. 33.

39 *Ibid.*

40 *Ibid.*, p. 36.

41 Cf. *ibid.*, p. 31.

42 *CD*, p. 43.

43 *CC*, p. 32.

44 *Ibid.*

45 *Ibid.*, pp. 33f.

46 *Ibid.*, p. 36.

47 *Ibid.*, p. 34.

48 *Ibid.*

49 *AB*, p. 141.

50 *Ibid.*, p. 139.

51 *Ibid.*, pp. 138f.

52 *LPP*, pp. 237f. (*LPPE*, pp. 381f.).

53 *AB*, p. 89.

54 *LPP*, pp. 243f. (*LPPE*, p. 391).

55 *CC*, pp. 38ff.

56 *LPP*, p. 162 (*LPPE*, p. 279).

57 Cf. n. 42.

58 *CC*, p. 31.

59 Cf. *CD*, p. 55.

60 Cf. *GS*, III, 107: "The pathway to this knowledge is action. I can know God only if I can effect an act—an act which makes me transcend the limits of myself, which carries me out of the circle of my self-hood in order to acknowledge the transcendent God. While it is obvious that I myself cannot effect such an act, there is, nevertheless, such an act, which is executed by God himself, and which is called 'faith'."

61 Cf. *LPP*, pp. 228, 232.

62 Cf. *AB*, pp. 139ff.

63 *Ibid.,* pp. 147f.: "To resume: in the knowing of the believer there is absolutely no reflexion. The question whether faith is possible can be answered only by faith's reality. But, since this reality retires from demonstration as an entity, any reflexion must obliterate it. Faith looks not on itself, but on Christ alone. Whether faith *is* faith can be neither ascertained nor even believed, but the faith which believes *is* faith."

64 Cf. *LPP,* p. 238.

V.
CHURCH AND WORLD

THE ECCLESIOLOGY OF *ETHICS*
AND THE PRISON WRITINGS

John Wilcken

IN THE SPRING of 1924, when Bonhoeffer was eighteen years old, he made a short visit to Rome, and the visit made a lasting impression on him. As he wrote in his diary, he began to understand for the first time the concept of church.[1] In his own home one had always spoken of "Protestantism," but seldom of "the Church." In Rome, as he attended the ceremonies of Holy Week, the theological significance of the concept of church penetrated his consciousness.

In a remarkable sermon preached in Barcelona four years later, he spoke movingly of the need for Protestantism to deepen its understanding of the word "Church":

> . . . our fate is sealed if we cannot win back again for this word a new, or perhaps the very old, meaning. Woe to us, if the word does not soon become once again important, yes, the main concern of our life.[2]

His own early theological writings were in fact concerned with the church. In his university dissertation, *Sanctorum Communio*, he examined the sociology of the church, while in his *Habilitationsschrift*, *Act and Being*, he presented a markedly ecclesiastical view of revelation. Then, in the lectures on Christology delivered at the University of Berlin in 1933, he simply identified Christ with the Word of the church's preaching, with the sacrament administered by the church, and with the church-community itself.[3] After the establishment of the Confessing Church in 1934, he devoted his energies to writing in its defense, even going so far as to declare that there was no salvation for those who knowingly separated themselves from it.[4] In the writings of the war years, one problem that occupied his attention was the relationship between church and world. So at all stages of his life he was concerned with questions of ecclesiology.

Moreover, Bonhoeffer's whole view of theology and of the role of the theologian was ecclesiastical. In *Act and Being* he wrote:

> *Theology* is a function of the Church, for Church there is none without preaching, nor preaching without remembrance, but theology is the memory of the Church.[5]

In an essay written in 1933, entitled "What should the Student of Theology Do?" he explained:

> The young theologian should realize that he is, with his theology, in the service of the true Church of Christ, which unflinchingly acknowledges its Lord and lives in this responsibility.[6]

In the outline for a paper entitled "Theology and Community," probably drawn up in 1940, he declared: "Theology does not rule in the community, but *serves*."[7] And finally, at the conclusion of his "Outline for a Book" (sent to Eberhard Bethge with the letter of August 3, 1944), he expressed the hope that this work would be "of some help for the church's future."[8] Thus in his view the theologian was someone who serves the church with his theology.

In short, there is an ecclesiastical dimension to all of Bonhoeffer's thinking, even that which does not directly concern itself with ecclesiological themes. His theology can be rightly understood only if it is seen as produced within the church and for the church.

Bonhoeffer's mature ecclesiology is found in the writings of the war years, notably in *Ethics* and the prison writings. All these writings have a fragmentary character. This is obvious in the case of the letters from prison, but it is also true of the book posthumously published under the title of *Ethics*. This work contains writings—some of them unfinished—which were composed over a period of years (roughly 1940-43). Eberhard Bethge, in his preface to the sixth German edition, describes the circumstances in which each section was written—as far as this can be known—and assigns a date to each.

In the chapter entitled "Ethics as Formation," written in September 1940, Bonhoeffer proposes "conformation with Christ" as a basis for ethics. Men are "conformed to Christ" not by their own efforts but when Christ "takes form" in them. This does not mean that a person must pretend to be something other than what he really is. Rather, a person becomes conformed to Christ, that is, Christ takes form in him, when he becomes more truly and more fully human:

> To be conformed to the Incarnate is to have the right to be the man one really is. Now there is no more pretence, no more hypocrisy or self-violence, no more compulsion to be something other, better and more ideal than what one is. God loves the real man. God became a real man.[9]

Thus a person becomes his "real" self when Christ takes form in him. Christ wants to take form in all people, but in fact this occurs in only a small group of people. These are the church:

> So the Church is not a religious community of worshippers of Christ but is Christ Himself who has taken form among men. The Church can be called the Body of Christ because in Christ's Body man is really taken up by Him, and so too, therefore, are all mankind. The Church, then, bears the form which is in truth the proper form of all humanity.[10]

Thus the church stands where all mankind should stand. It is both an example to all men and the representative of all mankind. What has taken place in the church should take place in every human being. We see here Bonhoeffer's richly christological view of the church, as well as the close relationship which he maintains between the church and all mankind.

In *The Cost of Discipleship* (1937) Bonhoeffer emphasizes the fact that the church occupies "space" in the world—space for its liturgy, for its organization, and for its daily life. This teaching he reaffirms in *Ethics*.[11] However, a difficulty arises for Bonhoeffer here. In the chapter "Christ, Reality and Good," probably written during the summer of 1941, he emphatically rejects what he calls "Thinking in Terms of Two Spheres," that is, the spheres of the holy and the profane. This kind of thinking means the division of reality into two areas, and Bonhoeffer holds very firmly that reality is one and undivided:

> There are not two realities, but only one reality, and that is the reality of God, which has become manifest in Christ in the reality of the world. Sharing in Christ we stand at once in both the reality of God and the reality of the world.[12]

The problem is that the church, in being visible and occupying space in the world, does seem to create a division in reality. Bonhoeffer refuses to solve the problem by denying the visibility of the church and reducing it to a merely spiritual force. Just as Jesus Christ was visible, so is the church; just as Christ occupied space in the world, so does the church. Bonhoeffer solves the problem by declaring that the church occupies space in the world not for its own sake but for the sake of the world:

> The space of the Church is not there in order to try and deprive the world of a piece of its territory, but precisely in order to prove to the world that it is still the world, the world which is loved by God and reconciled with Him.[13]

Bonhoeffer writes further:

> The only way in which the Church can defend her own territory is by fighting not for it but for the salvation of the world. Otherwise

the Church becomes a "religious society" which fights in its own interest and thereby ceases at once to be the Church of God and of the world.[14]

The members of the church must above all be witnesses to Jesus Christ before the world. This, rather than leading lives of personal piety, is their primary aim. However, Bonhoeffer hastens to add, this aim can be achieved only if the community leads a life of holiness. Where the church fails to give such testimony to Christ before the world, this is a sign that its inner life is not one of holiness but of corruption.

Bonhoeffer stresses that the church should not be thought of as separated from the world. Rather, the church *is* the world both redeemed by Christ and conscious of the fact that it is reconciled with God:

> It is implicit in the New Testament statement concerning the incarnation of God in Christ that all men are taken up, enclosed and borne within the body of Christ and that this is just what the congregations of the faithful are to make known to the world by their words and by their lives. What is intended here is not separation from the world but the summoning of the world into the fellowship of this body of Christ, to which in truth it already belongs.[15]

The church proclaims the fact that the world has been reconciled to God; this proclamation alone divides it from the world.

Further light is thrown on the church's proclamation in the chapter entitled "The 'Ethical' and the 'Christian'," which was probably written during the winter of 1942/43. This chapter contains the second treatment of the doctrine of the "mandates," and it includes a rather lengthy discussion of the church's mandate of proclamation. The content of the church's proclamation, Bonhoeffer declares, is "the word of the revelation of God in Jesus Christ." He emphasizes that this word comes from above, "from the will and the mercy of God." Hence a clear relation of superiority-inferiority is established, and Bonhoeffer uses this notion of superiority-inferiority in speaking of the church's ministry:

> Above there is the office of proclamation, and below there is the listening congregation. In the place of God and of Jesus Christ there stands before the congregation the bearer of the office of preaching with his proclamation. The preacher is not the spokesman of the congregation, but, if the expression may be allowed, he is the spokesman of God before the congregation. He is authorised to teach, to admonish and to comfort, to forgive sin, but also to retain sin. And at the same time he is the shepherd, the pastor of the flock.[16]

In this passage we see the mature Bonhoeffer's theology of the ministry. He emphasizes in a remarkable way the authority of the minister ("the spokesman of God before the congregation"). Further, he seems to limit the authority to forgive and retain sin to the ordained minister. Next, he sees the minister not simply as a preacher of the Word but also as a pastor of the flock.[17] He then writes of the divine institution of the ministry:

> This office is instituted directly by Jesus Christ Himself; it does not derive its legitimation from the will of the congregation but from the will of Jesus Christ. It is established in the congregation and not by the congregation, and at the same time it is with the congregation.[18]

Finally he describes in very emphatic terms the reverence due to the office of preaching:

> The congregation which is being awakened by the proclamation of the word of God will demonstrate the genuineness of its faith by honouring the office of preaching in its unique glory and by serving it with all its powers; it will not rely on its own faith or on the universal priesthood of all believers in order to depreciate the office of preaching, to place obstacles in its way, or even to try to make it subordinate to itself.[19]

This "high" doctrine of the ministry does not in any way imply a "triumphalist" ecclesiology. The mandate of the church is to proclaim God's Word. This does not mean that the church exercises a universal lordship over the world. The Word proclaimed by the church, not the church itself, exercises this lordship:

> The word of God, proclaimed by virtue of a divine mandate, dominates and rules the entire world; the "community" which comes into being around this word does not dominate the world, but it stands entirely in the service of the fulfillment of the divine mandate.[20]

Bonhoeffer here introduces the concept of deputyship (*Stellvertretung*) and says:

> The Christian congregation stands at the point at which the whole world ought to be standing; to this extent it serves as deputy for the world and exists for the sake of the world.[21]

He draws a comparison between the church and its Lord, "who was Christ precisely in this, that He existed not for His own sake but wholly for the sake of the world."

In *Ethics* Bonhoeffer presents a very rich doctrine of the church. The church consists of those people in whom Christ has "taken form." It is a visible community and occupies "space" in the world, but it does so solely for the sake of the world. It exists to give testimony to Jesus Christ and thus to proclaim to the world that it really is the world redeemed by Christ and reconciled with God. It can give this testimony only if its members live in holiness, and where this testimony ceases to be given, the inner corrup-

tion of the community becomes manifest. The ministry is of divine institution, and the minister stands as the "spokesman of God before the
congregation," one to whom respect and reverence are due. The church
proclaims the Word of God, and this Word rules all creation. But the church
itself does not rule; its task is to serve. It acts as deputy for the world, and
"stands at the point at which the whole world ought to be standing." It
exists for the sake of the world, and in this follows Christ its Lord, who
himself existed for the sake of the world.

The fairly clear outlines of this ecclesiology become a little blurred
in the prison writings. These latter certainly show a rapid development in
Bonhoeffer's thought. There exists a continuity between the theology of
Ethics and that of the prison writings; yet it is clear that in the latter
Bonhoeffer is attempting to examine at a deeper level the relationship
between Christianity and the world. The thinking of the prison writings
remains exploratory. Bonhoeffer is not stating conclusions he has reached
after mature consideration, but is, as it were, thinking on paper. He is not
so much solving problems as asking questions. And since his theology is
essentially ecclesiastical, some of these questions inevitably concern the
church. Thus, in the famous letter of April 30, 1944, he asks: "What do a
church, a community, a sermon, a liturgy, a Christian life mean in a religionless world?"[22] In this letter he gives no reply (apart from the enigmatic
reference to the "secret discipline" and the "distinction between the penultimate and the ultimate"). But in the paper "Thoughts on the Baptism
of D.W.R.," written in May 1944, he expresses some views on the future
of the church. He writes of the difficulty of preaching to the contemporary
world the traditional doctrines of Christianity—"reconciliation and redemption, regeneration and the Holy Spirit, love of our enemies, cross
and resurrection, life in Christ and Christian discipleship"—and he goes on
to say that this difficulty results from the church's own attitude:

> Our church, which has been fighting in these years only for its self-
> preservation, as though that were an end in itself, is incapable of
> taking the word of reconciliation and redemption to mankind and the
> world. Our earlier words are therefore bound to lose their force and
> cease, and our being Christians today will be limited to two things:
> prayer and righteous action among men. All Christian thinking,
> speaking, and organizing must be born anew out of this prayer and
> action.[23]

What he contemplates is a temporary silencing of the church's preaching,
not because the mandate to preach has been taken away but because the
church, through her own defensive attitude, has lost her understanding of
the gospel. However, the silence will be temporary only:

By the time you have grown up, the church's form will have changed greatly. We are not yet out of the melting-pot, and any attempt to help the church prematurely to a new expansion of its organization will merely delay its conversion and purification. It is not for us to prophesy the day (though the day will come), when men will once more be called so to utter the word of God that the world will be changed and renewed by it. It will be a new language, perhaps quite non-religious, but liberating and redeeming—as was Jesus' language.[24]

In the "Outline for a Book" sent to Eberhard Bethge with the letter of August 3, 1944, Bonhoeffer makes the same charge that the church (i.e., the Confessing Church) has been content with a defensive attitude:

Generally in the Confessing Church: standing up for the church's 'cause', but little personal faith in Christ. 'Jesus' is disappearing from sight. Sociologically: no effect on the masses—interest confined to the upper and lower middle classes. A heavy incubus of difficult traditional ideas. The decisive factor: the church on the defensive. No taking risks for others.[25]

The third chapter of the "Outline" is entitled "Conclusions," and significantly all these conclusions refer to renewal in the church. The chapter begins:

The church is the church only when it exists for others. To make a start, it should give away all its property to those in need. The clergy should live solely on the free-will offerings of their congregations, or possibly engage in some secular calling. The church must share in the secular problems of ordinary human life, not dominating, but helping and serving. It must tell men of every calling what it means to live in Christ, to exist for others.[26]

This is his final word on the relationship between church and world. It must be a relationship of utterly unselfish service, after the pattern of Christ. In fact, the best summary of Bonhoeffer's mature ecclesiology is the memorable sentence: "The Church is the Church only when it exists for others."

To the end of his life, Bonhoeffer remained faithful to the insight he had received on his visit to Rome in 1924, namely the theological significance of the concept of "church." It was not simply that he showed himself continually concerned with questions of ecclesiology. It was more than that. He saw that the Christian is essentially a member of a community. And this also applies to the theologian—precisely as theologian. He must carry out his task as a member of the community, and for the benefit of the community. Theology belongs to the church as a whole and is not simply an academic exercise for the individual. In practice Bonhoeffer always carried out his theological work as one conscious of his community obligations. In his early writings he attempted to solve some of the major theological problems facing the church at the time: the reconciliation of revelation and sociology, the nature of revelation. During the period 1934-1939 he was outspoken in his defense of the Confessing Church. Then during the war years he examined at greater and greater depth the problem of the relationship between church and world. This, he came to see, was the major problem facing the church in the mid-twentieth century. And the postwar popularity of his writings has no doubt been due to the accuracy of this insight.

I am not suggesting that the concept of "church" occupied a central position in Bonhoeffer's "theological system." In fact, he had no theological system. He remained a theologian of insights, not a systematic thinker. Moreover, for him theology was very closely related to life; he lived his theology. If one asks what was the center of his life and thought, the answer is contained in the name Jesus Christ. In his early thinking he saw Christ as closely related to the church. In *Sanctorum Communio* the phrase that recurs again and again is: "Christ existing as community." But in this early period the relationship between church and world was scarcely considered. During the time of the church struggle, Bonhoeffer saw the church as fighting against the world, fighting for survival. But in the final period of his life he recognized that church and world are very closely related. And so the three central ideas of his mature theology seem to be: Christ, church, world. And "these three are one." The church consists of those human beings in whom Christ has taken form; and the church, hearing and proclaiming God's Word, stands in the place where the whole world is meant to stand and acts as deputy for the world. The church serves the world and summons it into the fellowship of Christ's body. By acting in this way, by trying to live entirely for others, the church is following more and more closely in the footsteps of its Lord, who himself came to serve and not to be served, and to give his life as a ransom for mankind.

Notes

1   Quoted in *DB*, p. 87.
2   *DB*, p. 92 (*DBET,* p. 42).
3   See *CC*, pp. 52-60.
4   See *WF*, pp. 93-94.
5   *AB*, p. 143.
6   *GS*, III, 245.
7   *GS*, III, 425.

8 *LPPE* (3rd ed. London: SCM Press, 1967), p. 383.
9 *E* (London: Collins, Fontana Library, 1964), p. 81.
10 *Ibid.*, p. 83.
11 *Ibid.*, p. 201.
12 *Ibid.*, p. 197.
13 *Ibid.*, p. 202.
14 *Ibid.*
15 *Ibid.*, p. 206.
16 *Ibid.*, p. 293.
17 Cf. the letter to E. Bethge of 28th August, 1941 in *GS*, II, 412-413.
18 *E*, pp. 293-294.
19 *Ibid.*, p. 294.
20 *Ibid.*, p. 300.
21 *Ibid.*, p. 301.
22 *LPPE*, p. 280.
23 *Ibid.*, p. 300.
24 *Ibid.*
25 *Ibid.*, p. 381.
26 *Ibid.*, pp. 382-383.

BONHOEFFER AND OUR
THEOLOGICAL EXISTENCE TODAY[1]

Henry Mottu

DIETRICH BONHOEFFER was an irregular theologian, that is, a scholar converted to the concrete reality of the church who became a political conspirator, a witness of the historical collapse of Christendom and its structures, a prophet of what he himself called "the future of the church," and a very fine political analyst who understood—even before and better than men like Niemöller and Karl Barth—that as early as 1933 Hitler meant nothing else than war—an insight which for us is something like an understatement, but which at that time was an extraordinary view.

I confess that reading Eberhard Bethge's biography of Bonhoeffer was a human as well as a theological shock for me. Admittedly, we have to resist the somewhat infantile temptation to identify with him by means of a doubtful psychological transference; nevertheless, instead of showing the different "dangers" of a given attitude or position—as is done often enough by our professors—let us have the courage *not* to identify with him. Complete identification, by the way, would be impossible, because history never repeats itself in the same way. Rather, following Bonhoeffer, let us perceive the dangers and listen to his voice, drawing conclusions for ourselves as teachers or as students.

Therefore, I propose to develop four main foci:

1) the courage to be one-sided;
2) the quest for an institutional counter-model;
3) the search for an authentic language;
4) the global character of theology.

I. The Courage to be One-sided

Bonhoeffer was a seer. According to him, theology is prophetic or it is no theology at all. During the three main stages of his life, his theological reason, like a counter point stretching the given reality in which he lived, always functioned in direct dialectical connection with the given situation and its future dangers.

As Bethge powerfully reminds us, at the very moment when almost all others forgot the church, the concrete community through which every theological statement becomes either true or false, Bonhoeffer almost single-handedly rediscovered it as the river of fire for every theology as early as the mid-1920s, expounded it in his first work, *Sanctorum Communio*, and this in opposition to the liberal tradition represented by Troeltsch, Seeberg, and Harnack. Thus the classical passage in *Act and Being*:

> God is not free *of* man but *for* man. Christ is the Word of his freedom. God is *there*, which is to say: not in eternal non-objectivity but (looking ahead for the moment) "haveable", graspable in his Word within the Church. Here a substantial comes to supplant the formal understanding of God's freedom.[2]

Further, at the very moment when almost all others forgot—during the crucial years of the church struggle of 1932/33—that Jesus Christ is the living center of every church which pretends to be "the church," that Jesus Christ alone, the Jew, the prophet assassinated under Pontius Pilate, is the first and last criterion of the church's confession and witness, Bonhoeffer converted once more to Christ and costly grace. Bethge calls this period "The Theologian becomes a Christian."[3] Bonhoeffer wrote to his brother, the religiously sceptical physicist Karl Friedrich, in 1935:

> It may be that in many things I may seem to you rather fanatical and crazy. I myself am sometimes afraid of this. But I know that, if I were "more reasonable", I should in honour bound be compelled to give up the whole of my theology. When I first began, I imagined it quite otherwise—perhaps as a more academic matter. Now something very different has come of it. I now believe that I know at last that I am at least on the right track—for the first time in my life. And that often makes me very glad. . . . I believe I know that inwardly I shall be really clear and honest with myself only when I have begun to take seriously the Sermon on the Mount. That is the only source of power capable of blowing up the whole phantasmagoria once and for all. . . .
>
> I still cannot really believe you genuinely believe all these ideas to be so completely crazy. There are things for which an uncompromising stand is worthwhile. And it seems to me that peace and social justice, or Christ himself, are such things.[4]

Finally, at the very moment when almost all others considered the task of the Confessing Church accomplished, and felt that it was sufficient that the churches had been able to remain "intact" (that is, had been preserved only for themselves against the Nazi regime) he recalled, almost alone, that the confession of Jesus Christ as the only Lord requires a political commitment—and in this case, an underground commitment, one-sided and secular. *God is where men are.* The object of God's love is the world; thus the church has to completely reconsider its structures and its witness. Bonhoeffer was in a troop train on his way to Munich, after the meeting with Bishop Bell in Sweden, when he wrote in June 1942:

> My activities, which have lately been very much in the worldly sector, give me plenty to think about. I am surprised that I live, and can go on living, for days without the Bible; I should feel it to be auto-suggestion, not obedience, if I were to force myself to read it. I understand that such auto-suggestion might be, and is, a great help, but I am afraid that for me it might mean adulterating a genuine experience and not getting genuine help after all. When I open the Bible again, it is ever so new and cheering, and I should like just to preach. I know that I only need to open my own books to hear what there is to be said against all this. And I do not want to justify myself, for I realize that "spiritually" I have had much richer times. But I feel how my resistance to everything "religious" grows. Often as far as an instinctive revulsion, which is certainly not good. I am not religious by nature. But I always have to be thinking of God and of Christ, and I set great store by genuineness, life, freedom, and compassion. Only I find the religious trappings so uncomfortable. Do you understand? These ideas and insights are not new at all, but as I think I shall now be able to see my way through them, I am letting things take their course without resistance. That is how I understand my present activity in the worldly sector.[5]

Indeed, at every stage of his life Bonhoeffer was prophetic, because he was one-sided and precisely never "reasonable." And he was one-sided because he was a truly dialectic theologian—perhaps the only true disciple of dialectic theology. Indeed, only one-sided positions are true and effective and realistic in the long run. This is, I think, the greatest point we can and must learn from Bethge's biography. Thus a theological statement, according to Bonhoeffer, is not a mixture of this and that, not a weak melting pot—in academic English, a weak eclecticism—of a recognition of this fact or that fact with the addition that, of course, all things are far more "complex" than that; a theological statement is not therefore a blending of opposites (*complexio oppositorum*), where all things are grey and where every position neutralizes the former in a weak and nowadays more and more inadequate pluralism and atomism. Rather, a theological statement as a theological communal existence is the attentive and patient but decided search for the confessing stance (the *status confessionis*) here and now. Today one must learn again to call a spade a spade: imperialism, imperialism; injustice, injustice; what is unacceptable, unacceptable; and to draw all the consequences of such an insight. As early as 1933, Bonhoeffer insisted that one is either National Socialist *or* Christian. For us today this is almost a commonplace; but at that time it was exceptional. I am afraid that what has become a commonplace for us because it concerns the past, if transferred to our own situation as a statement about imperialism in our own time, would become an object of scandal. In other words, the hour approaches— and has already come—when the commonplace of the past will be transformed into the stumbling block of the present.

Now, the secret of Bonhoeffer's insight into political matters is none other than its prophetic, one-sided, dialectical theology. Today we do not have to be converted to Bonhoeffer, but rather converted once again to our primary task: God's Word within the concrete. As André Dumas emphasizes in his book:

> This is why Bonhoeffer's attitude at the beginning and end of his life remains so important for us. He recognized that neither life in the church, i.e., piety, nor action in the world, i.e., politics, can exempt us from a rigorous pursuit of the knowledge of God.[6]

Yes, neither the *praxis pietatis* (the worship) nor the political praxis (commitment) relieves us from the rigor of the knowledge of God; not only do they not relieve us from it, but precisely in our time do they compel us to it.

II. The Quest for the Institutional Counter-Model

In his winter course of 1932/33 on the history of systematic theology in the twentieth century Bonhoeffer concluded his lectures:

> Proclaiming the concrete Christ always means proclaiming him in a concrete situation. What is the foundation on which ethics can be constructed? Where is the principle of concretion in the general injunction to obey? The reason why our churchly pronouncements are so lacking in force is that they are half-way between general principles and the concrete situation.[7]

And in a letter of September 11, 1934 to his friend Erwin Sutz, some months before accepting the proposal of the Confessing Church to take up teaching at the newly founded underground seminary at Finkenwalde, he reveals "that he was in a state of mental flux, though his comments on the *place* of theology in the new Germany are far from equivocal":

> I no longer believe in the University, and never really have believed in it—a fact which used to rile you. Young theologians ought now to be trained throughout in conventual seminaries where the pure doctrine, the Sermon on the Mount and worship are taken seriously as they never are (and in present circumstances couldn't be) at university. It is high time we threw off a restraint grounded in theology— which is, after all, only fear—towards the conduct of the State.[8]

Berlin or Finkenwalde? It seems to me that our lives will be more and more explicitly centered on what is becoming more and more urgent today, namely, the creation and the theological structuring of counter-models on ecclesiastical, political, and university levels. What would such counter-models look like? Nobody can tell exactly today. But it is sure that they will include different emphases:

—the achievement of *one* ethical task (the praxis)
—doctrinal unity (the theory)
—a community of resources in whatever form they may be (including money)
—the reassertion of the whole human being

The new theology is still only a theology; we now need a new way of life, a world-wide adventure worth living for and dying for. People do not die for an idea; they die for their brothers and sisters. For the moment I have nothing else to say—nothing more, but nothing less.

III. The Search for an Authentic Language

According to Bethge again, "In contrast to *Sanctorum Communio* and *Act and Being*, which used a conceptual language taken over from others"—and I would add, taken over from a borrowed academic language—in *The Cost of Discipleship* and *Life Together* Bonhoeffer stated "in his own terminology the contributions he wished to make to theology and the Church."[9] Finally, the *Letters and Papers From Prison* marks a further step in Bonhoeffer's search for an authentic language by expressing his own political fighting as well as his new views on a nonreligious interpretation of the gospel. The academic language, the confessing language, the political and so-called nonreligious language—these are, at the level of his search for his proper language, the three stages of this man Bethge calls the theologian, the Christian, and the contemporary. I have already alluded to the transition from the theologian to the Christian; but one must not forget that the Christian in turn became a contemporary, that the pacifist of Fanö (1934) became the man of the resistance of 1943, and that the confessing Bonhoeffer became the activist. To separate one of these three stages from the others is, in my view, to be completely mistaken, for such a progression in his life as well as his theological language does not mean an evolution, but rather a dialectic. Thus nowadays we are not only questioned by the Bonhoeffer of the death of the God of Christian ideology but also and simultaneously by the confessing Bonhoeffer. Let us not assassinate Bonhoeffer a second time by making of him the insignificant interpreter of the so-called post-Christian era, while forgetting his fight *against* the bourgeoisie and *for* a confessing church because it is embarrassing to us for obvious reasons. While the so-called new hermeneutics goes on, private property, the academy, and imperialism also continue as if nothing has happened. In a fascinating part of his book, called "The Transition of the Christian to the Contemporary"[10] (which the English translation minimizes with "The Contemporary Christian"), Bethge writes:

> The year 1932 had put Bonhoeffer into a world where things were comparatively clear-cut, where it was a matter of confessing and denying, and therefore in his case of the one Church for the whole world and against its betrayal to nationalist particularism. The end of such a road was bound to be a fate like that of Paul Schneider. In 1939 he entered the difficult world of assessing what was expedient, of success and failure, of tactics and camouflage. The certainty of his calling in 1932 now changed into the acceptance of the uncertain, the incomplete, and the provisional. The new call demanded quite a different sacrifice, the sacrifice even of a Christian reputation.[11]

But my concern here is to emphasize the pedagogical significance of Bonhoeffer's search for his own theological expression. In being a passionately attentive student of the Word of God, he was, for this reason, a truly free man; he never was really anyone's disciple, even Harnack's or Barth's. He always remained himself precisely because of his concentration on the only subject matter which is necessary: listening to the Word within the given situation. In this connection, what does it mean to learn, if not to seek to appropriate for oneself the materials which teachers propose to us, and in turn, what does it mean to teach, if not to allow others to find themselves and their own expression of faith? I think more and more that the teaching relationship must today be reorganized in connection with what Bonhoeffer called the risk of "saying controversial things,"[11] so that the teaching relationship henceforth consists not only of a confrontation between teachers and students—although such a fruitful confrontation will necessarily be maintained—but also of a confrontation of both teachers and students with the risk of saying "controversial things" today. Thus we are able to discover together that doing theology today means accepting as a body—as a community of faith—taking the risk of becoming a "controversial" institution. And the teaching relationship could again become something dynamic and fruitful. Only those who are getting down to "the serious problems of life" today will become controversial; in turn, only a controversial theology is a theology that can really help people—whether teachers or students—in the serious problems of life today. We have to learn again to state clearly the life questions of university, church, and Christian life as the only true terrain of theological thinking today:

> The church must come out of its stagnation. We must move out again into the open air of intellectual discussion with the world, and risk

saying controversial things, if we are to get down to the serious problems of life.[13]

IV. The Global Character of Theology

Theology has a global character, a global theme, which again and again overthrows specialties and specialists, which again and again upsets the best experts and the most "competent" people. This theme is Jesus Christ, his work and his person, as the polemical encounter of God's reality with the reality of the world; it is Jesus Christ, the assassinated prophet, the priest charged with the fault, the Lord. Such a theme is synthetic, and thus the demand of Christianity is total, nonnegotiable. Such a theme is a unifying theme: nothing escapes it or everything escapes it. If there is among us and in us the slightest domain (money, for instance) which does not obey it, then all among us and in us becomes untrue. This is the theological reason we ask for interdisciplinary learning and teaching today. Theology is dead if it accepts being performed in isolated domains and fields without any center, without any epistemological center of decision. The *Römerbrief* of Barth was already a synthetic work of an exegete who was more than a pure exegete, of a dogmatician who was also an exegete—a work which therefore profoundly upset the professional exegetes. Jülicher thought he was executing Barth by speaking contemptuously of his work: "Much, perhaps even very much, may someday be learned from [Barth's] book for the understanding of our age, but scarcely anything new for the understanding of the 'historical' Paul."[14] But without realizing it, Jülicher paid the greatest possible tribute to synthetic interpretation, Barth's theological and global exegesis.

And following Barth, Bonhoeffer always stayed more or less between two poles in *Sanctorum Communio:* he tried to unite what he learned from dialectical theology with sociology. Hence the remark of his cousin, Hans Christoph von Hase, in 1930: "There will not be many who really understand it, the Barthians won't because of the sociology, and the sociologists won't because of Barth."[15] He was to encounter the same misfortune when he proposed his theological exegesis of Genesis 1-3, entitled *Creation and Fall.*

Bonhoeffer's incursion into the field of the Old Testament specialists was taken amiss. The *Theologischen Blätter* said: "At all events, it is no credit to Old Testament specialists that nowadays non-specialists should be the first to attempt to present us with such an exegesis of Genesis 1-3." As in *Sanctorum Communio*, Bonhoeffer had again fallen between two stools. The exegetes regarded the work as systematics and the systematicians regarded it as exegesis. The former were indignant and the latter took no notice.[16]

V. Conclusion

For all these reasons, I invite you to recognize Bonhoeffer as the future theological master whom we urgently need today. I have the impression that, despite all the literature set down about him (often isolating one aspect of his work from its totality), we are, by considering his life and his death, less post-Bonhoefferian than pre-Bonhoefferian. Still we have a lot of things to rethink and to do until we become able to live our theological existence with him today.

Further, I invite you to remember that Bonhoeffer's work and life was and still is a controversial event. Perhaps like the Idiot of Dostoevski, he never was really understood; theologians never have known what to do with the two of them. In succession, he was considered an Anabaptist and fanatic during his time with the Confessing Church, as an obscure pietist during his time at Finkenwalde, as a traitor during the war, and as an atheist in his latest period. Fanatic, pietist, traitor, atheist—all these characteristics together were and still are the theologian for whom we thank God today. For let us not forget that this theologian was never really recognized for what he was. There is something *a posteriori* incomprehensible for us, but unfortunately historically true, in the fact that Bonhoeffer's own church in Berlin-Brandenburg, and especially a group of Bielefeld pastors, "appealed to the Bonhoeffer family to protest against the naming of streets for Paul Schneider and Dietrich Bonhoeffer among those named for members of the resistance, *'because we don't want the names of our colleagues, who were killed for their faith, lumped together with political martyrs.'* "[17]

Such things can very easily happen again in the future. Therefore, I urge that we recognize Bonhoeffer for what he was, a political martyr because of his theological existence today, and a true Christian martyr because of his political engagement. Thus we cannot isolate from each other the three elements of his life: the theologian, the Christian, and the contemporary.

Notes

1 This address was given at a service to mark the 25th anniversary of the execution on April 9, 1945 of Dietrich Bonhoeffer (Union Theological Seminary, New York, April 8, 1970).

2 *AB*, pp. 90f., quoted in *DBET*, p. 98.

3 *DBET*, pp. 153ff.

4 *DBET*, p. 155.

5 *DBET*, p. 626.

6 André Dumas, *Dietrich Bonhoeffer: Theologian of Reality*, trans. Robert McAfee Brown (New York: Macmillan, 1971), p. 116.

    7 *DBET*, p. 140.
    8 *DBET*, p. 334.
    9 *DBET*, p. 130.
   10 *DBET*, pp. 580ff.
   11 *DBET*, p. 582. .
   12 *LPPE* (SCM, 1967), p. 378.
   13 *Ibid.*
   14 James M. Robinson, ed., *The Beginnings of Dialectical Theology*, Vol. I
(Richmond: John Knox Press, 1968), p. 21.
   15 *DBET*, pp. 58-59.
   16 *DBET*, p. 163.
   17 *DBET*, p. 834.

CONVIVIALITY AND COMMON SENSE:
THE MEANING OF CHRISTIAN COMMUNITY
FOR DIETRICH BONHOEFFER

Thomas I. Day

DIETRICH BONHOEFFER'S best-known letters are the least understood of his writings. Their lapidary formulations have served as springboards for sundry leaps in a variety of directions. If I ask you to consider them once again, it is to reread them in Bonhoeffer's context in order to see the direction in which he was moving when his penultimate questions suddenly became his ultimate ones.

The considerations that follow are drawn from my study of the meaning of Christian community for Bonhoeffer's ethics. It focuses on that point where ecclesiology and ethics converge, where churches become responsible, and where mature Christians remember and realize who they are.

I share with Bonhoeffer the conviction that all theology is ecclesial thought and that genuine theological statements can be understood only when set within and filled out by their specific social context. His recognition of the concrete communal locus of Christian existence and theological reflection is the richest and most radical of his insights. Its neglect has made of his theology a Ouija board; as many as have put their hand to it have read different messages, mutually contradictory and generally confusing.

Many have seen that Jesus Christ is the center of his thought. The best commentators recognize that for Bonhoeffer the location of this Christ-center in our world is the Christian community, the real church. However, in their desire to prove the continuity of his thought against eclectic interpreters who luxuriate in one period or emphasis and write off the rest as passing phases, *Schwärmerei*, or prison psychosis, even the best theological interpreters have stressed conceptual Christological continuities instead of their shifting social implications. Bonhoeffer is shoved back behind the academic podium he had left, or back into a church structure he had rejected.

213

Increased political engagement had concretized Bonhoeffer's theological concerns and facilitated his writing. Instead of emigrating as he had in 1933 to London, or immigrating from the political chaos to a rural community life like that of Finkenwalde, in 1940 he went into political incognito in the very midst of his familial world. When the Gestapo moved against their (correctly) distrusted rival intelligence service on April 5, 1943, he was thrown into jail. Bonhoeffer's imprisonment has been unduly romanticized. After ten days of solitary confinement that was cruel indeed, his family connections became known, and there began a swelling stream of privileges and amenities. His physical needs reasonably well met, the major problem was his experience of abrupt separation from his people and his past. His solitary existence was nonsensical.

I. Saving the Past

Bonhoeffer responded by structuring his isolation toward remembering, recouping the past. His whole existence was waiting, and his memory held the sole promise of a future. To remember the social bonds that defined his personal existence was a matter of identity or chaos, purpose or anomie. He tried to recapture his family experience in a play, then a novel. He read nineteenth-century literature and history. His study regimen centered on the Bible. The Old Testament, whose message resists "spiritualizing," was the context in and through which the New Testament should be approached. It proffers no religion of deliverance from the world, but a message of deliverance in this world, as does the New Testament insistence that "the Word became flesh."

Earthy Ethics

That God was in Jesus meant for Bonhoeffer that God suffers because of the misery in the world. To believe and to be Christian is to go to God in his suffering. The interpretation of Jesus' gospel consists in the articulation of this command. The primary task of Christian hermeneutics is ethical clarification. An immediate consequence of Bonhoeffer's Old Testament reading was his strong, new affirmation of the bodily reality of human community. For instance, the best Christological interpretation of the Song of Songs is simply reading it for what it is, an earthly love song. The flesh-and-blood needs of people determine what it means to tell the truth.

Bonhoeffer's ethical arguments had always been deductive. Now he began to stress exact observation and sensitivity. The major ethical problem was not maliciousness but stupidity and lack of perception, which he saw more as a sociological than psychological problem. Human solidarity is the source of sensitivity, creative imagination, inner alertness, and outer perceptiveness. Neutrality begets stupidity, solidarity begets insight.

Bonhoeffer was still trying to overcome the static disjunctions which spatial imagery so etched in his thought, looking for a way to overcome the distance between the "two realms" while saving the distinction. His affirmation of the earthiness of human life and the humanness of corporate existence led him beyond refurbishing his notions of the four mandates and his earlier distinction between the ultimate and the penultimates. He discovered a musical figure to express the multidimensionality of human life. Instead of the diametrical opposition between eros and agape, he understood love as a polyphony, in which the *cantus firmus* of God's agapeic love supports and pervades the whole, while fugal counterpoints of earthly love rise and fall in changing melody. This insight brought him to the threshold of what Bethge has termed the "new theology."

Bonhoeffer's remained an ethics for the elite. His questions were real for his own social stratum of academic aristocracy, whose failures had contributed to the Nazis' taking of power and who were divided and unwilling to act to change the situation. His ethical task was urging action rather than clarifying options. Not abuse of power but failure to take action was the greatest sin. He looked for the rise of a new elite who would rule well.

II. Shaping the Future

For the first year of his imprisonment, Bonhoeffer's whole existence consisted in waiting, ever waiting, as each hope for an early trial date and release was in turn dashed. He was dismayed by his lawyers' delaying tactics. His unrest peaked in December 1943 and continued through March of the next year, greatly hindering his study. In April 1944 he received word of the lawyers' definitive decision to put off his trial until after the coming putsch. Imminent release was no longer even a remote possibility. He had to reckon with a long spell of prison. Unable to change this, he accepted it and settled down to work.

After the long months of unproductivity, he now left behind his stalled literary attempts to recapture the past, and he felt a new surge of creativity.[1] Instead of nineteenth-century literature, he concentrated on social history, requesting works of Dilthey, Harnack, and Ortega y Gasset. He threw himself into an attempt to incorporate his and his people's past in "a thorough preparation for *a new beginning*, which would be characterized by marriage, peace and a new task."[2]

The church to which he had committed himself was clearly unfit for the coming tasks; it had to be born anew in praying and acting for justice.[3] He felt himself and his people thrown back to "the beginning of understanding."[4] His letters now overflowed with new, sharper questions. And though he could not answer them all, he instinctively knew that they were the coming questions, questions that would draw him ahead into the future and would also help to draw a future.[5]

He was kept informed of the timetable to inaugurate that future, that is, of the plans for the coup d'etat. When the putsch of July 20, 1944, failed, he shared the new danger to his family and friends. At very best, he could not hope for release prior to an Allied victory, which would be "total" and destructive to a degree as yet unimagined. His reaction was to use the time remaining to prepare a programmatic manifesto for a German church beyond ground zero, a study of not more than a hundred pages, which would take stock of the situation, inquire in what Christian faith consists, and draw its implications for a postwar church. During the months of August and September 1944 he did almost nothing else than work on the project.[6] When his situation was made more precarious by the Gestapo's discovery of a cache of documents implicating Dohnanyi and himself, among others, he rid his cell of illegal materials, sending many books and papers home for safekeeping. But the manuscript of his project he kept even when he was moved to the SS prison. The manuscript, like his body, is gone. We are left with the outline within which he had begun to frame the questions and insights which fill his letters to Bethge.[7] It would be presumptuous to try to rewrite the lost book. Still, we are well advised to study the new themes of his later letters in the framework within which he was working.[8] For this shows the direction which Bonhoeffer himself intended his thought to take.

Many have spoken of a caesura occurring in Bonhoeffer's thought in April 1944.[9] This unfortunate expression poorly characterizes the change which did take place. In the very letter which proclaims the "new beginning," Bonhoeffer wrote:

> I have the impression, however remarkable this may sound, that my whole life has proceeded in a straight-line continuity, at least in what concerns the outer direction of life. It has been an uninterrupted experiential enrichment, for which I can only be thankful.[10]

And a fortnight later he added:

> I have certainly learned much, but I think that I have not changed much. . . . The times which we are now living through will not constitute a break in the passive sense. Earlier I sometimes wished for such a break. Today I think otherwise. Continuity with one's own past is also a great gift. . . . Everything seems to me to be purposeful, necessary, straightforward, directed from on high.[11]

Bonhoeffer could now calmly assert the continuity that he had so recently struggled to retain. This continuity was the ground which he needed to feel beneath his feet. With the past secure, he could turn to the future, and he did. His shift of weight was slight, but he began moving. Peter Berger has well noted that "conversions" often consist in very small movements, but they are movements that cross some socially significant boundary and thereby take on the nature of vital watersheds, requiring almost inevitably the revision of one's previous biography.[12]

Whether we find such an epochal switch in Bonhoeffer's month of April 1944 depends on the significance we accord his slight shift. It is indeed a new beginning and one that would have changed his future life, though he did not find that it necessitated the revision of his biography. In Bonhoeffer's—and my—estimation, more important shifts had preceded this one.[13] And I see more carry-over of the reactionary elements in his thought than I had hoped for. However, more important than chronicling the changes (not caesurae) in Bonhoeffer's thought and measuring them on some kind of "Richter scale" is seeing how this fundamentally conservative person won ground on which to launch into the future, not by rejecting but by appropriating his past.

> Things against which one has desensitized oneself will be soon forgotten. Other things, which one has consciously or unconsciously worked through, will never be forgotten. Rather, these strong experiences take on the solid form of clear knowledge, purposes and plans, and as such they retain their meaning for future life.[14]

The Intent of Bonhoeffer's New Project

The letters from Bonhoeffer's final months in Tegel Prison are the best known of his writings. Their scintillating new thoughts have been used as cudgels in many an auto-da-fé aimed against the church that outlived him. They have become suitable indices of general theological knowledge in American seminaries. What they meant and what they mean remain contested questions, usually lumped into one, thus confusing matters the more. Most often forgotten is that these new insights led Bonhoeffer to devote the last months of his life to the writing of a theological tract for the Christian church after Germany's crushing defeat. Precisely because the church was so important to him, he kept the manuscript with him to continue working on it, and with him it was lost. However, the outline of the tract we do have shows us the directions and intent of the fragmentary excursions and exciting notions in the prison letters which otherwise seem to lead in all directions.

Misleading, too, is the catchy triptych of a thesis that in an early period Bonhoeffer gave to theologians, telling them that their subject was the church; in a second he spoke to the churchmen, telling them that their subject was the world; and in a third he addressed the world with the message that its subject was Christ. Though most interpreters reject Hanfried Müller's contention that Bonhoeffer moved "from the church to the world,"[15] they remain influenced by its force. They continue to interpret Bonhoeffer in the spatial categories he was trying to get beyond, speaking, for instance, of his early ecclesiology's "giving ground to" or "receding behind" his oncoming Christology.[16] Thus they contribute to a false picture of the secularization of Bonhoeffer. He is seen as moving from being a theologian of the established church to being a Christian in a minority opposition church, and later to being a contemporary in conspiracy.

This is too simple. It makes of Bonhoeffer an ideologist of each of his successive positions. He was more a Jeremiah than a court prophet.[17] His early high ecclesiology was indeed staid and conservative. It was drawn in the clear knowledge that the Prussian church did not measure up to it. It was a challenge whose consequence would be his steadfast opposition to that church. Neither did his increasingly Christological ecclesiology ever find a home in the Confessing Church. It was all too critical, even among the ever-decreasing minority of "Dahlemites." Nor was he in place in the conspiracy. Among lawyers and soldiers he was a pastor, hoping to be able to minister again but in a new church situation which the conspiracy would help shape. Thus there came out of his experience in political resistance and prison a new project.

Facing the imminent and total defeat that loomed as terminator of the past and harbinger of a future yet to be formed, he did not continue to work on his magnum opus, an ethics for the new age, but began to write a short ecclesiological treatise, which he saw as "calling for and to a certain extent anticipating" his continued work on *Ethics*.[18] The first priority was to shape in Christ a community in which further reflection on the ethical implications of the gospel would be possible and meaningful.

Thus Jørgen Glenthøj is right in pointing out the continuity of Bonhoeffer's later thought with the commission he had received at Sigtuna from Bishop Bell to prepare for the reshaping of church and social structures after the war.[19] His new project went far beyond the conservative restoration which he had proposed in the Freiburg Circle[20] and the minimal conditions which he had delineated in his 1942 proposals for church reorganization after a coup. Then he had still hoped for a conditional surrender and an intact Germany. The worsened situation demanded, and enabled, more radical measures. His tract drew conclusions in the light of his own and his people's recent experience, conclusions which he had not been ready to draw during the church struggle and which still somewhat frightened him.[21]

It is not the point of this essay to discuss in detail the many notions which found pregnant expression in his final letters and which have become the trademarks of sundry Bonhoefferisms. Nor is it my intent to blunt his incisive thought by reminding people of its church concern. Some "radical theologians" are suspicious of any such reminders, and not always without cause.[22] However, attempts to avoid the sharply critical force of Bonhoef-

fer's thought are easy to spot by their ignoring of the intention of his final
reflections. Only by seeing them in their social context and social intention
can we assess the force and direction of their cut and find the handle by
which to wield them honestly today. Bonhoeffer was clearly planning to·
take the conceptual scalpel to the body of the ecclesiastical establishment,
and "in this way to perform a service for the future of the church." Whence
the outline of his project and our next paragraphs: 1) taking stock of Christianity; 2) what is Christian faith today; 3) what does this mean *for the
church?*[23]

Taking Stock of Christianity

"But where is God in your system?" Napoleon had asked, and his wizard
answered, "Sir, I find no need for that hypothesis." Taking an honest look
at his own world, Bonhoeffer realized that it was getting on quite well
without the God preached by the Christian churches. In his historical studies he had traced a movement of secular autonomy from Herbert of Cherbury's postulation that the truths of faith could be adequately known by
reason.[24] Subsequent to the thirteenth century came increasingly liberated
reason's discovery of the laws of nature and the development of the autonomous sciences of physics and politics, art and ethics. Such disparate
notions as Nicolas of Cusa's teaching that the universe was infinite, Machiavelli's basing politics on "reasons of state" instead of moral theology,
and Hugo Grotius' notion of a natural law of nations which would remain
valid "even if God did not exist"—all these moved people in the same
direction of worldly autonomy. Deism generalized the particular conclusions: The world exists as a well-functioning mechanism without the need
of God's intervention. Pantheism, on the other hand, made God everything
and insignificant, all and nothing special. As the positive sciences explained
more and more the mysteries of nature and even human society, the God
of mystery was banned from more and more segments of human life. And
since Feuerbach, there is no need for God as a working hypothesis even
in philosophical and religious questions.[25] The empirical and philosophical
study of religious phenomena can explain them quite as well without the
God-premise as with it.[26] Thus it seemed for Bonhoeffer "a matter of
intellectual honesty to drop this working hypothesis, or to do away with it
as much as possible."[27] He saw the massive rejection of religion among
intellectuals of his own class as a sign of the inbreaking of a "completely
religionless era."[28]

The churches, whose whole proclamation had been aimed at fulfilling
men's natural religious need,[29] and which for nineteen hundred years had
considered Christianity as a form—albeit the highest—of religion, continued to fight a losing battle to secure room for religion in the world or
against it.[30] Particularly since the Enlightenment, apologetics had attempted

to show God as the answer to the ultimate, that is, still unanswered human questions.[31] Thus the church and the theologians strove to justify their existence.[32] But as the boundaries of human knowledge were pushed ever further, the "God of the gaps" was exiled to more remote reaches. Then came Protestant pietism as a last try to save God a place in the inner life.[33] Sensitive persons were offered the choice of "Jesus, or doubt!"[34] "The psyche became the modern pastor's hunting ground."[35] In a kind of "religious blackmail,"[36] troubled people in their weakness were overpowered by God the Answer.

But Christianity has no particularly forceful answers. "Christian answers are just as unconvincing, or just as good, as other possible solutions."[37] This conviction of Bonhoeffer is too often overlooked. Jesus did not come to provide answers to ultimate questions.[38] He did not *solve* suffering and dying; he suffered and died. Where human knowledge runs out, there is no Christian revelation waiting any more than when human strength runs out is there a *deus ex machina* hovering above.[39] Jesus died asking why![40]

Bonhoeffer realized that the church's attempts to keep humanity under its tutelage were doomed to failure. Pietism would smother in its murky inner world.[41] Even the Confessing Church had, in its fight to save itself, become nothing more than conservative reaction, incapable of bearing Jesus' word of reconciliation to people in the world.[42] The church had to get out of its self-centered stagnation and look beyond itself into the world,[43] where many good people are interested in what the church is about, where the arts and sciences are looking for their source.[44] But Christians must stop pretending that they understand the world better than the world understands itself.[45] Humanity is of age. Secularists are looking to the Christians for solidarity, not tutelage. They have rightly rejected the Christian religion which kept them too long in subservience.

I shall comment below on some of the limitations of Bonhoeffer's stocktaking, after the argument has been presented.

What Did Bonhoeffer Really Believe?

Bonhoeffer cast his project in the Hegelian form of thesis, antithesis, and synthesis. After his situational analysis, the second chapter was to have been an attempt to say "what Christian faith really is"[46] in the world he had described, to speak of "Christ in the world come of age."[47] He did not intend to draw up a creed which the church could use for advertising or for defining its own limits.[48] All too long the church's theologians had been telling people what they ought to believe. The question was, "What do we really believe? That is, so that our lives depend on it?"[49] Surely not every word of the Apostles' Creed, nor the sacred slogans which have mummified misunderstandings between Christians of yore and continue to hinder ecumenical cooperation today! Bonhoeffer was certain that biblical faith did not hinge on the questions of controversy between Lutherans and Calvinists, nor between Protestants and Catholics. Nor would it be nourished by rolling them out again. He thought that Confessing Churchmen had followed Karl Barth in granting those slogans too much importance, asking ever about "the faith of the church" rather than honestly examining their own beliefs. He respected the dialectical theologians' inability to state simply what they believed, since they did not themselves control the tenets of their faith. However, he contended that Protestants cannot simply identify themselves with the church so as to hide behind it.[50]

"The question which won't stop bothering me is what Christianity is, or who Christ really is for us today."[51] "Today" sharpened the question which had shaped Bonhoeffer's 1933 Christology lectures entitled "Who is Christ for us?" The intervening decade had changed not only the context of the question but the question itself, as we shall see from the answer it now evoked.

Who is Christ in our world come of age? Who is God? Bonhoeffer's addressing of the question began by his accepting Feuerbach's liberating critique of religion. "A general belief in God as omnipotence, etc. . . . is no authentic experience of God, but a bit of extrapolated world."[52] The stopgap God[53] whom we project after our own needs and desires has nothing to do with Jesus' God.[54] Jahweh does not respond to, but overturns and redirects, our whole human existence. We meet him in Jesus, whose whole existence was for others.[55] Faith in Jesus' God is not primarily an intellectual conviction nor the acceptance of some statement of "truth." Faith in Jesus and his God consists in sharing a new life of being for others. God became human in Jesus. "The transcendent is not the unattainable, the eternal, but the present given, tangible neighbor."[56] Jesus' God has nothing to do with "world forces," best imaginable beings, etc. He is

> God in human form! Not in the form of an animal symbolizing the terrible, chaotic, remote, abhorrent, etc., as in oriental religions; nor in the notions of the absolute, metaphysical, infinite, etc.; nor in the divine-human form of "autonomous man"; but as the "man for others!" and therefore the crucified.[57]

To be Christian is not to be in some specific way religious, but to participate fully in human life, to live as Jesus teaches us to live, that is, "in God and with God, as though God did not exist,"[58] "which is to say" (continues Daniel Berrigan), "as though God were indeed God, not score keeper, Band-Aid, bonbon, celestial oracle, Good Humor man."[59]

Unlike the gods of respectable religions, Jesus' God, Immanuel, God with us, is God who abandons us, as he did Jesus.[60]

God is powerless and weak in the world, and in this way alone is he with us and helps us. Matthew 8, 17 makes it very clear that Christ does not help in his omnipotence, but in the force of his weakness, his suffering. Here lies the decisive difference from all religions. Religiosity sends a person in need to the power of God in the world. God is *Deus ex machina*. The Bible refers one to the powerlessness and suffering of God. Only the suffering God can help.[61]

In the myriad concrete forms of belief in God related by the New Testament, Bonhoeffer saw the one common element of "participation in God's suffering in Christ,"[62] "participation in the suffering of God in secular life."[63] The difference between Christians and pagans is simply that Christians stand by God in his suffering.[64] Humankind is called to come to the aid of God, to share in his plight, to take up worldly responsibility to alleviate suffering. Christian belief frees from all false religious inhibitions, for social responsibility. Bonhoeffer still took literally Jesus' definitive statement, "When you have done it for one of the least of these my little ones, you have done it for me."

The emphasis on suffering was not born of masochism but of Bonhoeffer's realistic appraisal of what the immediate present held for him and his people. He did not propose suffering as a good in itself, nor as a method of being for others; but he knew that to be for others would entail suffering. Neither was his outlook defeatist. For Jesus' God, who needed all the help he could get, was in his very weakness the Lord of the earth,[65] and what he was up to was the establishment of his kingdom[66] right here below in the midst of human suffering,

> . . . a kingdom stronger than war and danger; a kingdom of power and force; a kingdom which will be for one person eternal horror and judgement, for another eternal happiness and justice; not an inner kingdom, but over the whole world and over the earth; not transitory, but eternal; a kingdom which makes its own way and which calls men to prepare the way for it, a kingdom for which it's worth committing one's life.[67]

Bonhoeffer hoped that a coming generation might be able to see more of that kingdom's justice and peace in the world.[68] In the meantime, Jesus' God might get some of the help he needs, if the misleading religious trappings of Christianity were helped to fall away.

But if Jesus' God is such a poor idol and Christianity basically so areligious, even antireligious, how is all the religious talk in the Bible to be understood? Or the centuries of Christian theology which have couched faith in exclusively religious terms?[69] Is it possible to speak of God without the dualistic propositions of Greek metaphysics or Renaissance "inwardness"?[70]

As early as 1932 Bonhoeffer had realized that abstract conceptions of God are much more deceptively anthropomorphic than the recognizably childlike imagery of the Bible's fairy-tale language.[71] Then he had proposed that, in order to be understood in the modern world, the old language of magic be translated into the new language of technology.[72] The German Christians soon demonstrated the danger of "updating" the biblical language, that is, the tendency to manipulate the text to one's own avail rather than to be challenged by it.[73] Thus in 1940 Bonhoeffer had changed his mind and rejected the "radical cure" of removing the terms "cross," "sin," "grace," etc., from Christian vocabulary. He preferred to stick to the biblical language and to pay more attention to the context of its utterance. He had often experienced, for instance, the biblical words about suffering, which rang so hollow in his mouth, filled with meaning when spoken by someone sick, or poor, or alone.[74]

In 1942 he was delighted with Bultmann's just-published theses on "demythologizing,"[75] but found that they did not go far enough.[76] He rejected the metaphysical and individualistic terms into which Bultmann wanted to translate the message. Further, he realized that it is not enough to identify and demythologize *some* aspects of the biblical message, such as the miracles and the ascension.[77] The Bible does not present a general truth clothed in a religious mythology, a message which can be unwrapped and repackaged in whatever modern terms. "The mythology (resurrection, etc.) is the heart of the matter."[78] The Bible's whole form and context is religious and so are its basic images and notions, for example, God and faith, as well as miracles and resurrection.[79] Rather than be translated into another inadequate language, which could then well harden into an impediment to understanding for other people or another age, Bonhoeffer thought that the whole content, including the mythical terms, must be kept. However, they must be interpreted in a way that does not make religion a condition for faith![80]

Christians instructed by Paul can no more insist on religion as a condition of, or criterion for, faith in Jesus' God than their brethren in old Jerusalem could insist on circumcision as such.[81] The whole Christian message needs to be interpreted in the sense of Old Testament worldliness (not Old Testament religion) and the New Testament emphasis that "The Word became flesh" (John 1:14)[82] in order to show its true secular, nonreligious meaning.

One need only remember Bonhoeffer's aim in 1927 as he wrote *Sanctorum Communio*, that is, to show "the social intention of all basic Christian notions,"[83] in order to appreciate the continuity of his theological effort as well as his shifting of priority from academic phraseology to political reality.

Whence will come this new understanding and new expression of the gospel? Not from theoretical reflection, nor from keener exegesis of biblical texts. Only in praying and doing justice! For the nonce, Christians have nothing to say; their words have proven empty, they have no meaning. Christians must stop talking religion, justice, everything, and begin working for social justice and praying quietly to God. Out of this communal praxis there *may* arise "a new language, a language of justice and truth, a language which speaks the peace of God with all men, and the nearness of his Kingdom."[84] Such a language *may* be fully irreligious, but it will be liberating as the language of Jesus was.[85]

How far Bonhoeffer came in working on his nonreligious interpretation we do not know. We are left with listings of terms to be translated and his hints as to the general direction of movement, from word to flesh. He suggested the secular notion of "meaning of life" as a translation of the Biblical notion of "promise."[86] And for "salvation" he proposed the "political" notion of a kingdom of justice on earth.[87] Jesus' resurrection did not turn his hopes to an afterlife, but to more intensive life here and now.[88] "Redemption" meant *historical* liberation, as it had to the Old Testament Jews.[89] "Transcendence is not infinite remoteness, but the neighbor."[90]

In his key study of Bonhoeffer's understanding of "religion," Bethge has helped greatly to specify the direction Bonhoeffer intended.[91] However, he did not intend a nonreligious interpretation as a desk-bound exercise in translation. Rather, the eventual new language would arise out of the life of Christians engaged together with their secular comrades in solidarity with Christ, suffering in the world. Interpretation was not the primary task at hand. The immediate need was the structuring of responsible communal life in secular society.

And thus Bonhoeffer's letters and his project outline repeatedly mention the need for reinterpretation but never get around to it. Only an outer liberation from the strictures of religion would effect the inner freedom necessary for a postreligious interpretation of Christian faith.[92] Only in full engagement in social life does one learn to believe.[93] "One must live a while in a community in order to understand how 'Christ takes shape in it' (Gal. 4:19)."[94] Thus Bonhoeffer's first priority remained the communal living of the Christian message, and his project climaxed in proposals for future church structures. His thought remained to the end incorrigibly Hegelian. The existent thesis (see his analysis of the present human situation) is met by an inbreaking antithesis (Christ's this-worldly revelation) and, instead of being destroyed or negated, is taken up into a new Christian-human synthesis.

Consequences for the Church

Herbert Gold did not have to destroy the Unitarian Jewish temple with its Unitarian rabbi on Euclid Avenue in Cleveland. He simply left it.[95] Doubtless, the rabbi was comforted. Doubtless, too, would many churchmen have been comforted had Bonhoeffer simply left the church or at least refrained from drawing the ecclesiastical conclusions from his ecclesial theology. So would those who applauded his later insights as a new, invigorating hermeneutics, a novel attempt to find common ground for discussion with secular contemporaries. Thus, particularly in the German church context immediately threatened by Bonhoeffer's conclusions, the theologians' discussion has centered on his *notion* of "nonreligious interpretation" as though he had been interested in theory for its own sake, instead of the consequential thinking through and forwarding of "nonreligious Christianity."[96]

Bonhoeffer's ecclesiology was left "up in the air." His outline for a tract lists but a few suggestions for reshaping the church after the Third Reich had been smashed. However, these suggestions may not be handled as something of a hasty postscript to his main point. They are Bonhoeffer's main point—and the purpose of his writing. They are the practical conclusions to his situational analysis and his beginnings at nonreligious interpretation of the Christian revelation. They are the practical steps he saw necessary to enable further development of theological understanding.

Can there be a nonreligious Christianity? What would this mean practically for the church? What would prayer mean? Or worship services? Bonhoeffer posed these questions not in an attempt to save the church by legitimating its prayers and services. Concern for self-preservation had been the church's capital sin.[97] He saw such tries at self-legitimation as hopelessly reactionary and futureless.[98] He put the questions so sharply because the church would soon face a new possibility itself to be real Christian community.

> The most important question for the future [is] how we are to find a basis for people's living together with each other, which spiritual realities and laws we shall accept as the fundaments of a meaningful human life.[99]

Reversion to the old clericalism would be a *salto mortale* back into the Middle Ages, both dishonest and impossible.[100] The only way forward was that of repentance, ceasing to be a church unto itself and becoming a community for others.

What would this mean concretely for the institutional church? It would mean scuttling the empty hulk of the national church. Bonhoeffer realized his proposals would be controversial.[101] He had himself long weighed them. In 1927 he had articulated the criterion which would now finally lead to his rejection of the structures of the Prussian *Volkskirche*:

> . . . [The] point in time when the church dare not continue to be a national church has come when the national church can no longer fight its way through to becoming a gathered church, but on the contrary is moving into complete petrification and emptiness in the use of its forms, with evil effects on the living members as well.[102]

During the church struggle he had often considered the option of leaving the national church and joining one of the "free churches." Instead he had tried to establish a new style of communal life and ministry within the Confessing Church, which was deprived of its rights and privileges but continued to claim them and to look toward regaining them in the re-establishment of the national church.[103] Now he rejected such restoration. Sixteen years before, he had said that the church of the future could not be a bourgeois church.[104] Now he concluded: "The church is only church if it is there for others. To make a beginning, it must give all its property to those in need."[105]

God's justice must not be preached as a hope for a later time, but must be seen nonreligiously as historical justice here and now. For Bonhoeffer this meant that his whole class would have to give up their privileges and share fully the life and sufferings of their fellow men. The church should be the first to shed its cushions and sit in solidarity with the poor. Had not Jesus said to the rich young man, "Go, sell what you have and give to the poor, and *then* come, follow me!" Thus the whole system of church tax and guaranteed salaries for the clergy should be abolished. Pastors should either be supported by the parishioners' free donations, or they should take jobs, the better to participate fully in the social life of their communities—not dominating, but helping and serving. Thus they might show people of all occupations what being for others is, what life in Christ is about.

The church had done enough preaching. What was needed now was paradigm. It would not be through new concepts and explanations, be they religious or not, that the church's word would gain power and emphasis, but through exemplary human existence, that human being for others which has its source in Jesus.[106] It was time for Christians to shut up and act, keeping their motives to themselves until, perhaps, someone impressed by their action might inquire. Rather than new eloquence, the church needed "moderation, authenticity, trust, faithfulness, steadfastness, patience, discipline, humility, contentedness, and modesty"[107]—a list of virtues Bonhoeffer drew from his family's catalog of human qualities.

These were his primary considerations for a re-formed church. They would necessitate a revision of questions of creed and theological controversy, and a very different preparation for the new shapes pastoral ministry would take. Common prayer and worship there would be, though any proposals for new forms which Bonhoeffer might have made have been lost. He himself continued to the end his regimen of Bible reading, prayer, and meditation,[108] and he proposed to ghost-write sermons for Bethge, should the latter get a chance to preach.[109] Only in prayer could he undertake and carry out the work he had sketched for the remolding of the church.[110] However, worship would be the private concern of the community of Jesus-believers. It would not be in the forefront of their activity, but it would constitute the basic background for it, a modern "arcane discipline." Bonhoeffer's students in Finkenwalde had been hard put to understand his interest in early Christianity's keeping its creed and liturgy secret. In the centuries since Constantine, the gala liturgy had been the church's most flamboyant public demonstration. But Bonhoeffer sensed that its time was—or should be—over. And, in fact, the post-Christians who most appreciate his devastating critique of the Christian religion tend to overlook his continued quiet piety and prayer. Surely he would have had it so. Those churchmen still misunderstand him who rush to "balance" his nonreligious interpretation with his notion of "arcane discipline," thus trying to preserve an "identity" for the Christian community which otherwise "identifies" itself fully with those suffering in the world.[111]

It is difficult for professional Christians to refrain from trying to save the church, to salvage a specifically Christian *something* in the world, a little acre for God amidst the secular wilds. Yet Bonhoeffer's point was that it is in identifying with the world that the church meets Jesus and finds its identity as community for others. Out of this commitment will come forms of worshipping the God who is suffering there, forms of prayer, however, which may not be allowed to become new conditions for Christian solidarity. The arcane discipline is not a balancing "corrective" to secular Christianity but the provisional expression of its faith that this, our time—and not some remote eon—is the age of Jesus; that this, our world—and none other—is the place where his kingdom is breaking in. The immediate task is to prepare its way in the world.

Jørgen Glenthøj well refers those prematurely interested in determining the proper forms of arcane Christian discipline and worship to the counsel of Christoph Blumhardt: "Wait for God. Don't be so religious!"[112]

The Failure of Bonhoeffer's Project

Bonhoeffer's was a program not of explanation but of prayerful action.

> Our being Christian will consist now in these two things, in praying and doing justice among men. All thinking, talking and organizing of the things of Christianity must be born anew out of this prayer and this action.[113]

His was a call for Christians to divest themselves of Constantinian privilege and crusty religion and to form paradigmatic communities living and working for social justice.[114] Despite widespread opinion to the contrary, Bonhoeffer was not optimistic about the prospects of what Harvey Cox has temporarily celebrated as the secular city. He mistrusted technology as an excessive rationality leading to a monolithic, monotonous organization of life. Technical organization had so nearly overcome nature as to become the primary context of decreasingly human urban life. Thus he saw deep meaning in the 1944 evacuations of German cities. It was with good reason that the Bible had called Cain their father. A mirage of life's pleasures, the cities had lured people into a morass of untold suffering and death. "The age of the big cities on our continent seems to be over."[115] Though some metropolises might remain, their false sheen would no longer tempt Europeans. Bonhoeffer looked to the country for contact with nature and possibility of natural human life, recognizing, however, that the great exodus from the cities would revolutionize the countryside as well.[116]

Looking ahead to war's end, he wondered whether the reorganization of society would be a heartless technological massification, or whether people with heart would be able to structure a personal society. Were these necessarily the alternatives? He insisted that they could not be. Responsible people must build community within the necessarily broadly woven international organization.[117]

> Within a very far-reaching uniformity of all material and intellectual living conditions, the qualitative feeling for the human values of justice, achievement and courage, which today runs through all the social strata, could effect a new selection of people who could be given the right to exercise strong leadership.[118]

Ever elitist, Bonhoeffer hoped for a natural selection of a new cadre to provide an "aristocratic order." It has been insufficiently noted that his increased appreciation of the development of intellectual maturity among people had not changed his rejection of all popular movements for political liberation.[119] To avoid this impression, he spoke most often of human "maturity" rather than of "autonomy."[120] The mature person respects and lives within the existing social relationships. The revolution that was fought and won at the barricades in France was so quickly crushed in Prussia that the ongoing contest there was waged across the philosophers' desks. As in his earlier essay on ethics, Bonhoeffer continued to condemn the people's revolution while affirming the philosophers' fight for intellectual honesty.

Bonhoeffer overlooked the confluence of interests that would prevent the realization of his own proposals. His senseless murder by the defeated Nazis in the closing days of the war brought tragically true his feeling that "it will be our lot to plan and hope, to hold out in this hope more than to move forward to its realization. A new generation will have to plan, build and shape a better life."[121] Indeed, his voice was not there to protest the bearing out of his worst fears for the postwar German church. With the military's traditional recognition of the useful function of religion, and apparently under the impression that whatever churchmen had been connected with the Confessing Church were ipso facto anti-Nazi, the Western Allies moved quickly to reestablish in their occupation zones the old national church structures, entrusting them to some of the very people whom Bonhoeffer had hoped could be kept out of power.[122] The formal Stuttgart confession of guilt, and later the more substantial Darmstadt Declaration, were ignored by too many churchmen in their impenitent rush to secure again their privileges in the shell of the same old state church.[123]

Meanwhile, religion flourished after World War II. Since then there has been a great upswing of participation in religious organizations. The years of Bonhoeffer's becoming known in the English-speaking world were years of social ferment in which many Christians moved to social action. Church seminaries and institutions became somewhat unwieldy and unwilling instruments of responsible secularity. Bonhoeffer's sayings were celebrated by the most popular of theologians. Near-sighted as usual, these latter, too, saw the end of religion near at hand. In the gloom of frustration following the political establishment's effective blocking of the "movements" of the 1960s, the swingback to "that old-time religion" among the loose-hanging social stratum of erstwhile secularists has made it popular wisdom to point out the failure in Bonhoeffer's analysis. "The Persistence of Religion," indeed, the fact that the conservative churches and myriad sectarian pietisms of East and West grow at the expense of the more liberal and activist denominations,[124] has led Andrew Greeley, for instance, to conclude that

> the basic human religious needs and the basic religious functions have not changed very notably since the late Ice Age; and what changes have occurred make religious questions more critical rather than less critical in the contemporary world.[125]

American religiosity in the last half-dozen years more closely resembles the Great Revivalism of 1787-1805 than it does the ecclesiastical conventionalism and pious activism of the 1960s.[126]

The response from too many theologians who had previously proclaimed the good news of secularity was to heave an audible sigh of relief, salute the age of Aquarius, and rush off to explore ways of folk religion, the occult, and the new groupy pietisms, in search of a new church, while others have tried to exploit the trends to corral people back into the old. Bonhoeffer's prognosis has proved to be overoptimistic, based as it was on a doubly limited analysis. Like all his ethical thought, it focused primarily— and more or less consciously—on the experience of his own social stratum of academic aristocrats. For them it remains, in the main, correct. It also shared their propensity to analyze the history of ideas without sufficient attention to their social context and impact. It would behoove Bonhoeffer's relieved critics to avoid his double mistake.

They would do well to heed his insights, too. He preferred a godlessness full of promise to a hopeless piety.[127] However "successful" Christian churches might be in building on the continuing religious need of our ever threatened and frustrated contemporaries, Bonhoeffer's writings are there to remind us that Christ is not to be found building successful religious organizations but informing human community among the poor and suffering of the world; and that faith in Jesus' God means full, active commitment in human solidarity. This is "the church [which] now stands in place of religion; and that is biblical."[128]

III. Penultimate Questions of Conviviality and Communal Sense

Dietrich Bonhoeffer saw that his church and his whole social world had come to the end of the road—not just a crisis or a turning point but a dead end! He had experienced the oncoming cultural collapse in 1928, when the Barcelona parish failed to constitute real community in the deepening chaos of the depression; and later in Berlin, when in its "twelfth hour" the church failed to stand up for those persecuted and destroyed by the Nazis. He had found meaning temporarily in the soon-squelched Finkenwalde community, and then in his family's solidarity amidst the contradictions of the anti-Hitler conspiracy. He had seen the symbols of Christian faith and culture emptied of meaning, reduced to ideological décor for doomed institutions. When the putsch failed on July 20, 1944, there was no more staving off the total collapse and destruction of the discredited whole. The only future lay beyond ground zero.

Christian theology had for centuries served as the major ideology of the world Bonhoeffer now saw expiring. Albert Memmi has written that the function of ideologies is as much to reassure as to explain; when they cease to convince, we feel abandoned to the chaos and fragility of our destiny. We can unmask the blindness of others: Marxists of Christians, the latter of Moslems, etc., and vice versa. But none can lay a hand to his own ideology without being accused of perversity.[129] The heretical traitor Bonhoeffer did just this as his world was going under. Amid the social disintegration, he called for fellow Christians to abandon the shelter of Christian religion to risk new, free forms of living together, and quietly to search the Bible together for resources for secular solidarity.[130]

Only those who realize they have come to the end of the road can make a new start. Bonhoeffer was ready to strike out anew, in a new direction. The majority of his fellow churchmen were not. Most of them were looking for light at the end of the long Nazi tunnel, hoping to re-establish the church of 1933. Bonhoeffer had given up his plans for restoration. He pinned his hope for Christian survival on recognizing that this was the end of the religious road.

Only those who are able to make new starts can admit to themselves that they have come to the end of a road. Bonhoeffer's concentrated study in prison had led him to new, liberating meaning in the very biblical tradition whose religious form he now recognized as perfidious. In Barcelona he had written that "Christianity contains within itself the seed of animosity to the church." This seed was the biblical revelation, and it was bearing fruit. Bonhoeffer looked to start anew with Christ toward human conviviality. But he perished, leaving us with a pack of questions he thought held the clues for a new beginning.

His questions were ever sharper and more instructive than the answers he could get—or yet give. Visser 't Hooft has written of a long conversation with him on a London station platform in 1939:

> I remember his acute questions better than his answers, but I think I learned more from his questions than from my answers. In the impenetrable world between "Munich" and "Warsaw" in which hardly anyone ventured to formulate the actual problems clearly, that questioning voice was a release.[131]

In 1944 Bonhoeffer knew that he had no clear answers, but he was equally assured that the questions he was putting were the "coming questions,"[132] the questions that would open people for a possible future.

I shall not postulate what his answers would have been. André Dumas has wisely noted that "a question receives its true answer from the one who asks it."[133] The fitting response to the cryptic queries of his last writings is to work them out, to lead them further. His work was broken off just as he was crossing the threshold of new insights. We have not to preserve them, but to try them. He considered them not as limit questions, which must always remain open, but as the beginnings of wholly new developments, bringing unforeseen duties.[134] At the end of his critical review of Karl Heim's *Glauben und Denken*, Bonhoeffer wrote in 1931:

> I think that the most honest way to express real gratitude for a great work is with all the resources at one's command to take up the questions it poses. Even if one comes to divergent conclusions, the appreciation for the work is surely not lessened.[135]

Indeed, the last questions we have from Bonhoeffer were still penultimate inquiries, made final only by the Nazi hangman. They were questions he had long been asking, questions we have seen come up so often that he would seem to have been going around in circles. Yet his renewed inquiry always received a new answer, and his circles became a helix moving from academic abstraction ever deeper into social reality.

Standing foursquare with his people and among his immediate Christian community, if a bit askew in the church, Bonhoeffer invited others into the social context where he found the Christian gospel meaningful. His ethical questions were calls beyond whatever social, religious, and other considerations toward joint action in response to human need and toward fellowship with all, of whatever class, color, or credal hue, who joined to meet that need. They were invocations to collaboration, conviviality, engagement, risk, and solidarity with others, which brings a bit of sensitivity and perspective.

Solidarity with other people, being with and for them, is self-transcendence in community; it enables thinking that is not entirely self-centered. It is the condition that distinguishes communal sense from group-think, whose narrow loyalties are more blinding than individual selfishness.

Christian ethics has been and will continue to be a partial and circumscribed view of reality, articulated in the best-conceived interests of Christian communities, whose vision extends more or less beyond themselves. Bonhoeffer was right to focus first energies on the shaping of communities which come into being in response to a Word from beyond themselves and which consist in service to others. Their communal sense will urge them toward conviviality; and their conviviality may lead to common sense.

Notes

1 Letter of 22-4-44, *WE*, p. 302.
2 Letter of 11-4-44, *WE*, p. 297.
3 "Thoughts on Baptism," May 1944, *WE*, p. 328.
4 *WE*, p. 327.
5 Letter of 8-6-44, *WE*, p. 356.
6 *DB*, p. 967.
7 Unfortunately, the letters written in September were destroyed by Bethge before his own arrest. Cf. *DB*, p. 941.
8 Bethge has done this in presenting the "New Theology" in his biography. Unfortunately, he has shortchanged the third chapter, which was least fully developed but nonetheless the conclusion of his main argument, instead of an appendix. Cf. *DB*, p. 571.
9 Cf. *DB*, pp. 959, 964ff.
10 Letter of 11-4-44, *WE*, p. 297.
11 Letter of 22-4-44, *WE*, pp. 300-301.
12 Peter Berger and Thomas Luckmann, *The Social Construction of Reality* (New York: Doubleday, 1967), pp. 157-162.
13 Letter of 22-4-44, *WE*, p. 300.
14 Letter of 26-4-44, *WE*, p. 302.
15 Hanfried Müller, *Von der Kirche zur Welt* (Leipzig: Koehler and Amelang, 1961).
16 Cf. John Phillips, *Christ for Us in the Theology of Dietrich Bonhoeffer* (New York: Harper and Row, 1967), p. 25, and H. Müller, p. 37.

17 Jeremiah 45 was the Bible text which recurred most often in his prison writings. Cf. *WE*, pp. 121, 246, 325, 402, 304.

18 Letter of 23-8-44, *WE*, p. 428.

19 Jørgen Glenthøj, "Was hat Dietrich Bonhoeffer zur Frage des Gottesdienstes . . ." (pamphlet, no pagination), also later in *MW*, V, 296.

20 Cf. *E*, pp. 332ff.

21 Letter of 23-8-44, *WE*, p. 428.

22 Cf. Thomas Altizer's alarum that the new edition of the prison writings might "quietly drop some of the more controversial, misusable sections, and add new material guaranteeing Bonhoeffer's stolid Lutheranism" (in his review of Bethge's Biography, *Journal of the American Academy of Religion*, XXXIX, 3 [September 1971], 361). Altizer's warning was not needed. If anything, the new, fuller edition of the letters shows Bonhoeffer to be less safe as a Lutheran.

There have been attempts to defuse Bonhoeffer, or domesticate his errant ideas. Cf., for instance, the dissertation of Rainer Mayer, *Christuswirklichkeit* (Stuttgart: Calwer Verlag, 1969). There Bonhoeffer's ecclesiastical thrust is "absorbed into Christology" and his arguments get twisted back into an apology for the national church. Cf. Mayer's "Volkskirch oder Friewilligkeitskirche? Überlegungen im Anschlusz an Dietrich Bonhoeffer," in *Zeitwende*, 41 (1970), 378-388.

23 *WE*, pp. 413ff.

24 Letter of 16-7-44, *WE*, pp. 392-393.

25 *Ibid.*, p. 393.

26 Letters of 8-6-44, *WE*, p. 356; 29-5-44, *WE*, p. 341.

27 Letter of 16-7-44, *WE*, p. 393.

28 Letter of 30-4-44, *WE*, p. 305.

29 *Ibid.* The church's preaching had been predicated on (no pun intended) the "religious a priori" which Bonhoeffer's professor Seeberg had so celebrated, and which Bonhoeffer had rejected from student days.

30 Letter of 8-6-44, *WE*, p. 359.

31 Letter of 30-6-44, *WE*, p. 374.

32 Letter of 8-6-44, *WE*, p. 357.

33 Letters of 8-7-44, *WE*, p. 377; 8-6-44, *WE*, p. 360. Bonhoeffer had rejected the "disgusting," "moldy underground" of Zinzendorfian piety by 1936 (cf. letter of 31-7-36, *GS*, II, 278). At that time "piety" seemed to him sometimes good (*GS*, IV, 346), parallel to "realistic" (*ibid.*, p. 377), and sometimes bad (*ibid.*, p. 357). I mention these points since this Finkenwalde time is usually considered his "pious period."

34 Karl Heim's expression, cited by Bonhoeffer in the letter of 8-6-44, *WE*, p. 359.

35 Letter of 8-7-44, *WE*, p. 376.

36 Letter of 8-7-44, *WE*, p. 378.

37 Letter of 29-5-44, *WE*, p. 341.

38 Letter of 30-5-44, *WE*, p. 342.

39 Letter of 30-6-44, *WE*, p. 374.

40 Cf. *GS*, V, 153.

41 Letter of 8-6-44, *WE*, p. 360.

42 "Thoughts on Baptism," May 1944, *WE*, p. 328.

43 Letter of 3-8-44, *WE*, p. 411.

44 Bonhoeffer himself found it more natural and easy to speak of God with nonbelievers than with his fellow Christians. Cf. letter of 30-4-44, *WE*, p. 306.

45   Letter of 8-6-44, *WE*, p. 360. Bonhoeffer did not always heed his own warning. Cf. letters of 8-6-44, *WE*, p. 360; 28-7-44, *WE*, p. 407.

46   "Outline for a Book," *WE*, p. 413.

47   Letter of 8-6-44, *WE*, p. 358.

48   See, for instance, his intention for the Bethel Confession of 1933. Cf. *GS,* II, 80ff.

49   "Outline," *WE*, p. 415.

50   *Ibid*.

51   Letter of 30-4-44, *WE*, p. 305.

52   "Outline," *WE*, p. 414.

53   Letter of 29-5-44, *WE*, p. 341.

54   Letter of 21-8-44, *WE*, p. 425.

55   Letter of 30-6-44, *WE*, p. 374.

56   "Outline," *WE*, p. 414.

57   *Ibid*.

58   Letter of 18-7-44, *WE*, p. 395.

59   Daniel Berrigan, "The Passion of Dietrich Bonhoeffer," *Saturday Review* (May 30, 1970), p. 20.

60   Letter of 18-7-44, *WE*, p. 394.

61   Letter of 16-7-44, *WE*, p. 394.

62   Letter of 18-7-44, *WE*, p. 396.

63   *Ibid*., p. 395.

64   "Christen und Heiden" (poem), *WE*, p. 382. Cf. *WE*, p. 395.

65   Letter of 14-8-44, *WE*, p. 421.

66   Letter of 5-5-44, *WE*, p. 312.

67   Letter of 21-5-44, *WE*, pp. 332-333.

68   "Thoughts on Baptism," May 1944, *WE*, p. 328.

69   Letter of 5-5-44, *WE*, p. 312.

70   Letter of 30-4-44, *WE*, p. 306.

71   *CFT*, pp. 45-49.

72   *Ibid*., p. 50.

73   "On Updating NT Texts" (August 23, 1935), *GS*, III, 303ff.

74   Letter of Spring 1940, *GS*, III, 42-43.

75   Letter of 24-3-43, *GS*, III, 45. Bultmann's theses had been published in 1941 by Ernst Wolf of Kaiser Verlag, Munich.

76   Interview with Jochen Kanitz, Berlin, November 1974. Bonhoeffer told Kanitz this in the latter's clearly remembered meeting with him on leave in Berlin in July 1942.

77   Letter of 5-5-44, *WE*, p. 311.

78   Letter of 8-6-44, *WE*, p. 360. In Marshall McLuhan's sharpest terms, the "myth is the message," *not* the "massage."

79   Bonhoeffer first slated for translation such praxis terms as church, arcane discipline, parish community, sermon, liturgy, Christian life, and prayer (letter of 30-4-44, *WE*, p. 306). Later he thought of theological terms such as repentance, justification, sanctification, faith, etc. (letter of 5-5-44, *WE*, pp. 312-313).

80   Letter of 8-6-44, *WE*, p. 360.

81   Letter of 3C-4-44, *WE*, p. 307.

82   Letter of 5-5-44, *WE*, p. 313.

83   *CS*: see his 1930 Preface, p. 11.

84   "Thoughts on Baptism," May 1944, *WE*, p. 328.

85   *Ibid*.

86   Letter of 21-8-44, *WE*, p. 426.

87   Letters of 5-5-44, *WE*, p. 312; 27-6-44, *WE*, p. 368.

88   Letter of 27-6-44, *WE*, p. 369.

89   Letter of 27-6-44, *WE*, p. 368.

90   Notes, *WE*, p. 408.

91   *DB*, pp. 979ff.

92   "After Ten Years," *WE*, p. 18. Cf. "Stations on the Way to Freedom," *WE*, p. 403, and the letter of 21-8-44, *WE*, p. 425.

93   Letter of 21-7-44, *WE*, p. 401.

94   Letter of 16-7-44, *WE*, p. 392.

95   Herbert Gold, "Apologia without Apology," *New York Times Review of Books* (23-1-1972).

96   Practically minded Anglo-Saxons have picked up his expression "non-religious Christianity" (which occurs only twice in the letters), while the ever-idealist German theologians have virtually overlooked that in their stress of "non-religious *interpretation*" (which is more often mentioned). The thesis of this essay is that the first is as basic as the second is indispensable.

97   Letter of 8-6-44, *WE*, p. 359.

98   *Ibid.*, p. 360.

99   Letter of 2-6-44, *WE*, p. 344.

100   Letter of 16-7-44, *WE*, p. 393.

101   Letter of 3-8-44, *WE*, p. 411.

102   *CS*, p. 180.

103   Cf. his proposals for ending the church struggle, *GS*, II, 433ff.

104   *CS*, p. 193.

105   "Outline," *WE*, p. 415.

106   *Ibid.*, p. 416.

107   *Ibid*.

108   Cf. letters of 8-21-44 and 8-23-44, *WE*, pp. 425ff.

109   Letter of May 1944, *WE*, p. 392.

110   Letter of 3-8-44, *WE*, p. 411.

111   This "balancing" is a possible misinterpretation of Bethge's handling of the "arcane discipline" in *DB* (pp. 988ff.), one which he has tried to exclude by introducing his (post-Bonhoefferian) paradox of identity/identification. "Christian identity can only be won and kept in total identification" (with the world, suffering). Cf. *Ohnmacht und Mündigkeit* (Munich: Christian Kaiser Verlag, 1969), pp. 130-131, 169.

112   Christoph Blumhardt in *Heute schauen wir vorwärts*, ed. Otto Bruder (Zürich: Zwingli Verlag, 1966), p. 175. Cf. Glenthøj's theses on "What Dietrich Bonhoeffer had to say on the Question of Worship Services in a Secular Age?" (Copenhagen: Frimodts Forlag, 1968).

113   "Thoughts on Baptism," May 1944, *WE*, p. 328.

114   This thought of paradigmatic communities has been picked up by Paul Lehmann and experimented with by Richard Shaull. Cf. Shaull's "The End of the Road and a New Beginning," *Marxism and Radical Religion* (Philadelphia: Temple University Press, 1970), pp. 35ff.

115   "Thoughts on Baptism," May 1944, *WE*, p. 323.

116   *Ibid*.

117   *Ibid.*, pp. 326-327.

118   *Ibid.*, p. 327.

119   Cf. *E,* p. 100.

120   The expression "autonomy" appears only twice, in letters of 18-6-44 and 16-7-44, *WE*, pp. 356, 392ff.

121   "Thoughts on Baptism," May 1944, *WE*, p. 325.

122   Helga Krüger Day, *"Christlicher Glaube und gesellschaftliches Handeln"* (Ph.D. dissertation; New York: Union Theological Seminary, 1973), ch. 1. Karl Kupisch relates how Karl Barth's hope for a new beginning of the church was dashed at the first church conference he attended after the war, in Treysa, August 1945, in which the majority of participants did not seem at all concerned with a new start, but with reconstruction and restoration of the church on the foundations as they were in 1933. Kupisch, "Introduction" to Karl Barth's *Der Götze wackelt* (Berlin: Käthe Vogt Verlag, 1961), p. 23.

123   Texts and commentary in F.-W. Marquardt, *Kirche der Menschen*, Unterwegs No. 16 (Berlin: Käthe Vogt Verlag, 1960).

124   Cf. Dean M. Kelley, *Why Conservative Churches are Growing* (New York: Harper and Row, 1972).

125   Andrew M. Greeley, *The Persistence of Religion* (New York: Schocken Books, 1972).

126   Cf. Sydney E. Ahlstrom, *A Religious History of the American People* (New Haven: Yale University Press, 1972).

127   *E*, p. 103.

128   Letter of 5-5-44, *WE*, p. 312.

129   Albert Memmi, "Review of Maxine Rodison's *Mohammed*" in *New York Times Book Review* (Nov. 7, 1971), p. 3.

130   This is the thrust of Richard Shaull's teaching at Princeton Theological Seminary, where I have benefited from much discussion with him concerning the resources of the gospel for freedom and creativity in the midst of social chaos, instead of its religious use as a shelter from the threat of personal and social disintegration, or in addition to this latter.

131   *DBET*, p. 551.

132   Letter of 8-6-44, *WE*, p. 356.

133   André Dumas, *Dietrich Bonhoeffer, Theologian of Reality* (New York: Macmillan, 1971), p. 96.

134   Hanfried Müller, *Von der Kirche zur Welt*, pp. 29-30.

135   *GS*, III, p. 159.

DIETRICH BONHOEFFER'S UNDERSTANDING
OF THE WORLD

Ernst Feil

IN CONTRAST to the other topics being dealt with at this congress, the one assigned to me looks remarkably apolitical. In Luther's doctrine of the two kingdoms,[1] which relies on Augustinian thought, the struggle between the *civitas Dei* and the *civitas terrena* has a primarily theological character. What this doctrine gets at is humanity's existence *coram Deo*. But that two-kingdom doctrine—and this does not appear to be an accident or a mere question of form—uses not cosmological but political terms and categories, relying on terms like kingdom, reign, battle, and so forth. Moreover, this doctrine certainly has political relevance, for Luther never permitted theology to be isolated from encompassing political questions; he did not believe in a peaceful division into the kingdom of God and the kingdom of the world. Hence a genuine Lutheran tradition can speak of the "politics of discipleship" as well as "politics and faith."[2] Such an outlook reflects the Christian's responsibility to the world in the sense of political-social responsibility as a concern for *systematic* theology while at the same time postulating and initiating it as *practical* theology.[3]

It can now be shown that the concept of a theological understanding of the world, not only in Bonhoeffer but in others as well, has immediate implications for our conception of the political responsibility of the Christian. In the case of the Third Reich, didn't the seemingly apolitical "orders of creation" have an essentially political function, even though they were always tied in with cosmological categories in our thinking? (The aim was to develop a world-picture embracing the entire cosmos and the divinely established natural orders.) The political function of those "orders of creation" lay not just in a certain application based on a time when the "orders" had a special role; rather, their political function was tied in with a basic interdependence of ethical and cosmological concepts.[4] Not even the concept of creation, which was originally used in the theological demythologizing of ancient (cosmological) mythology, can be abstracted from political

237

consequences; for those mythologically and cosmologically formulated depictions of the world were not isolated, apolitical speculations. On the contrary, they served the purpose of legitimizing political structures from the perspective of theology and the philosophy of law. In the case of the Third Reich, then, what we should brand as illegitimate was not the relationship between politics and "orders of creation" but the use of that relationship and the specific way it was defined.

This reminder about the connection between cosmological and political concepts and speculation is necessary as a foundation for an exploration of our topic. The question that cannot be pursued further at this point is: Why can anthropological, ethical, and political concepts be used to project a philosophical system in the sense of a cosmology?[5]

I propose to pursue the opposite question instead: What is the significance of a specific philosophy (Weltanschauung) for political-social ideas? I will use Bonhoeffer as my example in exploring this question. It will become evident that Bonhoeffer's theological understanding of the world is directly relevant to his statements about the political engagement of the church and Christians. In our exploration, the problem will be more precisely defined as we come to see that the relationship is not accidental, and that at the very point where it appears that there is no connection between an understanding of the world or a philosophy, on the one hand, and the determination of relationship to the state and society, on the other, we have good reason to suspect that some connection is indeed present. In hermeneutical terms, this connection can be expressed as the interdependence of cosmological and political ideas, which was mentioned earlier. Arnold Erhardt, prompted by his forced emigration from the Third Reich, investigated this problem in detail.[6] Only at first sight is metaphysics apolitical; but an apolitical metaphysics is also political in its own way. Thus, political relevance cannot even be avoided by making a deliberate attempt to avoid it, for political abstinence is also politically relevant.

Under the assumption that there is a correlation between our relation to the world and political forms of life, we may conclude—even from an external standpoint—that the question of Bonhoeffer's understanding of the world fits within the framework of a conference that focuses primarily on the "political Bonhoeffer" and thereby seeks to contradict those who, on the basis of their own presuppositions, appeal to Bonhoeffer as their witness in what they take to be a new church struggle.

I will now attempt to verify the connection between Bonhoeffer's understanding of the world and his political-social views. I am assuming here that Bonhoeffer's biography and his theology must be brought together; indeed, we must remember that his theology attempts, in special measure, to serve the purposes of faith in the concrete situation. It was not his intention to outline a theological system; rather, in intellectual honesty he hoped to render a service in a situation that called for reflection but could not be dealt with and resolved by means of thought alone. It is only by a decision that is well considered but then must be dared into the darkness of the future and of guilt that we can meet the demands of reality in a concrete situation of the world and of history. If we want to summarize Bonhoeffer's philosophical outlook on the world, we must recognize that this philosophy presupposes a relation to the world that cannot adequately be conceived by our intellect. Using a slogan, we might say that the theory necessary for practice will always fall short of an adequate judgment of this practice, not only in trying to prejudice it beforehand, but also in trying to catch up with it afterwards.[7]

On the basis of these assumptions, I will sketch Bonhoeffer's conception of the relationship between the Christian faith and the world. Possibly the most important exemplification of that relationship is the relationship between the church (in this case Christians) and the state. I have deliberately spoken of "sketching" this relationship, for anything more than a sketch would be impossible here.

To begin with, I will explain the starting point from which Bonhoeffer develops his understanding of the world (I). I will then go on to specify what theological foundation there is for such an understanding of the world (II). Only after this is done can an abbreviated version of Bonhoeffer's understanding of the world and his plea for a world-come-of-age be outlined. The form of the Christian faith in such a world-come-of-age, that is, religionless Christianity as service to this world, can then be revealed (III). Finally, I will outline the situation of church and state as Bonhoeffer saw it (IV).

I. Cultural Protestantism's (Religious) Understanding of the World as Starting Point and Opposition

When Bonhoeffer, in his *Letters and Papers from Prison,* pleads for a religionless Christianity in a world-come-of-age, we must bear in mind the background, for the religious understanding of the world contrasts sharply with the Christianity he postulates. The fact that the religious understanding of Christianity still (or again) plays a role, at least in theoretical discussions where the concept of religion is still defended[8] despite the protests of Karl Barth, keeps any examination of Bonhoeffer's statements on these matters from assuming an antiquarian character.

Bonhoeffer's opposition is kindled not so much by the theoretical formulation of this religious understanding of the world as by the basic practice of cultural Protestantism. His personal experience reaches back beyond the attack on "religion" enunciated by Karl Barth since 1922. In his student days Bonhoeffer was already preoccupied with Schleiermacher's lectures *On Religion* as well as with Naumann's *Briefe über Religion* (Letters about Religion). He regarded both authors as proponents of a form (*Gestalt*) of Christianity that one would have to call "religious."

This religious form of the Christian faith consisted of what Bonhoeffer had come to view as a false determination of the relationship between God and the world, namely, a precocious separation of God and the world, a separation that corresponds with a fallacious amalgamation of both that had occurred largely in the background and had therefore remained unrecognized. The result of this separation is that God is safely settled beyond the boundaries of our world and our reason (in the sense of theoretically known transcendence, which has been the model for theological transcendence since Kant). The separation corresponds with a restriction of God's relationship to inwardness. These dissimilations are ultimately based on a spatial division; as a result, God has no place *in* the world, and faith is compartmentalized as "religion." "For the psyche of the nineteenth and twentieth centuries religion plays the role of the so-called 'front room', into which one likes to retreat for a few hours,"[9] declared Bonhoeffer in the Christology lecture of 1928. This internalization corresponds with a total indifference to the world. "Liberal theology (especially Troeltsch, Naumann) understood the original gospel as a 'purely religious' power that changed the individual person's attitude, but at the same time took an indifferent, renunciating stance toward worldly orders and conditions. . . . This deficiency of the New Testament gospel prompted Naumann to make the statement that he could be Christian in only five or ten percent of his life insofar as he did not have contact with the worldly orders."[10] One can therefore measure in percentages how much "room" faith takes up. (Time can also be conceived of "dimensionally.") The remainder one can devote to the world—undisturbed.

Whether religion lets Christ have a "place" in the world, or wishes to leave "room for religion in the world or against the world,"[11] thus letting religion be "one area beside others in life,"[12] it always operates with a spatial scheme. In other words, "thinking in two spheres" is fundamental for religion. Characteristic of religion is a "cleavage of autonomy in culture, scholarship and politics" and—we may summarily add—of world "on the one hand, and heteronomy of Christianity, on the other."[13] This cultural Protestant relationship to the world and its reflected form, the understanding of the world in liberal theology, which Bonhoeffer designates the religious relationship and understanding of the world, is the background against which his own efforts must be understood.

Early in his career Bonhoeffer understood the concept of religion in its specific meaning as a concept in the history of thought. This is shown by a statement in the transcript of the first lecture: "In the post-Copernican world, the word *religio* shrouded the word faith, that is to say, filled it with its own meaning."[14] Thus the concept of religion as the cardinal concept for the Christian faith belongs to a specific period. But it appears that even during the time of "religion"—and this is of special significance—there was opposition to the religious understanding of the world, to the "religion of secularism," as Bonhoeffer put it in 1932. The opposition manifested itself as a call to withdrawal from the world as a protest against the secular addition to the world. But the withdrawal was itself a religion, namely, the "religion of otherworldliness," which belongs with the religion of secularism just as the two sides of a coin belong together. Withdrawal from the world is ultimately identical with a false attachment to the world. It might be asked whether Bonhoeffer was following a tradition in using this thesis. As early as 1932, in any case, and again in *The Cost of Discipleship* and *Ethics,* he expressly emphasized that the two positions, which at first glance are diametrically opposed—whether we call them secularism and otherworldliness, or secularism and enthusiasm (*Schwärmerei*), or compromise and radicalism, or cultural Protestantism and monasticism[15]—are ultimately identical. What the two positions have in common is that they do not believe in the kingdom of God as the kingdom of God on earth.[16]

The similarity between the two positions, which at first may seem to be opposites, is that withdrawal from the world ultimately brings about an association with the world. Otherworldliness cannot tolerate the world assigned to the Christian, and therefore it ends up with a self-made world. "He who escapes the world does not find God; he only finds another world, his own world, a better, nicer, more peaceful world, a different world, but never God's world, which dawns in this world."[17] The monastery is likewise a protest against the world; however, since Luther (according to Bonhoeffer's interpretation) denied everything except his own pious subjectivity when he entered the monastery, the monastery itself became the world.[18]

Therefore, being addicted to secularism and withdrawal from the world are "on the same plane. Neither is capable of thinking the thought of the end in Christ."[19] Thus, cultural Protestantism and Pietism are forms of religion.[20] Their characteristic feature is that God has nothing to do with the world but is to be settled somewhere beyond this world or, if in this world, then only on a reservation. In 1932, Bonhoeffer already opposed such thinking directly by writing: "The parish of the Church of Christ is the entire world."[21] Any division between God and the world is ruled out by the *Incarnation of Jesus Christ*; the Incarnation has made "thinking in two spheres" impossible once and for all. Therefore, an understanding of the world cannot be developed without a Christological foundation.

II. Christology as the Foundation for an Understanding of the World

At first it did not appear that Christology would become the cardinal point of Bonhoeffer's whole theology. In his dissertation, in his initial lectures, and in the seminary, he seemed to want to begin with ecclesiology, but it always led him back to Christology as the foundation for ecclesiology and of every other theological undertaking. Christology may therefore be regarded as the constant, the *cantus firmus*, with the understanding of the world as the most important of those "contrapuntal themes which have their full *independence*, but are still based on the *cantus firmus*."[22] Christology is the constant for Bonhoeffer's own theology too, beginning with the Christology lecture in Barcelona, continued in *Act and Being* (in contrast to *The Communion of Saints*), carried on during his lectureship in Berlin (especially in connection with the question of the concretion of the commandment), emphatically set forth in *The Cost of Discipleship* (where discipleship, as the discipleship of Jesus Christ, has a particularly Christological character), and finally climaxed in *Ethics* and *Letters and Papers from Prison*.

Since *Act and Being,* Jesus Christ is the boundary, the barrier, through which alone true transcendence is established. At the same time, he is the center on which faith is focused. "Boundary" and "center"—these two terms with opposite meanings must both be related to Jesus Christ. As the center, Jesus Christ is the simultaneous mediator to both God and the world,[23] although no similarity between the two mediations can actually be established. In any case, there is no such thing as direct prayer to God, according to Bonhoeffer's express, repeated declaration. Only through the mediation of Jesus Christ can the praying person reach God.[24]

It is of fundamental importance for our topic that a Christian understanding of the world can be developed only by beginning with Jesus Christ, as Bonhoeffer pointed out programmatically in his letter to Theodor Litt.[25] But before we come back to this point, we must consider the components in the concept of the more formal statements about Jesus Christ as center and mediator. Jesus Christ is the center of existence, of history, and of nature,[26] for in him alone is the unlocking of the self-confinement of the world and man accomplished; in him alone can God be near to man. In him God is no longer present as an idea but as the absolute mystery—indeed, he is "here today" ("heute und hier"), as it is formulated repeatedly when Bonhoeffer wants to express the concretion of the reality of God in the world.[27]

Jesus Christ rescues man from his self-imposed guilt, his self-sufficiency, his closedness, his lack of mystery in life—in short, from his one-dimensional reality. Jesus Christ is the eternal son with the Father, the risen and ascended Lord,[28] of whom the Chalcedonian Confession speaks not in order to unlock a mystery but to keep it ever present. God, the *concretissimum,* has entered the world in Jesus Christ so that man can see God and the world as one in Jesus Christ. Precisely because of this, the man who clings to Jesus Christ is relieved of the brokenness of "man between God and world" (F. Gogarten) and therefore no longer faces the choice between addiction to the world and withdrawal from the world, for

God himself has accepted the world. "If you want God, keep to the world"—
this is the imperative for the Christian.[29] Only maintaining the "multidimensionality"[30] made possible and commanded by Christ is appropriate
to reality, for reality is not purely factual and without mystery, but is "created, sustained, contained in laws, reconciled, and renewed."[31] The positivistic understanding of the world is an "idea," an "abstraction," in that it
cannot and does not want to see this. Therefore, one can risk saying—even
though such a statement is easily misused as a basis for authoritarian demands—that by faith the world is understood better than it understands
itself. This superior understanding is based on Jesus Christ. A theological
understanding of the world must be developed on that basis.

III. Plea for a World-Come-of-Age (Worldliness of the World) and the Religionless Christianity Appropriate to It

When we survey the efforts Bonhoeffer made over many years to formulate
an understanding of the world which did not rest content with rejecting
proposed positions and formally outlining the boundaries within which
concrete statements were to be made, we are inclined to suppose that
Gerhard Ebeling was not justified in expressing his suspicion about Bonhoeffer's Christology. Ebeling wondered whether Bonhoeffer "did not
sometimes speak of Jesus Christ too quickly, too self-evidently, too dog-
matically—simply covering theological problems through the formalized
use of this name while leaving a great lack precisely where an explication
is very much needed."[32] Bonhoeffer had difficulty enough developing his
Christology, and had still more difficulty in conceptualizing his Christologically mediated understanding of the world, which not only rejected the
cultural Protestant understanding of the world but also overcame the acosmicism of dialectical theology, which was the price Karl Barth in particular
had to pay to register his protest against liberal theology.

This was Bonhoeffer's dilemma. Barth's decisive attack on "religion"
was indeed the only ray of light that Bonhoeffer, along with many others
in his time, could glimpse; for in Barth the *deus dixit* was set forth in all
clarity. (Barth's "religion," as Bonhoeffer knew Barth, was certainly a systematic concept rather than one referring to the history of thought, in
analogy to "law.") Very early, in *Act and Being,* Bonhoeffer asks how the
Word of God is to reach man in his history. He sees the danger that instead
of meeting man in the world, the Word of God may establish a second,
heavenly subject, a "heavenly double."[33] Even in the later letters published
in *Letters and Papers from Prison,* Bonhoeffer maintains this reproach under
the frequently misunderstood concept of a "positivism of revelation." What
he means by this term, according to an explicit statement in *Ethics,*[34] is a
"metaphysical-religious positivism" that takes the place of empirical posi-

tivism and, as a "system of orders and values," is to establish an authorization for ethical discourse. In this metaphysical positivism, an authorization is abstractly attempted through a principle, but it only leads to "the paralysis of real life." Such a "metaphysical-religious positivism" might be behind Bonhoeffer's criticism of the positivism of revelation. What this positivism consists of, more simply stated, is that Barth's justified criticism of religion must be redeemed by theological abstraction, that it to say, by abstract theology dealing with the "virgin birth, the Trinity, or whatever there is, each . . . an equally meaningful and necessary part of the whole." The central error of the positivism of revelation is that the world is, "to a certain degree, left to its own devices and abandoned."[35] Thus the positivism of revelation turns out to be only the inner theological side of Barth's acosmicism, on the basis of which his thinking is still determined by liberal theology, even if only in a negative way.[36]

Bonhoeffer seeks to overcome the worldlessness that results from the isolated otherworldliness of God. He cannot agree that all revelation leaves on earth is something like a single "bomb crater," namely, "religion"; for this would mean that God's Word can never reach man directly and that everything earthly is always only emptiness (*Hohlraum*).[37] God thereby remains outside the world ultimately, and the believer is actually a heavenly double of himself, for in his earthly existence he is always only the "pious one," the religious one. In this situation Bonhoeffer could only follow Karl Barth; nevertheless, he felt obliged to criticize a central point from the outset, which is why Barthians correctly regard him as suspect to this day. In his opinion, Barth did not attach enough significance to the reality of the Incarnation of God in the world and in history.

This point of departure made it impossible for Bonhoeffer to come up with quick solutions. He laboriously developed his Christology with this configuration, going contrary to Barth and challenged by the quest for the concretizing of the law *in* a specific historical situation (1932/33). Supported by Christology, Bonhoeffer found it easier instead to offer negative criticism of false forms that were being touted as solutions around 1933. First he critiqued "secularism," which used the worship service as the "front room" for Sunday and on the basis of the orders of creation could not only tolerate but even sanction discrimination against Jews. (This was a result of the separation of faith and world without a recognition that through faith an effort was being made to sanction worldly conditions that were directed against faith.) On the other hand, he also criticized religious fanaticism, which wanted to turn away from the world entirely and turn completely to God. Bonhoeffer saw clearly that the two were equally wrong in the end. He was looking for the "worldly" decision that the Sermon on the Mount commanded. He feared that "Christians who only had one foot on earth also only had one foot in heaven."[38] The Christian resembles the giant

Antaeus, who has his power only as long as he is standing on the earth.[39] Not just as a human being but also as a Christian, Bonhoeffer sought firm ground on which to stand.[40]

Bonhoeffer's first faltering attempts at a theological understanding of the world are found in the sermons at Barcelona, although they are still without Christological mediation. The warning against withdrawal from the world (in the ethics lecture), therefore, remains quite unmediated, and the challenge to serve the times still has no real foundation.[41] Nevertheless, it must be appreciated that Bonhoeffer points to the responsibility believers have for the world and also to their solidarity with mankind. Reminiscent of his reading of Nietzsche, whose influence is underestimated to this day, he speaks of "our disdainful attitude toward the earth."[42] His questionable, often recurring motto of this period is: "God loved the earth and made us out of earth; he who is our Father made the earth our mother."[43] Not until 1932 does an extensive discussion of the topic "world" occur, and then quite expressly for the sake of the Christian's political responsibility. The challenge to "remain true to the earth" (which was probably also prompted by Nietzsche), the warning against dreaming of a better yonder and in the meantime forgetting the present, the warning against "being cloud dwellers" and "losing the ground under one's feet"[44]—all this is now based on the cross and resurrection of Jesus Christ as the dawn of God's kingdom on earth.

This, then, was the basis of the protest against secularism and other-worldliness, mentioned above. "What belongs to Christ is not a holy, sacred area of the world but the whole world."[45] The Incarnation, therefore, is related to the world; it is "universal." Thus it has implications not just for the universe in general but also for man and society. The Incarnation, cross, and resurrection are characterized by universality and world-relatedness— not by partiality and withdrawal from the world.[46]

The result is a necessarily strained, multifaceted relationship between church and state. The state is the guarantor of the orders of preservation— which are also Christologically based, however, for the world is created and sustained for Christ's sake. As the guarantor of the orders of preservation, the state—and not the church—must determine history. "The action of the state remains free from intervention by the church."[47] The church has a threefold function in her relationship to the state: 1) to ask the state "whether its actions can be accounted for as legitimate actions of a state"; 2) in case the state violates its responsibilities, to "offer assistance to the victims of the state's action"; and 3) in the most extreme emergency situation, to move to "direct political action," meaning that when it is no longer sufficient to dress the wounds of the victims of the state's actions, the church must put a stick in the spokes of the wheel itself.[48] Thus we can speak of Bonhoeffer as favoring an engagement of the church versus the state that is both political and apolitical, which means that the actions of the church are not immediately political, although they are indeed politically relevant. In case of extreme emergencies, it is no longer sufficient to criticize the state; it then becomes necessary to take political action. This political action is not undertaken by the church as church but as a subsidiary for the state, even while respecting the state as the state.

It is significant that only W. Dress noticed an important printing error in these Bonhoeffer texts:[49] the correction he calls for is that the text should speak of "indirect political action" in two instances where it reads "direct political action."[50] According to information from Bethge, however, the Bonhoeffer original clearly speaks of "direct political action" on the part of the church in both cases. To what extent this thesis of Bonhoeffer's expresses something true can be seen from Karl Barth's belated correction of his own thinking: Barth rebuked himself for having regarded the church struggle as far too much an "inward" struggle and having thereby neglected the Jewish question.[51] Bonhoeffer's own actions in the later Resistance may therefore be understood not just as Christian encouragement for the participants in the Resistance but as active participation, with Bonhoeffer using the means at his disposal.

The challenge Bonhoeffer raised in 1932/33 did not lead to any results. This prompted him to retreat to London, where he concentrated theologically on *The Cost of Discipleship*. Here Jesus Christ remains the center, though the search for a positive understanding of the world remains futile, except for a few hints.[52] The picture is dominated by distance taken from the world, the break with the world, on the basis of which the believing community passes through the world like "a sealed train in foreign territory," like "the ark in the flood," without a constructive relationship to the surrounding world and focusing only on its future in Christ.[53]

Only in his letter to Theodor Litt, mentioned above, does Bonhoeffer make a second attempt at a constructive understanding of the world. This second attempt determines his future theological reflections up to the time of the last letters. In answer to two of Litt's publications, Bonhoeffer writes to him that he has "presumably deliberately neglected to express, as it should be expressed, the Christian faith's ultimate reason for its relationship to the world, namely, the name of Jesus Christ."[54] Thus Jesus Christ—not God and his order of creation—is the reason for the Christian's relationship with the world. Bonhoeffer develops this train of thought further, stating that it is not sufficient to develop an understanding of the world on the basis of Jesus Christ, for such an understanding might be negative. Rather, the Christian must accept a positive understanding of the world for the simple reason that he accepts the world through the "fact of the incarnation of God." "Because it is a fact that in the Christian faith the 'uncertain is indeed included in the certain'; . . . the 'beyond' [*Jenseitige*] has entered the 'present' [*Dieseitige*]. Therefore the believer is not torn between the two;

rather, in this one place in the world he finds God and man in one."[55] This statement would also fit into Bonhoeffer's *Ethics*. It verifies the Christological foundation of his theological understanding of the world.

I will not sketch the historical sequence of Bonhoeffer's theology any further. I simply wish to demonstrate, on the basis of Christology as the *cantus firmus* and the understanding of the world as the most important contrapuntal theme, that the development of Bonhoeffer's theology cannot be portrayed as described by H. Müller.[56] In spite of all the differences in their interpretations, subsequent writers subscribed to Müller's thesis. They speak of a "caesura,"[57] and even of a "collapse of Christological ontology as a system."[58] The fact of the matter is that the *cantus firmus* of the Christology lecture in Barcelona on *Act and Being* is maintained right into the letters written in prison, although the counterpoint is inserted once again in 1939. There is no caesura in *Letters and Papers from Prison* as far as any basic theological concept is concerned.

On the basis of this fundamental assumption, the most important points with regard to the topic of "world" can be summarized as follows:

A.

To begin with a negatively formulated point, there is the rejection of thinking in two spheres. We have seen earlier that Bonhoeffer rejected any interpretation in terms of "spheres" as characteristic of "religion." He guarded against any radical separation of faith and the world in which faith is confined to a reservation. Naumann states that the "Lutheran separation of the spheres [of reason and faith] has proved to be right for us, too. We return to the great old doctor of the German faith when we regard political affairs as being outside the sphere of the proclamation of the gospel."[59] Bonhoeffer rejects any such division into two spheres, especially in his *Ethics*. There are not two spheres; rather, there is only "one sphere of the realization in Christ." "Thought which is conducted in terms of two spheres regards such pairs of concepts as secular and Christian, natural and supernatural, profane and sacred, and rational and revelational as though they were ultimate static antitheses."[60]

Such a division makes the mistake of limiting Christ to one sphere, whereas in fact the whole world belongs to Christ.[61] Christian and secular are not identical, of course, but the two are inseparable and form one polemical unity, as Bonhoeffer puts it:

> Luther was protesting against a Christianity which was striving for independence and detaching itself from the reality in Christ. He protested with the help of the secular and in the name of a better Christianity. So too, today, when Christianity is employed as a polemical weapon against the secular, this must be done in the name of a better secularity and above all it must not lead back to a static predominance of the spiritual sphere as an end in itself. It is only in this sense, as

a polemical unity, that Luther's doctrine of the two kingdoms is to be accepted, and it was no doubt in this sense that it was originally intended.[62]

Perhaps Bonhoeffer's reason for not proposing a two-kingdoms doctrine was that he wanted to sidestep the inevitable misunderstandings. He draws on it only incidentally, largely in criticizing the false two-kingdoms doctrine that had been so widely propagated. In his later theology, he preferred to use the concept of "worldliness" instead, which had already appeared in the lectures of 1932/33 as "worldliness of the church" and then as "worldliness of man."[63]

B.

In our effort to summarize Bonhoeffer's understanding of the world, we turn next to the concept of "worldliness." "Worldliness" (used with regard to the church in 1932, and in the negative sense in *The Cost of Discipleship*) is the central concept in the last section of *Ethics,* where Bonhoeffer attempts to express a positive characteristic of the world which cannot be constituted without Jesus and his cross. In this case the cross has a double function. In the first place, the world got rid of God, which is the negative side of the godlessness of the world. At the same time, the cross is the cross of reconciliation, of "setting free for life before God in the midst of a godless world"; it is "the setting free for life in genuine worldliness." The world is protected from every "vain attempt to deify the world" only by the crucified Reconciler. Thus "a life of genuine worldliness is possible and real only through the proclamation of Christ crucified."[64] To the extent that the Christian faith indeed lets the world be worldly and keeps it from the "deification of the worldly," which is unavoidable without God and results in a deterioration into "inauthentic half-worldliness," to that extent it is the foundation and guarantee of genuine, complete worldliness and bestows freedom and courage on worldliness. Yet Bonhoeffer did not want this to be misused as a basis for making false claims to power over the world.

The formal aspect of genuine worldliness is worked out here as the world's independence, which is understood as freedom from self-deification. Bonhoeffer was not able to work out the material aspects in writing, for it was at this point in his work that he was arrested. That he was concerned with the material aspect, or the concrete content, is clear: his reflections about reality, initiated within a Christological framework, came under the heading "The Concrete *Law* and the Divine Mandates." Thus these reflections were to serve the purpose of a concrete ethic.

C.

The same topic comes up in an earlier section of Bonhoeffer's *Ethics,* where he deals with the ultimate and penultimate things and also with the natural.

That section is especially important because Bonhoeffer there attempts—avoiding express confrontation—to replace two-sphere thinking with a positive proposal, namely, the historical concept of the ultimate and the penultimate. Indeed, the ultimate "entirely annuls and invalidates the penultimate." There is no way or method whereby the ultimate can be reached from the penultimate, but "the penultimate must be dealt with precisely for the sake of the ultimate."[65] The penultimate is not determinative for the ultimate; rather, the ultimate is determinative. Ultimate and penultimate are connected in Jesus Christ. "What must be done, therefore, is to fortify the penultimate with a more emphatic proclamation of the ultimate, and also to protect the ultimate by taking due care for the penultimate."[66] Therefore, "the ultimate—the last things—leaves open a certain amount of room for the penultimate, the things before the last."[67] The tension between the ultimate and the penultimate can only be resolved in Christ. Because the ultimate came to the world in Jesus Christ, the penultimate is really pen-*ultimate:* the world which is preserved for Christ and his coming.

What this formal designation, the "preservation of the penultimate,"[68] is getting at is also expressed in Bonhoeffer's plea for "the natural," a phrase that can be used as a synonym for the penultimate. The natural is not a preliminary step on the way to the ultimate, which is what *theologia naturalis* attempts to prove. Bonhoeffer rejects *theologia naturalis* along with its religious a priori. The natural should instead be viewed as a preserved reality in a relationship determined by the ultimate. Therefore, it cannot be abridged. All the word *natural* includes, namely "the form of the preserved life itself, may not be disregarded for the sake of the ultimate." According to Bonhoeffer, "the natural" expressly implies "an element of independence and self-development."[69] To the extent that the natural is not without the ultimate—and actually, as penultimate, only becomes visible through the ultimate, thereby gaining a new status because it can only be seen in its full reality in this way, namely, as not being the ultimate—to that extent it is identical with what Bonhoeffer speaks of in a later section of *Ethics* as "genuine worldliness." "The natural" does sound less secular than the concept of "worldliness," and this may be why Bonhoeffer later preferred the concept of "worldliness."

All these concepts—ultimate and penultimate, the natural, worldliness—are of renewed significance in *Letters and Papers from Prison.* Instead of abstract "worldliness," the preferred term here is "the world" or, better yet, "the world-come-of-age."

D.

Bonhoeffer's letters from prison have aroused continuing controversy among theologians. Whether the controversy can be settled, at least to a degree, remains to be seen. At the beginning of 1944, Bonhoeffer wrote some surprisingly colorful theological letters. Those letters have given rise to talk about a caesura, if not a "qualified leap" (Müller), which was followed by a "new theology" (Bethge, and actually Rainer Mayer as well). Such talk is correct insofar as it shows that Bonhoeffer, without giving up the continuity of his theological thinking, opened himself to Wilhelm Dilthey's arguments taken from the history of thought.

There is a complicated and highly differentiated set of issues facing us here. For one thing, Bonhoeffer tried to think historically to an ever-increasing extent; this was a countermove to "idealism" on his part. He was extremely interested in properly understanding the concretion of faith in the world: "Reality is the sacrament of the commandment."[70] For the sake of this reality, Bonhoeffer was open to the world. The world was to be an integral part of faith because in Jesus Christ the world is really the world accepted by God. On this basis Bonhoeffer could unreservedly accept Dilthey's interpretation of modern times, only to use this interpretation to protest against Dilthey's thesis of an inward, universal, unecclesiastical Christianity.

Bonhoeffer read especially Dilthey's *Weltanschauung und Analyse des Menschen seit Renaissance und Reformation.* From this volume he gathered the historical materials he needed to interpret the modern process of autonomy, ranging all the way from Herbert of Cherbury to Grotius, to certain statements of Giordano Bruno and Spinoza, as well as examples from the worldly Middle Ages, where Dilthey pointed to a Christian but anticlerical worldliness. In Dilthey he also found his central idea of the modern movement toward autonomy, as well as the "coming-of-age" concept, which had until then not appeared in Bonhoeffer with this full meaning.[71] Together with Dilthey, Bonhoeffer arrived at the thesis: "It is a great development that leads to the autonomy of the world."[72]

It may be that Bonhoeffer was still ambivalent in *Ethics,* but we certainly find an unequivocal, positive attitude toward the modern development and also the Enlightenment in his *Letters and Papers from Prison,* a work that was surely influenced by his experiences in the "worldly realm," for example, his participation in the German resistance. Bonhoeffer also agreed with Dilthey in his criticism of metaphysics, but he protested firmly against Dilthey's separation of inwardness from worldliness and his reduction of faith to inwardness. Yet Bonhoeffer did not direct his criticism with regard to this point directly at Dilthey; instead, he directed it against Barth, who, to put it bluntly, perpetuated an important tenet of liberal theology when he talked about the unworldliness of Christian faith.

Bonhoeffer's efforts to make reality concrete are evident in his earlier writings as well as in his prison letters, in that he preferred to work with historical categories. Whenever possible he writes about the "world-come-of-age" *(mündig gewordene Welt)*. (Only once does he speak simply of the *mündige Welt,* or "adult world.") He relinquishes any abstract understanding of secularization, as we can see from a comparison with F. Gogarten, who relied on the same books Bonhoeffer did (Volume II of Dilthey's *Gesammelte Schriften,* as well as C. F. von Weizsäcker's *Zum Weltbild der Physik*),[73] but apparently came to entirely different conclusions. Gogarten represents a Diltheyan, ultimately idealistic acosmicism and a corresponding inwardness. Bonhoeffer guards against such a "religious"—in the sense of pantheistic-subjective—concealment of the true godlessness of such a world-come-of-age, which in itself is ambivalent. He pleads "that we have to live in the world *etsi deus non daretur.* And this is just what we do recognize—before God! . . . God would have us know that we must live as men who manage our lives without him."[74] Not to misuse God as a "stopgap" or "working hypothesis," but to become involved in life in the world "before God and with God . . . without God"—that was Bonhoeffer's challenge.

Bonhoeffer's polemic against "religion" is valid in view of the world-come-of-age, but it is also valid for "religious" Christianity, which is characterized by metaphysics, inwardness, and the associated false concept of transcendence, which might be summarized as a false understanding of God and the world. The religious understanding of the world is based on the twofold, contradictory error already mentioned, namely, that God is on the one hand edged out of the world and settled somewhere beyond the boundaries of the world and our understanding, while on the other hand he is always inserted as a working hypothesis in our worldly calculations to solve our inward problems when they do not disappear. God is thus degraded to a *deus ex machina.*

This religious Christianity, Bonhoeffer thinks, is now finished. Religion is clearly not a systematic concept. (Here he differs with Barth.) Just as circumcision is not a condition for faith, although in a certain epoch it was seen as such, religion is not a condition for faith. During a certain period, rather, when certain assumptions were in effect (metaphysics, inwardness), religion was the *form* of faith. Hence it is to be viewed as a "garment" that has now been worn out. And there is no sense in mending the garment. The assumptions of religious Christianity have been updated in the face of a world-come-of-age. How the new garment or new form (i.e., the religionless, "worldly" Christianity and its inward side, the secret discipline) is to take shape was Bonhoeffer's most urgent problem during the summer of 1944. As far as content is concerned, he was able to realize almost nothing, not just because the "Outline for a Book" could not be realized but especially because such a topic can only be mastered in practical terms, not theoretical ones. Therefore, there are only a few allusions of a formal nature to be found.

In *Letters and Papers from Prison,* Bonhoeffer speaks in various ways of the "form" of this new Christianity and its accompanying interpretation, the nonreligious interpretation or worldly interpretation, which is synonymous with it. (Contrary to Ebeling, I maintain that this sequence is convincing and significant.) Bonhoeffer's way of speaking about this matter is reminiscent of an early letter he wrote at the time he was planning to visit Gandhi in India: "Since I am becoming daily more convinced that in the West Christianity is approaching its end—at least in its present form, and its present interpretation—I should like to go to the Far East before coming back to Germany."[75] Both these key terms, "form" and "interpretation," are used again in *Letters and Papers from Prison.* In addition, this is where Bonhoeffer confirms that "we who are in the middle, between East and West, are the ones who will be left with an important task."[76]

I would like to venture the thesis that in Gandhi's way of life—however politically relevant—Bonhoeffer found an active passiveness or passive activity, a *vita communis,* something definitely Christian, a model for Christianity, which was not "Westernized to the extent" that it now is.[77] For Bonhoeffer, liberation from the Western way of life and thought, which in our day has the same significance that liberation from circumcision had for the primitive church, that is, as a liberation from occidental "religion," is a basic presupposition for the new form of the Christian faith in a world that is no longer determined solely by the West. The nonreligious interpretation thereby becomes a "program of translation." The translation involved here is not so much from the mythological into late occidental, secularist "language," but into all languages, all forms of culture in the world, as a contribution to the "profaning of the world" that is still largely due. Through such a program Christianity can make a contribution to the world's coming of age, its emancipation from false gods, but not by beginning with the image of God as leading his "children." Rather, it must present God as letting them go, as followers of Jesus Christ, to live responsibly in a "world-come-of-age," a world in which God is near only in his absence.

IV. Toward the Political Engagement of the Church

To link religionless Christianity to the renunciation of any relationship to political-social reality would be to misunderstand it, for that would involve leaving the world to itself, which was something Bonhoeffer opposed "religiously." Rather, the new form of Christian faith in the world requires substantial—even fundamental—changes on the part of the church. "The church is only church when she exists for others."[78] That this is a difficult, if not impossible, demand is evident: the church is told to forego using its power as an institution. Although it is indeed an institution, it is asked not to use power in the way institutions do. The church can no more waive selfless service to the world than the individual can separate his being a Christian from his being a citizen. And the concern here is definitely not the "Christianizing of politics."[79] Bonhoeffer's understanding of the world has immediate consequences in the *political* realm inasmuch as the service to the world, the state, and society which faith demands does not bring about a Christianization in which state and church converge.

Just as Bonhoeffer does not advocate a church-state, he is not in favor of a state-church. In fact, one of the important political functions of the church is to prevent the state from wanting to be the church, or even wanting to be lord over the church. Since the incarnation and the cross, there is neither separation nor amalgamation of church and state but only a "dualism of church and state"[80] based on Christ. "Only in the genuine interrelationship and separation of both is the kingdom of Christ realized." Thus the church is "political and apolitical simultaneously, in an eminent sense."[81] The church must acknowledge this political responsibility, and it must recognize that no one who acts responsibly can evade the guilt.

Not acting at all, however, would really lead to guilt, which was why Bonhoeffer was working in 1942 on the church's confession of guilt to be used after the coup. Bonhoeffer's motive as an individual for becoming involved in the resistance was to diminish the church's guilt as much as he could, given his situation and limitations. For him, the decision to join the resistance meant venturing into the darkness of guilt. After some doubting, Bonhoeffer was sure that "it was really for the cause of Christ" that he was imprisoned. In a very unassuming way—unconcerned about whether he was now a political conspirator or a martyr—he embodied what he had said in a sermon of 1932, namely, that times requiring the blood of the martyrs would probably come again. "But this blood, if we then actually still have the courage and faithfulness to shed it, will not be as innocent and shining as that of the first witnesses. On our blood will be our own great guilt, the guilt of the unprofitable servant who was thrown out into the darkness."[82]

Notes

1   Cf. U. Duchrow, *Christenheit und Weltverantwortung: Traditionsgeschichte und systematische Struktur der Zweireichelehre. Forschungen u. Berichte der Ev. Studiengemeinschaft,* XXV (1970), 525.

2   Cf. the topics of the addresses by P. Lehman and G. Casalis at the Bonhoeffer congress.

3   Cf. Duchrow, XXV, 509f.

4   Here one should examine the cosmological tradition in the fragment of Anaximander, where there is talk of things "paying the penalty" for their "un-

righteousness" (*Die Fragmente der Vorsokratiker,* ed. H. Diehls and W. Kranz, I [8th ed., 1956], 12 B 1).

5 Cf., for example, the correlation between microcosm and macrocosm, taking note that *cosmos* originally indicated a purposeful human order. Cf. W. Kranz, "Kosmos, I," *Archiv für Begriffsgeschichte,* II (1955), 8. In any case, this question might be considered in connection with the rejection of "cosmocentric thought" in favor of "anthropocentric thought."

6 *Politische Metaphysik von Solon bis Augustin,* I-III (1959-69).

7 This thesis, like the other theses in this essay, is expounded in detail in my *Die Theologie Dietrich Bonhoeffers: Hermeneutik, Christologie, Weltverständnis* (Munich: Christian Kaiser Verlag, 1971). References to this work (hereafter *ThDB*) will be provided only in exceptional cases. Bonhoeffer quotations will be identified by means of the usual abbreviations.

8 Cf. C. H. Ratschow, "Standort-Bestimmung gegenwärtiger Evangelischer Theologie," *Theologische Zeitschrift,* XCIV (1969), 723.

9 Quoted in *ThDB,* p. 158, n. 5.

10 *Ek,* p. 342.

11 *WE,* pp. 218f. (*WEN,* p. 359; *LPPE,* pp. 326f.).

12 1931/32, *DB,* p. 1053; cf. *GS,* V, 298.

13 *DB,* pp. 1051f.; cf. *GS,* V, 210ff.

14 *DB,* p. 1048; cf. *GS,* V, 185.

15 *ThDB,* p. 307, n. 69.

16 1932, *GS,* III, 173; 1941, *GS,* III, 471.

17 *GS,* III, 273.

18 Cf. *ThDB,* p. 276.

19 1933, *GS,* II, 119.

20 *WE,* p. 258 (*WEN,* p. 413; *LPPE,* pp. 381f.).

21 *GS,* I, 159.

22 *WE,* p. 192 (*WEN,* p. 331; *LPPE,* p. 303).

23 Cf. *ThDB,* p. 176.

24 Cf. *ibid.,* p. 182.

25 1939, *GS,* III, 31-33.

26 1933, *GS,* III, 194f.

27 Cf. *ThDB,* p. 428, on "hier und heute."

28 *Ek,* pp. 313ff.

29 Sermon in Barcelona, September 23, 1928, quoted in *ThDB,* p. 244; cf. *GS,* V, 464.

30 *WE,* p. 210 (*WEN,* p. 341; *LPPE,* p. 311).

31 *Ibid.,* p. 184 (*WEN,* p. 312; *LPPE,* p. 286).

32 "Die nicht-religiöse Interpretation biblischer Begriffe," *MW,* II (1956), 19.

33 *AS,* p. 77.

34 *Ek,* pp. 292f.

35 *WE,* pp. 184f. (*WEN,* pp. 312f.; *LPPE,* pp. 286f.).

36 Cf. *ThDB,* p. 237; *WE,* p. 221 (*WEN,* p. 360; *LPPE,* pp. 328ff.).

37 K. Barth, *Der Römerbrief* (1922; new edition: Zurich, 1967), p. 12.

38 In a letter to his fiancée, quoted in *ThDB,* p. 316.

39 Sermon in Barcelona on September 23, 1928, quoted in *ThDB,* p. 247 (cf. *GS,* V, 467), and again in the fragment of a drama of 1943, *GS,* III, 494.

40 Recurring throughout Bonhoeffer's entire work. Cf. *ThDB,* p. 247, n. 39.

41   Cf. *ThDB*, pp. 244f.
42   *Ibid.*, p. 247.
43   Sermon in Barcelona, see n. 39.
44   *ThDB*, p. 253.
45   1932, *GS*, I, 144.
46   Cf. *ThDB*, p. 255.
47   1933, *GS*, II, 45.
48   *Ibid.*, pp. 46ff.
49   As of now, *GS*, II, 48, reads "indirect political action," and p. 49 "direct political action."
50   "Widerstandsrecht und Christenpflicht bei Dietrich Bonhoeffer," *Luth. Monatshefte*, III (1968), 199, ns. 12, 14; cf. *ThDB*, p. 264, n. 105.
51   Letter to Bethge in *Evangelische Theologie*, XXVIII (1968), 555f.
52   Cf. the interpretation of the story of Abraham in *N*, pp. 75f. (*CD*, p. 251).
53   *CD*, pp. 252f.
54   *GS*, III, 31ff.
55   *Ibid.*, p. 32.
56   *Von der Kirche zur Welt: Ein Beitrag zu der Beziehung des Wortes Gottes auf die societas in Dietrich Bonhoeffers theologischer Entwicklung* (Leipzig, 1966), pp. 8ff.
57   *DB*, pp. 964ff.
58   R. Mayer, *Christuswirklichkeit: Grundlagen, Entwicklung und Konsequenzen der Theologie Dietrich Bonhoeffers* (1969), pp. 226f.; cf. J. A. Phillips, *The Form of Christ in the World: A Study of Bonhoeffer's Christology* (London, 1967), pp. 181ff.
59   With an appended plea for the German Kaiser's fleet, "Briefe über Religion," *Werke* (1964), I, 626.
60   *Ek*, p. 210 (*E*, pp. 197-98).
61   *Ek*, p. 218 (*E*, p. 205).
62   *Ek*, p. 212 (*E*, p. 199).
63   Cf. *ThDB*, pp. 308f.
64   *Ek*, p. 314 (*E*, p. 297).
65   *Ek*, p. 133 (*E*, pp. 125-26).
66   *Ek*, p. 151 (*E*, p. 142).
67   *Ek*, p. 141 (*E*, p. 133).
68   Here again (*Ek*, p. 155 [*E*, p. 146]) we have the differentiation between "formal" and "material."
69   *Ek*, p. 154 (*E*, p. 145).
70   1932, *GS*, I, 147.
71   Cf. *ThDB*, pp. 355ff.
72   *WE*, p. 239 (*WEN*, p. 392; *LPPE*, p. 359).
73   *ThDB*, p. 369, n. 65.
74   *WE*, p. 241 (*WEN*, p. 394; *LPPE*, p. 360).
75   1934, *GS*, II, 158 (*DBET*, pp. 329-30).
76   *WE*, p. 182 (*WEN*, p. 308; *LPPE*, p. 282).
77   1934, *GS*, II, 182.
78   *WE*, p. 261 (*WEN*, p. 415; *LPPE*, p. 382).
79   1932, *GS*, III, 270; *Ek*, pp. 369, 350 (*E*, pp. 342, 333).
80   1932, *GS*, III, 279.
81   *GS*, III, 282, 289.
82   *GS*, IV, 71.

VI.
RELIGION AND SECULARIZATION

RELIGION AND REALITY IN THE
WORK OF BONHOEFFER

André Dumas

I. Disgust for Religion

IN A LETTER of June 25, 1942, Bonhoeffer wrote to Eberhard Bethge:

I feel how much my resistance against all that is "religious" is growing. This resistance is becoming almost an instinctive disgust, which is surely not good. I am not of a religious temperament. But on the other hand, I must think unceasingly of God, of Christ. I am also strongly attached to authenticity, life, liberty and mercy. Religious dress is what bothers me most. Do you understand this? In truth these are not new thoughts or new perspectives, but I believe that I am now hung up on this point and that I should let things take their course.[1]

Bonhoeffer was free when he wrote this letter. He was participating in the German resistance and composing the fragments of *Ethics*. Thus the theme of faith in God and Christ going hand-in-hand with the growing disgust for religion is not a wholly new one that sprang up in the solitude of prison, appearing only from the letter of April 30, 1944, and marking a rupture between *Ethics* and *Letters and Papers from Prison*. Even if the later Bonhoeffer both accentuated and made famous this theme, his whole work, from its very beginnings, is marked by the refusal to confuse Jesus Christ with the founder of a religion, or the church with a religious association, or Christians with religious people. "Religion" always had a pejorative and painful connotation for Bonhoeffer, deceitful and repulsive at its worst, while we shall see that the word "reality" represents all that Bonhoeffer believed about God and hoped for man.

Let us try to characterize the misdeeds of religion according to Bonhoeffer, beginning by collecting some texts from throughout his works and then synthesizing their implications. First, the older texts, prior to the rise of Nazism. Vicar at Barcelona, Bonhoeffer wrote on August 7, 1928, to his friend Rössler:

Here one meets men as they really are, far from the masquerade of the "Christian world"; impassioned people, good-for-nothings, little people with little goals, little impulses, and little offenses, real people. I can only give my impression: These very people seem to me to be more under grace than under judgment, while the Christian world, finds itself, I believe, more under judgment than under grace. . . . That's the judgment of all religion . . . and that is why as a theologian one suffers doubly.[2]

Three years later, as a student at New York's Union Theological Seminary in 1931, Bonhoeffer developed his thought, explaining that religion is the category opposed to grace:

God's work with man does not begin as a continuation or a perfection of man's highest, although, as every decent man will admit, imperfect enterprises, such as religion and morality, but on the contrary, it begins as the irrefragable limitation of man. . . . The category which Barth tries to introduce into theology in its strict sense and which is so refractory to all general thinking and especially religious thinking, is the category of the Word of God, of the revelation straight from above, from *outside* of man, according to the justification of the sinner by grace. . . . It is, in the final analysis, the great antithesis of the word of God and the word of man, of grace and religion, of a pure Christian category and a general religious category.[3]

Next, let us take some texts contemporary with the great "religious" rise of Nazism.

As the community of Jesus Christ, the church separates itself from this Protestantism which confuses the church with a national, cultural and religious movement. . . . To understand the action of Luther as the irruption of the Germanic spirit, or as the origin of the modern feeling of liberty, or as the foundation of a new religion, is to fly in the face of his own words.[4]

The second synod of the Confessing Church meeting at Dahlem on March 4 and 5, 1935, warned the parishes "against the mortal danger of a new religion." On February 22, 1931, H. Rössler wrote to Bonhoeffer: "Here is the greatest tragedy of the church and our people: A burning nationalism tied to a new paganism, harder to fight than the religion of the free-thinkers, because it wears Christian clothing. . . . The grounds of this neo-pagan religion is the pretension of unity manifest between the religion and the race."[5] Bonhoeffer himself qualified Nazi anti-Semitism as "religious" because it sought to ground itself among Christians on the basis of a "pious and arbitrary experience,"[6] instead of listening to the Holy Spirit speak when and how it wants through the whole of Scripture.

Finally, there are the texts that are dominated by the search for a nonreligious Christianity, exactly as in *Letters and Papers from Prison.* They are to be found from the beginning of his writings. Their formulation—but not their content—becomes more and more striking. The class of November 19, 1932, "Thy rule is coming. The prayer of the community with regard to the Kingdom of God on earth," is a long and remarkable development of the necessary struggle against the religious escapism of those who become unfaithful to the earth and pass into another world of religion. For Bonhoeffer this struggle is the counterpart of another struggle, just as necessary, against the "secularists," that is, the pious Christian secularists who have joyously replaced the eschatological cause of God on earth with their own cause of moral and religious progress. These two groups, the seekers of another world (*Hinterweltler*) and the secularists (*Sekularisten*), are equally religious in Bonhoeffer's eyes. Neither of them believes that the Kingdom of God is coming on earth.

> Either we are enemies of the world, because we want to be better than it, or we are the enemies of God, because He has stolen from us the earth, our mother. We flee before the power of the earth, or we clutch at it. . . . We have lived in another world ever since we discovered the bad trick of being religious and even "Christian" at the expense of the world. As soon as life becomes painful or bothersome, we make an audacious leap into the air and rise up relieved, without a care, into what is called the "eternal abode". . . . But Christ does not lead man into another world of a religious flight from the world, he returns him to earth as a faithful son. Do not live in another world, but be strong. . . .

Similarly:

> We have fallen prey to secularism, I mean, "pious Christian secularism," not atheism or bolshevism, but the Christian renunciation of believing that God is the Lord of the earth. . . . Man, yes, religious man, takes pleasure in exciting himself this way and in manifesting his strength. . . . Escaping from God himself in calling ourselves ready to establish his rights in this world, loving the earth for itself, for the struggle that we make there, such is the Christian way to surrender to the secular spirit. However, we do not escape God. He brings man back under his lordship. Become weak in the world and let God be Lord.

Bonhoeffer judges these two religious subterfuges by the reality of God, that of the flight to another world as much as that of the exaltation of secularism.

> He who runs away from the earth does not find God, but only another world, his own world, better, more beautiful, more peaceful. He never finds the world of God which comes in this world. He who runs away from the world to find God finds only himself. He who

escapes God to find the earth does not find the earth as God's earth;
he finds the pleasant theater of a war between good and evil, between
religion and impiousness, a war that he started himself, he finds only
himself. He who loves God loves him as Lord of the earth, such as
it is; he who loves the earth loves it as God's earth. He who loves the
Kingdom of God loves it wholly as the Kingdom of *God*, but he loves
it also wholly as the Kingdom of God *on earth*.[7]

I know of no better illustration of this disgust with religion, other-
worldly or secularist as opposed to a terrestrial and theocentric faith, than
the reflections of Bonhoeffer on Sunday, June 18, 1938, in New York,
where he heard two sermons in a row, the morning one bad—"religious"—
at Riverside Church, the afternoon one good—Christological—at Broad-
way Presbyterian Church. Bonhoeffer found the sermon at Riverside Church
"simply insupportable. . . . The whole affair is a religious festival, decent,
flourishing, self-satisfied. With such religious idolatry the flesh lives again,
the flesh which is used to being disciplined by the Word of God. Preaching
like that makes one a libertine, an egoist, indifferent. Don't these people
really know that one gets out of this mess much better without religion—
if only God himself and his Word didn't exist!" On the other hand, Bonhoeffer liked the "wholly biblical" preaching of the afternoon on "our likeness with Christ. . . . We are blameless like Christ, we are tempted like
Christ." He predicted that "later there will be a center of resistance here,
while Riverside Church will long have become a temple of idols."[8] Bonhoeffer added some words in the margin of his diary of his last three weeks
of travel in the United States in June 1939, before returning to the German
"reality," far from American "religion": "The church is a religious (philosophical, cultural) province, a means for an end (pedagogy, morals, ap-
peasement of religious needs, harmony of existence, just like science and
art). Religion, church, private affair, private satisfaction."[9]

Before this degeneration of faith into religion, let us recall what the
young Bonhoeffer had already explained in 1930 to the students of Union
Theological Seminary:

> The Christian faith is absolutely different from every other religion.
> One often hears it said: If grace is all and man nothing, then the
> natural consequence is that all ethical life is made impossible. But
> this argument is a relapse into the psychological interpretation. . . .
> Grace makes man free from himself (from his trust in his religion, in
> his ethical life . . .) and free for God, for hearing his Word.[10]

We have now seen enough texts to try to say why religion is more
and more discouraging and disgusting in the eyes of Bonhoeffer. First of
all, religion is often bound up with idols. More dangerous than atheism, it
is the disguising of man's pretensions with regard to false absolutes in a

terrible piety. Nazism was dangerous in proportion to its religious power, seducing patriots, the masses, and the church. To make something secular religious is to constitute it as a mortal peril for human discernment. It is to manipulate God in the service of our finitude, instead of serving him at the heart of our limitations and our responsibilities.

But this first meaning of religion as idolatry is not the most specifically Bonhoefferian sense. Religion is also the pious climb toward heaven, the coveting of salvation which one wants to conquer by exalting oneself and not to receive by grace. Such is the accursed meaning of religion, for example, in the *Commentary on Romans* of Karl Barth, who in the 1919 edition denounced romanticism and pietism, and concentrated the attacks of the 1922 edition on religion: "Religion and grace are as opposed to each other as life and death." Religion is the "over-stepping of the limit which is fixed for us," the "drunken confusion of distances," the "establishing of romantic immediacy," the "false divinization of man and the humanization of God," the "lewd grasping" of that which can come to us only from God. Religious man is "the most stiff-necked species of the whole human genus," the "sinner in the most visible sense of the word." Surely Bonhoeffer always shared this Barthian attack against climbing up to heaven, the religious ascent of man as opposed to the nonreligious condescending of God's grace. But that is not, in my opinion, Bonhoeffer's specific understanding of religion either; the proof is that he never participated in Barth's majestic assumption of religion under grace (in the *Commentary on Romans* just as in the *Dogmatics*), when religion, ceasing to be vain ascent against grace, through grace becomes realized truth and fruitful for man. Bonhoeffer never assumed religion under grace. He had the impression, on this point as on many others, that Barth's *Dogmatics* restored dialectically what he had only begun to attack.

Religion for Bonhoeffer, it seems to me, means above all else *unreality*. It is a flight out from the confines of earth to a place where is neither God nor man, a desertion of the earth where God is located along with man. It is a longing for the ideal in a renunciation of reality. It hopes to get something better than what it already has. Religion is the snake's proposal to Adam and Eve: Disobey the concrete commandment of God by the imaginary supposition that the divine creation could become better religiously. Religious man searches and lives elsewhere. He is fundamentally unfaithful to earth, and at the same time to God, the Lord of the earth. He is, as Feuerbach said ironically, the "student of the beyond," the "beggar after eternity." However, we should remember, over against Feuerbach, Bonhoeffer's attack on religious secularism, which also prefers the ideal world of human speculation to the real world of God. Thus religious man, in Bonhoeffer's eyes, detests reality; he wants either to embellish it or to evacuate it. The good boundaries of the concrete become insupportable barriers to desire. He leaps, he crosses them, and he finds himself alone with himself, having deserted his reality and his neighbor, God and the world.

When the Christian church becomes religious, as it does unceasingly—since the serpent is never more persuasive than when he succeeds in subtly twisting the Word of God for his own profit as in the temptation of Jesus—it transforms itself into an association cut off from the earth. The church then cultivates religion for the sake of those who have a fondness for such things. It becomes a province—either small or large, but in either case unreal—which no longer points to God, the Lord of all the earth. Entering a church becomes a synonym for leaving not the world of sin, but the profane earth, which is nevertheless the veritable site of the divine benediction. Religion sacralizes outside the realm of the profane; it no longer sanctifies the profane. Religion isolates man, apparently for God but really for piety's egocentrism. God himself is annexed by the religion of the beyond, which thus takes away from him his power of critical judgment and recreative resurrection here on earth. Religion is abstract, vain, and misleading. It is a mortal danger for faith to replace sin by the fall, salvation by escapism, eschatology by gnosis, man by the ego, and God by an ideal.

Thus the "double suffering" of the theologian (that is, of all people of the church, all parishioners) was evoked in 1928 by the young vicar of Barcelona: he believed that faith is not religion, and yet he saw clearly that religion remains one of the most obvious motivations of those people who gather in the church. Just as Goetz in Sartre's "The Devil and the Good Lord" had to take on the appearance of a religious man—though an atheist himself—in order to become one with the revolting peasants of the sixteenth century, who had chosen him as their leader, so the theologian wonders unceasingly if his combat for the faith does not also constantly risk to consolidate the escapism of religion. His suffering is double: suffering of the truth, which is to fight in the reality of the world along with God (Jesus experienced this suffering); and also suffering of the equivocal, which is to seem to flee toward God outside the real of the earth. Jesus also experienced this second suffering, dying in a multiple equivocation, seeming to some to be a sublime otherworldly man and to others to be a secularist in revolt. "The servant is not greater than his master" (Matt. 10:24).

Bonhoeffer's veracity seems to me to be in his clear consciousness both of the profoundly nonreligious character of faith and of the perpetually religious appearance of this same faith. Perhaps one must even say that to a great extent religion was and still is an aspect of the reality of earth that faith ought not to distort, but for which it ought to be responsible. Faith ought at the same time to unmask and to support the treason of religion which accompanies it like its own shadow.

From there on, things become clear: Bonhoeffer sees metaphysics as having the appearance of transcendence while in reality being an idealist escapism and an immanentalist annexation. Inwardness has the appearance of discipline, while really it is an interior escape and an egocentric extension. Christian religion, which is related to metaphysics and inwardness in *Letters and Papers from Prison*, is an appearance of Christianity, but in reality it is just a parenthesis in the history of Western culture. Today the parenthesis is being closed. Certainly we are in a great perplexity. Some (the partisans of another world) would like to save the faith by the permanence of religious needs; others (secularists) no longer know how to distinguish between faith in God and their immanentalist optimisms (or pessimisms). But let us remember that the Old Testament, more clearly than the New, shows the struggle of the faith in Jahweh against the surrounding religions—idolatrous religions, covetous religions, but especially religions of the unreal. They feed on speculation about the beyond and the soul, while Jahweh the living God meets the whole person, soul and body, on the earth of living humans. The divorce between faith and religion thus does not only come from the present weakening of religion besieged by secularist attacks. This divorce is biblically fundamental. The revelation of God to the biblical witnesses took place in this context of reality. However, today God no longer lives in reality with the same compelling obviousness that he had for Abraham and Moses, for Paul and Peter. Therefore, after having evoked the sources of Bonhoeffer's disgust with religion, it is important to analyze in what sense he lived the love of reality.

II. Love of Reality

"Real" (in German *wirklich*, from the root *Werk*, work, *wirken*, to do, to work) reappears constantly in Bonhoeffer's vocabulary. It is opposed to a series of words that define the ineffective and illusory; among them I would name "religious," "possible," "idealist," "abstract." Reality is our concern with an event that precedes us and a responsibility that calls us. In this sense, according to Bonhoeffer, theology is the science of reality because it reckons with the pronounced Word of God and the realized incarnation of God. Philosophy, on the contrary, is a science of the possible. In a 1931 article "concerning the Christian idea of God," Bonhoeffer wrote:

> Christian thinking has to be conscious of its particular premise, that is, of the premise of the reality of God, before and beyond all thinking. . . . But philosophical truth always remains truth which is given only within the category of possibility. Philosophical thinking can never extend beyond this category—it can never be a thinking in reality. . . . Thinking does violence to reality. . . . Thinking always means system and system excludes reality. Therefore, it has to call *itself* the ultimate reality, and in this system the thinking ego rules.[11]

In a word, the young Bonhoeffer sees no other fate for philosophy than the circle of the absolute idealism of the transcendental ego, while he assigns theology the vocation of rendering the realism of *Christus praesens* in the church and the world.

This reality of God, which is the methodological presupposition of the realism of theology, determines its characteristics. Theology is always concrete. Theological ethics is not concerned with general and abstract principles but with particular and concrete commandments. We are here at the antipodes of religion, which loves to escape toward the borders of the indefinite.

> As the Word issued from the omnipotence of *Christus praesens*, the Word of the church must be a valid Word, compelling here and now. The only Word which can be said to me with omnipotence is a Word which reaches me here and now from the base of the most profound knowledge of my humanity in my total reality. All other words are impotent. . . . The church ought to be able to say the Word of God, the omnipotent Word, here and now from the most concrete knowledge of the thing itself. Consequently, the church should not preach principles which are always true, but only commandments which are true today. For, that which is "always" true is not true "today." For us, God is "always" God "today."[12]

Concreteness is opposed to religion, commandment to ideals, obedience to vacillation, the sacramental to the conceptual. Ethical and sacramental realism expresses itself in surprising formulas: "The sacrament is to the preaching of the Gospel what the knowledge of reality is to the preaching of commandment. Reality is the sacrament of the commandment."[13] Throughout his works and all through his life Bonhoeffer sought the concretion of thought and of conduct. He combated without mercy the abstractness of knowledge, source of and alibi for the indecision of will as for the weakness of action.

But it is difficult to conform to reality if we give this term the full meaning that it has in Bonhoeffer's writings: unity between God and the world in Jesus Christ, unity indivisible, polemical, oriented, combative, suffering, and blessed. In effect, we no longer know reality in its natural state. In 1931, Bonhoeffer characterized sin as the loss of this reality: "Man 'before' the fall must be thought of as being able to think of 'reality', that means to think of God and of the fellow man as realities. Man 'in' and 'after' the fall refers everything to himself, puts himself in the center of the world, does violence to reality, makes himself God, and God and the other man his creatures."[14] Thus for lack of reality man "after" the fall, that is, the man that we all are, runs after two abstractions, either the ideal and the religious, or the factual and the pragmatic.

It would be to misunderstand conformity to reality to confuse it with the "servile devotion to the given" (Nietzsche) which always surrenders to the strongest pressure, which in principle justifies success, which chooses the opportune as though it were always the real. According to this misunderstanding, conformity to the real becomes irresponsibility. Neither servility toward the factual (*faktisch*) nor opposition in principle, as refusal in principle, in the name of whatever ideal, can lead to the responsible grasping of the conformity to reality. The two extremes are equally far from the essential.[15]

To recognize the factual and to be opposed to it are indissolubly bound together in all authentic conduct towards reality. For the most original reality is that of God becoming man. All factualness receives from this reality its final grounding and its final suppression, its final justification and its final contradiction.[16]

From this point on we see what separates the responsible man from the ideologue, that is, the believer from the religious man:

The ideologue sees himself as justified by his idea. The responsible man lives by the grace of God into whose hands he commits his action. . . . Jesus Christ did not hold himself before reality as a foreigner to it, as a reformer, a fanatic, a founder of a religion. But he carried and experienced in his own body the essence of reality; he knew how to speak out of reality as no other human being on earth.[17]

Bonhoeffer's love for reality was not an avid realism nor a rigid stoicism. It was the pursuit of the reconciliation of the world in Jesus Christ. This reconciliation in its depths is a tension. It passes through the cross where Jesus Christ conformed totally to the reality of man so that man might become totally conformed to the reality of God, which is the new creation of the world through the resurrection on earth. Without a doubt, it is our understanding of the resurrection that best shows the divergence between faith in the real world and religion in an unreal world. If we imagine a resurrection that removes us from the earth with Christ toward God, we transform Christianity either—as in the past—into a celestial gnosis, or today into transcendental idealism. But if we understand the resurrection as the recreation of the here below and as the announcement of the ultimate creation of the coming kingdom, then we are living in the biblical faith. The reality of the resurrection is thus neither its inward or metaphysical religiosity nor its objectifying factualness, but the presence of Christ in the church and the world. The category of reality is a category of presence, here and now; it is a category for faith. Faith is action in the world and hope for the world.

In conclusion, in Bonhoeffer's eyes, religious Christianity unrealizes, provincializes, interiorizes, and makes Jesus Christ remote. A nonreligious Christianity realizes, universalizes, and makes Jesus public and present, at once extraordinary and hidden, to use the two favorite adjectives of *Nach-folge*. It is almost inevitable that the paradoxical affirmations of Bonhoeffer should engender misunderstandings. Some people believe that nonreligious Christianity would end up in the muteness of faith; others believe that conformity to reality opens into an unconditional realism. Certainly Bonhoeffer's life and work are living refutations of both of these erroneous conclusions. But it is true that some texts remain so compressed that occasionally their meaning escapes us. In commemorating the thirty-fifth anniversary of his death we have no need to deny the difficulties of interpreting certain of his themes. Rather we should salute with an immense gratitude the man whose disgusts, like his loves, awaken, instruct, and delight us daily. I would like to apply to Bonhoeffer himself some of the phrases he pronounced as a young student in Berlin, June 15, 1930, at the grave of Harnack:

> He was always ready to listen and to respond. The only thing that mattered to him was the truthfulness of the answer. In his person it became clear that truth is born only from freedom. It was his way to say little, preferring to say too little about such things than to say one word too much. *Non potest non laetari, qui sperat in Dominum.*[18]

Notes

1 *GS*, VI, 568 (author's translation).
2 *GS*, I, 51-52.
3 *GS*, III, 115-117.
4 *GS*, II, 95.
5 *GS*, I, 57.
6 *GS*, II, 94.
7 *GS*, III, 270-273.
8 *GS*, I, 300-301.
9 *GS*, I, 302, n. 1.
10 *GS*, III, 98.
11 *GS*, III, 100-101.
12 *GS*, I, 144-145. Cf. "Because God is reality he is absolutely free of all theoretical generalization" (*GS*, III, 102-103).
13 *GS*, I, 147.
14 *GS*, III, 101.
15 In *LPP*, Bonhoeffer illustrates the two extremes, servility in principle and refusal in principle, by the two figures of Sancho Panza and Don Quixote.
16 *GS*, III, 458-459.
17 *GS*, III, 461, 465.
18 *GS*, III, 59-61.

WORSHIP IN A WORLD-COME-OF-AGE

Larry Rasmussen

WORSHIP IN a world-come-of-age is a topic given very little attention thus far in the area of Bonhoeffer studies and in the spate of literature on liturgical renewal. Perhaps this is just one of those oversights that occurs even in thirty-five years of close scrutiny. But should we not be rather amazed at the omission, for the question of worship in Bonhoeffer's last years was unmistakably very much on his mind. In the very first of those pathfinding theological letters from prison, after he raises what is for him the leading question ("what is bothering me incessantly is the question what Christianity really is, or indeed who Christ really is, for us today"), he goes on to say that "today" is a religionless time: "People as they are now simply cannot be religious any more."[1] That uncovers a whole series of questions for Bonhoeffer, among them the meaning of worship "for us" in such a time. He writes: "The questions to be answered would surely be: What do a church, a community, a sermon, a liturgy, a Christian life mean in a religionless world?"[2] Further along Bonhoeffer again asks: "What is the place of worship and prayer in a religionless situation? Does the secret discipline . . . take on a new importance here?"[3]

Even more indicative of the importance of this topic is the place it is given in Bonhoeffer's work plans for the future. When he came upon what was for him the momentous insight of the world's coming-of-age, he set aside for the time being what he had only recently stated was his major life task, writing his *Ethics*, and with great energy and concentration set out on a new book. However, to our poverty, only the outline survives. There "cultus" is listed as one of the main sections in the critical chapter, "The Real Meaning of Christian Faith." For us considerable frustration accompanies the notes, for Bonhoeffer scribbled simply: "Cultus. (Details to follow later, in particular on cultus and 'religion'.)."[4] But the point is that when Bonhoeffer's thoughts turn to the future and he stakes out his own theological project, cultus in a religionless time has a place that is far from peripheral for him. Thus it is a surprise that the treatment of our subject is virtually absent from the crowded shelves of these thirty-five years of Bonhoeffer studies.

The surprise is underscored if we note the pattern of Bonhoeffer's life, and not only the stated priorities in his writings. Striking in those letters and papers from the jail cells is the intense piety: Paul Gerhardt hymns, a memorized stanza of "Froelich soll mein Herz springen" commended to a friend, daily use of the Herrnhuter *Losungen*, prayers, a sermon or two, poetry, and so on. Yet even these constitute a second-order example. The telling point is that in prison, while he lamented "religion" and applauded the world's coming-of-age, Bonhoeffer practiced regular prayer and meditation (surely part of what was included under *Arkandisziplin*). He in fact lived by the church year, often dating his mail by the ecclesiastical calendar. His last action in community was to conduct a worship service among fellow prisoners on the way to the last concentration camp; and his last action in solitude was to quietly pray, on his knees and naked, before the steps of the gallows. Cultus counted for Bonhoeffer in his life and thought, in his last days, and for the future he envisioned. It is a surprise, then, that worship in a world-come-of-age has been given so little attention by so many scholars.

Or is it? In that first letter about religionless Christianity, just after those questions about "the place of worship and prayer in a religionless situation," Bonhoeffer goes on: "I must break off for today, so that the letter can go straight away. I'll write to you again about it in two days' time. . . ."[5] The succeeding discussions are equally abbreviated, and the typical outcome is the same postponement as noted in the book outline: "details to follow later. . . ." Thus we come away nearly empty-handed, with apparently little more than a clear indication of the importance of the topic to Bonhoeffer. So it is hardly a complete surprise that there has been little follow-through, since Bonhoeffer himself supplied so little.

Again, if we look to Bonhoeffer's life and not just to his unfinished thoughts, we are faced with that common situation in which, while actions certainly do speak louder than words, they often do not tell us what we most need to know. Bonhoeffer did indeed worship in the world-come-of-age, and that says much. But what shall we make of that for his own answers to his own questions about cultus in a religionless time? Perhaps he, like many of us, is anachronistic, talking and sometimes acting radically, but when the pressure is most intense responding in the familiar; speaking freely and excitedly about the new setting of a religionless world, but under stress and facing death answering in a manner marked by the most traditional cultic forms. Thus Bonhoeffer's actions, which speak so movingly, still do not interpret for us what we most need to know. Perhaps.

There is a final reason our topic did not become Bonhoeffer's in the space of those pages he left behind. He held some convictions about prior questions and attendant ones. And until the former are answered, the latter cannot be. Bonhoeffer was serious when he asked that question, "What is bothering me incessantly is what Christianity really is, or indeed who Christ really is, for us today."[6] Or, in another place, "The question is: Christ and the world that has come of age."[7] When these first-order questions are answered, then perhaps from the answers will emerge the clues to church renewal, meaningful worship forms, and the actions of a Christian style appropriate to a drastically altered setting. The ordering of topics in the outline of Bonhoeffer's new project is not arbitrary: 1) A Stocktaking of Christianity; 2) The Real Meaning of Christian Faith; 3) Conclusions (for the Church).[8]

Answering the first-order questions will take a long while. In the baptismal sermon from prison, Bonhoeffer includes the following:

> Today you will be baptized a Christian. All those great ancient words of the Christian proclamation will be spoken over you, and the command of Jesus Christ to baptize will be carried out on you, without your knowing anything about it. But we are once again being driven right back to the beginnings of our understanding. Reconciliation and redemption, regeneration and the Holy Spirit, love of our enemies, cross and resurrection, life in Christ and Christian discipleship—all these things are so difficult and so remote that we hardly venture any more to speak of them. In the traditional words and acts we suspect that there may be something quite new and revolutionary, though we cannot as yet grasp or express it. That is our own fault. Our church, which has been fighting in these years only for its self-preservation, as though that were an end in itself, is incapable of taking the word of reconciliation to the world. Our earlier words are therefore bound to lose their force and cease, and our being Christians today will be limited to two things: prayer and doing justice [trans. corrected] among men. All Christian thinking, speaking, and organizing must be born anew out of this prayer and action. . . . We are not yet out of the melting time [trans. corrected] and any attempt to help the church prematurely to a new expansion of its organization will merely delay its conversion and purification. It is not for us to prophesy the day (though the day will come) when men will once more be called so to utter the word of God that the world will be changed and renewed by it. It will be a new language, perhaps quite nonreligious, but liberating and redeeming—as was Jesus' language. . . Till then the Christian cause will be a silent and hidden affair, but there will be those who pray and do right and wait for God's own time. May you be one of them. . . .[9]

If "the Christian cause" is "a silent and hidden affair" for the foreseeable future, waiting "for God's own time" and awaiting the conversion of the church, and if Christians are being driven by the world's coming-of-age "right back to the beginnings of [their] understanding," then it is surely little surprise that the matter of worship in a religionless time must join the long labor and endure the hard pangs of the church's rebirth. That will be a while, for clearly the answers to those priority questions of what Christianity actually is and who Christ really is for us today are not armchair discourses. We cannot simply think through to the answers.

So perhaps it is no surprise at all that worship in a world-come-of-age has been given so little attention by so many scholars. Bonhoeffer's own utterances dictate a necessary restraint. But if the topic is to be pursued at all, at least the place to begin is clear. We must discern the meanings of "world-come-of-age" and "religion."

In a rich discussion of Bonhoeffer's later thoughts, Roger A. Johnson sorts the thoughts about religion and world-come-of-age by clustering them around three distinct themes that interplay in the prison writings. Sometimes the discussion by Bonhoeffer comprises what is virtually a psychological typology of religious and mature, or world-come-of-age, personalities. These are distinct personality types for which the psychological traits are sharply contrasting ones.

Other remarks sketch or comment on a movement of Western history that locates us in a "religionless situation" or is leading toward "a time of no religion at all," in Bonhoeffer's terms. Here the contention is that of a particular historical development on a grand scale in Western history, beginning about the thirteenth century and reaching a certain culmination in the present or near future.

Finally, many of Bonhoeffer's remarks and ruminations compose a theological-biblical critique of religion and a theological-biblical search for an understanding of, and response to, the world-come-of-age.[10]

Discussing the first two of these three (religion and world-come-of-age as personality types and as historical movement) can be explored profitably under the rubric of "consciousness." The term is vital here and in need of definition, all the more so because it is not Bonhoeffer's own way of explicating his own categories. By "consciousness" is meant that configuration of values, knowledge, feelings, judgments, and opinions that makes up the picture of reality or the "sense" of reality of any given individual or group. Our consciousness sets our angle of vision on things and so determines the way we see life, think about it, and live it out, selecting and sorting and interpreting our experience.

Several notations need to be made. The first is that the content of consciousness is historically mutable. Pictures of reality often vary greatly from time to time and place to place, from one age to another and one society to another, often from one person or group to another, and not rarely within the course of the life of the same person or group. Discontinuity as well as continuity characterizes consciousness. Its content changes.

The second notation is that occasionally a widely shared consciousness—a "collective consciousness"—undergoes massive changes, and a new way of seeing life, thinking about it, and living it out comes about for a people or a nation, a society or a group within a society. A revolution of consciousness occurs, and, however long it is in coming, a new sense of reality dawns for large numbers of people.

The third item is that consciousness is a basic shaper and interpreter of human needs. Of course, there are some basic physiological determinants of our needs, and we all have "needs of first necessity"—the survival needs of food, clothing, and shelter that cross and influence all varieties of consciousness. But beyond these elemental stipulations, and other genetic ones, what we regard as our needs is very much a function of our perception of things, our "reading" of reality, our consciousness.

What does this highly simplified profile of consciousness have to do with Bonhoeffer and worship in a world-come-of-age? Almost everything. For him, "religion" belongs to a longstanding, now changing, and for many, a *passing consciousness;* "world-coming-of-age" belongs to an *ascending consciousness.* He surmises that we are living in something approaching an axial period and that many people are moving from a "religious" consciousness to a "world-come-of-age" consciousness. These are fundamentally different ways of seeing life, thinking about it, and living it out. Both the psychological dynamics of the people and the *Zeitgeist* of a whole period are undergoing a mutation that is massive. When Bonhoeffer says, "We are moving toward a completely religionless time; people as they are now simply cannot be religious any more,"[11] his reference is to the eventual historical outcome of major changes of content in a previously widely shared consciousness.

The implications are startling, even for Bonhoeffer. He is rejecting a religious a priori supposedly constitutional to human nature. There is no inborn God-shaped blank that must be filled if a person is to lead a life of meaning, purpose, and integrity. More accurately stated, if some set of religious needs exists that only God, or at least "religion" can meet, such needs are integral to, and relative to, that person's consciousness or the collective consciousness of the community. A need for God and for religion is not a "given" of being human. Humankind qua humankind is not *homo religiosus*, although some men and women are, depending upon their sense of reality.

Bonhoeffer is not saying that some people no longer have a felt need for God and religion. He is saying that such needs are those of people possessed of a particular consciousness, one with a very long history, but one currently on the wane. He is saying further that the consciousness of some others has already altered in such a way that they get on well without religion, indeed they fare better than religious people. These are people of world-come-of-age consciousness. In part that means that their way of seeing life is such that God and religion are not indispensable to a satisfactory vision of life, to a humane morality, to living lives of meaning, purpose, and integrity.

There is more. Bonhoeffer observes that Western Christianity in all aspects—doctrine, liturgy, ethics—has cast its content in the material and forms of "religion." The edifices that support Christianity in the West rest on religious foundations. Thus if ours is indeed a religion*less* time, "the foundation is taken away from the whole of what has up to now been our 'Christianity'. . . ."[12] In different words, Christians in the West have been— and are—people of a religious consciousness who now find themselves in a world in which that consciousness is in the process of slow expiration.[13]

It is clear why Bonhoeffer calls for a religionless Christianity for a world-come-of-age. It is also clear why he thinks it will be a long time before that is worked out, before religious Christians become world-come-of-age Christians. And it is clear why he asks how worship, which has been encased in religious rubrics for so long, will appear and what meaning and place it might have in a time of no religion at all.

What criteria would mark "religionless" worship in a world-come-of-age? How would it be characterized? Answering such questions would require an exact description of what Bonhoeffer means by "religion" and "world-come-of-age." Since thirty-five years of Bonhoeffer scholarship have attended to this with a now happy outcome,[14] we need not undertake more than a sketch here. In this sketch the reader should be particularly attuned to the way in which the elements of religious and world-come-of-age consciousness sharply contrast on point after point.

For the person of religious consciousness, God is a working hypothesis for explaining whatever is unexplainable, or he seems so. Contrasting with this is a characteristic of the world-come-of-age, the growth of human autonomy through the increase of human knowledge and powers. Mankind in a world-come-of-age, using its autonomous reason, can and does interpret natural and social processes and can and does face and answer life's questions without the tutelage of a divinity, from premises which need not and do not posit God. Where God or the gods were once employed to account for almost everything, now other explanations suffice—or they suffice at least as well as do religious ones. God is not necessary to those understandings that enable us to come to terms with our world and its matrix of obligations. The ensemble of explanations in sphere after sphere is assembled without God's necessary participation in our consciousness.

All this may be so commonplace as to be a dull statement of fact. But the implications for "God" and "religion" in a world-come-of-age are nonetheless momentous. Because for religious consciousness God is a working hypothesis for explaining the unexplainable, God becomes associated with, or situated in, the unknown rather than in the known. Thus as the known increases, God is removed farther and farther from the center of life and pressed ever outward toward the boundaries, boundaries which themselves move back as human knowledge and powers increase.

What happens to religion? It becomes a separated sector of life, a diminishing sector of the unknown and unexplainable rather than the critical dimension in the overriding sense of reality. It becomes a certain genuinely alienated—and alienating—division in life.

The God of religious consciousness is also the *deus ex machina*. Whenever the normal course of human events in the plays of antiquity simply could not muster some action essential to the plot, a god or goddess intervened and did his or her job. The business of life and the plot then moved on to the next dramatic episode. Bonhoeffer is contending, in effect, that people of religious consciousness turn to God and religion only (but always) when their human resources fail to accomplish what they want or need done. God and religion function to secure "solutions" of sorts to problems that exhaust us or that we regard (or choose to regard) as insoluble or interminable. God and religion "rescue" us from dangers we encounter but cannot face or control. Or they function, in some grand theodicy, to right sooner or later all those wrongs we are too tired to right when our passion for justice wanes but our apathy does not.

The contrast with characteristics of world-come-of-age consciousness is stark for Bonhoeffer. The growth of human autonomy through the increase of human powers and accountability means that human destiny falls into human hands in ever greater measure. And people possessed of world-come-of-age consciousness (whose answers are arrived at without recourse to God and religion in the first place) regard themselves irrevocably accountable for their answers to life's questions, together with the consequences of the answers chosen and acted on. When there is failure, as there will be, there is no recourse to God and religion. The buck is not deposited with "God" or "circumstances" or "fate" or any other religious or quasi-religious account.

(It should be noted in passing that by world-come-of-age Bonhoeffer does not mean moral maturity. He means psychological maturity and moral accountability, or responsibility. When he speaks of the adulthood of the world, he does not mean humankind has achieved a degree of moral ripeness never before attained. He means humanity is responsible for the uses of increased knowledge and powers, whether they are exercised in a morally mature manner or not. And he means world-come-of-age people accept that responsibility. There is no returning to an adolescent dependence on a father—even a heavenly father—on whom final responsibility falls. For world-come-of-age people, mankind's future or lack of future rests in human hands.)

When God is the *deus ex machina*, the consequences for religion can be readily seen. God is not experienced by people in their achievement and strength; God is experienced in their weakness and resignation. Religion then is for people in their trouble, not for people at their best; at their best people are nonreligious. Since God is at the periphery and depended on only (but always) when human powers peter out, then people at their most religious are people at their most exhausted, defeated, and self-denigrating, though also most self-serving and turned in on themselves. But on its own, humankind is self-confident, responsible, and strong, exercising powers in full consciousness of a common destiny of all with all. For religious consciousness, humanity is "less" when it is most with "God," and "more" when most godless.

One last matter must be extracted from Bonhoeffer's thought. There are two poles in religious consciousness. At the one pole is a God who is located beyond the world rather than in the midst of it. At the other is an interior realm within the individual that serves as the place of contact for the self with this God beyond. Religion then, as Bonhoeffer says, is a matter of "individual inwardness." God is removed from the world except for a speaking place in the recesses of the soul, and religion is removed from critical engagement in the self's public life in various communities. Religion again becomes a separated thing, now located in some inner sanctuary to which one withdraws from the world in order to encounter God. Thus Bonhoeffer jotted in the outline for the new book, "Pietism as a last attempt to maintain evangelical Christianity as a religion. . . ."[15]

This is, admittedly in skeletal form, Bonhoeffer's delineation of religion and the God of religious consciousness. He laments such religion and he applauds the world's coming-of-age. Thus he laments religious Christianity and religious worship and calls for religionless Christianity and the nonreligious interpretation of biblical concepts.

Bonhoeffer is aware that a certain irony and tragedy wait in the wings; for the church will fight the world's coming-of-age and do all in its power to save a place for God and religion. The clergy will, in Bonhoeffer's language, use all their "clerical tricks" to retain religion as a sector of life by marketing certain questions and problems—death and guilt, for example—"to which [supposedly] only 'God' can give an answer."[16] The irony is that world-come-of-age people are, in their godlessness, actually closer to confronting the God of the Bible than are religious Christians and the church in their alliance with the "God" of religion. The tragedy is that the church will be the strongest opponent of the rediscovery of Christianity in its nonreligious biblical roots and will be the ablest opponent of its own conversion (conversion here in the precise sense of an altered consciousness). Bonhoeffer's language is anything but timid at this point.

> The attack by Christian apologetics on the adulthood of the world I consider to be in the first place pointless, in the second place ignoble, and in the third place unchristian. Pointless, because it seems to me like an attempt to put a grown-up man back into adolescence, i.e. to make him dependent on things on which he is, in fact, no longer dependent, and thrusting him into problems that are, in fact, no longer problems to him. Ignoble, because it amounts to an attempt to exploit man's weakness for purposes that are alien to him and to which he has not freely assented. Unchristian, because it confuses Christ with one particular stage in man's religiousness, i.e. with a human law.[17]

But what does all this mean for worship? First, to satisfy Bonhoeffer, worship in a world-come-of-age must strive to be nonreligious worship for religionless Christians. If it does not become this, that is, if it remains religious worship in a world-come-of-age, it will participate in that ignoble, pointless, and unchristian "Christian" apologetics that tries to soften up a place for God and religion in world-come-of-age people. In Bonhoeffer's language, worship will try to communicate to such people that they are dependent on things on which they are, in fact, no longer dependent, thrust them into problems which are no longer problems to them, and play on their weaknesses in such a way as to smuggle God into some last secret and vulnerable place in their lives. Or, if world-come-of-age people choose to ignore the church altogether, religious worship may well continue, but it will be part of the world-view baggage of people in quiet retreat from the world, people who tragically believe themselves to be preserving Christianity in the very act of fortressing themselves against those forces that offer opportunity to rediscover and recover it. Worship will then continue to be meaningful, to be sure, but precisely because it is part and parcel of a dying consciousness. Its meaning to some people will be the flipside of its irrelevance to the world that surrounds them. Worship then is meaningful precisely because it is protective against the promising vulnerability that world-come-of-age consciousness includes. (Etsi deus non daretur!)

Secondly, and a quite different point: religion for Bonhoeffer does not refer to the liturgical elements as such—sermon, sacrament, Scripture, doctrine, prayer, meditation, confession, and so on. Any and all of these may be interpreted and employed in either a religious or a nonreligious manner.

As the conclusion of the foregoing we can now contrast religious worship and nonreligious worship, using familiar phrases from the prison letters. Nonreligious worship would, using the liturgical elements, help us "find God in what we do know," not "in what we do not know" (the latter would be religious worship). Nonreligious worship would help us, through the liturgical elements, to realize God's presence in those problems that are solved, not simply in "unsolved problems" (that would be religious worship). Nonreligious worship would help us speak of God "at the center of life," not "on the boundary" (that would be religious worship). It would help us discern "the beyond in the midst of life," not point away to some other life in some beyond (that would be religious worship).

Nonreligious worship would thrust us "unreservedly [into] life's duties, problems, successes and failures, experiences and perplexities" in such a way as to take seriously "not our own suffering, but the sufferings of God in the secular life." By contrast, religious worship would aid and abet our efforts "to try and make something of ourselves, whether it be a saint, a converted sinner, or a churchman . . . a righteous man or an unrighteous one, a sick man or a healthy one." Nonreligious worship would help us, through the liturgical elements, experience God in the meeting with the neighbor and being for him or her in that meeting; by contrast, religious worship would experience God in a private encounter of the single self and God in some interior sanctuary of the individual.

Surely more could be said. It would include Bonhoeffer's theological-biblical critique of religion and his efforts at nonreligious interpretation of biblical concepts for religionless Christianity (e.g., Jesus as "the man-for-others"). Yet further discussion would soon find its limits, for the reason cited earlier: Bonhoeffer's conviction that Western Christianity is so soaked in religious consciousness that the answers to those prior questions of what Christianity really is, indeed, who Christ is for us in a religionless time, will be answers a long time in process. And we cannot be clear about the gestalt of religionless Christianity, including the gestalt of religionless worship, until we are well into the struggle that might yield those first-order answers.

Still we would be amiss in drawing the curtain here. Bonhoeffer does leave a last trace of how the movement toward religionless Christianity and religionless worship might proceed. Two earlier cited quotations can serve as "texts":

> What is the place of worship and prayer in a religionless situation? Does the secret discipline . . . take on a new importance here?[18]
>   . . . [O]ur being Christians today will be limited to two things: prayer and doing justice among men. All Christian thinking, speaking, and organizing must be born anew out of this prayer and action. . . .[19]

If we set these few lines in context within Bonhoeffer's own life, they become suggestive for the rhythm of Christian living in a world-come-of-age. In fact, they reflect a lively dialectic Bonhoeffer lived out in the *Kirchenkampf* of the 1930s and the resistance movement of the late thirties and early forties.

What are the poles of the dialectic? Naming the first is easy because Bonhoeffer does so, taking the early Christian community's name: the hidden, or arcane, discipline. Naming the second is not as easy because Bonhoeffer does not provide the term. It has to do with "doing justice among men" or, viewed in its theological dimension, with participation "in the sufferings of God in the secular life." For lack of a better term, we shall here call it "costly worldly solidarity." "Costly deputyship" might suffice equally well.

Arcane discipline. Bonhoeffer says "back to the conventicles" more than once. The goal is focused inner concentration for deputyship. Bonhoeffer sees the church of the future as a kind of low-profile order in the world as the world-come-of-age. In this order, arcane discipline is the focused inner concentration. Bonhoeffer's continuing fascination with Gandhi was in part because he wanted to learn from Gandhi the disciplines for a discipleship community. Also, his visits to certain Anglican communities were in preparation for his own community of arcane discipline, the seminary at Finkenwalde. His look to the future in the "Outline for a Book" is on the same track.

Arcane discipline means that worship in a world-come-of-age is not for everyone. It is only for small groups of clearly committed Christians who comprise an intense community on the basis of their intense loyalty to Christ; and their expression of the meaning of that loyalty as members of the one Body is communicated with one another in worship, but not to and with all. Worship as arcane discipline is not for the streets, the posters, the media, or the masses. It is certainly not Hollywood Bowl and drive-in Easter sunrise services, nor Sunday East Room exercises in American civil religion, nor Astrodome rallies of religiosity. It is not bumper-sticker and slick-paper Christianity. If Bonhoeffer were to have his way, the church would begin by giving up its property for the sake of the needy, would be devout in its practice of disciplines and demanding in its stipulations for participation. It would be a poor and apparently powerless church that would dispense costly grace, rather than a rich and privileged church that would offer only cheap grace.

Arcane discipline means a concentrated nurturing of the varied elements of the Judaeo-Christian heritage. At the time the secular theologies were in their heyday, worship and tradition were often neglected, occasionally forthrightly downgraded. At a critical point those theologies missed Bonhoeffer almost entirely, even when they were in part inspired by him. They overlooked one focus in the dialectic: his genuinely pious observing of the liturgical traditions. Bonhoeffer did not want less to do with the ancient symbols and archaic confessions of the church. Nor did he want less to do with the lives of all those bizarre saints, with the details of that hoary tradition, with all the "gesimas" of the church year. He *did* want to know what we still really believe of all that. And more importantly for our topic, he wanted it clear that the materials involved, including the biblical materials, were in need of nonreligious interpretation. They must not be retained in such a way as to make religion a necessary condition for salvation, as they have in the past.

The concentrated nurture includes worship, both in solitude and with others. (Bonhoeffer's own daily meditation and prayer in prison is an example of the first; the personal confession of one brother of Finkenwalde to another and the common celebration together in communion is an example of the latter.) Thus one ongoing element in the rhythmic process of answering the first-order questions is the arcane discipline of intense nurture and disciplined worship of small groups of strongly committed Christians who make up the church as a kind of low-profile Christian order in the world-come-of-age.

The other element, costly worldly solidarity or deputyship, refers to the engagement for which arcane discipline was nurture. It means groups of Christians operating rather incognito in the world, making common cause with the non-Christian and the nonreligious, all without ecclesiastical and theological pretense and qualification. (Bonhoeffer's resistance activity is itself paradigmatic here.) This second pole is doing justice in secular ways in public arenas. It is above all doing justice as "mitleiden," for the informing vision is that of the *theologia crucis*, and the mission is understood as part of the *missio Jesu*. It is costly deputyship as participation in the *sufferings* of God in the secular life.

The dialectical movement here is critical. Arcane discipline left to itself would easily revive the worst of the sectarian style. The Christian ingroup would become the pious and self-righteous ghetto. Its "otherness" would become fetid particularism. Costly worldly solidarity by itself would result in Christianity as a soon burnt-out case. The rich paths in spirituality of arcane discipline would soon lose themselves in the worthy—but eventually shallow—crusades of a one-dimensional secularism. Arcane discipline by itself would soon become just another form of spiritual tribalism and worldly solidarity by itself another round of exhausting partisan involvement.

But in dialectic, arcane discipline provides the sustenance for suffering with non-Christians for the common good. And costly deputyship provides the mode of public engagement for that hidden concentration. Even more, costly worldly solidarity provides the very means and materials necessary for discovering religionless Christianity in a world-come-of-age. The "otherness" of arcane discipline brings to expression the transcendent elements of worldly solidarity (being-for-others as the "realization of reality"); and the solidarity with others breaks again and again the easy propensity of the (necessary) Christian particularism to close in upon itself.

An edited look at an earlier excerpt may suffice as a summary:

[O]ur being Christian today will be limited to two things: prayer [shorthand here for arcane discipline] and doing justice among men [shorthand for costly worldly solidarity]. All Christian speaking, thinking and organizing must be born anew out of this prayer and action.

In the end we do not know for certain the gestalt of nonreligious worship in a world-come-of-age. That awaits our conversion from religious consciousness to world-come-of-age consciousness, the renewal of our minds in an axial age. Yet if we would take our cues from Bonhoeffer, we are inheritors of a rich fund of resources and we are pointed the way of proceeding.

Notes

1   Dietrich Bonhoeffer, *LPPE*, p. 279.
2   *LPPE*, p. 280.
3   *LPPE*, p. 281.
4   That only the outline survives happened because Bonhoeffer took the remainder of the manuscript along to the Gestapo prison. That among the very few possessions the manuscript was included is indicative of its importance to him. *LPPE*, p. 382. From: "Outline for a Book."
5   *LPPE*, p. 281.
6   *LPPE*, p. 281.
7   *LPPE*, p. 327. From the letter of 8 June 1944.
8   *LPPE*, p. 380. From "Outline for a Book." Words in brackets mine, in keeping with Bonhoeffer's content.
9   *LPPE*, pp. 299-300. From "Thoughts on the Day of the Baptism of Dietrich Wilhelm Rüdiger Bethge."
10   Roger A. Johnson, Ernest Wallwork, Clifford Green, H. Paul Santmire, and Harold Y. Vanderpool, eds., *Critical Issues in Modern Religion* (Englewood Cliffs, N.J.: Prentice-Hall, Inc., 1973), p. 287.
11   *LPPE*, p. 279.
12   *LPPE*, p. 280.
13   More precisely, Christianity in the West has been clothed in a variety of forms of consciousness, all or virtually all of which have shared certain common "religious" strains.
14   See especially Feil, *ThBD*, as well as Bethge, *DB*.
15   *LPPE*, p. 381.
16   *LPPE*, p. 326. From the letter of 8 June 1944.
17   *LPPE*, p. 327.
18   *LPPE*, p. 281. From the letter of 30 April 1944.
19   *LPPE*, p. 300. From the baptismal sermon (trans. corrected).

BIBLICAL AGNOSTICISM AND THE
CRITIQUE OF RELIGIOSITY

James W. Woelfel

FOR THE BONHOEFFER of the prison writings, one of the marks of religiosity is a pious familiarity with God and the easy chatter about him which is its linguistic expression. In the letter of November 21, 1943, written at a time when he was reading the Old Testament with new interest and insight, he wrote to Bethge: ". . . my fear and distrust of 'religiosity' have become greater than ever here. The fact that the Israelites *never* uttered the name of God always makes me think, and I can understand it better as I go on."[1] In the letter of April 30, 1944, which initiates his "nonreligious" reflections, Bonhoeffer observes: "I'm often reluctant to mention God by name to religious people—because that name somehow seems to me here not to ring true, and I feel myself to be slightly dishonest. . . ."[2] Throughout the prison writings he is concerned on the positive side, of course, with Christian existence as fully human rather than narrowly "religious," and with a "new" language of faith which will be an adequate expression of such an existence.

I want to suggest that an important if underdeveloped element in Bonhoeffer's characterization of religiosity is this confident familiarity with the divine which expresses itself in religious chatter. I use the word "chatter" quite deliberately to evoke Martin Heidegger's analysis in *Being and Time* of the understanding expressed in "everyday" human speech. Speech, which is properly disclosure, the bringing to light of reality, is distorted in everyday life into "chatter" or "idle talk" *(Gerede)*. Chatter conceals rather than discloses, while it pretends to knowledge; it trivializes and tranquillizes. Chatter is the linguistic expression of inauthentic existence.[3]

In the religious sphere of life, inauthenticity manifests itself in a self-assured knowledge of God, a familiarity that is in the last analysis blasphemy. Religious chatter thinks it reveals but actually conceals the true reality of the infinite and holy mystery which is God. It trivializes the divine name by using it so frequently and knowingly, as if "God" were "Jones" next door instead of a hushed and ignorant syllable stammeringly pointing to the numinous inexhaustibility within and surrounding all things of which human beings hardly dare speak. Religious chatter tranquillizes by anaesthetizing people against genuine openness to the mystery and scope of this fathomless ground of the universe and ourselves—openness in wonder and awe, in surprise and shock, in fear and trembling, in humility and *metanoia*—an openness which quite clearly can take forms that are not conventionally "religious."

I am assuming that we can infer the affirmative from Bonhoeffer's negation of religiosity: If religious inauthenticity is self-deceptive familiarity with and trivializing and tranquillizing chatter about God, religious authenticity will be marked by a deep awareness of divine mystery and our own finitude and by a linguistic reticence that will not lightly utter or invoke the holy name of God, and then only in a way that will reveal rather than conceal. At the heart of authentic faith is a reverent *agnosticism* for which it is talk rather than silence that must justify itself—talk that can justify its breaches of silence only by humble, careful, sparing, finally "ignorant" disclosure.

Bonhoeffer did not develop this aspect of religious authenticity in his remarks on "nonreligious interpretation" and Christian "worldliness." All we have are hints here and there. Furthermore, for Bonhoeffer theology was Christology; and his overriding Christological emphasis was a vigorous restatement of Luther's insistence on the utter "haveability" of God in Christ, his concretely and intimately making himself known in this man, so that to encounter the Christ of the New Testament in his words and deeds is to have to do with God in the fullest sense possible. This is the basis of Bonhoeffer's "nonreligious interpretation" of the transcendence of God as Jesus' "being there for others."[4] The whole drift of this sort of theological method might seem to run counter to a concern for the agnostic elements in faith and for verbal reticence in the presence of the truly holy. And a cursory examination of Bonhoeffer's remarks on "nonreligious interpretation" in *Letters and Papers* suggests just that. He seems to highlight and intensify God as surely known, manifest, "given over to us" in the Incarnation. His brief attempts at starting on a "nonreligious" Christology appear to humanize and domesticate the divine otherness in terms of the man Jesus almost to the point of reducing it and flattening it out.

And yet we know well that this monopolar impression is inaccurate. Steeped in the biblical literature, in Reformation and Neo-Reformation theology, Bonhoeffer's thought is from beginning to end intensely *dialectical*. The God who reveals himself in Christ is at the same time profoundly concealed just there; Kierkegaard's classic theme of the divine incognito in the Incarnation runs throughout the pages of Bonhoeffer's chief Christological study, the lectures posthumously published as *Christ the Center*.

The God who makes himself utterly "haveable" to us in Christ is precisely the infinite, eternal, incomprehensible mystery which grounds and controls the universe. And that is just why his condescension toward us in the man Jesus is both astonishing and scandalous. These themes are there just as surely, if less obviously and frequently, in the pages of the prison writings as is his emphasis on God "near at hand" and manifest. To neglect or collapse Bonhoeffer's intense theological dialectic is simply to miss the point of "nonreligious interpretation" entirely; and, of course, the early years of Bonhoeffer studies produced a fair amount of hopelessly misguided "reductionizing" of the prison writings.

While we must certainly concede that the accent in *Letters and Papers* is on language rather than silence, on reinterpreting the known in Christ rather than reaffirming the *mysterium Christi*, we cannot neglect these elements of agnosticism and reticence in a total view of "nonreligious interpretation." We must, I believe, infer the significance for authentic Christianity of reverent agnosticism and linguistic reticence about God from Bonhoeffer's critique of the familiarity and chatter of religiosity. We must further take quite seriously the thoroughly dialectical character of his biblical interpretation and theology as providing an ample framework within which such agnosticism and reticence have an integral place. What I want to do in the remainder of this essay is simply to recall to the reader some profoundly agnostic elements in biblical faith with which I believe Bonhoeffer would entirely concur, and to highlight along the way some more of his own remarks in this vein. I do so because I believe that the theme is vitally important; Bonhoeffer—at least indirectly—makes it integral to Christian authenticity; and it still does not receive the attention it deserves among Christians.

The agnosticism about which I have been speaking has come to pervade contemporary religious faith and thought to an admirable degree. Modesty, reticence, tentativeness—a sense of the relative and fragmentary character of our apprehension of transcendent reality—increasingly typify talk about God. But Christian faith has not gone far enough in the direction of really accepting religious ignorance viscerally as well as intellectually. The religious ethos rooted in the biblically witnessed events has been, understandably but regrettably, so utterly preoccupied with the manifest, revealed God that it has neglected the divine hiddenness and mystery and our human *a-gnosis* (our "not-knowledge") concerning the transcendent. So preeminently a preached faith, Christianity has always believed that it has something to *tell* everybody about God. Preaching about a revelation has made Christianity a garrulous, quarrelsome, highly conceptualized religion. Preoccupation with the Word has produced a great deal of wordiness. The Christian preacher or theologian still tends to find reticence, ignorance, and silence concerning the divine somewhat unfamiliar and even embarrassing, and further he or she seems to believe that his or her congregation or students cannot bear it.

But the fact is that there is a profoundly agnostic strain at the very heart of the biblical sources to which Christian faith looks for witness to divine self-disclosure. In calling attention to it, I am definitely not doing anything new; it has all been said before, and by some of the greatest and wisest minds in Christian history. I am suggesting that the Bonhoeffer of "nonreligious interpretation" said it, quietly but significantly, in our recent history. But it needs to be said again and again, simply because the church has on the whole never taken it with the seriousness it deserves. It has never become sufficiently rooted in the very center of Christian existence and faith. If this awesome and stammering sense of the mystery of God proclaimed in parts of Scripture and by some of the most sensitive theologians and mystics down through the centuries had been taken with the full significance it has always deserved, the history of Christian faith might have been spared some of its darkest and ugliest aspects.

It tends to be the trend nowadays for Christianity to learn intellectual humility from encounters with certain other religious traditions (such as Zen Buddhism, with its radical sense of the inadequacy of words to describe reality) and with the general relativism and fragmentation of modern knowledge. It may be that the agnostic dimension within Christianity's own roots and tradition is one which is so overlaid that it cannot be heard—at least at the moment—as a native source of illumination. But it is a dimension that lies at the very center of what Christian faith calls "revelation," and it is therefore well worth recalling.

From its primitive origins to its most exalted expressions, the biblical understanding of God contains at its center a "cloud of unknowing." The key to biblical agnosticism is the Hebrews' profound sense of the utter *transcendence* of God, his radical "otherness" or difference from man and his world. In what follows I want to draw out two of the chief manifestations of this biblical apprehension of the divine transcendence that express a reverent agnosticism, an awed sense of human ignorance before the fathomless mystery of God, which is at the heart of the Judaeo-Christian tradition: 1) divine revelation and 2) divine freedom.

We begin with revelation—with God as manifest, as "open" to man—because that is where biblical faith itself, for obvious reasons, begins. Here we seem at the outset to be at the farthest remove from any notion of divine mystery or human ignorance. Yet it is precisely the biblical apprehension of revelation that makes room for the whole biblical *a-gnosis* about God. It is precisely a thorough attention to all that is implied by Israel's belief in the self-manifestation of God in their midst that quickly dispels any notions of divine self-disclosure as divine familiarity or "chumminess." Such notions bear no relation whatsoever to the Bible's dreadful sense of how weighty a thing it is to speak of the "nearness" of God. It was also for Israel, to be sure, a supreme joy and celebration to believe and affirm "God with us." But the profundity and reality of the joy lay on the far side of the solemn recognition that this incredible business was, in the words of Kierkegaard, "the paradox of life and existence."

For biblical faith, revelation means the self-unveiling of the God who because of his transcendence, his intrinsic otherness from man and his created environment, would otherwise remain utterly hidden from man. "Revelation is essential," writes George Hendry in a standard exposition of the subject,

> because the realm of God is exalted above this world (I Tim. 6.16); he dwelleth on high (Isa. 33.5); he is the high and lofty one that inhabiteth eternity (Isa. 57.15); he is in heaven, and we upon earth (Eccles. 5.2). In modern language, God is transcendent. He is not accessible to our observation in the world. He cannot be "imaged" in the categories at our disposal (Exod. 20.4).[5]

Revelation is a very partial "lifting of the veil" of the depthless mystery of being; in the words of Ignatius of Antioch, it is "a word out of silence."

God the transcendent one is for biblical faith *essentially* (that is, in his proper being) hidden from human beings; ultimate reality is in itself unknown to us. Only by God's own free forth-proceeding activity by which he relates to humankind does he make the "fringes of his ways" known to us. Revelation is to be understood precisely in terms of God's transcendent hiddenness. "Revelation" is properly used of that which apart from being revealed would remain completely hidden or unknown.

For the biblical writers it is thus the case that the very self-disclosure of God through Israel's law and prophets proclaims the essential mysteriousness of the transcendent: ". . . even in his revelation God remains hidden; for while he makes himself known, he does not explain himself to men. He is hidden in respect to his ways, which are 'past finding out' (Rom. 11.33, Isa. 55.9)."[6] This statement by Professor Hendry is important. A common misunderstanding in much Christian thinking about revelation, as well as in critical opposition to Christian claims, has been the idea that the self-disclosure of God to man as witnessed in the biblical literature provides "answers" to all the basic questions of life: What is the basic structure of reality? What is the nature of man? Why is there evil and suffering? Skeptical critics of Christian thought have always seen that biblical revelation as an "explanation" of the big questions is severely wanting in some important respects, and they have thus rejected it as a tenable world-view. Their Christian opponents have too often joined battle in defense of the explanatory character of biblical faith when they should have listened more attentively to the Scriptures' own refutation of the idea that *any* "ultimate explanation" is possible to finite man surrounded by infinite reality. Both have argued on the wrong level.

There is never the suggestion in the biblical writings that God in his self-disclosure "explains" everything, or even very much, to human beings. This is just as true of the New Testament affirmation of God's supreme self-disclosure in Christ as it is of the Old Testament. The problem of evil, the ultimate purpose of things, the nature of God—these issues remain fundamentally mysterious. To be sure, some light is shed on all of them by the self-disclosure of God; but it is a decidedly refracted light, not a pure beam. Man is given sufficient guidance to live his life in obedience to God amid its changes and chances, its mysteries and tragedies. He is not given neat, clear answers which he can happily stick in his hip pocket for instant reference. Bonhoeffer had something of this in mind when he wrote from prison, "As to the idea of 'solving' problems, it may be that the Christian answers are just as unconvincing—or convincing—as any others."[7]

To the biblical writers God is in his inexhaustible depths utterly transcendent, beyond the range of finite man's grasp. Biblical faith finds in certain events, persons, and symbols in human experience what the existentialist philosopher Karl Jaspers calls "ciphers": fragmentary, often ambiguous and enigmatic, but compelling manifestations of the awesome and incomparable mystery of God. These revelatory ciphers disclose something of God-himself-in-relation-to-us, God *pro nobis*. But it is precisely the point of Israel's faith to recognize that from beginning to end God in himself— the holy, the majestic, the eternal—remains even and especially in his self-disclosure the utterly transcendent one.

So it is that the writer of I Kings 8 has Solomon say, at the dedication of the Temple in Jerusalem,

> The LORD has set the sun in the heavens,
> but has said that he would dwell in thick darkness. (v. 12)

In the prayer that follows, Solomon praises God by affirming that "heaven and the highest heaven cannot contain thee" (v. 27). Chapters 40-51 of Isaiah, the first portion of the writings of the great anonymous prophet of the postexilic period and certainly a high point of Old Testament theology, are in part a sustained paean to the utter transcendence of God:

> Who has measured the waters in the hollow of his hand
>   and marked off the heavens with a span,
> enclosed the dust of the earth in a measure
>   and weighed the mountains in scales
>   and the hills in a balance?
> Who has directed the Spirit of the LORD,
>   or as his counselor has instructed him?

Whom did he consult for his enlightenment,
   and who taught him the path of justice,
and taught him knowledge,
   and showed him the way of understanding?
Behold, the nations are like a drop from a bucket,
   and are accounted as the dust on the scales;
   behold, he takes up the isles like fine dust.

. . . .

To whom then will you liken God,
   or what likeness compare with him? (Isa. 40:12-15, 18)

And surely there is no more agonized yet exalted affirmation of the depthless and inscrutable mystery of this transcendent God than the book of Job, which reaches its climax in chapters 38-42:6. God overwhelms Job with the infinite and mysterious divine wisdom manifested in the created order: " 'Where were you when I laid the foundation of the earth? Tell me, if you have understanding.' " (38:4) Job penitently replies, "I have uttered what I did not understand, things too wonderful for me, which I did not know." (42:3b) Significantly, Job's "comforters" are examples of religious chatter: they think they *know* and can *tell* Job why he has been visited with such suffering. These are simply a few better-known examples of many biblical references to the divine transcendence as hiddenness and mystery. Important aspects of this biblical *a-gnosis* are also to be found in the central ascription to God of *holiness*, the root meaning of which is "separateness" or "otherness" from the earthly or profane; and the belief, extending from Exodus to the Gospel of John, that "no man can see God and live."

In the later history of Israel the special name by which the Israelites knew God, Yahweh, ceased to be pronounced. The pronouncing of a name conveyed something of the reality and power of that which it named, and the holy name of God denoted a reality and a power too holy, too awful, to be lightly used. As we have seen, Bonhoeffer became increasingly impressed by the implications of the Jewish refusal to speak the divine name. It stood in sharp contrast, he believed, to the Christian religiosity which trivializes and blasphemes the name "God" by an easy familiarity. The chatter of much religiosity about the divine has none of the biblical sense of the mystery and majesty of the reality about whom it speaks, and therefore it conceals rather than reveals. Bonhoeffer went on to write that "it is only when one knows the unutterability [*Unaussprechlichkeit*] of the name of God that one can utter [*aussprechen*] the name of Jesus Christ. . . ."[8]

In the New Testament there is of course a decisive new emphasis on the nearness of God to man, with the faith that in the man Jesus of Nazareth God has supremely disclosed himself in the most intimate manner possible.

This man is at the same time believed to be Emmanuel, "God with us." But precisely in the apprehension of the person of Christ we find in the New Testament the same deep-rooted sense of the transcendent mystery of God and the stammering inadequacy of our speech. For here it is the very mystery of this man, who is so obviously a human being but also believed to be the very presence of God with man, which provokes awe and wonder before the infinite divine mystery on the part of the disciples and the early Christians. In the four Gospels, ignorance of who Christ really is runs deep until the very end, even and especially among those closest to him. Only the demons, those evil spirits who are themselves supernatural, seem to recognize his divine status. The varied writings of the New Testament use numerous images to try to describe the mystery of Christ's person, but all of them in the final analysis fall short of a mystery which, it is believed, can only be encountered and acknowledged. As John Courtney Murray aptly put it in his Terry Lectures:

> The Son is here with us. With him the Father, who sent him, inseparably comes to us. Here with us, Father and Son breathe into us the Holy Spirit who is their Gift, now given to us. The Three are here as who they are, mysteriously the one God, the triunely Holy One. As triune, God is more hidden than ever, more unknown, his Name more mysterious. Yet his Name has been revealed. As Father he is [at the same time] more intimately known. . . . The Old Testament structure of the problem remains unchanged. . . .[9]

The affirmation that God is free flows directly from the remarkable biblical grasp of his transcendence, and may be, when considered in its full scope, the most exalted concept of deity ever projected. The freedom of God was a neglected idea in modern theology, under the dominance of the immanentalism of which Friedrich Schleiermacher was the fountainhead, until the writings of Karl Barth emphasized it as central to the biblical apprehension of God.

God the radically transcendent, who reveals himself as essentially and hiddenly "other" than man and the world, thereby discloses himself as a wholly *self-sufficient* being. God, the eternal source and goal of everything else, is entirely independent of that which he has created. This divine *a se esse* is the divine freedom: God exists and acts entirely out of himself, independent of any external constraint.

"In the beginning" the sole reality, God, according to biblical faith, freely chooses to create beings other than himself. There is no necessity in this; God does not have to create as an intrinsic expression of his nature. The biblical God is not Plotinus' One, from which the universe emanates of necessity. In the depthless mystery of his hidden being God has a "life of his own," as it were, which is gropingly pointed to by Christianity in trinitarian terms. For biblical faith, his creative activity thus becomes the sublime primordial freedom out of which the universe is born, which can be expressed by man only in inadequate human analogies that speak of God as "willing" or "deciding." The universe and man are created out of a "free decision" on the part of God, a mysterious act of his independent "will" which biblical faith thanks as an act of love. In the creation story in Genesis 1, God is viewed as so utterly transcendent and self-sufficient that he has but to "speak" and creating takes place: "Let there be . . . ," *fiat*, a supreme decision of sovereign freedom.

As being which is in its essence *a se esse*, God is seen to be free also in his relations with his creature man. In his self-disclosure in Israel's history, God is never at man's disposal: precisely in his revelation is his utter independence made known; his "unveiling" is his "hiding"; his self-disclosure is as sovereign Lord over man. In the biblical writings God's activity is creative, dynamic, full of surprises. Israel is always running at least three or four steps behind the free God, who is out in front "doing new things." In this view, man can never anticipate or domesticate God; he never has a firm handle on the divine. Those whom Israel came to call its great prophets were men who intuited that the most nearly authentic human relationship to transcendence is an openness to "depth" meaning in the events and experiences unfolding around us in that unpredictable interplay of the free God and self-transcending man called history. The prophets were at the same time men who were able to see this through a creative interpretation of those "ciphers" from Israel's past and present which pointed, however fragmentarily, to a sovereign and creative freedom at the mysterious heart of reality which was mirrored finitely in the historical freedom of man.

The biblical writings do not explicitly use the term "free" in speaking of God. But they point to the reality of the divine freedom in a wealth of other ways. It must be emphasized again that the hidden self-sufficiency of God and his free activity with regard to his creation are for biblical faith clear implications of his self-disclosure as the radically transcendent one. Biblical talk about God's "willing," his majestic kingship over human beings and events, his "power and might"—these are simply a few of the images by which Scripture speaks of the divine freedom.

Even in the New Testament, with its emphasis on God's intimate "handing over" of himself to man in Christ, the radical transcendence and corollary freedom of God continue to be vigorously affirmed. This is a fundamental dialectic of the early Christian experience which lies at the root of the doctrine of the Trinity. Despite their perfect unity, the Father remains transcendent over the incarnate Son: it is the Father who calls the shots, as it were, and Jesus who responds in active obedience. Jesus confesses his ignorance of so basic an issue as the time of the Last Day (see Mark 13:32). It is the Father who in his freedom and power raises Jesus from the dead. God remains elusive, somewhat unpredictable, and surprising both in the teaching and the mystery of the person of Christ. Indeed, we can see Jesus' ethical teaching of "radical obedience"—over against the prevailing Torah-legalism—as a crucial affirmation of the freedom of God with regard to man.[10] Jesus' preaching of the kingdom of God, and the unforeseen revisions which its postponement has created for Christianity, are powerful if enigmatic pointers to the idea of the kingly freedom of God. Bonhoeffer nicely epitomized the divine freedom in Christ when he wrote: "The God of Jesus Christ has nothing to do with what God, as we imagine him, could do and ought to do."[11]

The human correlate of Israel's grasp of the fathomless mystery of God is the whole Hebraic understanding of man as a thoroughly finite psychophysical unity, whose uniqueness lies not simply in his reason but more completely in his "addressability" as a whole being by God. In this view, man's reason is limited to the finite, and his grasp of the infinite is always a concrete, ethically oriented response to what he trusts to be the partial self-disclosure of the One who is essentially mysterious, holy, transcendent.

There are isolated figures in the history of Christian thought who have reemphasized the divine mystery in striking ways: for example, the sixth-century theologian Pseudo-Dionysius, influenced by Neoplatonism, with his *via negativa*, or approach to the knowledge of God by way of negation; those mystics who, following Dionysius, through the violently paradoxical use of language tried to point to the experienced fathomlessness of the divine by speaking of God as "not-good," "not-wise," and even "not-being"; to some degree Luther, with his profound sense of the *deus absconditus* behind the *deus revelatus*; Søren Kierkegaard, with his remarkable insights into the biblical affirmations of divine otherness and human limitation; Albert Schweitzer, who found himself rationally unable to link together God as the enigmatic creativity behind a nonmoral nature and God as ethical will in human life; and Karl Barth, insofar as he dramatically reemphasized the sovereign freedom of God. In quite varying and often very partial ways, these have been among the voices within the biblically rooted tradition who have attempted to recall Christianity to a sorely neglected, deeply agnostic element in its most fundamental understanding of God and his relationship to man.

Building on hints in the prison writings and the vigorous dialectical character of Bonhoeffer's theology even in its "nonreligious" phase, I have suggested that the biblical agnosticism of "fear and trembling" before the inexhaustible hiddenness and freedom of the holy God in his self-disclosure, expressing itself most appropriately in an awed reticence about speaking of God, is integral to the structure of an authentic Christian existence.

I believe that Bonhoeffer would have done well to emphasize it even more than he did, but that is the important and never-finished task for those who have been inspired by and seek to carry on in the spirit of his work. For faith to be authentic, it must learn again and again "in the heart and reins" how little it knows and speak tremblingly only out of silence. The opening passage from Bonhoeffer's Christology lectures of 1933 (with which there is no reason whatever to suppose he would have disagreed later and indeed some good reasons to suppose he reaffirmed) is a fitting charter for such Christian agnosticism and expresses that agnosticism in his characteristically Christocentric and dialectical manner:

> Teaching about Christ begins in silence. "Be silent, for that is the absolute" (Kierkegaard). This has nothing to do with mystical silence which, in its absence of words, is, nevertheless, the soul secretly chattering away to itself. The church's silence is silence before the Word. In proclaiming the Word, the church must fall silent before the inexpressible: Let what cannot be spoken be worshipped in silence (Cyril of Alexandria). The spoken Word is the inexpressible: that which cannot be spoken is the Word. It must be spoken, it is the great battle cry of the church (Luther). The church utters it in the world, yet it still remains the inexpressible. To speak of Christ means to keep silent; to be silent about Christ means to speak. The proclamation of Christ is the church speaking from a proper silence.[12]

Notes

1 *LPPE*, p. 135.

2 *Ibid.*, p. 281.

3 *Being and Time*, John Macquarrie and Edward Robinson, trans. (N.Y.: Harper & Row, 1962), pp. 203-224.

4 *LPPE*, p. 381.

5 In Alan Richardson, ed., *A Theological Word Book of the Bible* (London: SCM Press, 1957), p. 196.

6 *Ibid.*

7 *LPPE*, pp. 311-312.

8 *Ibid.*, p. 157.

9 *The Problem of God: Yesterday and Today* (New Haven: Yale University Press, 1964), pp. 28-29.

10 See, e.g., Rudolf Bultmann, *Jesus and the Word* (New York: Scribner's, 1955).

11 *LPPE*, p. 391.

12 *CC*, p. 27.

VII.
ETHICS

AN EXAMINATION OF BONHOEFFER'S ETHICAL CONTEXTUALISM

James T. Laney

IN CHRISTIAN ethics a contextualist approach rests on the assumption that the will of God is not to be derived from principles or generalized from the past, but is to be discerned within each specific concrete situation or immediate context. A careful consideration of such a claim reveals that the avowed reliance on the concrete situation to provide the necessary components for ethical decision and action in fact presupposes several contexts of interpretation and evaluation within which alone the situation is morally intelligible and ethically viable. For purposes of clarity these several contexts might be classified as: 1) a context of interpretation establishing the theological grounds for recognizing the will of God; 2) a context of decision comprising the concrete encounter where perception in light of that understanding and existential moral judgment occur; and 3) a context of action indicating the area in which the objective consequences of personal decision are related to public responsibility.

In view of the great and continuing influence of Bonhoeffer's *Ethics* on recent developments in Christian ethics, an examination of his major ethical work, especially in regard to its heavy emphasis on a contextualist approach, seems appropriate. This essay then is an attempt to sort out, along the lines of the schema indicated above, the various interwoven and overlapping "contexts" employed by Bonhoeffer in order to better understand his ethical thought and more adequately reassess our reliance upon it.

I. The Context of Interpretation

The "Ethical," Reality, and the Good

The starting point of ethical understanding for Bonhoeffer lies not in an ideal to be realized, a norm to be approximated, or even essentially in a command to be obeyed, but in a reality to be expressed. This reality consists of the "recovered unity" and reconciliation established in Christ and in which the Christian is called to participate.[1] Because the actions of a Christian do not reflect the "irreconcilable cleavage between vitality and self-denial, between 'secular' and 'Christian' or between 'autonomous ethics' and the 'ethics of Jesus,' " but rather spring from joy in the accomplishment of the reconciliation of the world with God, they already move in a sphere which lies beyond the fatal antinomies in which traditional ethics is embroiled.[2] They are, in short, expressions of the true ethos of life, a life whose origin, essence, and purpose has been revealed and established in Christ. Such reality "discloses itself" only within the concrete world, a world now seen to be "already sustained, accepted, and reconciled in the reality of God."[3] As a result, the question of the good is posed and resolved "in the midst of each definite, yet unconcluded, unique and transient situation of our lives, in the midst of our living relationships with men, things, institutions and powers, in other words in the midst of our historical existence."[4] The unity of life, concrete good, and essential reality, all accomplished in Christ, are seen to be repeated and realized ever afresh in the lives of men.[5] Christian life is based on a fundamental acceptance of and trust in the reality that man encounters in these concrete relations and events of life. This means that man is permitted to share in life, not under the alien domination of "shall" and "should" but from the "full abundance of vital motives, from the natural and the organic" in free acceptance rather than "humorless hostility."[6]

The "ethical," on the other hand, not only is incapable of prescribing action but is ruled out of all but the periphery of life. To be sure, Bonhoeffer admits, there is a time and place in human life for "the so-called 'ethical phenomenon', that is to say, the experience of obligation, the conscious and deliberate decision between something which is, on principle, good and something which is, on principle, evil, the ordering of life. . . ."[7] However, at the same time, unless the ethical is carefully delimited, he feels, there is the very real danger of "a pathological overburdening of life by the ethical" which can only result in a moralistic and speciously critical attitude. The ethical is properly called into consideration only when there is disruption and disorder, and once harmony is restored the ethical has no more to contribute.[8] For these reasons, ethical discussion is never appropriate or even legitimate as an abstract consideration of the good and the right; it is appropriate and legitimate only with specific reference to concrete situations by those who carry responsibility for a decision reached in reference to them. On any other terms, ethics is hardly more than meddling, an attempt by "ineffectuals" to exert a spurious influence over the affairs of others.[9] With Barth, Bonhoeffer would say that man's greatest enemy is the abstract "I"[10] conceived in ideal terms, which so easily becomes a "Moloch" to which real life and liberty are sacrificed. Consequently, any ethics that begins theoretically or on principle is a priori incompatible with the Christian understanding of life and reality.

The Command of God

In contradistinction to the "ethical," the command of God embraces the whole life and is expressed in the "total and concrete claim" on man by a merciful God.[11] The qualifying adjectives "total" and "concrete" provide the key to an understanding of what Bonhoeffer means by the term "command." It is total in the sense that it not only limits and forbids but also permits. It sets life free from all impositions that are not themselves concrete expressions innate in the command as it upholds and sustains life. More especially, the command delivers life from the watchful and critical eye of self-consciousness; it allows and enjoins "unreflected doing."[12] It sets man in the concrete nexus of life, amid continuing relationships, and authorizes a free participation in all the fullness of that life. It is not a jealous guard over life's frontier but is the ground of power by which one is enabled to live from life's center. Seen in this way, the command is an authorization for life, a mandate to live, a warrant for "man to be man before God" as an expression of and participation in the new reality which has been reaffirmed in Christ.[13]

The command is also concrete. This means that it eludes categorization, defies conceptualization. It does not come to man as a verbalized law but manifests itself within the matrix of life, in the given realities and actual historical relationships of men among men. In this way the command upholds and legitimates the countless actions which flow freely apart from any self-conscious control.[14] The command, in a word, "mandates" certain definite relations among men, even orders of superiority and inferiority, which undergird the essential structure of social life. The mandates Bonhoeffer finds in Scripture relate to home and family life, the church, labor and culture, and government.[15] The command thus establishes these continuing relationships which embrace all of life and yet exist independently of any specific embodiment or institutionalization. As such they constitute the basis for mutual and reciprocal responsibility, and therefore are the locus for the concrete command of God which is heard by the individual. By relating the command of God, seen now in general terms, to the mandates, Bonhoeffer seeks to eliminate abstracting the good or duty from the immediate expression of authority and obedience already structured within the spheres of life defined by the mandates.

Understood in this way, the command does not make man a "critic and judge of himself and his deeds, but allows him to live and act with certainty and with confidence. . . ."[16] By encompassing all of life, the so-called ethical dimension is no longer the primary concern, and man is thus permitted a full and spontaneous life free from intrusions of conscious contrivance or artificial imposition. The true ethical, being generic to the situation, now finds expression in intrinsic reality, a reality seen to be grounded in Christ himself. The result is a freedom that moves unselfconsciously within life's human relationships in the confidence that it is already discharging its responsibilities and affirming its true meaning.

Specific commands by those in authority, though not absolute, are warranted by God's command and call for simple obedience. Since the Christian accepts as holy these mandated spheres, there is no conflict or schism, but a free and joyous acceptance of the rightful order of life.[17] It is, in short, for the Christian, a deliverance from self-torment and doubt into a "freely accepted and self evident" life.[18] On this level, the question of higher accountability, the problem of the rightful exercise of the mandates themselves, is avoided. Bonhoeffer claims that the mutual interaction, limitation, and support of the mandates make the problem of abuse less than critical. If it should occur that the countervailing relations existing among the mandates by which mutual limitation and balance are achieved were upset, it would, he declares, mean simply that they are no longer mandated of God.[19] But this contingency raises the whole problem of responsibility extending beyond the "given" aspects of life, which must be considered after all.

Reflection, Responsibility, and Understanding

Up to this point our discussion of Bonhoeffer's understanding of Christian action has moved solely within the sphere of the "pre-ethical,"[20] that field or ethos wherein life and its structured expression in the mandates are simply affirmed and expressed. Quite obviously, however, this view does not exhaust the possibilities of free action and responsibility but rather is seen to underlie them. On a more deliberative level, Bonhoeffer speaks of the concept of responsibility as referring to the "response to the reality which is given to us in Jesus Christ."[21] This response is not based so much on Christ's life, according to which our lives are patterned, as it is grounded in the awareness that the whole of life which confronts us and to which we respond is already itself life in Christ.[22] Because the command undergirds life and is a mandate to live, we encounter it not as an articulated imperative to be obeyed, but as a "reality" to which we respond in Christ.

Therefore, ethical response is to *that* reality itself, not to any imperative which is abstractable from it. In this view, responsibility is understood to depend on 1) an appreciation of this dimension of life, this "reality," extending beyond but not severed from the empirical, and 2) the freedom from any constraint that might foreclose the spontaneity and immediacy with which we meet that reality and by means of which our actions "correspond" to it. In light of this reality, responsible life is the life of "deputyship," lived in acknowledgment of its reciprocal and interrelated nature.

Furthermore, all responsible action is guided by the understanding that the relationships between people have final priority over all norms or values. Again, since responsibility is grounded in the concrete relationships in which life is enmeshed, there can be no escape from direct responsibility to others by appeal to extrinsic purposes, nor can one contrive his initial actions in light of such goals in lieu of a response to this immediate encounter.[23]

Ethical reflection, to the extent that it is legitimate, arises from within this encounter among people, and seeks to illuminate what action will best contribute a true response to that situation which is now enclosed within the reality of Christ.[24] Instead of being primarily directed toward God and undertaken in awareness of accountability to him, it deals with the nature of one's responsibility among people in primary reference to the situation. Reflection will forego all attempts to establish proper conduct or behavior in advance, and it will do this because there is no longer a concern over the rightness of one's action considered in principle. The responsible person is free from any necessity to impose on the situation even something presumed to be good, and as a result his reflection on the situation deals with the elements of that situation seen under the aegis of Christ. Since the movement of reality from its true origin to its true end is discerned by the Christian, he can respond accordingly. Not an examination of a lifeless cross section severed from the dynamic present, but an immersion in that present is the basis for, and provides the ingredients of, response to Christ.

Responsible action is action "set free," free from self-regard concerning its goodness, free from preconceptions about what ought to be, free from any goal that would subordinate the present to any future. Although not entirely unreflective, it is nevertheless nondeliberative insofar as this implies a conscious weighing of duties or values not immediately intrinsic to the situation. True reflection consists rather in a repeated reminder of the total context of interpretation which provides the clue to a knowledge of reality, and which thereby allows one's response to be as direct and uncalculated as possible. It provides a rehearsal of the decision "already behind" one, a decision which gives the confidence that life is now grounded on the goodness and freedom of God's command.

Thus the context of interpretation rests on the command of God, interpreted and known in its nature but not in content. Its nature is expressed in, and is congruent with, the recovered unity of life in the world and of the Christian found in Christ. Its primary mood is not the imperative, mandating certain actions or abstentions; it is permissive, authorizing life. Structurally, it is expressed in and through the mandates that provide the proper limits and establish the bases for continuing relations among people. Appropriate action consists in a response to life in the given situation interpreted with respect to its true reality in Christ. The human, therefore, no longer stands under the critical scrutiny of either himself or God but is free to act in correspondence with this "reality" and with his true nature as known in Christ. Right action does not stand under the fatal antinomy of an ideal "ought" and a condemned "is," but consists of the appropriate response to be given in terms of what is actually possible, with primary attention to the persons involved. Responsibility is defined, then, in terms of the acceptance of the existing reciprocal obligations of life, where people act in and for others in deputyship. Reflection has value insofar as it addresses the context of action, bringing to it an awareness of what reality means for life. Good action is expressive of the essential unity of a person no longer divided within himself and fearful of his own justification; it is directed toward the recovered unity of the real world in Christ.

By its very nature, this approach does not provide criteria for evaluating or testing Christian action. The ethical question is ruled out a priori as an expression of—if not outright identification with—mankind's "defection from Christ." Certain questions do arise, however, regarding the place of understanding and reflection. For instance, on what basis does Bonhoeffer distinguish the understanding that is legitimate and required in order for action to correspond with reality from the understanding that would intrude on intrinsic reality and thereby stultify one's free response? Certain key conceptual patterns are already operating in his discussion of "reality." How can action be seen to correspond with reality understood in this sense without employing certain ideas and even ideals by which "correspondence" is judged, ideas or ideals that one brings *to* that situation?

Further, can the ethical question be avoided so easily? Bonhoeffer's descriptive approach rests on a postulation of proper Christian response rather than a specification of its direction or an acknowledgment of its moral necessity. What moves one to make that response or to assume the responsibility entailed by his concept of deputyship? Does ethical or "good" action simply flow from the encounter with the situation in such a way that conscious decision about the nature of the action rather than its constituent parts is rendered unnecessary? These questions provide the basis for an examination of a second "context."

II. The Context of Decision

The Assumption of Responsibility

Although Bonhoeffer himself never makes distinctions among the various meanings denoted by the term "responsibility," there would appear to be at least four different usages in his *Ethics*. The first and most obvious one has to do with the objective duty or obligation inherent in concrete relationships. The second usage refers to the perception of responsibility, including not only the acknowledgment of concrete claims themselves but also an understanding of these claims in the light of faith. The third sense of the term describes one's conscious acceptance of duty and willing assumption of the larger dimensions of "free responsibility" which faith-perception entails. Finally, there is the use of the term as it deals with the execution or discharge of responsibility.[25]

The importance Bonhoeffer attaches to the concrete grounding of responsibility is revealed by this statement: "We are set objectively in a definite nexus of experiences, responsibilities, and decisions from which we cannot free ourselves again except by abstraction."[26] We have already noted how the mandates are seen to uphold this nexus in the various spheres and how the term deputyship is used to describe this interrelatedness of life in its various dimensions. The point here is that life is set within operating claims and counterclaims that do not require conscious support or theoretical understanding for their existence. These could be called empirical obligations. No one denies, for instance, that within the family various demands and needs all press upon a father for some kind of response. Simply to assert the existence of such duties and responses, however, says nothing about how they are understood or how adequately they are met. The term "father" can be no more than a biological or sociological description; or it can mean all that is conveyed by a sense of divine paternity. What it *does* mean and the corresponding responsibility it entails rest on the understanding brought to it by the person and his conscious decision to fill the role in light of that understanding. Bonhoeffer never acknowledges this distinction.

Indication of such an unconscious transition is found in the claim that because of Christ, "whether or not life resists, it is now always deputyship . . . just as the father is always a father, for good or for evil."[27] Here is an assertion about life which makes objective claims that are somehow supposed to have ethical consequences. The problem is not whether life is "really" deputyship; the problem is whether people understand it to be such and act in accordance with that understanding. In any case, there is an unjustified identification of the objective reality of fatherhood with a nonempirical assertion about the *nature* of life. Nothing of any consequence at all has been said by this identification unless deputyship means the consciousness of being "for" others, and this is of course what Bonhoeffer does mean by it, even to "being for all mankind."[28] Quite obviously if, as he says, deputyship involves the "complete surrender of one's own life to the other man,"[29] this can be said to characterize life only in a highly exaggerated sense, whether or not it "resists." Simply to claim that it does says nothing whatever about the ethical question about whether one *ought* to act in accordance with this understanding of life. Further, to claim that this identification is a parallel of fatherhood assumes that the inherent dynamics of a concrete situation that operate on a father also provide impetus and motivation on this higher, more voluntary level.

When Bonhoeffer asserts that "only the selfless man lives responsibly" and thereby is truly a "deputy," what does this imply for ethics? Is there an implicit demand that all people are to understand and assume this larger role of deputyship that runs far beyond any understanding derived from the mandates? Since the mandates themselves are grounded in the concrete claims and demands of life, what is the relationship of this extended role of deputyship to them? Does this entail a new command that supersedes the command underlying the mandates? If not, is Bonhoeffer saying that it is simply a question of individual perception and understanding with no imperative implied at all? It would appear that some crucial decisions about one's conscious understanding of responsibility and its acceptance have either been assumed or overlooked. Since a person is not simply a reflection of the forces that play on him, his discharge of responsibility will rest on his understanding of its meaning and will entail a decision, a conscious acceptance of it on those terms. Bonhoeffer's descriptive approach, although it begins with the objective situation, imperceptibly moves to include a "reality" that is a product of his own understanding and interpretation. At the same time he assumes that the concrete "mandate" found in human relations is either adequate for this larger role of responsibility, or else that individuals when apprised of this larger sphere of responsibility will respond voluntarily. In any case, a descriptive approach such as Bonhoeffer's cannot give answers to these questions because it does not address these problems.

"Proving" the Will of God

Manifesting, or "proving," the will of God in a given situation requires a decision taken in "free responsibility." Such a decision presupposes, as we have noted above, both an awareness of the dimensions of responsibility and a consciously assumed stance to make it responsible. It also presupposes a freedom from self without which it is impossible really to "see in the situation" what the right decision would be.[30] As a corollary to the selflessness which true deputyship involves, perceiving the will of God in the specific instance entails ultimate ignorance of oneself, a freedom from all inner need to justify one's actions, or to impose alien demands on the situation.[31] "Free responsibility" is possible only from within a stance that reflects a freedom from self which in turn enables one to be "for" others. In this double freedom, one perceives reality and makes a decision that manifests the will of God.

The role and place of conscience in discerning God's will becomes somewhat ambiguous in light of this new freedom. Ordinarily, Bonhoeffer observes, the conscience functions with a supreme eye to avoiding personal guilt. It is in the service of the self, which seeks to justify itself in terms it knows and can accept.[32] This means that actions dictated by conscience are not taken in primary response to the situation but with regard to how well the actions accord with the demands conscience imposes. As a result, this "ungodly self-justification" distorts reality and subverts personal relations. Only when the conscience is freed by Christ and thus becomes open to the situation can there be a "total and realistic response . . . to the claims of God and of our neighbor."[33] Liberated from the curse of guilt-calculation, the Christian not only can act freely but is set free to identify with the pariahs of society whom others shun. Further, he is set free to act decisively and with assurance because he is no longer paralyzed by fear that he will incur guilt in his action. Free responsibility eschews any knowledge of one's own good and evil, and refuses to seek any judgment in light of an ethics based solely on principles.

Given the preconditions necessary for proving the will of God, namely, a responsible stance toward the situation coupled with a freedom from self, the question must still be asked, what is the basis for a concrete decision? It would be a serious error to infer that for Bonhoeffer the will of God is known intuitively within the situation once these preconditions are met. On the contrary, because the proper act, word, or deed may lie concealed beneath many possibilities, each person in every situation "must ever examine anew what the will of God may be."[34] To this end, "intelligence, discernment, attentive observation of the facts" all come into live operation, and the actual alternatives and the possible consequences are clearly and carefully assessed.[35] Only after this kind of consideration may a decision be made in confidence and freedom.

In what sense does such a decision "prove" the will of God? Obviously not by its correspondence to some norm or generalized view of God's will, for that will, in principle, cannot be formalized. Nor are the empirical consequences taken by themselves the basis for such an evaluation, for this would also imply some means by which God's will could be measured or quantified. Proving the will of God, contrary to all these, consists in a decision about what is responsible under the circumstances, with due regard for reality. That decision is to be accompanied by a self-examination, which will "always consist precisely in our delivering ourselves up entirely to the judgement of Jesus Christ. . . ."[36] Any further attempt to determine its congruence with God's will is illegitimate, reflecting a desire to know one's own goodness or evil. Since the substantive aspects of the decision cannot be tested, manifesting or proving the will of God would appear to refer back to the preconditions of perception, namely, the orientation of the self and its unity with Christ. While the ethical value of the deciding self remains uncontested, are we to assume that, even for dimensions of responsibility involving the welfare of great numbers, no guidance is really permitted other than "correspondence with reality" subjectively discerned? There are, he affirms, the limits set by God on people's actions that are found both in the mandates and in the Ten Commandments.[37] But the realm of "free responsibility," though grounded in the mandates, extends beyond them and is not finally limited to them. Also with regard to the Ten Commandments, certain "necessities" may arise which compel a decision that will entail a violation of these commandments. The proviso Bonhoeffer offers is that "extremely serious consideration" must be given to any action that would violate the law of God. Yet because the law as given is expressive of the will of the lawgiver, his direct command can enjoin an action that contravenes the stated law itself.[38]

On what basis is such a decision to be reached? Objectively, only the "ineluctable necessities in the lives of men" can warrant or mandate a decision such as this, which not only leaves all principle and convention behind but violates them as well.[39] In the nature of the case, no further support can be adduced, since it is *ultima ratio*. The results are left to providence. Subjectively, as to the mode of action, when such a decision is taken, public acknowledgment of the validity of the law—even though the law is violated—will serve to affirm its integrity. In such a way, even a violation can serve to hallow the law, Bonhoeffer declares.[40] The decision itself, however, is taken in free responsibility by the one who has authority. Thus, aside from counseling self-examination to insure against the intrusion of subjectivity, Bonhoeffer offers no criteria by which even the exceptional case may be tested either for its consequences or for the validity of the command which is presumed to be the basis of that decision.

Discernment and Decision: An Example

The most comprehensive illustration of Bonhoeffer's approach to the situation in which the proper decision is reached after "due consideration of reality" is contained in a brief essay entitled "What is Meant by 'Telling the Truth'?"[41] Since the ethical cannot be detached from reality, "continual progress in learning to appreciate reality is a necessary ingredient in ethical action."[42] Before one can "speak the truth," therefore, there must be an assessment of the total situation, involving in particular an awareness of the nature of the claim put forth by the person with whom one is in conversation. Certain limits on and demands for the truth are established by the kind of relationship represented by the two parties. The more complex the actual situation of a person's life, the more involved will be the task of speaking the truth in any given moment. In any case, however, truth is to be a faithful expression of the "reality of the relationship."

Instead of using the negative criterion that defines lie as a conscious discrepancy between thought and speech, Bonhoeffer introduces the idea of truth as a correspondence with reality. For this reason he rejects calling the deliberate deception employed during wartime a "lie" because, as he notes, it does not convey a discrepancy in the reality that exists among the parties in question. Furthermore, to call it a lie and then justify telling the lie by referring to the exceptional conditions war entails would give the term "lie" a moral sanction that is indefensible. The most sensitive illustration Bonhoeffer gives is of a teacher questioning a child about his family before the class. Because a true answer to the question will compromise his father, the child replies with an evasion. Though the actual words of the child are factually misleading, Bonhoeffer comments, they faithfully reflect the child's loyalty to his family, and are therefore "true." Moreover, his refusal to give the "truth" to the teacher reveals that the question was illegitimate under those circumstances. With this illustration Bonhoeffer show how "truth" rests on the context and is not simply judged in reference to an abstract or objective norm.

The degree of sensitivity and responsibility Bonhoeffer displays in his discussion of truth-telling makes his position both cogent and compelling. Nevertheless, certain reservations about this approach remain. One has to do with the presupposition on which it rests, namely, that truth-telling not only requires ethical sensitivity but also a high degree of self-awareness. Due to this subjective reliance, the possibilities of self-deception are very great. A principled approach seeks to avoid this danger. Another reservation has to do with the private or subjective determination by each of the participants of the right of the other to the truth, depending on how they interpret the relationship. While it is true that all speech leaves large areas of expression open, not only in terms of the choice of words but also in terms of nuance, inflection, gesture, expression, and so forth, it may still be asked whether there remains no objective criterion at all to which both the speaker and the addressee are related. The question here is whether there is more at issue than the immediate context of the people involved. Bonhoeffer himself acknowledges this when he indicates that certain prior loyalties, for instance, the boy's relationship to his parents, can influence the freedom to speak. But he fails to mention that the relationship of the self to the other stands beneath, and is comprehended by, the claim of God on both, which is not simply intrinsic to that relationship as either one of them understand it. However wooden seems Kant's logical conclusion that the truth must be told under all circumstances, nonetheless that position points to the existence of the total human community, which also lays a claim on all people at all times to tell the truth. Finally, Bonhoeffer's refusal to term even a deception a "lie" if it is justified by the situation reveals a basic problem in his entire ethical position, namely, the refusal to admit the tragic antinomies of existence without attempting premature resolution. In any case of war, the fact that lying is necessary points to one of war's morally debilitating aspects; to deny that results in more confusion than clarity because it blunts the meaning of truth itself. There is, in other words, an objective dimension of ethical reality that stands in tension with the concrete situation and cannot be abstracted from it or collapsed into it. In this case, it results in a prima facie claim for truth regardless of the relationships involved, with the burden of any exception falling to the agent.

III. The Context of Action

On the basis of the assumption that the Christian 1) has consciously accepted a role of responsibility, and 2) has assumed that posture which frees him from paralyzing self-regard, fear, and guilt, he is then granted the requisite perception and ethical sensitivity to decide and act within a given situation with a "due consideration of reality." This total direction, decision, and action in the nexus of personal relationships is itself, taken as a whole, the "realization" of the Christian life, the concrete "proving" of the will of God. Under the context of action we turn to an examination of how this subject-oriented understanding of responsibility relates to the objective demands and requirements of the world at large. Since the Christian's attitude accords with reality only if he allows the world ever anew to disclose its essential character to him,[43] we are particularly interested in the terms for action set by its "essential character"—how these relate both to the mandates and to the free responsibility of man under the command of God.

The Penultimate and the Natural

Bonhoeffer repeatedly affirms the importance of allowing the world to be the world.[44] Seen within the comprehensive reality of Christ, this means that it is not merely instrumental to the kingdom of God on the one hand, nor is it an autonomous self-sufficient realm on the other. Rather, the world has its own unique place. A due regard for reality will seek to avoid either imposing a "higher" order on the world, thereby violating its integrity, or abandoning it to its fate outside Christ. Only the perception that is possible in Christ can lead one to accord the world its rightful place in the total economy of God, taking with full seriousness the inherent laws and conventions of life that have been achieved through the experience of many generations.[45]

Methodologically, Bonhoeffer gives proximate, but not relative, value to the world by means of the concept of the "penultimate." By this he means that the world, while not severed from the ultimate in a final sense, nevertheless is accorded its own provisional independence and justification. Its relationship to the ultimate is that of anticipation and preparation, which means that although it is oriented to the "coming" of the ultimate, the ultimate for its part does not exercise a determining voice in the form of its preparation.[46] The ethical implications of this are that the Christian is not to overleap this world by a premature claim presumptively derived from the ultimate. There is no ethical principle that stands in transcendental relation to the world. Nor can any action claim a divine warrant that disregards worldly order and structure. Bonhoeffer offers two basic criteria as intrinsic to the world seen under the aegis of Christ. These two are: to be human and to be good.[47] Although the realization of either of them establishes no claim for divine justification, even so he insists that for the Christian "it makes a difference in God's sight" whether a person acts justly and serves the good.[48]

Although neither the fulfillment of man nor the attainment of the good is bound in a deterministic sense to the world as a system or by nature, both are grounded in the "natural" and are thus given shape and content there. Formally, life is directed toward Christ, and this dimension of reality is known to the Christian. Substantially, however, life has its own relative freedom and self-development which is "entirely appropriate" to its nature, and this content element is perceptible by reason.[49] Put in its simplest terms, the natural is self-validating and self-sufficient, maintaining and preserving created life through a natural order that always reasserts itself.[50] Violations of the natural are always organized, arbitrary contrivances that are imposed upon, not emergent from, the natural. Ethically, this dictates certain rights that are inherent in life, and certain corresponding duties that accord with the direction and purpose of the natural.

The Adequacy of "Natural" Rights

The fundamental right, "innate" to the nature of things as they are, is the right to bodily life. Preservation of the life of the body is the foundation of all natural rights "without exception" and applies to all people without any qualification whatsoever.[51] While the positive realization of all that bodily life implies is itself worthy of ethical consideration, Bonhoeffer devotes most of his discussion to the possibility of any legitimate limitations to the right of the body against arbitrary killing. His conclusion is that all deliberate killing of innocent life is arbitrary.[52] The two qualifiers in this statement are "deliberate" and "innocent." Thus there is "nothing arbitrary" about killing civilians during a war so long as it is not directly intended but is only "an unfortunate consequence" of a measure which is "necessary" on military grounds.[53] Nor is it arbitrary to kill the enemy in war, or a criminal convicted of a deed "worthy of death."

While each of these positions has been upheld within the Christian church, this rather simplistic disposal of the question reflects the basic inadequacy of a doctrine of natural rights itself to specify the terms of its exercise. Further, it does not reflect whether there is a commanded *duty*— and not just an innate ethical pressure to uphold all life against any killing.

Considered solely from within the context of natural rights, what is to keep the key term "necessary" from becoming a blanket legitimation for any military action under any circumstances? Or to take another example, by what means does one determine that a criminal act is worthy of death? The "inherent laws and conventions" which result from many generations' experience are no sure or adequate guide to the resolution of this kind of supreme ethical problem. If they are claimed to be, which culture's experience is to be taken as normative? While there is some basis for claiming certain natural rights for all, the problem of the guarantor and the terms of support for these rights remains highly conjectural.[54]

When Bonhoeffer turns to a consideration of euthanasia, he declares that the destruction of the life of another is to be undertaken "only on the basis of an unconditional necessity." When such a necessity is present, "the killing must be performed, no matter how numerous or how good the reasons which weigh against it."[55] Two questions arise: On what basis is necessity postulated as the *sine qua non* for euthanasia but not for war itself or the execution of criminals? Doesn't this reveal the ambiguity of supporting "natural rights" on conventional interpretation? That is, ethical "necessities" are built in and assumed, without requiring new examinations in light of new demands. Second, on what basis is euthanasia "necessitated" to the exclusion of all reasons? Is there a self-authenticating dimension to necessity which validates itself apart from reason? If this is true, doesn't this reveal the bias of Bonhoeffer, that while claiming to avoid intuitive judgment,[56] rational ethical thinking is so closely allied to self-justification that the possibility of its providing real service and testing for serious issues is undervalued? Ordinarily, a "necessity" that transcends rational formulation is perceptible by an individual. Public discussion by its nature requires reason. Presumably, Bonhoeffer is seeking to insure that the decision will allow no hiding behind reason as an evasion of responsibility. That does not in itself, however, guard against the arbitrary factor from entering the decision-making process in its place.

Bonhoeffer's primary concern in dealing with the problem of euthanasia is to deny that life can be quantified or evaluated in utilitarian terms. In rejecting the "social value" theory, he points out that the strong person, confident of his position, need not inquire about the usefulness of the weak. Only the weak themselves think in these terms. The strong person, he avers, sees in the weak a stimulus to "loftier achievements," not a source of diminution of strength. Thus the idea of destroying socially "useless" life is one that "springs from weakness, not from strength."[57] If this appeal to the higher sensibilities of the "strong" is intended as a primary support for the right of bodily life which otherwise would have no worldly justification, it reveals eloquently the ethical impoverishment of the attempt to ground human life on a naturalistic basis. As though in implicit acknowledgment of this fact, Bonhoeffer asserts that the "inherent right" once postulated vis-à-vis the natural can now only be affirmed under the sovereignty of God. Without this secure foundation, the right to life would finally be adjudged by society itself, and thereby become subject to "arbitrary decisions."[58]

Therefore, while attempting to establish natural rights solely within the sphere of the natural, and while denying that there is any pressure of the penultimate from the ultimate for any ethical value, Bonhoeffer has nevertheless been driven to acknowledge that God is the ultimate guarantor of rights. He steadfastly maintains that although God is the guarantor, "He continually makes use of life itself," which sooner or later gains the upper hand "in spite of every violation of the natural."[59] But to say that life always returns to an equilibrium over the long run does not solve the problem of the infringement of individual rights or the violation of life itself. To affirm the foundation of inherent rights in life, when one's life is itself being unjustly taken, is not only poor consolation but poorer justice. And to ignore this as a problem of the first order in Christian ethics appears to be a defect of corresponding magnitude. It is precisely here that the "one way traffic" which Bonhoeffer insists on maintaining between the world, nature, and the penultimate and the ultimate and God seems to prove most inadequate. To refuse any demand, ideal, or normative law, legitimate authority within the world, while at the same time requiring that all ethics be emergent from within the world, would seem to foreclose on responsibility. It is at this point that the problem of the divine mandates in relation to the natural and the world becomes most acute. Although under certain extreme conditions of imbalance the mandates lose their divine warrant, they themselves are unable to provide any leverage over the world and the natural which would restore balance or offer an adequate basis for justice.

Another problem arising from a view of natural rights is that of the adjudication among conflicting rights. Ironically, the closest Bonhoeffer comes to admitting an ethical principle is found in his use of the classical *suum cuique*. Although as a principle *suum cuique* is an attempt to uphold all rights limited only by the corresponding rights of others, it unfortunately does not in itself define the bounds of "what is due" and thus leaves open the question of balance, harmony, and order. Therefore, to achieve this adjudication of interests requires the imposition and formulation of positive law.[60] There is no discussion, however, of why it is "incumbent upon reason" so to take account of the rights of others, unless it is prompted by conscience. It is true that in one place Bonhoeffer does indicate that the natural conscience contains certain striking similarities to the "law of life," but he does not imply that this includes an anticipation of the law of love.[61] Presumably, then, reason prompted by conscience is the basis for upholding natural rights in the most general sense, and is the ethical basis for the formulation of positive law as an expression of *suum cuique*. How such naturally arrived at positive law is corrected or supported by Christian understanding, or whether in principle it can be, is never discussed specifically.

Responsible Action

The question we must now ask is whether "responsible action," for Bonhoeffer, is defined entirely by the situation seen with a "due regard for reality." This question really has two foci: 1) whether there are any demands through revelation or Scripture which are attributable to the will of God and which arise apart from the situation as perceived by the agent, and 2) whether such demands which are seen to arise within the situation by the individual Christian have any binding power on people other than the agent. The foregoing discussion has questioned the adequacy of a general view of the natural either as a basis for the just adjudication of rights or for their guarantee. Within the context of decision it becomes clear that responsible action is not as concerned that the "world should be made better" as that "the reality of God should show itself everywhere to be the ultimate reality."[62] To this degree, responsible action carries the possibility within itself of its own validation, not, to be sure, as establishing the goodness or rightness of the agent but as manifesting the will of God. Thus the true criterion of action is in the nature of a witness or sign, and its "rightness" consists in the degree to which it "corresponds" to the reality of Christ.

However, since action itself has objective consequences, Bonhoeffer allows for a proximate rightness which obtains in relation to the nature of the created world and the natural. But this does not take into sufficient account the inadequacies of the established order of life or the conditions of the fallen world. At times he seems to be saying that the only warranted action is that which is "necessary at the given place,"[63] with the implication that whatever is truly necessary will be readily discernible. On other occasions he admits to certain overriding necessities which stand in conflict with the established order and which require a "free decision."[64] He fails to indicate, however, how one distinguishes between the two levels of necessity, and whether it would be possible for a Christian to perceive in a given situation a "necessity" that is not apparent to everyone else. The question must then be raised whether such "ineluctable necessities" rest on such grievous social disorder or ills which obviously "necessitate" emergency action, or whether the Christian is ever given a mandate to declare in advance certain minimal conditions as essential to justice, even though they do not commend themselves intrinsically to all.

This brings us to the second dimension of the problem. On what basis, if ever, is one "mandated" to declare that certain basic conditions must be met and thus to enjoin certain actions toward their realization upon the world? The apparent discontinuity between the penultimate and the ultimate, between the world and the will of God, is such that any attempt to ascertain by rational consideration what the conditions of justice are and how they might apply to a given time would constitute a violation of integrity of both the "world" and other people. But this view rests on a very narrow understanding of the term "situation." Even Bonhoeffer acknowledges that reason and reflection are to play a part in shaping "pertinent" action. At what point, then, does the use of reason become illegitimate? In this case the concern for selfless action and the desire to avoid spiritual imperialism, laudable as they are, would appear to determine the limits of responsible action and thereby seriously foreclose on the adequate discharge of responsibility viewed in a larger context than that of the immediate situation.

The final problem has to do with the terms of responsibility themselves. Although Bonhoeffer upholds the Decalogue and the divine mandates as "inviolable limits" of the "manifest will of God," he refuses at the same time to allow any ultimate authority to these expressions.[65] For those upon whom responsibility devolves, simple obedience to these limits does not constitute observance of God's will, and most certainly does not "manifest" that will. There may well be occasions when it is necessary to violate the limits, and these violations will be done to God with full cognizance of the guilt involved. At the same time, he declares, such an occasion will be seen to be justified before other people in terms of the necessity that prompted the action.[66] This of course requires acknowledgment and concurrence on their part, and the inevitable conclusion is that we are now in an area of ethical calculation for which Bonhoeffer is unprepared. What if the necessity is not generally agreed on by others or acknowledged by them? Is this a return to a consensual ethic? More importantly in terms of justice, does a general agreement about necessity suffice to validate it, assuming of course that there is a willingness to assume responsibility for the act? The dangers of this need no emphasis before one who suffered under a regime established upon such a principle. Yet it is curious that Bonhoeffer in fact admits of no final safeguard in terms of objective demands and principles. The willingness to make decisions and take responsibility for them considered *in itself* yields no basis for ethical policy. It may be true that "the natural" guards its own frontiers. But that guard can come a whole generation too late.

IV. Conclusion

The sprinkling of questions throughout this essay has already pointed to the issues that seem unresolved within the scope of Bonhoeffer's ethics as

we have received it. What follows is in part a summary and in part a reminder to those of us most indebted to the German martyr that his incon-
clusiveness can no longer be accepted as a basis for subsequent ambiguity
and confusion. These are issues with which Christian contextualists must
come to terms.

One of the most widely accepted ideas of Bonhoeffer is that the
Christian life is to be seen as "free responsibility." The element of responsibility appeals to the self-image of maturity in modern man, and the qualification "free" is attractive in that such responsibility is not imposed from
without but is assumed within the context of life. Conceived in terms of
deputyship—life for others—it becomes an exalted contemporary understanding of Christian responsibility. Yet for all this, there is no acknowledgment of the necessity for its development and nourishment among men.
Put epigrammatically, for Bonhoeffer such responsibility is not an obligation. Christian ethics today must address this from a developmental view
of the moral life.

Again, moral perception does not entail being claimed by an imperative as much as seeing what really is, and then acting in correspondence
with that reality. Questions of motivation, readiness, and attitude are all
subsumed under the need to see and understand. Motive is thus a correlate
of the perception itself or an unrecognized response to a demand within
the situation that is never specified. Such a position requires a highly developed prior awareness of how the concrete present is interpreted as "reality." It also presupposes that, without reflection, there is a direct
correspondence between such reality and the intentional life of the person.
In discussing specific cases Bonhoeffer implies that this ethical perception
is very much akin to artistic sensitivity. One is left wondering about those
who fail to develop such sensitivity or lack the capacity to begin with. Does
this tend to become an insider's ethic after all? A careful phenomenological
examination of the ethical situation could point to dynamics within relationships in a given situation that could assist us here. This would enable
contextual ethics to have a more objective handle and avoid a too ready
ascription to personal—and indefinable—qualities.

Finally, despite the creative attempt to move beyond the age-old tension between law and gospel by transposing it into the penultimate/ultimate
dialectic, we sense that Bonhoeffer's Christian remains a citizen of two
worlds, but fully franchised in neither. This is evident in the fact that while
he wants mankind to act in light of the world itself, seen in terms of its
true origin and purpose, such a "natural" response has to be supplemented
by the need to stand as deputy with Christ, suffering in one's own body
the agony of conflict. The very distance between these two worlds may
make it unlikely that a helpful connection between salvation and worldly
justice can be effected. Such distance is also seen in the perennial temp-

tation for the more exalted aspects of ethical life to withdraw into an arcane discipline, leaving the world and its responsibilities to be exercised on its own terms.

The very fact that questions like these, so integral to Bonhoeffer's *Ethics*, still define the major issues Christian ethics must address today is a remarkable tribute to the suggestiveness of this thought and a continuing testimony to the vitality of his legacy.

Notes

1 *E* (London, 1955), p. 150.
2 *Ibid.*, p. 191.
3 *Ibid.*, p. 61.
4 *Ibid.*, p. 185.
5 *Ibid.*, p. 65.
6 *Ibid.*, p. 237.
7 *Ibid.*, p. 233.
8 *Ibid.*, p. 234.
9 *Ibid.*, p. 235.
10 Karl Barth, *Church Dogmatics*, III/4, 388.
11 Bonhoeffer, *E*, p. 344.
12 *Ibid.*, p. 247.
13 *Ibid.*, p. 250.
14 *Ibid.*, p. 247.
15 *Ibid.*, p. 255.
16 *Ibid.*, p. 250.
17 *Ibid.*, p. 247.
18 *Ibid.*, p. 250.
19 *Ibid.*, p. 257.
20 *Ibid.*, p. 249.
21 *Ibid.*, p. 192.
22 *Ibid.*, p. 193.
23 *Ibid.*, p. 197.
24 *Ibid.*, p. 195.
25 Conspicuously absent is that dimension of responsibility most prominent in Barth, namely, direct accountability to God.
26 *E*, p. 24.
27 *Ibid.*, p. 195.
28 *Ibid.*
29 *Ibid.*, p. 196.
30 *Ibid.*, p. 197.
31 *Ibid.*, p. 204.
32 *Ibid.*, p. 211.
33 *Ibid.*, p. 214.
34 *Ibid.*, p. 161.

35 *Ibid.*, p. 163.
36 *Ibid.*, p. 165.
37 *Ibid.*, p. 220.
38 *Ibid.*, p. 229.
39 *Ibid.*, p. 207.
40 *Ibid.*, p. 229.
41 *Ibid.*, pp. 326-334.
42 *Ibid.*, p. 327.
43 *Ibid.*, p. 202.
44 *Ibid.*, p. 200.
45 *Ibid.*, pp. 206-207.
46 *Ibid.*, p. 88.
47 *Ibid.*, p. 96.
48 *Ibid.*, p. 97.
49 *Ibid.*, pp. 102-103.
50 *Ibid.*, pp. 104-105.
51 *Ibid.*, p. 112.
52 *Ibid.*, p. 116.
53 *Ibid.*
54 Barth's dependence in *Church Dogmatics*, III/4, on Bonhoeffer is striking here, even though he surrounds the concept of "necessity" with more careful qualifications than Bonhoeffer was able to in his fragmentary writings.
55 *E*, p. 116.
56 Cf. *ibid.*, p. 163.
57 *Ibid.*, p. 119.
58 *Ibid.*, pp. 120-121.
59 *Ibid.*, p. 111.
60 *Ibid.*, p. 109.
61 *Ibid.*, pp. 215-216.
62 *Ibid.*, p. 55.
63 *Ibid.*, p. 203.
64 *Ibid.*, p. 208.
65 *Ibid.*, p. 228.
66 *Ibid.*, p. 216.

ORDERS AND INTERVENTIONS: POLITICAL ETHICS IN THE THEOLOGY OF DIETRICH BONHOEFFER

Tiemo Rainer Peters

CERTAIN VISIONS of the kingdom of God and the kingdom of earth form the background to Dietrich Bonhoeffer's political ethics.[1] In *Sanctorum Communio,* Bonhoeffer's dissertation, we read that only the kingdom of Christ, the church as "the kingdom of God realized in history since Christ,"[2] is empirically visible. The visible church can indeed be understood as such a "kingdom," but only "from above to beneath, from within to without, not in the reverse order."[3] Despite the ecclesiocentricity of the early Bonhoeffer, one must note that the church as the kingdom of Christ, that is, "as the new humanity,"[4] is a sketch of the world, of society, and that it finally relates to the questions of human—not just religious—society. *"Per analogiam ecclesiae,* the human society that has been disjointed in the complete reorganization can again achieve sensible order."[5] When Bonhoeffer describes the church in dogmatic-sociological terms, he is at the same time criticizing "individualistic social atomism" (*Gesellschaftsatomismus*).[6]

In his Barcelona lectures, Bonhoeffer discovers the kingdom of the earth and the sovereign "decalogue"-creating freedom of the Christian, but he does not yet succeed in theologically integrating the new aspects.[7] He does, however, attempt such an integration in "Charakter und ethische Konsequenzen des religiösen Determinismus" (Character and Ethical Consequences of Religious Determinism), a thoroughly "German" paper delivered at Union Theological Seminary in 1930. Over against the metaphysical determinism that is always concerned with the justification of God before the world, Bonhoeffer places a Christian determinism in which God and man, rather than universal principles of good and evil, confront each other. The sinner is touched "from without" by God's free and exclusive act of justification: "The question here is the freedom or bondage of man in relation to the ultimate, to salvation."[8]

The ethical consequences are obvious. In relationship to the ultimate, to grace and salvation, mankind is in bondage; nevertheless, he is free within the nonultimate, within the "relativity between good and evil, between God and man," or, as he had previously put it in the Barcelona lecture and had probably already read it in Karl Barth at the time he was working on his dissertation,[9] within the "penultimate." (In his later work he was to use the term "penultimate" repeatedly.) The ultimate and the penultimate belong together. Mankind is rendered creative through his believing recognition of his bondage regarding the "ultimate"; at the same time he is made free in the "penultimate," free "from the world before God," even while remaining in the midst of the world. In other words, all relativities of the penultimate receive their ethical qualification through the ultimate.

This is where Bonhoeffer's theological argument with the "social gospel" begins. On the one hand, he complains in his study report[10] about the *theology* of the social gospel. This theology omits the eschatological understanding of the kingdom of God and introduces the idea of evolution in its place, regarding the end of history as the realization of the kingdom of God on earth. As a result, the progressive ideology of the social gospel cannot give proper weight to the commandment of God, which, according to Bonhoeffer, presupposes a fundamental distinction between the kingdom of God and the kingdom of the world. On the other hand, he appreciates the *practical aims* of theological thought in America and sympathizes with the formula "God is not only valid truth, but also operational truth." He also wants to fully emphasize the basic assumption of the social gospel: "Taking the kingdom of God seriously as a kingdom on earth is truly biblical and correct in comparison to an other-worldly conception of the kingdom." Finally, "the impression I received from today's advocates of the social gospel will be determinative for me for many days to come."[11]

If Bonhoeffer's Barcelona ethic breaks down theologically when the freedom of man and his "faithfulness to the earth" is finally determined by eschatology ad absurdum, the theological ethic of the social gospel's advocates breaks down, as he sees it, when they declare the kingdom of God to be an immanent ethical principle of progress or improvement, thereby eliminating it. For Bonhoeffer, the significance of American theology is that it brings the kingdom of God down to earth; it is here that he finds powerful inspiration.[12] His question will be: How can one think of the kingdom of God as the kingdom on earth without at once having it become a kingdom of grace on earth?

The new experiences precipitate new, turbulent questions. In a letter to H. Rössler, Bonhoeffer writes: "The invisibility exhausts us ... this senseless, persistent being thrown back on the invisible God himself—no man can endure that."[13] In his lecture on the history of systematic theology Bonhoeffer outlines the problems to be solved more clearly. "On what basis can one formulate an ethic? Where is the principle of making the demand for obedience concrete?" How can the law be preached? "The messages in our churches are often so powerless that they remain halfway between general principles and the concrete situation."[14] A little later, at a youth peace conference in Cernohorske Kupele, Bonhoeffer said: "The church may proclaim no principles that are always true; rather, only commandments that are true today. For what is said to be true always is not true exactly today."[15]

The demand for obedience, therefore, can apply to the side of the gospel as well as the law. It can be a liberating gift, but it can also be an abusive fetter and thereby become law. Bonhoeffer speaks of a theological criterion for distinguishing between commandment and law: reality itself is not something one can inquire behind or a God-ordained sign of assurance (sacrament) but is "the sacrament of the commandment." This sacrament is based on the relationship of reality to the reality of creation.[16] Paradoxically, this relationship can only be seen by looking ahead to where the new creation originates. (This reversal is typical of Bonhoeffer.) "The commandments can originate nowhere else than where prophecy and fulfillment originate—in Christ."[17] Reality is an ethical sacrament, not a *factum brutum*. (Here creation and sin are indistinguishably interwoven.) Reality as a sacramental sign of assurance is only accessible through faith in the new creation in Christ.

Bonhoeffer develops a critical concept of reality and the present while resisting the liberal temptation to map out an ethic of adaptation.[18] Yet he is equally critical of a strongly dialectical interpretation: reality—the present—is not canceled by the future of God. On the contrary, the will of the coming God—his commandment—shows itself nowhere else than in the ever-concrete present. "God is always God for us precisely today."[19] The notion that the "penultimate" receives its ethical qualification through the "ultimate" is now varied and concretized to the extent that the reality in which we live becomes qualified, through the eschatological future of Jesus Christ, as an ethical sacrament to the point that the commandment of God can thereby be perceived.

But how is the dignity and ethical validity of the continually experienced present to be expressed without again sanctioning "from above" that which is important and dominant at any time? The answer to this question is to be sought in Christology, which makes a dynamic and critical concept of reality possible as it sets the kingdoms in motion toward one another. In Christ both "the earth and God" can be loved as one, for "Christ entered the cursed earth" and established "the kingdom of Christ as the kingdom of God on the cursed field." Faithfulness toward the earth, which, according to Eberhard Bethge's fitting characterization, appeared quite "gigantic" in Barcelona, is now synonymous with "faithfulness toward misery, hunger, death . . . and entirely with evil and the guilt of our brother." "God's kingdom is the kingdom of resurrection on earth." It is the kingdom of "the breakthrough of death to life."[20]

With this Christological statement, Bonhoeffer enters the discussion of "orders of creation" current at that time. "In Christ, God affirmed the orders, subordinated himself to them, and simultaneously relativized and broke through them."[21] Bonhoeffer's battle cry is: "Not orders of creation, but orders of preservation."[22]

— All orders of the world can break and be broken. "They are not to be addressed as orders of creation which are 'very good' as such. Rather, they are God's orders of preservation," orders utilized in "formulating objectives against sin in alignment with the gospel."[23] Using Christ as our point of orientation, we can say that the orders of the world that are most likely to retard the decay of the world through sin and death must be preserved, while we are to intervene in the orders that are not open regarding the gospel. Bonhoeffer's concept of the orders of preservation bears on the given earthly reality as well as the new reality that arises out of Christ.

International peace is interpreted as the most urgent order of preservation. The conventional vindication of the just war, which Bonhoeffer had still offered in Barcelona,[24] is given up. The modern war contradicts the commandments of God in every case. War is "self-assertion";[25] modern, mechanized war is "absolutely devastating" and results in "the sure self-destruction of both warring factions."[26] Here Bonhoeffer manifests considerable personal engagement, almost as though he were a pacifist. For that very reason, his careful discrimination in his handling of this matter is somewhat surprising. Social and international peace, he declares, is not an absolutely ideal condition, not "a part of the kingdom of God." Rather, it remains an order of preservation directed toward truth and justice. "Wherever a community of peace endangers or suppresses truth and justice, the peace community must be broken and war declared."[27] The temporarily commanded, unwarlike battle that results is "a battle out of love for the other"; it is "a battle prompted by the Spirit, not by the flesh."[28] "Battle" in the sense in which Bonhoeffer uses the term here is also—but not only—"passive resistance" (Gandhi).[29] It is always a risking of oneself "for the holiest brotherhood of humanity."[30]

Bonhoeffer sees revolutionary war not only as a possibility but, in certain cases, as a *necessity*. He opposes Gogarten's conservative concept of the state by arguing that since the state is capable of assuming a form of evil, a revolution can become necessary. In a certain sense, of course, the existing order has right on its side over against the revolutionary. "The existing state has its rights not *qua* order but as an allusion to the God who alone can create order and revolution"[31] and who broke through and relativized all orders in relation to Christ and the "better righteousness" of that which is Christian. As Bonhoeffer sees it, Christian conservatism goes wrong in failing to take this "better righteousness" into account.[32]

Bonhoeffer's political ethic corrects the Lutheran two-kingdom doctrine, which the Pauline indifference to the world had never quite discarded. At the same time, it corrects his own earlier ecclesiocentricity. The kingdom of God is announced in double form: first of all as church, and thereby as the kingdom of resurrection and miracle that breaks through and overcomes all kingdoms of the world,[33] and secondly as state, as the kingdom of order which subdues and preserves the earth and its history. The two belong together: "The miracle as the breaking through of all orders, and order as the preservation of the miracle."[34] Thus there is no peaceful coexistence of church and state, nor does the church "function as the cultural arm of the state," as a moralistic-pedagogical institution. Bonhoeffer clearly sees the danger of this liberal arrangement. "Every strong state needs such allies . . . and will grant them a certain reserved encouragement. With insight into the finer art of statesmanship, this paradox and its relative significance can be used for the state's own good." No, "the church must continue calling the state into question through eschatology."[35] Therefore, she is "political and apolitical simultaneously in an eminent sense." Only in this way, as the critical boundary of the state and politics, can she remain critical and free. But this does not mean that her politics are free and independent of partisan concerns. "One wrong move here damages the political substance of the church and thereby her substance generally."[36]

Although the church cannot primarily take "direct political action,"[37] there is, under certain circumstances, a commandment to take sides, to intervene directly in the political situation. Indeed, it may even become necessary for the church "to get entangled in the spokes of the state's wheel, to replace the state politically. . . . Here the church would find herself in *statu confessionis,* and the state would find itself in the act of self-abnegation."[38]

Does the church possess criteria by means of which it can recognize this act of self-abnegation by the state and venture to intervene? If so, wouldn't such recognition prove her basic ecclesiastical-political superiority? The state does not possess any such criteria. The recognition must come as a result of the way "leadership" takes place in the state. "Leadership occurs through dominance in something essential, through office, ability and expert knowledge in the field." This means that the authority of a political leader is always "from above," limited by office, and also that such authority is only "penultimate authority compared to the authority of God," for "worldly courts are built by men and therefore do not have absolute

authority."[39] Leadership and office are legitimate only when they are prepared to "lead the individual into actually coming of age first."[40] "Whenever
leadership and office deify themselves, mocking God and the one who
stands alone before him, they must be broken."[41] To recognize this and to
remain alert, independent, and critical is the essence of the fraternal service
which the church is to render to political leadership. The church involved
in politics must show solidarity with the interests of the citizens and must
confine her own political interest to their coming of age.[42]

This brings to light the importance of Bonhoeffer's political-theolog-
ical ethic. Through the incarnation God and the world must be loved "in
one." Wherever the kingdom of the "penultimate," the kingdom of earth,
the orders and offices, is set up as absolute, the Christian ethicist must
intervene and point out to the earthly political powers that the "ultimate"
is still on the way, and that one must believe in the resurrection on earth.
This means, as the Christology lecture summarizes it, that "Christ is at once
the destruction as well as the fulfillment of all the messianic expectations
of history."[43]

Bonhoeffer's theology of orders becomes silent in 1933—though not
the concern it expresses—and is only taken up again in *Ethics.* Although
the political ethic of *The Cost of Discipleship,* written during the troubled
intervening years, has heretofore received little attention, it does deserve
special mention in this context. Bonhoeffer begins with the Sermon on the
Mount, which "negates all *Beheimatung.*"[44] In the dialectic of the "extraordinary" and the "natural," he believes he can sum up Matthew 5 and the
whole ethic of *The Cost of Discipleship.* "The natural is τὸ αὐτὸ (one and
the same) for heathen and Christian; the distinctive quality of the Christian
life begins with the περισσόν. It is this quality which first enables us to see
the natural in its true light."[45] According to Matthew 5:13, the disciple
community is "the salt of the earth." Bonhoeffer explains:

> The disciples, then, must not only think of heaven; they have an
> earthly task as well. Now that they are bound exclusively to Jesus
> they are told to look at the earth whose salt they are. . . . But only
> so long as it remains salt and retains its cleansing and savouring prop-
> erties can the salt preserve the earth.[46]

Thus the world and the church belong together. The church does not keep
itself undefiled by the world for its own sake; rather, its concern is to keep
the world pure—a case of intervention by keeping one's distance!

In the chapter "The Simplicity of the Carefree Life," Bonhoeffer
again comes upon this dialectic between the "extraordinary" and the "natural," but without reviewing the terms once more.[47] The follower looks
"simply" to Christ. The "world" no longer stands between them. Where

earthly goods are accumulated and the heart is set on the acquired treasure, man spoils not just the gift but himself as well. His accumulated wealth becomes "a barrier between himself and God."[48] "Treasure" is "everything which hinders us from loving God above all things and acts as a barrier between ourselves and our obedience to Jesus."[49] Only through the extraordinary does the world become what it really is—thing, gift, and not treasure. Faith manifests itself in objective detachment, as freedom from anxiety, for "anxiety creates its own treasures and they in turn beget further care."[50]

The issue here is the self-evident use of the things of the world. Faith in Jesus Christ makes the world what it really is—a thing. As a thing that can and should be used in complete objectivity, the world is "natural."[51] To realize this in actuality is the aim of the church's political ethic. Bonhoeffer shows us more of what this ethic entails in his chapter "The Saints."[52] The church itself is a *polis,* a city set on a hill. Hence its sanctification has a "political" character. The political ethic of the church finds its sole basis in her sanctification. It is important that the world be the world and the church the church, so that the world does not become the church or the church the world. The concern is that the world, which has become worldly and objective to such an extent that it has been freed from ideological and messianic expectations, remain open to the ultimate, total truth that "the earth and all that is in it is the Lord's" and no one else's.

In *The Cost of Discipleship* the "ultimate" is introduced as an ethically determined "extraordinary" in place of the "penultimate," in order that the latter may appear and be preserved as such (the "natural"). During this period theological service regarding the penultimate could only be rendered by a rigorous disenchantment and detachment from the world, a detachment bordering on the appearance of contempt. But the purpose of this theology and ethic is not the destruction of the world for the sake of the eternal but the reduction of the natural to the natural, of the extraordinary to the extraordinary—in short, the reduction of everything that is to its own unadulterated truth. The distance involved in the extraordinary life is a political element in society.[53]

In the letters from prison this understanding is posed as a question that must be answered anew: "In what way are we 'religionless-secular' Christians, in what way are we the ἐκ-κλησία, those who are called forth, not regarding ourselves from a religious point of view as specially favoured, but rather as belonging wholly to the world?"[54]

Bonhoeffer's theology of orders reappears as a new concept in the ideas about the natural in his *Ethics.*[55] The fourth revision of *Ethics* takes up this topic in its entire scope. It is dealt with in connection with the question of the divine mandates.

The doctrine of the mandates comes up the first time when Bonhoeffer deals with the idea of the realization of Christ in all that is real.[56] The second time it comes up, the topic under discussion is the concept of law,[57] and the third time the topic is the relationship between the worldly orders and the church.[58] The main concern in the first instance is for the concretization of the dynamic ideas of reality and order. In the second instance, the main concern is for the representation of the sovereign commandment "from above," the commandment that can criticize institutions. In the case of the third instance, the main concern is for the liberation of the orders for genuine worldliness. In the light of all that has been said so far, we see that the three concepts are closely interrelated. They will therefore be treated as a unit here and can thus serve to summarize the whole.

Through God's commandment, life is somehow ordered in specific "estates" and "offices." "For lack of a better word," Bonhoeffer chooses the term "mandate," for "institution" or "order" is too easily associated with "a divine sanction for all existing orders and institutions in general and a romantic conservatism," while the word "estate" is too suggestive of "human prerogatives and privileges." As for the concept of "office," finally, it has been "so completely secularized" and is too closely "associated with institutional bureaucratic thinking." All these negative connotations are to be excluded and overcome by the concept of "mandate," which at the same time is only of a "temporary" nature and finally serves "to renew and to restore the old notion of the institution, the estate and the office."[59]

The mandates of labor, marriage, government, and church[60] (or perhaps church, marriage and family, culture, and government respectively)[61] do not receive their commission "from below," from the given reality of creation or from history. Thus they are not static, available statements of reality: "they are not earthly powers, but divine commissions." "They are introduced into the world from above as orders or 'institutions' of the reality of Christ."[62] Accordingly, the bearers of the mandate are not commissioned "from below" but "from above." They are "deputies" and "representatives of the Commissioner." Therefore, the mandate must always be fulfilled anew by adapting "the concrete form of the divine mandates to their origin, their continuance and their goal in Jesus Christ."[63] What is it, precisely, that constitutes the "from above" of the mandates? It is not an other-worldly but a this-worldly "from above"; the "from above" expresses the living, boundless relationship of Jesus Christ to the world. Hence the adaptation of the mandate to its origin, its continuance, and its goal is a deeply living, this-worldly, "political" process in the truest sense. Its alignment with Jesus Christ, with the "from above," takes place in the "with," "for," and "against" one another of the mandates. The responsibility to the divine commission in the mandates consists in maintaining this living relationship between the mandates, which embraces all of life, and also in making it productive for action.[64]

Let us point out the functions of the mandates briefly. Labor is concerned with fulfilling the biblical commission "to dress and to keep" (Genesis 2:15). As "responsibility for a thing," labor excludes "narrow pragmatism" as well as the deification of things. The mandate of labor is concerned instead with the world of things "in their original, essential and purposive relevance to the world of persons,"[65] finally grasping their fulfillment in Christ.[66] The mandate of marriage integrates man into God's creative domain[67] and is far removed from any "purely social, economic, religious, or biological obligation."[68] The mandate of government already presupposes labor and marriage, and therefore may never become their subject but must always serve to protect them. "By the establishment of law and by the force of the sword the governing authority preserves the world for the reality of Jesus Christ."[69] Finally, the church has the mandate, without "constant covert interference in the domains of the other mandates,"[70] to proclaim that man is not divided by the mandates and to proclaim how it can be said that he is not divided by them. The church proclaims that what man is confronted with is precisely "the one whole reality which is manifested to us in Jesus Christ."[71] In actual relationship to the mandates at any given time, what the proclamation declares above all is a "setting free for life in genuine worldliness"[72] and a liberation from every form of alien rule ("laws, ideologies and idols").[73]

It is significant that every mandate is subject to the others.[74] Thus there can be no "retreating from a 'secular' into a 'spiritual' sphere. There can only be the practicing of the Christian life under these four mandates of God,"[75] in situations of "with," "for," and "against" one another.

This warning against "retreat" could be understood as a further theological reflection of the sociological process, in which the individual is more and more rarely integrated into just one institution,[76] the process in which increasingly general criteria for action must be sought, those criteria that make it possible to critically ponder the standard specifications of the various systems of action. The question that immediately arises here is whether Bonhoeffer's universal mandates are sufficiently large and manifold. Or must we conclude that there are conservative elements resonant in these visionary presentiments (as is more often the case with Bonhoeffer), elements that ultimately serve as a secret protest against the increasing fragmentation and differentiation of society?[77]

Bonhoeffer was not oblivious to the problems in his theological thought; in fact, he made many corrections on his thought. In early attempts at a doctrine of the mandates, which have been discovered in the first draft of a catechism in 1931,[78] and above all in the first edition of the Bethel Confession[79] (Part IV, 2), which was strongly influenced by Bonhoeffer, the "orders of sex, marriage, family, nation, ownership (labor and economy), vocation, and government"[80] still face each other in unresolved tension, which is understood as a "visible indication of the lostness of the world."[81] In *Ethics* the mandates and their "with," "for," and "against" relationship are duly dealt with. However, economy, ownership, and culture are subordinated to the mandate of labor. In the letters from prison Bonhoeffer calls into question this subordination, which can be understood only against the background of the social ideas of the past century,[82] along with much else in the whole theory. There we read that friendship, culture, and education "belong, not to the sphere of obedience, but to the broad area of freedom, which surrounds all three spheres of the divine mandate."[83]

From the fact that Bonhoeffer revises the doctrine of the mandates one can conclude that political ethics at all times critically arranges the mandates within the concrete, historical context, based on a specific sociological past and adjusted to a specific sociological future, which at the very least must be open for the new, which was begun in Christ and is still to be expected. Thus the doctrine of the mandates is not to be understood as an alternative social theory in which the *etsi deus non daretur*[84] were valid but as a socio-theologically transmitted pattern of thought with whose help the concrete social relationships could be seen in the light of the "extraordinary," that is, the liberating reality of Jesus Christ.[85]

Does Bonhoeffer at least allude to what this liberation and breakthrough might consist of, and does he indicate the point at which the political theological ethic can consequently intervene? In the letters from prison he asks whether it might be possible to reestablish an understanding for the area of freedom (art, education, friendship, play) through the concept of the church.[86] In my opinion, this question of Bonhoeffer must be seen as a hint that is of interest even today. At the same time, it shows us how he finally understood the doctrine of the mandates. It is the task of the church to keep aware of the meaning of the mandates, along with their "with," "for," and "against" interrelationships, in that she proclaims the one commandment of God that abolishes all fragmentation. In his last letters Bonhoeffer indicates from whence the church can live according to the mandates as she makes others aware of their meaning, namely, from the area of freedom. When we put all of this together, we see that he is saying that freedom is the key to the mandate and to the doctrine of the mandates, and also to their meaning today.

This comes out in an especially beautiful way in Bonhoeffer's poem "The Friend."[87] In this poem he compares friendship, freedom, art—the aesthetic existence—with the "blossom" in the ripe "cornfield" of the mandate:

> Beside the staff of life
> taken and fashioned from the heavy earth,
> beside our marriage, work, and war
> the free man, too, will live and grow towards the sun.
> Not the ripe fruit alone—
> blossom is lovely, too.
> Does blossom only serve the fruit,
> or does fruit only serve the blossom—
> who knows?

From the perspective of the prison letters, this appears to be the line of questioning that Bonhoeffer wanted to introduce and keep open in the doctrine of the mandates—and thereby in his entire political ethic for life in our time. In a world of technology, completely organized and operated by planning and rationalization, the bearers of the mandates are to be made aware of this living, moving relationship between freedom and obedience.[88] Here the restorative and visionary aspects of Bonhoeffer's thinking appear simultaneously.

Obedience does not mean a slavish submission to the forces of coercion; rather, it means a new objectivity and coming of age,[89] a proud composure,[90] and a this-worldly seriousness through which life can be lived unreservedly in all its "duties, problems, successes and failures, experiences, and perplexities,"[91] made possible by the area of freedom.

The integrating, liberating ingredients for objectivity, composure, seriousness—in short, for "genuine worldliness" in social life—are education, art, play, friendship, which constitute the *area of freedom*. *Education* here implies "the relationship to the whole of natural and intellectual being (without specialization),"[92] the "mastery of language,"[93] "knowledge about other countries going beyond politics, business, snobbishness";[94] education implies "memory"[95] and "multidimensionality."[96] *Art and play* represent the most actualized subjectivization of human existence, the expression of "the underlying right to the conservation of bodily life,"[97] and, at the same time, "distance from oneself" (*hilaritas*).[98] *Friendship,* finally, is the chance of the "active, working, lonely man" to "return" and find himself in another[99] or in a "small circle" of friends, to gain distance, perspective, and new impulse for action.[100]

With this our topic of "orders and interventions" has reached its final formulation. The church, according to Bonhoeffer, moves in the area of freedom and in this way experiences the redeeming presence of Jesus Christ. With the "with," "for," and "against" of the mandates, she at once witnesses and proclaims that this redeeming freedom is the deepest meaning of all divinely willed orders. In our overly organized age this witness must be understood as a critical intervention. The acceptance of this criticism would mean that contemporary society, which appears to be a mesh of institutions, is open to the eschatological future and thereby has room for the kingdom of the resurrection on earth.[101]

Notes

1 Because this essay was written over ten years ago, it is impracticable to incorporate all the important contributions made to Bonhoeffer's theology and ethics during that time, both in print and at the congresses of the International Bonhoeffer Committee. The author's own publications should be noted, since they supplement the present text, and supersede it on one or two points: T. R. Peters, *Die Präsenz des Politischen in der Theologie D. Bonhoeffers: Eine historische Untersuchung in systematischer Absicht* (Mainz/Munich, 1976); "Theologie am Ort politischer Gefangenschaft: Das Beispiel D. Bonhoeffer," *Concilium*, 14 (1978); "Jenseits von Radikalismus und Kompromiss: Die politische Verantwortung der Christen nach D. Bonhoeffer," in *Verspieltes Erbe: D. Bonhoeffer und der deutsche Nachkriegsprotestantismus*, ed. E. Feil (Munich, 1979).

2 *SC*, p. 105.

3 *SC*, p. 154.

4 *SC*, pp. 81ff.

5 E. Lange, "Kirche für Andere: D. Bonhoeffers Beitrag zur Frage der verantwortbaren Gestalt der Kirche in der Gegenwart," *Evangelische Theologie*, XXVII (1967), 521. Cf. H. Müller, *Von der Kirche zur Welt* (Leipzig, 1966), pp. 69ff. According to *SC*, the church is the prototype of the new humanity through the *Ineinander* of "spiritual multiplicity, community and unity" in the church (*SC*, p. 111) and the new ethic made possible by the deputyship of Christ (deputyship is the "principle of life for the new humanity" [*SC*, p. 98]), and is characterized by the "with," "for," and "in place of" of believers (*SC*, pp. 127ff.).

6 *SC*, p. 15.

7 Cf. *GS*, III, 48ff. At the end of the lecture, the kingdom of grace is inverted over the kingdom of ethic. The cry "Our world ceases, Thy kingdom come" suppresses all faithfulness to earth and love of freedom in the earlier ethic and lets it break down theologically.

8 *GS*, III, 85ff.

9 Cf. Karl Barth's book *Auferstehung der Toten* (1924), pp. 97f., referred to in *SC*, p. 105: "As yet, it [the last sovereign act of the Son] is not accomplished. His power is used in battle with the other penultimate powers, and to that extent we are now in his kingdom, expecting the ultimate. . . ."

10 *GS*, I, 84ff.

11 *GS*, I, 102. Cf. H. H. Schrey, "Soziale Verkündigung oder social gospel?" *Zeitschrift für evangelische Ethik*, I (1957), 24ff. (hereafter *ZEE*).

12 Cf. R. Niebuhr in *Union Seminary Quarterly Review*, I, 3 (March 1946), 3: "He felt that political questions in which our students were so interested were on the whole irrelevant to the life of a Christian. Shortly after his return to Germany

he became very much interested in ethical and political issues and for a time considered going to India to study Gandhi's movement. . . . Once very unpolitical, he became a very astute political analyst."

13   *GS*, I, 60ff.; cf. *GS*, IV, 60ff.

14   *DB*, pp. 1047ff.

15   *GS*, I, 144f.

16   *GS*, I, 147.

17   *GS*, I, 150; see also *SC*, pp. 35f.; *SF*, p. 7; *E*, pp. 268, 298.

18   Cf. *GS*, III, 303ff.: "That something is against us—is waiting against us—says that the present is determined from without . . . by something approaching, by the future. The present is determined not primarily by the past but by the future, and this future is Christ; it is the Holy Spirit." Later he says: "Christ is our hope—that is the ultimate simplification of eschatology" (*GS*, IV, 358).

19   *GS*, I, 144f.

20   *GS*, III, 270ff.

21   *DB*, p. 1084.

22   Cf. *GS*, I, 128. For the difference between Künneth and Bonhoeffer, see W. Schweitzer, "Die Beziehungen zwischen Politik u. Geschichtsdeutung in theologischer Sicht," *ZEE*, I (1957), 21ff.; J. Moltmann, *Herrschaft Christi u. soziale Wirklichkeit nach D. Bonhoeffer* (Munich, 1959), p. 45; R. Mayer, *Christuswirklichkeit: Grundlagen, Entwicklungen u. Konsequenzen der Theologie D. Bonhoeffers* (Stuttgart, 1969), pp. 124ff.

23   *GS*, I, 151.

24   Cf. *GS*, III, 56; *DB*, pp. 230f.

25   *GS*, III, 263.

26   *GS*, I, 155.

27   *GS*, I, 153. This does not sound like the Lutheran "battle motif"! Bonhoeffer does not understand the world as an eternal battleground between good and evil (cf. *Ek*, pp. 19ff., 217), for it is precisely the "evil" world that is reconciled to God in Christ. The "evil" world has its ultimate and deepest foundation in Christ, and not in the devil.

28   *GS*, I, 169.

29   Cf. *GS*, III, 263.

30   *GS*, III, 269.

31   *DB*, p. 1083.

32   *DB*, p. 1084.

33   *SC*, p. 37 already speaks of the "miracle of the concept of Christian community," which is the church.

34   *GS*, III, 279.

35   *DB*, p. 1085.

36   *GS*, III, 290; cf. *GS*, III, 270ff.; *DB*, pp. 1071ff. Cf. A. A. van Ruler, "Die prinzipielle geistliche Bedeutung der Frage nach dem Verhältnis zwischen Kirche und Staat," *ZEE*, III (1959), 220ff. In this connection, see also *SC*, p. 135.

37   *GS*, II, 46.

38   *GS*, II, 48f.

39   "Christus und der Friede," introduction to discussion in J. Glenthøj, "Dokumente zur Bonhoeffer-Forschung, 1928-1945" (Munich, 1969), *MW*, V, 70.

40   *GS*, II, 36.

41   *GS*, II, 37f.

42   Here Bonhoeffer still thinks of "coming of age" as "responsibility for self," as "self-adaptation," as "ordering one's own life," as "allowing oneself to be

limited" (*GS*, II, 36), which is outstanding and certainly not yet accomplished. Although Bonhoeffer also speaks of "coming of age," the other impression has become dominant and aroused much controversy, accusing Bonhoeffer of not speaking to the being but only to the deceitful consciousness of modern man, and leaving him to his nonenlightened misunderstanding of self (cf. H. Schmidt, "Das Kreuz der Wirklichkeit," *MW*, IV, 95ff.). It appears that their criticism is beating the air. In fact, Bonhoeffer did not think of being first of all as the experienced present, whose nonenlightenment he precisely did not want to overlook. Rather, he thought of that consciousness of freedom and "coming-of-age" that can be betrayed, suppressed, but behind which one cannot go back, because, as the legacy and promise of Enlightenment (*DB*, p. 973), this true "heir" of the Christian West (cf. *Ek*, pp. 102f.) must progress and be led toward its historical realization. *Ethik*, p. 290 (*E*, p. 274) speaks of the Enlightenment as "a corrective."

43   *GS*, III, 197.

44   Cf. E. Bethge, "Ohnmacht u. Mündigkeit," *Beiträge zur Zeitgeschichte u. Theologie nach D. Bonhoeffer* (Munich, 1969), pp. 88ff.

45   *N*, p. 128 (*CD*, p. 137).

46   *N*, p. 90 (*CD*, p. 104).

47   *N*, pp. 147ff. (*CD*, pp. 154ff.).

48   *N*, p. 149 (*CD*, p. 156).

49   *N*, p. 150 (*CD*, p. 156).

50   *N*, p. 152 (*CD*, p. 158). Cf. also J. Glenthøj, "Christus und der Friede," p. 70; *GS*, I, 216: "There is no peace on the path of security. To demand guarantees of security means to harbor distrust, and distrust brings forth war."

51   Cf. *GL*, pp. 58f.

52   *N*, pp. 246ff. (*CD*, pp. 252f.).

53   A. A. van Ruler, *ZEE*, III (1959), 232f., speaks of the "theocratic claim of the church," in which "the essence of theocracy . . . is relativity." On the topic of worldliness and distance, see J. B. Metz, *Zur Theologie der Welt* (Munich-Mainz, 1968), pp. 92ff.

54   *WEN*, p. 306 (*LPPE*, pp. 280-281). The first attempt at *Ethics* shows the marked influence of *The Cost of Discipleship*. In this connection, it is interesting to note the second fragmentary chapter, "The Church and the World" (*Ek*, pp. 59ff. [*E*, pp. 55ff.]). "It is the refuge in Christ, sought amid persecution, that is now representative of the relationship between the church and the world" (*Ek*, p. 63). Here Bonhoeffer's political ethic is "conservative" in the truest sense. It is an inculcation of that which was regarded as great during the great times of Western history, in order to save it from the decay and devastation of nihilism (cf. *Ek*, pp. 94ff. [*E*, pp. 88f.]). When Hitler had won his most spectacular battle, Bonhoeffer wrote the church's "Confession of Guilt." In the background is the consciousness that "the Church alone can be the place of personal and collective rebirth and renewal of the Western world" (*Ek*, pp. 123ff. [*E*, p. 111]).

55   *Ek*, pp. 152ff. (*E*, pp. 143f.).

56   *Ek*, pp. 220ff. (*E*, pp. 207f.).

57   *Ek*, pp. 303ff. (*E*, pp. 285f.).

58   *Ek*, pp. 350ff. (*E*, pp. 332f.).

59   *Ek*, p. 305 (*E*, p. 288).

60   *Ek*, p. 220 (*E*, p. 207).

61   *Ek*, p. 303 (*E*, p. 286).

62   *Ek*, p. 306 (*E*, p. 288). Thus, "it is characteristic of the divine mandate that it corrects and regulates the earthly relations of superior and inferior power

in its own way" (*Ek,* p. 306 [*E,* p. 289]). Here, as in *DB,* p. 1083, Bonhoeffer's allusion to the biblical basis of the mandates (*Ek,* pp. 220f. [*E,* pp. 207f.]) strikes a note critical of the Lutheran concept of orders. *Ek,* p. 350 (*E,* p. 332) expressly turns against Luther's doctrine of three states and substitutes "the doctrine of the four divine mandates, derived from Scripture."

  63 *Ek,* pp. 221f. (*E,* pp. 208f.).
  64 *Ek,* p. 308 (*E,* p. 291); cf. *SC,* pp. 127, 132; *SF,* p. 43. For the function of the mandates, see J. Moltmann, *Herrschaft Christi,* pp. 58ff., and his article "Die Wirklichkeit der Welt und Gottes konkretes Gebot nach D. Bonhoeffer," *MW,* III, 58ff.

  65 *Ek,* p. 241 (*E,* p. 227).
  66 *Ek,* p. 222 (*E,* p. 209).
  67 *Ek,* p. 223 (*E,* p. 209).
  68 *Ek,* p. 185 (*E,* p. 173).
  69 *Ek,* p. 224 (*E,* p. 211).
  70 *Ek,* p. 309 (*E,* p. 292).
  71 *Ek,* p. 225 (*E,* p. 212).
  72 *Ek,* p. 314 (*E,* p. 297).
  73 *Ek,* p. 351 (*E,* p. 330).
  74 *Ek,* p. 349 (*E,* p. 329).
  75 *Ek,* p. 220 (*E,* p. 207).

  76 Bonhoeffer himself stresses this most strongly in regard to the institution of the church, which has now definitely become a mandate among mandates (*Ek,* p. 224; *E,* p. 211). Cf. K. M. Beckmann, "Die Mandatenlehre und die nicht-religiöse Interpretation bibl. Begriffe bei D. Bonhoeffer," *Evangelische Theologie,* XXVIII (1968), 202ff.

  77 Cf. Karl Barth, *KD,* III/4, 21ff.; J. Moltmann, *MW,* III, 63; H. Müller, *Von der Kirche zur Welt,* p. 291; W. Pannenberg, "Zur Theologie des Rechts," *ZEE,* VII (1963), 4f. Cf. also n. 54 above.

  78 *GS,* III, 248ff.
  79 *GS,* II, 99ff.
  80 *GS,* II, 99.
  81 *GS,* II, 100.
  82 Cf. *Ek,* pp. 222, 303ff. (*E,* pp. 209, 286). Here "labor" and "culture" are obviously used as synonyms. Cf. J. Moltmann, *MW,* III, 63.

  83 *WEN,* p. 216 (*LPPE,* p. 193).
  84 *WEN,* p. 393.
  85 One should not be too timid in bringing Bonhoeffer's doctrine of the mandates into dialogue with sociological questions. Bonhoeffer obviously did not shy away from it. Even though he did not endeavor to construct an ideal system of social orders, he was concerned, since *SC,* to describe the "new humanity" as concretely as possible. *SC* is more directly connected with the theology of the doctrine of the mandates than R. Mayer thinks (cf. *Christuswirklichkeit,* p. 184). A simultaneous encouragement and warning for the dialogue between sociology and theology may be derived from H. Schelsky, *Auf der Suche nach Wirklichkeit* (Düsseldorf-Cologne, 1965), pp. 276ff. Cf. T. R. Peters, "Gebot und Verheissung: Die Ethik in der theologischen Entwicklung D. Bonhoeffers," Diss. Walberberg 1969, pp. 194ff.

  86 *WEN,* p. 216 (*LPPE,* p. 193); cf. *Ek,* pp. 59f. The radical break between the doctrine of the mandates and the letters from prison, which J. A. Dvorácek presumes in his "Christusherrschaft und weltliche Ordnungen" (*ZEE,* XII [1968], 285), cannot be substantiated from the text.

87 *WEN,* p. 422 (*LPPE,* p. 388).

88 In his "Outline for a Book," Bonhoeffer notes: "What protects us against the menace of organization? Man is again thrown back on himself. . . In the last resort it all turns on man" (*WEN,* p. 413 [*LPPE,* p. 380]). In the "conclusions" one reads: "The church is the church only when it exists for others. . . . The church must share in the secular problems of ordinary human life, not dominating, but helping and serving" (*WEN,* p. 415 [*LPPE,* p. 382]). Cf. H. Schelsky, *Auf der Suche nach Wirklichkeit,* p. 410: "To gain and maintain the permanence and purity of small groups, of personal human relations in marriage, family, friendship, among colleagues and co-workers, etc., today, is a task that the individual must fulfill without significant assistance from the larger social system, and indeed, often contrary to it."

89 Cf. *GS,* 1, 51; *Ek,* pp. 250ff.; cf. n. 42 above; cf. D. von Oppen, "Die unbewältigte Freiheit," *ZEE,* III (1959), 75ff.

90 *WEN,* p. 215 (*LPPE,* p. 191).

91 *WEN,* p. 402.

92 *Ek,* p. 199; cf. *Ek,* p. 252; *WEN,* pp. 224, 246.

93 *Ek,* p. 199 (*E,* p. 187).

94 *WEN,* p. 259.

95 *WEN,* p. 288.

96 *WEN,* p. 340. Cf. H. H. Schrey, "Das Geschichtsbewusstsein als Voraussetzung für das Socialverhalten des Menschen," *ZEE,* VIII (1964), 76ff. In this connection see also the "memorial thesis" of J. B. Metz in H. Peukert, ed., *Diskussion zur "politischen Theologie"* (Munich/Mainz, 1969), pp. 284ff.

97 *Ek,* p. 168 (*E,* p. 156).

98 *WEN,* p. 257. Cf. O. Hammelsbeck, "Spiel und Sport in ihrer Bedeutung für die moderne Gesellschaft," *ZEE,* IX (1965), 298ff.

99 *WEN,* p. 423.

100 Cf. *Ek,* p. 199; *WEN,* p. 22. Cf. W. von Trott zu Solz, *Widerstand heute oder das Abenteuer der Freiheit* (Düsseldorf, 1958), pp. 103ff.

101 Cf. *WEN,* p. 401. The political ethic of Bonhoeffer offers the most meaningful understanding of the thesis of religionless Christianity. Cf. E. Feil, "Religionsloses Christentum und nichtreligiöse Interpretation bei D. Bonhoeffer," *Theologische Zeitschrift,* XXIV (1968), 40ff. Cf. n. 88 above; W. D. Marsch, "Kirche als Institution in der Gesellschaft: Zur Grundlegung einer Soziologie der Kirche," *ZEE,* IV (1960), 73ff.; E. Lange, *Kirche für Andere,* pp. 513ff.; J. B. Metz, "Über Institution und Institutionalisierung," *Zur Theologie der Welt,* pp. 122ff.; J. Moltmann, "Die 'Rose im Kreuz der Gegenwart': Zum Verständnis der Kirche in der modernen Gesellschaft," in *Perspektiven der Theologie* (Munich-Mainz, 1968), pp. 212ff.; E. Bethge, "Ohnmacht und Mündigkeit," pp. 152ff.

FREEDOM IN BONHOEFFER

Donald S. Bachtell

IN JULY 1944, Bonhoeffer offered a poetic version of a theme in his life
and theology that played no small part in his theology as a whole—the
phenomenon of freedom. In these verses, entitled "Stations on the Road
to Freedom," he describes the phenomenon of freedom that is shaped
through "discipline," "action," and "suffering," and which is only ultimately
revealed at "death." While in these verses Bonhoeffer emphasizes the mysterious and "hidden" quality of freedom in the Christian life, a careful study
of his theological writings as a whole would show that he was forever
struggling to give the concept description and theological clarity. His struggle with the church in Germany during the decade of the 1930s and continuing until his death, along with his growing restlessness with the
theological thought and language of his day, provided the context in which
Bonhoeffer was to give shape and clarity to his theology, and in particular,
his concept of freedom. The raw history of Bonhoeffer's own experiences
forms the background against which we can view the phenomenon of freedom and the descriptions he carefully gave it.

While Bonhoeffer describes his concept of freedom at many points
in his theological development, one does not find a systematic treatment
of the subject. Scholarship has correctly pointed out that while Bonhoeffer
has given careful structure to most of his thought, he purposely avoided
closed theological systems. This unsystematic style becomes clearly observable in his treatment of the subject of freedom. In his lectures on
Genesis 1-3 he gives freedom its theological basis but no clearly defined
systematic outline. He comes closest to a theological structure of freedom
in his writings on ethics, but even there the concept keeps appearing in a
variety of ethical contexts. The reason for this lack of system in Bonhoeffer's thought as a whole might be traced to his existential understanding
of the theologizing process. Bonhoeffer reflected theologically out of his
own existence and from within his own peculiar history. He was suspicious,

330

therefore, of all theological systems that remained unchanged while existence was ever being transformed within history.

However, the main reason Bonhoeffer never gave his concept of freedom absolute system can be found within the nature of freedom itself. For Bonhoeffer, freedom by nature does not lend itself to system. It is the untranslatable and enigmatic quality that enables persons to "be in relation." The freedom that Bonhoeffer saw both between man and God and between man and man was observable within reality but never graspable. One does not "have" freedom; rather, one *participates* in it. Thus there is always the elusive and mysterious nature of freedom within history that transcends and at times defies our fixed symbols. The ontological and existential definitions Bonhoeffer gave to his concept of freedom, which we will discuss later, will clarify why he never gave his idea of freedom final systematic outline.

To say that Bonhoeffer viewed reality on the whole in an unsystematic fashion is not to say, however, that he left us without rational structures. Freedom, for Bonhoeffer, has clearly definable and observable characteristics which function within the Christian reality. In what follows we will attempt to show how he defines freedom as an essential element within the Christian reality by describing a variety of dimensions which give clarity and unity to his concept. These dimensions are distinguishable by their *theological*, *Christological*, *ontological*, and *existential* characteristics.

I. Theology—the Origin of Freedom

Freedom is a concept that belongs wholly within the realm of theology. For Bonhoeffer, all freedom originates in God, becomes reality through the revelation of the living God, and can ultimately be understood only in relation to the living and personal God. To find the source of this freedom, one must go back to the God of creation. The God of creation is the one who creates the world out of freedom. Bonhoeffer's lectures on Genesis 1-3 clearly establish this premise. When the Bible says, "In the beginning God created . . . ," Bonhoeffer makes the revelational claim that this is "God's free affirmation, free acknowledgment, free revelation of himself."[1]

Bonhoeffer refutes the theory that God's contingency in revelation is based on the law of cause and effect. There is a contingency in revelation, but only understood as God's freedom to create a world and freely bind that world to himself. In this free act of creation there is only the beginning "out of freedom, out of nothing."[2] Bonhoeffer performs a fascinating theological feat with the biblical account "the earth was without form and void." It is the "void," the nothing, that corresponds to the freedom of God in his creation. The "void" and freedom are exchangeable terms for Bonhoeffer. This establishes the ground for understanding not only the freedom out of which creation is born but points to the unconditional freedom of the one who creates. The void then is not a void for nothing. It is the void that corresponds to the freedom of the Creator who unconditionally creates.

Bonhoeffer views this unconditional freedom in still another way. The Word is free in its speech. The Word of the Creator, like the Creator, is free: "God *speaks*; this means that he creates in freedom and in his creating remains totally free vis-à-vis his work. He is not bound to his work, but binds the work to himself."[3] Theoretically speaking, this means that the created world has two possibilities: it can live in the void with and for God, that is, in his freedom; or it can live in isolation from his Word, which is to fall back into nothingness. The second possibility does not really occur, since it is God's preserving Word that sustains creation and keeps it from falling into nothingness.[4]

We notice here that transcendence becomes an important factor in revelational freedom. God, as the transcendent one, comes to his creation through his Word but always remains outside his creation. Transcendence is a description of the one who creates the world through his Word but always stands beyond that creation as the free transcendent one. Transcendence always implies that God is free in and for his creation but is never to be substantially identified with it.

Having established the freedom of the one who creates and the freedom out of which he creates (the void), we need now to follow to a logical conclusion the freedom that creates man, that is, the image of God. We must give God's freedom concrete expression in the creation of man and observe how the creatureliness of man is God's freedom in the new context of *analogia relationis*.

The Word of God that calls being out of nonbeing so that it might be, takes on a special meaning for Bonhoeffer. He focuses on the *personal* quality of the one who speaks his world into being. Speech here is not only a creative power but a personal word. This personal word seeks a personal response. God chooses to find that response through the creation of man. The image calls for personality. Here we see a most important dimension of God's created freedom. We become aware that God's freedom is not freedom for itself or for God but for man and for the relationship between people.

Bonhoeffer views God as the one who in his freedom seeks to see himself:

> Only that which is itself free is not dead, is not strange, is not torn away as an event that has happened. Only in something that is itself free can the one who is free, the Creator, see Himself. But how can creation be free? The creation is fixed, bound in law, determined and not free. If the Creator wills to create his own image, he must create

it in freedom; and only this image in freedom would fully praise him and fully proclaim the honour of the Creator.[5]

The "likeness" of man to God, in Bonhoeffer's theological conclusion, is "that man is like the Creator in that he is free."[6] However, two essential claims made by this freedom in "likeness" must be understood from the outset. The first claim recognizes that created freedom is a gift of the Creator and cannot be possessed by man:

> Freedom is not a quality of man, nor is it an ability, a capacity, a kind of being that somehow flares up in him. Anyone investigating man to discover freedom finds nothing of it. Why? Because freedom is not a quality which can be revealed—it is not a possession, an object, nor is it a form of existence—but a relationship and nothing else.[7]

The second claim of freedom follows from the first. That is, freedom is only real in relationship and can never be understood as a special quality within the individual person. In this claim the broader dimensions of *analogia relationis* open up before us. This relational nature of freedom is the very essence of creatureliness. To be a creature—a person—is to be free for others and free for God. It is a freedom over which man has no control. "It is simply the event which happens to me through the other."[8] The analogy, then, of human likeness to God is the analogy of relation, the relationship that people find with other people and with God. The conclusion is that freedom is the event that makes relation to God and to fellow humans possible.

With this theological background, we are now prepared to consider what happens to this original freedom as a result of sin (the Fall). The sin of the Fall, for Bonhoeffer, is the loss of original creaturely freedom. The disobedience of sin forfeits the claim to this freedom, and man must now walk in the unfreedom of his isolation from God and fellow man.[9] This Adamic person in his fallen state no longer participates in the newly created freedom *for* God and *for* man. Man chooses the "middle" for himself—which belongs exclusively to God in original freedom—and thus loses his creatureliness, that is, his original freedom before God. The Fall describes the new status of man as unfreedom. The rediscovery of this lost freedom, for Bonhoeffer, is the special function of Christology.

II. Christology—the Rediscovery of Original Freedom

The recovery of the original freedom of creatureliness lost in the Fall is the special task of Christology. Christ and Christ alone restores and re-establishes the original freedom that was forfeited as a result of the Fall. The language in *Act and Being* is unmistakably clear:

If, through man's self-incapulation, *Dasein* in Adam was in subjection to his *Wiesein*, the sight of Christ brings the loosening of the bonds: *Dasein* becomes free, not as if it were able to stand over against *Wiesein* as independent being, but in the sense of escaping from the I's domination into the lordship of Christ, where for the first time in original freedom it recognises itself as the creature of God. . . . Only in Christ does man know himself as the creature of God. . . .[10]

In Jesus Christ the original freedom of creatureliness is restored and defined. He is the reality of the new mankind.[11] As the "New Creature," he brings, establishes, and claims the original creatureliness that was lost in the disobedience of fallen man.[12] He is the "new being" who invades our being with the recovered reality of original freedom.[13] Christ is the one, then, who restores the Creator-creature relationship to its proper form.[14] In Christ God again becomes Lord and Creator of the creature, and the creature becomes new creature because he has been reestablished in the original freedom of creatureliness before and under God's lordship.

How does Christ effect this new mankind? He accomplishes it in *who* he is and in the *work* he performs. The person and work of Jesus Christ are responsible for the new mankind. Christ as the "Vicarious One" and as the "Mediating One" are developed in Bonhoeffer's Christological lectures of 1933. Through his vicarious action Christ reconciles man to God and man to man; as Mediator he redeems the whole of creation. In both cases we are concerned with the recovery of freedom for the whole of creation.

The vicarious role Christ fulfills in restoring original freedom is defined by Bonhoeffer through incarnation, humiliation, and resurrection. Each of these three aspects of Christ's vicarious role is viewed in light of God's freedom. Referring to the incarnation, Bonhoeffer says:

God's incarnation is no necessity which may be derived from God himself. . . . The incarnation is the incomprehensible, the impossible; it remains in God's freedom.[15]

In reference to Christ's humiliation (suffering and the cross), Bonhoeffer says:

. . . the form of scandal is the very one which makes belief in Christ possible. In other words, the form of humiliation is the form of the *Christus pro nobis*. In this form Christ means and wills to be for us in freedom.[16]

In the interpretation of the resurrection the same theme of freedom is at work:

The fact that Christ was dead did not mean the possibility of the resurrection, but its impossibility; it was the void itself, it was the *nihil negativum*. There is absolutely no transition or continuity between the dead and the resurrected Christ except the freedom of God which, in the beginning, created his work out of nothing.[17]

At every stage in the historical life of Jesus Christ—his incarnation, crucifixion, and resurrection—we are confronted with the God who moves toward his creation not from necessity but out of his unfathomable freedom.

With these careful delineations within the person and work of Christ, Bonhoeffer is attempting to bring us to the reality of freedom itself and its availability for the new mankind. As defined in his ethical writings, freedom becomes a reality for man within the *formation (Gestaltung)* of Christ in the world.[18] In this form the full personal structure of Christ's being is revealed, that is, his incarnation, crucifixion, and resurrection. Freedom is restored to man by identifying with this form of the living and present Christ. In Bonhoeffer's words:

> ... the Holy Scriptures speak of formation in a sense which is at first entirely unfamiliar to us. Their primary concern is not with the forming of a world by means of plans and programmes. Whenever they speak of forming they are concerned only with the one form which has overcome the world, the form of Jesus Christ. Formation can come only from this form. But here again it is not a question of applying directly to the world the teaching of Christ or what are referred to as Christian principles, so that the world might be formed in accordance with these. On the contrary, formation comes only by being drawn into the form of Jesus Christ. It comes only as formation in His likeness, as *conformation* with the unique form of Him who was made man, was crucified, and rose again.[19]

What this means for man is that creaturely freedom has been restored to him *in* Christ. By conforming to the living and present Christ, a person is now free to be a person before God and before other people.[20] In conformation with the risen and living Christ, humans are now set free for life.

Keeping in mind these very distinct theological and Christological descriptions of freedom, the ramifications of which go far beyond these brief outlines, we will consider now the very important ontological character of freedom.

III. Ontology—Being in Freedom

The ontological argument as a tool for defining the reality of freedom comes into Bonhoeffer's thinking at the point where he recognizes that revelation is to be conceived in terms of being:

> It is the *esse* which we have to interpret; the business of ontological analysis is to understand the continuity of man and revelation. It has

to establish of revelation that God "is" in it, and of man that he "is" before he acts, and acts only out of that "being."[21]

Within this ontological framework Bonhoeffer describes the reality of fallen man. This newly acquired reality for man is his being in Adam. The Adamic personality is the ontological equivalent of *esse peccator*.[22] This living in the middle for fallen man now gives him the ontological status of *religious being*. That is, fallen man lives in the middle as a god.[23] His being a god means he has his own way: "He is himself a creator, a source of life and of the knowledge of good and evil."[24] This person who now lives *sicut deus* is ontologically defined as a being toward death and nothingness.[25]

Bonhoeffer is careful, however, not to leave us with just this one side of his ontological argument. He brings us to the new ontological reality which is centered in the person and work of Jesus Christ. In *Act and Being* he describes the possibility of "being in Christ." This new reality of man-being-in-Christ is the cornerstone upon which Bonhoeffer develops the whole of his Christology. Not until his Christological lectures of 1933 do we gain a full appreciation of this ontological dimension: "That Christ is *pro me* is not an historical or ontical statement, but an ontological one. That is, Christ can never be thought of in his being himself, but only in his relationship to me."[26] There is only one question for Christology, according to Bonhoeffer, the question "Who?":

> The question of the being, the essence and the nature of Christ remains. That means that the christological question is fundamentally an ontological question. Its aim is to work out the ontological structure of the "Who?"[27]

A proper interpretation of the recovery of original freedom as effected by Christ would then necessarily include the ontological definition of "being in Christ." Freedom for man must now be informed by the personal being of Jesus Christ. The question "Who?" is the question of the existing and personal Christ in the world. This ontological character of freedom is essential to Bonhoeffer's understanding of the formation *(Gestaltung)* of Christ in the world. Christ is the personal being, the one who stands central to the form of all reality. The question Bonhoeffer asked from his prison cell in April 1944 contained this same ontological formula: "What is bothering me incessantly is the question what Christianity really is, or indeed who Christ really is, for us today."[28]

These observations should keep us in constant tune with the frequent references to the ontological understanding of reality, and in particular the reality of freedom. Freedom originates in the being of God; it is recovered from the Fall in the being of Christ, and it is ultimately defined historically as being-in-relation. Freedom, finally, is defined as the *event* that takes place within the reality of being-in-relation to God, Christ, man, and the world. The personal structure of freedom is the ontological basis for all reality.

As one begins to grasp the ontological basis of Bonhoeffer's Christological statements, one gains a greater appreciation for how he was beginning to understand the reality of Christ in the later years of his life. Beginning with the Christology in *Communion of Saints* and following the development through the prison years, one might conclude, as did John A. Phillips, that Bonhoeffer held more than one distinct Christology.[29] The "two Christologies" which Phillips describes, however, do not appear to take into consideration the ontological basis for Christology. A more faithful account of Bonhoeffer's Christological distinctions throughout his writings should consider the ontological framework that allowed for and contributed to his broadening Christological understanding. The "Who?" of Christ in April 1944 is merely an expanded view of "Christ existing as the Church" in *Communion of Saints*. The Christ "for the world" in his ethical writings was an ontological extension of his Christ for the church during the years of the church struggle. What we see here in Bonhoeffer's ontological description of Christology is the *radical freedom* of the person of Christ himself. This dynamic rather than static personal structure of Christ's freedom is a movement toward the world as an ontological movement of freedom that is limited only by the personal structure of Christ himself. The "Who?" of Christ, according to Bonhoeffer, continues to be with us with all of its pregnant meaning and far-reaching application.

With these theological, Christological, and ontological distinctions before us, we are now prepared to consider the concrete expression of freedom, that is, its existential character.

IV. Existence—Concrete Freedom

Within a theological framework Bonhoeffer has described for us his ontological Christology and his Christological ontology. We must now consider a final dimension of freedom, which focuses on the character of existence. That is, creaturely freedom necessarily expresses itself as a concrete form of existence. In this discussion of freedom's concreteness, Bonhoeffer completes his theological argument for freedom through three distinct features: Christological, ontological, and existential. That is to say, freedom is rooted in ontology, is interpreted by Christology, and is formed by existence. Or, in other words, authentic creaturely freedom is grounded in personal being, receives its reality through the personal structure of Christ in the world, and is shaped by the concrete situation. Each dimension particularizes an aspect of the life of freedom, and together they form the boundaries within which the concept is to be understood.

As we consider this third dimension, the concrete expression of freedom in human existence, we have only to keep in mind our earlier ontological and Christological definitions. We have already established the personal structure of Christ as the form which Christ takes within history. The *pro me* of Christ necessarily includes the existential reality. We recall that Christ is free *for* man and for all creation and that in this availability he binds himself to existence. This personal structure of Christ-for-me also includes the ontological implication. That is to say, the ontological question of the *pro me* structure is also the existential question.[30]

Confronted with the existential element of the *pro me* structure, we recognize the freedom of Christ for each new concrete situation. What this means is that Christ is not for me once and for all. He is Christ for me in each new situation. When he addresses me in his Word, the address and the response create the new situation: "The word lies wholly at the disposal of the person who speaks. So it is always new."[31] In similar fashion, "the commandment of God in Jesus Christ is always concrete speech to somebody. It is never abstract speech *about* something or *about* somebody."[32] In these assertions Bonhoeffer only wishes to make clear that while Christ is free in his being, his freedom is only *realized* in each new concrete situation.

As Bonhoeffer moves toward more precise ethical discourse, we observe the emphasis he chooses to place on responsible freedom. The personal structure of Christ in existence necessarily calls for responsibility:

> The structure of responsible life is conditioned by two factors; life is bound to man and to God, and a man's own life is free. It is the fact that life is bound to man and to God which sets life in the freedom of man's own life. Without this bond and without this freedom there is· no responsibility. Only when it becomes selfless in this obligation does a life stand in the freedom of a man's truly own life and action. The obligation assumes the form of deputyship and of correspondence with reality; freedom displays itself in the self-examination of life and of action and in the venture of concrete decision.[33]

In this statement Bonhoeffer is pointing to four aspects of existential freedom that we will observe as *deputyship*, *correspondence with reality*, *the free act*, and *commandment*.

Briefly, deputyship *(Stellvertretung)* is "the obligation to act in the place of other men."[34] The deputy is the one who stands there as an advocate for other men. This authentic deputyship is epitomized in the person of Jesus Christ.[35] Following the form of the one who is the supreme deputy, authentic freedom, then, is realized at the place where a human cares for his brother.

Correspondence with reality is a central theme that emphasizes the importance of "conformation" with the form of Jesus Christ in the world. Since Christ's form is historically conditioned, ethical freedom will be shaped by the reality of Christ in a given concrete context. It is Jesus Christ in his living presence who determines that given situation.[36] This is the concrete given situation out of which man responds freely in accordance with the form of Christ in the world. The process moves from concretion to concretion and from freedom to freedom with responsibility shaping the process.

This responsible structure of life places a human in a position where he is capable of what Bonhoeffer calls "the free act." With no apparent assistance from established ethical norms, each person must venture forth freely—weighing, examining, assessing, and ultimately acting—based on the only reality that is given in that situation. He acts freely "with a due consideration for the given human and general conditions . . . he himself must observe, judge, weigh up, decide and act."[37] As a result of this careful evaluative process, the deed is then rendered as a free act in response to the reality so defined.

At what point, then, does one measure the propriety or "good" of one's deed? Such a deed, for Bonhoeffer, points only to the "good" of God, not to any human knowledge of good and evil:

> The man who acts in the freedom of his own most personal responsibility is precisely the man who sees his action finally committed to the guidance of God. The free deed knows itself in the end as the deed of God; the decision knows itself as guidance. . . .[38]

A final word on the responsible life falls under the category of commandment. Contrary to the view which holds that commandment thwarts freedom and places heavy restrictions on people, Bonhoeffer invites us to observe the commandment that enlarges rather than restricts our freedom: "Commandment embraces the whole of life. . . . It does not only bind; it also sets free; and it does this by binding."[39] Commandment differs from all human laws in that it "commands freedom."[40] The new liberation that comes to man who lives under the commandment is that he now lives without being conscious of it (commandment), moving and acting freely, and is thus freed from the fear of decision and the fear to act.[41] Commandment frees a man for certainty, quietude, confidence, balance, and peace.[42]

Bonhoeffer expands his view of commandment to include what he calls "mandates." By mandates he is referring to God's commandment as manifested in Jesus Christ which comes to us in the church, in the family, in culture, and in government. The same liberty applies to these mandates as in all of God's commandments, that is, under these mandates man is now free to live freely and obediently before God.[43] In sum, commandment is the instrument God has used to reveal his will for man; and in that revelation man is both free *to* obey it and freed *in* obeying it.

With these references to the responsible life and the corresponding reality of concrete freedom we conclude our commentary on Bonhoeffer's existential understanding of freedom. His description of the phenomenon of freedom is now before us. His concept of freedom is framed in theology, rooted in ontology, interpreted and realized in Christology, and shaped by each existential situation. To disregard any one of these dimensions of freedom would miss the full scope which Bonhoeffer wishes to place within our view.

Now we need to ask how these thoughts on freedom can stand the close scrutiny of modern critical thinking. Such a question would involve a more careful critique of Bonhoeffer's Christological/ontological/existential structure of freedom than this essay will allow. Indeed, there are serious critics who would challenge the tight Christological circle within which he defines freedom, not to speak of those who would do battle with his ontological ethic, which leaves little or no space for measuring ethical action. The theoretical ethicist quickly becomes frustrated with an ontological ethic which is rooted solely in the personal being of Christ in the world. With similar perturbation, the situational ethicist who establishes love as the *summum bonum* of ethical action is not at ease with Bonhoeffer's all-encompassing reality of Christ, which at times appears to diminish the place of love, giving it a secondary status within the larger sphere of Christian reality. These and other criticisms form part of the fruitful debate which continues with Bonhoeffer's theology of freedom.

Beyond these criticisms, however, we need to ask in what way these thoughts on freedom share in the important legacy which Bonhoeffer has passed down to us. It would appear that he has given us some viable functional structures by which we can observe the phenomenon of freedom and then test these structures over against the reality of freedom as we understand it.[44]

Bonhoeffer's theological structure of freedom, with its corresponding Christological, ontological, and existential dimensions, is clearly before us. His theological framework forces us to deal with the origin and nature of freedom. If freedom does not originate with God, then what is its origin? Bonhoeffer's Christological formulation of freedom forces us to recognize the personal structure of Jesus Christ in the world. The freedom which obtains from "being in Christ" compels every serious Christian to consider at what point freedom has anything to do with Jesus Christ. If not "being in Christ," then in what manner does Jesus Christ effect—if he does—our understanding of freedom? When Bonhoeffer insists on the ontological roots of freedom, he cautions us to be aware of theoretical ethics, which functions with absolutes and abstract norms. An ontological ethic, while it is not based on an ethic of subjective disposition on the one hand, will not tolerate an objective ethic which ignores the dynamic of ethical freedom which evolves from "being-in-relation" on the other hand. Bonhoeffer's ontological and Christological understanding of freedom, which is informed by existence, also presents a challenge to the situational ethic, which is governed by horizontal relatives that have no transcendent frame of reference. One of Bonhoeffer's major contributions to contemporary ethical conversation, in this writer's opinion, is his argument for transcendence.

Another valuable feature of this structure of reality is the manner in which freedom provides *interrelatedness* within the total sphere of reality. The broad theological sweep of Bonhoeffer's concept of freedom includes and interprets the sociological, political, ethical, ecclesiastical, and cultural dimensions of reality. Conversely, it can be said that these historical categories of sociology, politics, ecclesiology, ethics, and culture inform and shape the concept of freedom. Across these disciplines one observes an interrelatedness and a participation which demonstrate the breadth, depth, and balance that freedom gives to reality as a whole. To illustrate this unity within the concept, we have only to recognize that for Bonhoeffer theological freedom, for example, implies ethical freedom. That is to say, ethical freedom is not a part of reality that exclusively has to do with the human sphere of people's relationships. On the contrary, ethical freedom is always a freedom before God as well as before mankind. And since all freedom is realized before God, before humans, and in relation to human institutions, it is thus wholly ethical at the same time that it is wholly theological. There is no sense in which Bonhoeffer limited authentic freedom to a special category of relationships within existence. At every point freedom includes, affirms, informs, and unifies people's relationships with their total environment. This element of interrelatedness within Bonhoeffer's structure of reality should serve as a caution to ethicists, sociologists, anthropologists, and ecclesiologists who choose to define freedom within special categories of relationships—for example, the human, the social, the ethical—and in the process exclude the broader dimensions of freedom's relationships.

In measuring the legacy of this structure of reality, we also ought to ask at what point it provides valuable dialogue, if any, with a non-Christian audience. The strong Christological argument within the structure would at first appear to discourage such dialogue. Indeed, it is virtually impossible to imagine that Bonhoeffer would have ever given credence to any form of authentic freedom outside Christ. That is to say, without his particular Christology, the structure he describes would fall apart. With that acknowledgment in mind, however, we could then consider his paradigm of existence, the Christological/ontological/existential characteristics, in its distinguishable parts. This would mean that if we suspend the Christological element, we are still left with the important ontological/existential descriptions of reality. While Bonhoeffer would undoubtedly object to this kind of surgery, it would seem that two valuable points of argument remain exposed to a non-Christian audience. First, freedom understood ontologically would raise the important question of being-in-relation, which could open up possibilities for a non-Christian approach to the subject. The relational mode of freedom could provide dialogue with any number of theological or extratheological methodologies. Secondly, the characteristic existential quality of freedom within Bonhoeffer's paradigm could also suggest the direction of freedom's concreteness. When freedom is conceived within each new concrete situation, shaping and being shaped by that new situation, a new level of information may well enter productively into conversation with serious observers outside of the Christian point of view. Without intending to do violence to Bonhoeffer's total view, we are merely suggesting that his paradigm of reality may continue to inform a broader audience at points other than his Christology.

Two more helpful insights emerge from this legacy, which we will touch on briefly. First, let us observe this structure of reality and its distinct *openness to the future*. Depending on the formation of Jesus Christ in the world, and reliant on the ever-changing concrete situations of life, freedom is ever open to the new shapes of reality that belong totally to the future. A freedom operating within such a structure of reality neither anticipates the form nor does it predict the locus. It is ever open to the form and to the place as a waiting for the concrete reality of Christ in the world. Such a freedom conceives new ethical contexts and demands new methodologies to interpret these contexts. It calls a great multiplicity of human forms of life to participate in the reality of Jesus Christ in the world.

Secondly, this structure of freedom preserves the mysterious balance between freedom's *revealedness and hiddenness*. This mysterious balance between secrecy and revelation can be recognized through a reality that both gives and does not give freedom. That is to say, within the Christ-reality man does not *have* freedom; man *participates* in freedom by being in relation. Thus, freedom is shared, not possessed. It is human but not limited to the human. It is divine but not limited to the divine. It is historical but not confined to history.

The life of freedom so conceived also maintains a mysterious quality by which it is acted out but not ultimately defined; concretized but not absolutized; structured but not systematized. It lays claim but cannot be claimed. Yet, though we cannot grasp or manipulate freedom, somehow it is the promise of Christ's coming and the guarantee that he is here. Freedom reveals life to us while it remains the hidden mysterious mode by which God comes to the world and by which the world recognizes God. Freedom is a significant part of the whole of reality, but is a part which must ever be free to be known and free to be unknown. Bonhoeffer's Christological/ontological/existential structure of reality, according to this interpreter, preserves this important balance between secrecy and revelation within the life of freedom. We have here a foundation for understanding freedom on which other structures may be built. Our task is to expand

and develop this structure of reality beyond what Bonhoeffer was only able to sketch for us.

Notes

1 *CFT*, p. 11.
2 *Ibid.*, p. 16, which reads: "God is free regarding the world. The fact that he lets us know this is mercy, grace, forgiveness and comfort. . . . He does not need us men to prepare his glory; he creates worship himself from the silent world which slumbers, resting mute and formless in his will."
3 *Ibid.*, p. 19.
4 *Ibid.*, p. 32.
5 *Ibid.*, pp. 33-34.
6 *Ibid.*, p. 35.
7 *Ibid.*
8 *Ibid.*
9 *Ibid.*, p. 34.
10 *AB*, pp. 170-71.
11 *CS*, p. 111.
12 *CC*, p. 59.
13 *Ibid.*, p. 37.
14 *AB*, p. 172.
15 *CC*, p. 84.
16 *Ibid.*, p. 114.
17 *CFT*, p. 16.
18 *E*, pp. 80-84.
19 *Ibid.*, p. 80.
20 *Ibid.*, p. 81.
21 *AB*, p. 108.
22 *Ibid.*, p. 155.
23 *CFT*, p. 74.
24 *Ibid.*, p. 92.
25 *Ibid.*, p. 95.
26 *CC*, p. 47.
27 *Ibid.*, p. 33.
28 *LPP*, p. 139.
29 John A. Phillips, *Christ for us in the Theology of Dietrich Bonhoeffer* (New York: Harper and Row, 1967), p. 74.
30 *CC*, p. 33.
31 *Ibid.*, p. 51.
32 *E*, p. 279.
33 *Ibid.*, p. 224.
34 *Ibid.*
35 *Ibid.*
36 *Ibid.*, p. 228.
37 *Ibid.*, p. 248.

38   *Ibid.*, p. 249.
39   *Ibid.*, p. 277.
40   *Ibid.*, p. 281.
41   *Ibid.*, p. 280.
42   *Ibid.*
43   *Ibid.*
44   The emergence of a new liberation theology in Latin American countries is a case in point. One of the Third World's most representative voices which has won the attention of the entire theological world is that of Gustavo Gutierrez. It is more than a coincidence that this revolutionary thinker from the Third World of the 1970s borrows from the thought of Bonhoeffer on the subject of freedom. Gutierrez views with Bonhoeffer the personal structure of freedom in Christ as the basis for much of his liberation theology. He quotes these words from Bonhoeffer: " 'In the language of the Bible,' writes Bonhoeffer, 'freedom is not something man has for himself but something he has for others. . . . It is not a possession, a presence, an object . . . but a relationship and nothing else. In truth, freedom is a relationship between two persons. Being free means "being free for the other," because the other has bound me to him. Only in relationship with the other am I free.' " Gustavo Gutierrez, *A Theology of Liberation*, trans. and ed., Sister Caridad Inda and John Eagleson (Maryknoll, New York: Orbis Books, 1973), p. 36.

THE ROLE OF THE "ENEMY" IN BONHOEFFER'S LIFE AND THOUGHT

William Jay Peck

THAT ADOLF HITLER encountered no direct, successful political resistance in spite of painstaking, risk-filled months and years of conspiracy—indeed, in spite of actual assassination attempts—cannot but interest the student of Bonhoeffer's life and thought. The discrepancy between effort and outcome touches the depth of Bonhoeffer's concept of and behavior toward what he termed the "enemy."[1] Granted, his work in the resistance movement converged with that group's heroic expression of moral outrage.[2] He shared their nobility of motives and their inefficacy of results. But in the *disciplina arcana*, which he shared only with some, he came to the resistance from a starting point in Christology. From this starting point he gained a rich perspective on the "enemy."

The purpose of this essay is to supplement existing discussions of resistance[3] and martyrdom[4] by construing Bonhoeffer's death as an interaction with the enemy, a concept that he uses as a set, minimally including the Devil, Satan, and Antichrist in the iconic-mythic realm, and Hitler as well as the "German Christians" in the sphere of political interaction. From a position of wide separation between theology and politics as defined by the traditional Lutheran theory of the two realms, Bonhoeffer moved steadily toward an ever closer relation until at his death politics and theology had become virtually indistinguishable.

Even in recent years the theme of the enemy has been recrudescent in the Manfred Roeder incident, which in a bizarre way catches in a single net of falsehoods most of what was true about Bonhoeffer's death. On July 27, 1976, at the local courthouse in Heilsbronn, Roeder lost his case and was fined 5,000 DM for defamation of the dead. He had accused Bonhoeffer of being "in our eyes no innocent Christian who had to suffer for his convictions but a dishonorable traitor to his country who misused his ecclesiastical office . . . to work for the downfall of the German Volk."[5] Each of these charges—unchristian activity, treason, and misuse of office—is devious or false.

Indeed, the Heilsbronn court, on the basis of the original records of the night-time trial of April 8-9, 1945, ruled that Bonhoeffer had not been a traitor to his country, because he was hanged under a category of crime no longer possessing legal status—"traitor to the War."[6] Through the profound irony of deputyship, Bonhoeffer took on himself the other false charges and in a sense made them true: although innocent, he accepted the national guilt;[7] and though he by no means abused his ecclesiastical office, he did use it as a mask behind which to seek cessation of the war[8] and justice for the oppressed.[9]

And he was too obedient to the triple imperative of patriotism, human decency, and his understanding of the divine command to evade the task of working for Hitler's downfall. Nevertheless, Roeder's views reawaken the realization that a "stab in the back" theory might be dangerously alive today had the plot against Hitler succeeded. Instead, it was Hitler who, in still another of his long series of stunning successes, outlived the chief conspirators. Thereby he unwittingly put to the test one of Bonhoeffer's injunctions from the Sermon on the Mount: "The only way to overcome evil is to let it run itself to a standstill. . . . Then evil cannot find its mark, it can breed no further evil, and is left barren."[10] But Bonhoeffer immediately qualifies this command not to resist the enemy: "Patient endurance of evil does not mean a recognition of its rights";[11] and "to make non-resistance a principle for secular life is to deny God, by undermining his gracious ordinance for the preservation of the world."[12] In short, resist mightily but do not depend on success in resistance.

The double-sided command to resist and not to resist echoes exactly the discrepancy, already noted, between efforts and results in the resistance against Hitler. On the one hand, Bonhoeffer's intention to succeed in the resistance against Hitler was unambiguous. Indeed, he even spoke of success as a criterion for responsible action. The question was not whether Hans Bernd von Haeften, a conspirator with access to Hitler, "may" shoot him but whether he "should." The difference between these two options is that "may" is a matter of conscience while "should" includes consideration of consequences.[13] Bonhoeffer became convinced that this particular tyrant "may" in conscience be assassinated, all other means being exhausted;[14] but he also demanded that the conspiracy, to be approved as responsible, must demonstrate a reasonable chance of succeeding. Ironically, consensus on this very criterion of success plunged the conspirators into years of planning and risky negotiations in the construction of a full-scale shadow government.

On the other hand, an array of evidence assembled here will show that the command not to resist evil did not belong simply to the ecclesiastical phase in the 1930s, to be outgrown in the 1940s, but was fundamental to Bonhoeffer's whole involvement in the theme of the enemy.[15] He explored that involvement always in the context of a search for the concrete command. Not general principles but the rhythm of resistance and submission throbs beneath the surface in all his dealings with the enemy.[16] It is a rhythm ever surprising, ever veiled in the ways of providence. And Bonhoeffer might well have defined providence as fate, or the enemy's success, processed by trust in God.

I. A Paradoxical Theme

The interplay between resistance and submission in Bonhoeffer does not set up an abstract dialectic but, on the contrary, takes form concretely throughout the whole extent of the enemy theme. This theme, therefore, escapes the reproach rightly meted out to minor themes, that to work seriously with the Bonhoeffer materials now means to work diachronically with the entire corpus. The concrete exploration of the theme leads to the discovery of a paradox. The paradox lies in a tantalizing contrast between the relative unimportance of the theme—virtually none of the major commentators deems it worthy of a place in an index—and its pervasive presence both in the biographical and primary sources.

The theme of the enemy lingers in the shadow of all the central theological issues, which by general consensus[17]—though not a consensus as to details—govern the interpretation of Bonhoeffer's thought: Christology and person, ecclesiology and community, reality and concreteness, *actus directus* and worldly faith.[18] The other side of the paradox, the relative unimportance of the enemy, harbors an intriguing irony. This unimportance is calculated; it has to be fought for and vigilantly guarded.

Bonhoeffer kept the enemy unimportant in three ways: first, by the sheer force of his temperament; second, by a network of visual metaphors; and third, by the theological and political strategy implied in the exceedingly subtle command of Jesus not to resist evil. The evidence about politics and theology needs chronological treatment, while temperament and imagery belong to the relatively stable realm of feeling and language.

II. Temperament and Imagery

Bonhoeffer's temperament was aristocratic, disciplined, at once authoritarian and deeply reticent. But he also had an impressive physical vitality and a delight in the polyphony of life. His musical talent, his athletic ability, but, more than anything else, his warmth and sensitivity round out the picture of his temperament as sketched by most observers.[19] In spite of some periods of *accidie* earlier in his life, and a few days of understandable depression upon imprisonment,[20] Bonhoeffer was temperamentally incapable of groveling before his enemies.

Even an encounter as dramatic as the Gestapo's threats of torture he dismissed during a prison conversation with Fabian von Schlabrendorff with a single word: "repulsive."[21] This reaction expresses both his aristocratic nature and his sense of reticence and shame, his feeling that fear should be counted among the *pudenda* and kept out of sight.[22] Therefore, his interpreters have, in a sense, followed a correct instinct in avoiding the theme of the enemy.

The imagery by which Bonhoeffer expresses this achieved unimportance of the enemy is strongly perceptual. Bonhoeffer's language implies that for him the enemy hovers continuously within the range of peripheral vision, yet rarely if ever comes naked into central focus. In the presence of the enemy "we do not know what we should do, yet our eyes are turned toward thee."[23] Here, like Perseus, one does not look directly at the enemy. Conversely, Adam and Eve "saw that the tree was . . . a delight to the eyes," and looked forward to the knowledge of good and evil. But when their eyes were opened, they had lost the simplicity of the *fides directa* and were in the power of the enemy. References to this passage appear repeatedly throughout Bonhoeffer's works.[24]

A vivid instance of perceptual imagery occurs in the *Cost of Discipleship*. Peter can walk among the dangerous waves without sinking just so long as he keeps his eyes fixed on the figure of Jesus.[25] There are also frequent visual terms in *Ethics*, such as these: "It is precisely because he looks only to God, without any sidelong glance at the world, that he is able to look at the reality of the world freely and without prejudice."[26] Again, "to be simple is to fix one's eyes solely on the simple truth of God."[27] These examples show how at the level of imagery one can "slight" the enemy, not even give him a sidelong glance, and thus carry out part of the command: "Resist not him that is evil." In these examples, not to resist means not to engage. Thus a sovereign freedom, implicit in the metaphor of sight averted, keeps the enemy unimportant.

III. The "Phraseological" Period: 1924-1932

These perceptual metaphors form a component in a many-faceted and, over time, increasingly complex yet unified theological vision, in which "whoever sees Jesus Christ does indeed see God and the world in one."[28] But this consummate perspective took time to develop, and in the period 1924-1932 the relationship to the enemy is aptly described as "phraseological."[29] In *Sanctorum Communio*, Bonhoeffer spells out the structures of the person, the community, and God.[30] By implication, the function of the enemy is the converse—yet not simply the converse—of each. The enemy is that which diminishes or destroys personhood, undermines true community, and seeks to defeat the command of God. The enemy is whatever or whoever improperly substitutes *it* for *thou*.

Just such a substitution takes place in the fall of Adam. In that narrative the knowledge of good and evil replaces simple trust in God.[31] The *it* of overweening knowledge replaces the *thou* of concrete ethical encounter. But the enemy is more than the mere converse of the person, the community, and God, because the encounter with the enemy contributes to the dynamic unfolding of these concepts. Because "the person-forming activity of the Thou is independent of its personal being,"[32] the enemy can become the occasion for decision and responsibility.[33] In this way the enemy becomes a barrier and can serve as a preliminary form of the encounter with the divine *thou* as transcendent barrier.[34]

One encounters in the enemy as barrier a demand for creative response. Later on Bonhoeffer would reformulate this demand: it would become his call for costly grace. By never rewarding unwariness the enemy is person-forming. Therefore, "the person, as a conscious person, is created in the moment when a man is moved, when he is faced with responsibility, when he is passionately involved in a moral struggle, and confronted with a claim which overwhelms him."[35] Thus the enemy defines the contours of the concrete situation. Later, in the letter of February 23, 1944, Bonhoeffer refers back to this discussion by writing of the *it* of fate. The task is to transform that *it* into a *thou*; only a transition to perceiving the enemy as *thou* renders the relationship humanizing and creative.[36]

But in *Sanctorum Communio* he only lays the groundwork. Clearly he already saw that the person-destroying potential of the enemy is the criterion which defines the *it* of fate as enemy. This person-destroying aspect constitutes God's call to resistance; the conception of the barrier, the link between *it* and *thou*, sketches out the logic of the command not to resist evil. For the transition from the *it* of fate to the *thou* which lies hidden in that *it* is mediated by the barrier. The encounter with the other as barrier breaks the circle of the self-enclosed ego and provides access to the other as *thou*. Submission to God as *thou*, not to the enemy as *it*, will later become Bonhoeffer's way of keeping the enemy unimportant. The transition to the enemy's unimportance presupposes that the *it* of fate, even though obdurate in itself, is open to the *thou*, indeed, secretly constituted by the *thou*. Later Bonhoeffer restates this openness of the *it* of fate in the language of the orders of preservation, which hold the created world open to the future, toward the *thou* who is Christ the center of life.[37]

But during the period 1924-1932 the orders were still the traditional Lutheran orders of creation. The state's authority derives its finality from being rooted in the creation. Although even for Luther himself the "two kingdoms theory" allowed for mutual criticism between church and state, traditional German Lutheranism had increasingly separated the two.[38] Therefore, it is no surprise to learn that the young Bonhoeffer turned a blind theological eye toward the concrete political enemy. So separate were the two realms that he could indulge in a mild and untutored nationalism, pleading the German case for bitterness over Versailles,[39] flirting briefly with the youth movement,[40] and, during his year in America, virtually ignoring the ominous progress of the National Socialists.[41] The idea of submission had not yet acquired its nuances but still meant simply obedience to the powers that be. The enemy during the "phraseological" period was unimportant to Bonhoeffer—but only because of naivete and neglect.

In retrospect the scholar can see parallels and parodies already forming, unbeknownst to either, between Bonhoeffer and Hitler. During the Weimar period both men staked their future on the problem of community. Bonhoeffer chose the church; Hitler chose the sphere of nationalistic politics. In *Sanctorum Communio* Bonhoeffer states the issue bluntly, yet without so much as a hint that he might be referring to Hitler: "The confusion of community romanticism with the communion of saints is extremely dangerous."[42] He selected his dissertation topic not only in the glow of an enthralling trip to Rome,[43] but also in concern for a transition from the *it* world of individualistic liberalism to the *thou* of concrete community. Meanwhile, as Bonhoeffer would soon understand, Hitler's community romanticism already foredoomed the Third Reich to become a bitter parody of the Last Reich.

IV. Politics Through Ecclesiology: 1932-1939

On February 1, 1933, two days after Hitler came to power, Bonhoeffer's potential relationship to the political enemy became actual and public. He attacked directly and not under ecclesiastical cover. His radio talk warned against exchanging the personalistic and nonrational authority of the Fuehrer for the neutral, practical, and rational authority of traditional leadership.[44] In this tactic Bonhoeffer applied to politics the distinction of the coming Christology lectures,[45] between the *who* of personhood and the *how* of theological explanation. He was accusing the Fuehrer of usurping the *who* status while his office conferred only the dignity due the impersonal and technical craft of the statesman.[46]

The danger in this usurpation lurked in the tendency of the personalistic to depersonalize, to take away the citizens' power of choice and concentrate it in one "personality." Bonhoeffer fought depersonalization in 1933 through rational, legal, and moral theories of legitimacy. In 1940 he would write that these very criteria—duty, rationality, conscience, and moral fanaticism—were exhausting and misleading the forces of resistance, which, like a bull, were "rushing at the red cloth instead of the man who holds it."[47]

During the brief flurry of direct political resistance in 1933, limited almost entirely to the radio talk, it was Bonhoeffer who waved the red cloth of traditional values. In 1940 he had assigned Hitler the role of the toreador in this image drawn from Barcelona days. The difference between the two uses of the image, both reflecting Bonhoeffer's intention of direct resistance, is that the first aims to keep the enemy unimportant by traditional means while the second admits the failure of that policy and advocates instead the dread deed of free responsibility.[48]

But in the summer and fall of 1932, about a year before Hitler seized the chancellorship, Bonhoeffer was coming to grips with another form of the enemy. The first impact of the Sermon on the Mount and the injunction not to resist evil applied to France as the enemy, to war as the evil. Not Hitler but the problem of war first evoked Bonhoeffer's discovery of II Chronicles 20:12: "We do not know what to do, but our eyes are on thee."[49] This means that access to the enemy is indirect, mediated "through prayer to the Lord of all people."[50] As long as the world is alienated from God, there will be war.[51] But the church is to follow Christ in simple, unflinching obedience, not knowing good and evil. This obedience means that the command to "love your enemy" is to be stated in concrete terms. Contradictions will arise, mistakes will happen, but these can be absolved by the divine forgiveness. In the examples Bonhoeffer offered at a number of conferences, one can find advocacy both of resistance—"Go to this war, or do not go to this war"[52]—and of submission: "pure love . . . would rather see a defenseless brother killed, than have his or our soul stained with blood."[53]

But in these examples one submits to God's command, not to the enemy. The same is true in the relationship to Hitler and to the question of the enemy's successes. Because access to the enemy is indirect, and because "God is in the facts themselves,"[54] the success of the enemy, surprisingly, becomes a component of the *actus directus*. The success of enemies, familiar in the Old Testament as the rod of God's anger,[55] becomes an intimate source of faith's concreteness.[56] Here Bonhoeffer follows Nietzsche into the abyss beyond good and evil only to show that Nietzsche had, in his own strange way, understood Adam's condition before the fall, a condition of simple faith apart from the knowledge of good and evil.[57] Thus the role of the enemy is that his fate-like success serves as a person-forming barrier, an *it* which hides the transcendent *thou*.

In the face of the enemy's success, the task of the Christian is not to convert the enemy but to be converted. For example, Bonhoeffer wrote in 1934 that "Hitler ought not and may not hear; he is obdurate. We, not Hitler, should be converted."[58] Conversion means repentance. Therefore, when news came to London of Hitler's success in the Roehm Putsch of June 30, 1934, Bonhoeffer preached a sermon on the following Sunday calling for repentance, for refraining from moral judgments, for sorrow over lack of sufficient faith and love.[59] Only thus does one overcome the "world."[60]

Again in 1940, when news arrived of Hitler's stunning victory over France, Bonhoeffer told a group of pastors that this event called for an altered understanding of God's will.[61] He thereupon composed a confession of corporate guilt for the West's defection from Christ. A sample from this liturgy of vicarious appropriation of guilt follows: "The Church confesses that she has taken in vain the name of Jesus Christ, for she has been ashamed of this name before the world and she has not striven forcefully enough against the misuse of this name for an evil purpose. She has stood by while violence and wrong were being committed under cover of this name."[62] This is a moving and profound way of making the encounter with the enemy fruitful for the growth of faith and in that way keeping him unimportant in himself.

Meanwhile, throughout the ecclesiological period the Barmen Declaration, originally the Confessing Church's response to Hitler's successful manipulation of the National Church, served Bonhoeffer as an example of a victory for his own side. Success on either side thus serves as the starting point for the Christian's action and reflection. Success structures the givenness of reality; all thought and obedient action must therefore begin with that givenness. That is how one gains access to the concrete command.

Bonhoeffer's ecclesiastical tactics during the 1930s moved between ecumenical action and theological reflection. These two tasks, the realms of politics and theology, are still clearly distinguished during that period yet much closer together than they were during the "phraseological" stage. Bonhoeffer exactly stated the distinction between the political enemy and the iconic-mythic figure of Antichrist in the remark which Eberhard Bethge remembers as follows: "No, he is not the Antichrist; Hitler is not big enough for that; the Antichrist uses him, but he is not as stupid as that man!"[63] Here again Bonhoeffer holds the enemy in a position of unimportance. Bonhoeffer showed the same sense of balance and aplomb in his unremitting struggle with Bishop Heckel, whose language of reasonable doubt again and again successfully foiled the efforts to organize a declaration by the Ecumene on behalf of the Confessing Church as the only true church of Christ in Germany.[64]

The ambiguity between theology and politics, the element of incognito, in this struggle also comes to the fore in Bonhoeffer's fierce standoff with Baumgärtel over the interpretation of Nehemiah-Ezra. Baumgärtel, a neutral in the church struggle and professor of Old Testament at Greifswald, launched a double attack on Bonhoeffer's homily about "The Rebuilding of Jerusalem." First, it was unscientific and arbitrary, because one can adduce evidence for state aid to the "church," offered or granted by the Persian kings, while Bonhoeffer, on the basis of only a few passages, pictured a church independent of state aid and steadfast in resistance toward the enmity of the local populace. Second, Bonhoeffer's treatment of the church of Ezra as continuous with the church of today overlooks the role of the Jewish community in the death of Jesus. "The church is one, then and now?" asked Baumgärtel with undisguised sarcasm.[65]

On the first point, a complex methodological discussion, though technically legitimate, can blind one to the acute difficulties of Bonhoeffer's situation: Baumgärtel wins by an epistemological ploy that ignores the concrete *Sitz im Leben* of Bonhoeffer's text. Of course, their different purposes define their *Sitze im Leben* differently. Bonhoeffer was applying his Christological method of reading the Old Testament and doing so at a "moment" in German history when the church was in the *status confessionis*. He used the story of Ezra as a modern parable, almost a cryptogram. Had he spelled out the hinted similarity between the aid from Cyrus to Ezra and the state aid toward the church before 1933, he could have drawn the charge already adumbrated by Heckel of treasonous thought.[66] Most probably that is why he did not openly identify the "adversaries" who offer help and fatal compromise. He allowed his readers to draw the parallel to the Kerrl committees.[67]

Baumgärtel, whether naively or not, claimed strict neutrality toward church politics in the course of his attack. One may doubt the neutrality; one may also doubt that critics of Bonhoeffer have fully considered his concrete situation at the time. The truth is that if he had written the homily during normal times, it would correctly be judged eisegetical and one-sided.[68] But to apply that criticism in his own extraordinary situation is to deny him his idea of the concrete command and take him to task for doing what he declared he was doing.

The second part of Baumgärtel's charge is far more serious, for he was in fact disparaging Bonhoeffer's attempt to speak out on behalf of the Jewish people. The King David homily and the Nehemiah-Ezra study, both written in 1936, carry the clear message of a direct continuity between the Christian community and the Old Testament community of faith. The atmosphere of the times accounts for Bonhoeffer's caution. His critic, however, could freely speak, because his point supported the traditional Lutheran view of the death of Jesus, a view approved by the regnant ideology. The reply Bonhoeffer might have given concerning the death of Jesus is to be read off from his texts on the role of the enemy. Bonhoeffer did not hold any subgroup in the church or in world history responsible for Golgotha. Jesus was not simply a man, according to Bonhoeffer, but man—representative man. He was betrayed and killed by man, as much by the church of today as by the church of Ezra. This is Bonhoeffer's stand in opposition to the neutral theologians in a debate that leads from politics to the iconic-mythic issues of theology.

In Bonhoeffer's theology, Christ's death and resurrection manifest—not without a due concealment—an ultimate victory over Satan; therefore, in the encounter with the enemy the church becomes "realized."[69] The terror of that victory permeates Bonhoeffer's handling of the imprecatory Psalms. How, he asks, could the Christian condescend to offer up such horrifying incantations? He answers that Christians are not good enough, rather than too good, to pray these curses against God's enemies.[70] Only Christ can pray such prayers; only Christ can manifest God's ineluctable righteousness in dealing with enemies. But finally Christ *becomes* the enemy and accepts the full wrath of the divine righteousness, thereby overcoming the enemy through identification rather than through alienation.[71] Here in the depths of the iconic-mythic center of reality the transition from *it* to *thou* is fought through and, indeed, constituted.

God transcends Satan in Christ's full identification with the enemy at the climax of the drama of salvation. The blood of these enemies is his own blood; behind the *it*-world of slaughter looms the gracious person-forming *thou*. But this theology of grace had, in Bonhoeffer's view, become cheap. Early and late he used the role of the enemy to provide a barrier to cheap grace. In the *Communion of Saints* he declared that "the ultimate antagonists in history will forever be the *sanctorum communio* and the *Antichrist*."[72] Therefore, no human activity within history can escape contending with the hard transcendence posed by the enemy. The harshness of the *it* of fate acts as a catalyst for confession and the renewed discovery of God as *thou*.

A summary of events from 1933 to 1939 would reveal a threefold development. First, Hitler came to power, thus achieving a *success* that defined and constituted the concrete situation. Second, the Confessing Church came into existence through the success of Barmen. This ecclesiastical event decisively shaped the ensuing five years for Bonhoeffer; Barmen created the space and form for the appropriate *resistance*. The hints of direct political resistance—the radio speech of February 1, 1933, and the advocacy of grabbing the wheel of the car driven by a madman[73]—preceded Barmen and represent preliminary explorations into the question of resistance rather than a concerted response. The central response was confession, by founding the Confessing Church. Thus, thirdly, Barmen combines resistance to the tyrant with *submission* to God; the resistance is not direct.[74] By retaining it within the ecclesiastical structure, Bonhoeffer and the entire Confessing Church witness to a power greater than Hitler. By doing so they obey the command "do not resist your enemies." Consequently, the enemy remains paradoxically both all-pervasive and unimportant. The church looks only to Jesus, confesses only within the fellowship, "not to the enemy,"[75] preserves the pearls within the *arcanum*,[76] refuses to talk to the Devil about its sins.[77] Here one has a sequence: success, resistance, and submission. Thus in the second period Bonhoeffer moves far beyond the speculations of the first period about an abstract and still-absent enemy, through a brief phase in 1932, when France and war loomed as the enemies, to a concrete ecclesiological engagement accompanied by several sallies into theological reflection.[78]

V. Incarnational Participation: 1939-1945

What is the significance of the enemy as parody? In 1940, Bonhoeffer had come to believe that the personalistic parody of the truly personal now required nothing less in reply than the act of free responsibility by the man who "tries to make his whole life an answer to the question and call of God."[79] In the essay "Ethics as Formation," Bonhoeffer unmasks "the tyrannical despiser of men. . . . Fear he calls responsibility. Desire he calls keenness. Irresolution becomes solidarity. Brutality becomes masterfulness. . . . His secret profound mistrust for all human beings he conceals behind words stolen from a true community."[80] This description of Hitler as a parody of his own claims fits into the wider discussion of the two kingdoms in *Ethics*.

The state turns enemy by mistaking itself for something it is not. Germany was claiming to be the Third Reich, a parallel to the kingdom of God, the Last Reich. Both Reichs evoke apocalyptic ardor; both place themselves beyond the limitations of the penultimate, beyond ordinary legal and traditional restraints; both seek true and lasting community; both perceive that their communitarian goals are endangered by enemies. The Third Reich pitted itself in mortal combat against communists and Jews; the Last Reich pits itself against the ultimate embodiment of evil, Satan. Thus the Third Reich becomes a parody of the Last Reich. In its search for community it makes a shambles of community; in its hatred of the devil it becomes diabolical; in its desire to provide a millennium of peace, law, and order it ends after twelve years in the violent flames of its own war.

Bonhoeffer sought to contravene this parody through the steadily increasing prominence he gave in his ethics to the penultimate. The penultimate exists only by the patience of God.[81] Bonhoeffer's bestowal of blessing on the autonomy of the world and his rediscovery of the natural sprang from the secure grounding of the penultimate in the patience of God. Lack of patience created the Third Reich's tragedy: in its lust for accomplishment it overlooked its penultimate status and believed itself ultimate. Lack of patience with the concrete, unique world of persons and things, of trust, responsibility, and social justice, in short, lack of patience with the stranger—particularly the Jewish stranger—rendered the Third Reich a parody. But Bonhoeffer precisely advocates patience when he puts forth as a concrete command of God the saying "resist not evil."

By this he means: Struggle against the enemy, but avoid idolizing him. Keep him unimportant. Failure to struggle is submission to the enemy and not to God; nonresistance toward the enemy, on the contrary, can bring participation in the suffering of God along the way to the cross.[82] Along this path Bonhoeffer descended from worldly defeat to worldly defeat. He lost his post at the university; his seminary was closed down; he was forbidden to speak in public, then to write for publication. He went underground and became a conspirator. He was imprisoned. Finally he lost his life.

Meanwhile Hitler piled success on success. Three important successes during the 1940s dragged Bonhoeffer ever deeper into their fateful entanglements. The dates are well known: June 17, 1940, the fall of France; July 20, 1944, the assassination attempt; and April 9, 1945, Bonhoeffer's death at the hands of his enemies. These dates form a sequence. Bonhoeffer's reaction to the fall of France has already been described: in the enemy's success God presents the community of believers with a new situation, which included new and enlarged risks for Bonhoeffer. Next, July 20, 1944, meant submission in the already cramped cell at Tegel, but submission to the ways of God, not to the enemy's astounding tenacity.

The dark and tangled forest of historical change swallowed Bonhoeffer, but not before he left the outlines for interpreting his death.[83] In part his last letters break ground toward construing the whole recent history of the West as a success,[84] wrought by providence precisely through complete independence from providence, through science's very autonomy. In such a world men and women live before God without God. God is enemy to the world and to mankind until in weakness and forsakenness he calls forth the autonomy of the world and the strength and dignity of humans. Humans can share in this suffering. One of them was Bonhoeffer. His death took place under urgent orders issued by Hitler, and was therefore not an accident but another victory for Hitler.[85] Others were saved from this fate by the Allied troops who accidentally arrived in time. But for Bonhoeffer every accident is also a providential event, not because a manipulative God sits at the controls but because in the beginning there is success. And the success is fate until the response of a person transforms fate into providence.

The assessment of Bonhoeffer's death needs to follow the lines of his own theory of the enemy, a theory built around success, resistance, and submission. The lines of thought and action formed by a study of the enemy theme converge at the point of this death. The death was a supreme political witness to the necessity for direct action against tyranny. That witness does not conflict with a Christian witness but exactly clarifies what Bonhoeffer meant about seeing the reality of the world in God and the reality of God in the world.

Here the two kingdoms, separated during Bonhoeffer's "phraseological" period, and adjusted quite precisely at a certain distance in the period of political ecclesiology, briefly coincide in a final closeness of theology and politics at Flossenbürg. To Manfred Roeder it may be said that Bonhoeffer was a patriot and a true Christian martyr, but a twentieth-century martyr who knew he could not be a Christian without acting on his solidarity with the victims of National Socialism. Bethge correctly points to the deed in place of the word: only qualified silence fits—at this time in history—the scale of suffering inflicted by Western Christendom on the Jewish people. Current political conflicts, current demands for compassion toward another circle of victims, need not and ought not obscure the unfinished task which the genuine convergence of theology and politics in Bonhoeffer's death assigns to the Christian community.

In summary, to this convergence belongs also the evidence about Bonhoeffer's whole relation to the enemy: his temperament, which quite instinctively holds the enemy in a state of unimportance; the perceptual imagery which refuses the enemy so much as a sidelong glance; the naive ignorance of politics during the "phraseological" period; the direct resistance of the second period—masked, yet conveyed through ecclesiastical struggle; the enemy's parody of the kingdom of God, transparently false in its lack of patience and of grounding in the penultimate world; the concrete diminution of his prison inquisitors in the essay on truth-telling; the fact that telling the truth means not to discuss one's sins with the devil. This evidence on the paradoxical importance and unimportance leads directly to the conclusion that nonresistance remained a lifelong issue and thus contributes to the interpretation of his death.

In one sense the act done in free responsibility is an act of resistance without parallel, for that act sets aside all obstacles that would yield the last word to the enemy. There must be a concerted resistance aimed at success. Such is the concrete command of God. But an equally valid command of God is this: do not resist; do not make the enemy important; let the evil exhaust itself as it will do if it meets no exacerbating resistance.

This discrepancy or conflict finds its resolution in the turn toward the *actus directus*, the recovery of simplicity and wisdom. Concrete simplicity replaces the abstract knowledge of good and evil, of principles ruthlessly applied and of ethnic stereotypes carried to the point of slaughter and holocaust. Granted that the resulting priority of expressive over instrumental considerations in the resistance movement extended Hitler's time of personal survival, still his successes ultimately crushed him.

Bonhoeffer's life task—and his Christology supports the conclusion—was to encounter the enemy in the *it* of fate-as-success and transform that *it* into a *thou*. He wished to discover the person-forming barrier in the *thou* by first accepting the barrier which the *it* of fate had erected in the form of the enemy's success. Simultaneously he obeyed both of these commands by leaving the results to providence. His own death expresses equally the most clear-eyed resistance and yet the most profound submission. On his own principles, his death should stand as a given and as a starting point for thought, not as an object of speculation. The thought it prompts is the memory of his own call for repentance, for utter honesty, for letting go, indeed for that joy at the final victory of human dignity harbored in the phrase "resist not your enemies."

Notes

1   The quotation marks designate a technical term coextensive with the evidence in the text as a whole. They belong to each separate use of the term but are omitted hereafter for reasons of style.

2   Larry L. Rasmussen, *Dietrich Bonhoeffer: Reality and Resistance* (Nashville: Abingdon Press, 1972), pp. 188, 197. C. Abercrombie, "Barth and Bonhoeffer: Resistance to the Unjust State," *Religion in Life*, XLII (Autumn 1973), 344-360.

3   Rasmussen *passim*, but esp. pp. 32-73, 174-211.

4   Eberhard Bethge, *Bonhoeffer: Exile and Martyr* (New York: Seabury Press, 1975), pp. 155-166.

5   Eberhard Bethge, "Bericht von Roederprozess, Heilbronn, 27 Juli, 1976," *Bonhoeffer Rundbrief* (Mitteilungen des Internationalen Bonhoeffer-Komitees Sektion Bundesrepublik Deutschland), Düsseldorf, Nummer 3, 11. Februar 1977, pp. 5-8. The quotation is from the *Heilbronner Stimme*, 23 June 1975. Manfred Roeder, age 47, is not to be confused with Manfred Roeder, chief investigator of Bonhoeffer at Tegel.

6   *Ibid.*, p. 7.

7   Bonhoeffer, *E*, pp. 110-119, esp. p. 112; see also *GS*, I, 405.

8   *DBET*, pp. 661ff.

9   *Ibid.*, p. 651. Operation 7, arranging the escape of a handful of Jews to Switzerland, illustrates the priority of expressive over instrumental aims in the resistance.

10   Bonhoeffer, *CD* (New York: Macmillan Paperbacks, 1963), pp. 157-158.

11   *Ibid.*, p. 158.

12   *Ibid.*, p. 161.

13   Rasmussen, pp. 140f.

14   *DBET*, p. 699.

15   Contra Rasmussen, pp. 28, 35. Tiemo Peters is right in correcting the view that Bonhoeffer was narrowly ecclesiological in the 1930s, rather than political throughout: *Die Praesenz des Politischen in der Theologie Dietrich Bonhoeffers* (Munich: Chr. Kaiser Verlag, 1976), pp. 44, 57. Bonhoeffer's statement in *Ethics*, p. 59, that the "cross of Christ makes both sayings true: 'He that is not with me is against me' and 'He that is not against us is for us,' applies throughout his career. The *disciplina*

arcana carries the ecclesiological commitment right to the end. Matthew 12:40 and Mark 9:40 are related as 'resistance' and submission."

16 *LPPE* (Macmillan Paperbacks Edition, 1972), letter of February 21, 1944, p. 217. The stanzas entitled "action" and "suffering" in the poem "Stations on the Road to Freedom" of July 21, 1944, following the assassination attempt, express the same dialectic or interplay.

17 See David Hopper, *A Dissent on Bonhoeffer* (Philadelphia: Westminster Press, 1975), p. 71, contra.

18 The bibliographical leads to the issue of unity in Bonhoeffer's thought, including a variety of titles which have been offered to express that unity, are listed in Feil, *ThDB*, p. 128, n. 6.

19 This picture derives mainly from *DBET*; supplemented by W.D. Zimmerman, ed., *Begegnungen mit Dietrich Bonhoeffer* (Dritte Auflage, Munich: Chr. Kaiser Verlag, 1965); and Mary Bosanquet, *The Life and Death of Dietrich Bonhoeffer* (New York: Harper and Row, 1968).

20 *DBET*, pp. 420, 734-736.

21 The version of Bethge, *DB*, p. 1008, "kurz and bundig widerlich," appears to be a misreading of "kurz und bündig: 'widerlich!'" (*Begegnungen*, p. 188). If so, then "kurz and bündig" are Schlabrendorff's words and the English of *DBET* (p. 803), "frankly repulsive," is incorrect. Doubtless, Bonhoeffer spoke more than a single word about the torture threats. Bethge surmises, "It is possible that Bonhoeffer's own personality may have had an effect on his examiners," to account for an improvement in the atmosphere. This serves as an example of the (possible) effect of temperament in a specific case of dealing with the enemy.

22 *LPPE*, Letter of Nov. 27, 1943, p. 146.

23 II Chronicles 20:12 (RSV); *GS*, I, 31, 138, 148; *GS*, II, 133.

24 Genesis 3:5-7 (RSV). See esp. *E*, p. 20: "Instead of seeing God man sees himself"; also p. 233: "A man's attitude to the world does not correspond to reality if he sees in the world a good or an evil which is good or evil in itself. . . ." Here the visual imagery combines with the fall of Adam from *fides directa*; *AB* (New York: Harper & Row, 1961), p. 158: "Man in Adam . . . continues to 'seek himself in himself'"; p. 181 (under *fides directa*): "He sees only Christ"; also pp. 161, 170, 176, 177, 178, 179, 180, 182. Finally, *CS* (New York: Harper and Row, 1963), p. 196: "'We live by faith and not by sight'" applies to Adamic "knowledge" and to peripheral vision in relation to the enemy. The terms "revelation," "theory," and "self-regard" also belong to this complex of visual imagery. Other aspects appear in *GS*, I, 163, 334; *GS*, V, 163; and *CFT* (London: SCM Press, 1959), pp. 79f.

25 *CD*, p. 72: "If we fix our eyes not on the work . . . Peter. . . ." See also *CD*, p. 105: "eyes fixed on him alone"; p. 304: "looking only to their Lord"; and p. 175.

26 *E*, p. 68.

27 *Ibid.*, pp. 68, 69. A gripping counter-example, which illustrates Dietrich's point, is found in Klaus Bonhoeffer's note, written after torture and before the death sentence: "I am not afraid of being hanged, but I don't want to see those faces again . . . so much depravity. . . . I'd rather die than see those faces again. I have seen the Devil, and I can't forget it" (*DBET*, p. 832).

28 *E*, p. 70.

29 *LPPE*, p. 275. See Clifford Green, *Bonhoeffer: The Sociality of Christ and Humanity* (Missoula, Montana: Scholars Press, 1972), pp. 145, 207.

30 *CS*, p. 22.

31 *CS*, pp. 71f.

32   *CS*, p. 36.
33   *CS*, p. 30.
34   *CS*, p. 33.
35   *CS*, p. 31.
36   *LPPE*, p. 217. This passage in the letter of Feb. 21, 1944, is pivotal evidence for the writer's argument: "We must confront fate—to me the neuter gender of the word 'fate' (*Schicksal*) is significant—as resolutely as we submit to it at the right time. One can speak of 'guidance' only on the other side of that twofold process, with God meeting us no longer as 'thou', but also 'disguised' in the 'It'; so in the last resort my question is how we are to find the 'Thou' in this 'It' (i.e., fate), or, in other words, how does 'fate' really become 'guidance'? It's therefore impossible to define the boundary between resistance and submission on abstract principles."
37   *GS*, I, 129, 150ff.; *GS*, II, 45; *GS*, III, 278ff.; *GS*, V, 292.
38   William W. Butler, "A Comparison of the Ethics of Emil Brunner and Dietrich Bonhoeffer with Special Attention to the Orders of Creation and the Mandates" (Ph.D. diss., Emory Univ., 1970), pp. 15-30.
39   *GS*, I, 68-74.
40   *DBET*, p. 18.
41   *DBET*, pp. 104, 108.
42   *CS*, p. 195.
43   M.F.M. van der Berk, *Bonhoeffer, boeiend en geboeid: de theologie van Dietrich Bonhoeffer in het licht van zijn persoonlijkheid* (Meppel, Netherlands: Boom, 1974), pp. 48-52; Thomas Day, "Conviviality and Common Sense: The Meaning of Christian Community for Dietrich Bonhoeffer" (Ph.D. diss., Union Theol. Sem., 1975), p. 45.
44   *GS*, II, 27; the clarification on p. 28 was not in the original radio talks.
45   *GS*, III, 170-175.
46   *GS*, II, 29, 32.
47   *E*, p. 66.
48   *Ibid*.
49   See *GS*, I, 31, 148.
50   *GS*, V, 361; a slightly different version of the essay "Christ and Peace" is published in *DBET*, p. 159.
51   *GS*, V, 360.
52   *GS*, I, 146.
53   Bethge, *DB*, p. 254; translation by the writer, for the accuracy of nuance in the term "wehrlos."
54   *LPPE*, p. 191, Letter of January 23, 1944; see Heinrich Ott, *Reality and Faith: The Theological Legacy of Dietrich Bonhoeffer* (Philadelphia: Fortress Press, 1972), p. 303.
55   Martin Kuske, *The Old Testament as the Book of Christ: An Appraisal of Bonhoeffer's Interpretation* (Philadelphia: Westminster Press, 1976), p. 151.
56   Kuske, p. 155.
57   *GS*, III, 50.
58   *GS*, I, 42f.
59   *GS*, V, 524-527.
60   *GS*, V, 521.
61   *Begegnungen* (3 Aufl., Wilhelm Niesel's recollection), p. 130, is corrected by W. Rott, as quoted in *DBET*, pp. 586-587.
62   *E*, p. 113.

63 *DBET*, p. 627; see *GS*, I, 254, 358, 398; see also *CS*, p. 199.

64 *DBET*, pp. 274-281.

65 F. Baumgärtel, *Die Kirche ist Eine—die alttestamentlich-jüdische und die Kirche Jesu Christi? Eine Verwahrung gegen die Preisgabe des Alten Testaments* (1936), *passim*. Kuske's otherwise excellent study sides with Baumgärtel (p. 83) on both of these charges.

66 *DBET*, p. 279.

67 *DBET*, pp. 404, 407.

68 Kuske, p. 83; see *DBET*, pp. 436-439.

69 *CS*, pp. 106-114; *T*, p. 22.

70 *GS*, IV, 413-426, 566-568.

71 *Ibid.*, 420.

72 *CS*, p. 199.

73 *GS*, II, 48.

74 *DBET*, p. 285: "Bell understood how it was that Bonhoeffer had to keep political and theological judgements apart yet relate them closely to each other."

75 Bethge, *DB*, p. 1065 (the writer's translation). The version in *GS*, V, 259 has: ". . . not to be utilized against the enemy." Since both versions are based on student notes, a reliable preference is difficult to arrive at.

76 *Ibid.*

77 *T*, p. 43.

78 Some of the major instances already indicated are: *GS*, III, 167ff.; *CF*, pp. 73ff; *T, passim*; *GS*, V, 21ff. Other important passages include: *GS*, I, 253, 254; *GS*, II, 235, 340; *GS*, III, 258ff., 280, 376; *GS*, IV, 49, 327ff., 370, 417, 427ff., 430, 433, 447, 566ff.; *GS*, V, 294-295, 360-361, 388-389; *GS*, VI, 304-353; *CD*, pp. 162ff., 177, 160, 167, 226, 242-243, 297.

79 *LPPE*, p. 5; see *CD*, p. 87 for a similar view in 1937.

80 *E*, p. 73.

81 See the logic of *GS*, III, 409. Also MS #395, Filmfile #1, p. 50: "Time . . . the patience of God."

82 *LPPE*, p. 361, July 18, 1944; p. 370, July 21, 1944.

83 *DBET*, p. 790: "This 'borderline case' is suddenly made visible and validly interpreted as an *example* of being a Christian today" (the writer's italics).

84 Kuske, p. 155.

85 *DBET*, p. 827.

DIETRICH BONHOEFFER ON WAR AND PEACE

Herbert Jehle

THE 1933 CHURCH STRUGGLE did not drive the Confessing Church into the catacombs. For those who wanted to hear and who could still think logically despite the uproar in the street and noise from the loudspeakers, the message was available, not only at Dietrich Bonhoeffer's symposia but also throughout the entire country. When this became too uncomfortable for the Nazis in the following years, the church had to become literally migrant. Many of the loyal ministers found it difficult to provide for their families since the state had confiscated voluntary relief offerings. In spite of the impossible circumstances which threatened to throw the church into a state of confusion, this new situation certainly gave us all opportunity for renewed reflection on the message, and it had a vitalizing influence on the life of the church.

Soon the lecture room that housed Bonhoeffer's seminars had to be exchanged for unauthorized, primitive quarters in the attic of the University of Berlin. And that was only the beginning of the nomadic journey which the training centers of the Confessing Church had to make. We searched throughout the country for a place for the student seminary, until finally in 1935 a temporary accommodation was found in Finkenwalde.

In the intellectual and spiritual devastation, amid the confusion of ideas of what it means to be human, and in the unscrupulousness of people who wanted to erect their nationalistic Reich without and against God, people became bewildered, stolid, despondent, inwardly paralyzed, terrified, and frustrated. Then one was glad to hear Dietrich Bonhoeffer in Berlin's Trinity Church. As early as 1932 and 1933 he had fearlessly dared to speak a clear message, which imparted courage and confidence to us.

He spoke of the persecution of the Jews—not a timid, compromising message, but a clear rejection of anti-Semitism along with every other racial delusion. He reported about the racial hatred in South Africa, which Gandhi checked in a magnanimous way. That was an incentive to us, and instead of timidly and silently watching this cancer grow, he began a work that soon won the confidence of the best people within and without Germany. Together with Dietrich Bonhoeffer, Martin Niemoeller, and many others, the Confessing Church spoke a courageous and clear word about the persecution of the Jews, as a result of which the brave legal advisor of the Confessing Church, Dr. Weissler, was murdered at the beginning of 1937. Bonhoeffer proclaimed this calling of the church and of Christian charity toward other races throughout his life, though it was dangerous to speak of such matters. He wondered why churches compromised in order to procure Aryan identification papers. Dietrich was fearless, and he disliked the way many colleagues, under the cloak of erudite scholarship, weighed the alternatives with "but," "however," and "but" again, evading clear decisions. It was uncomfortable for many a churchman to place himself openly on the side of all the so-called non-Aryans. Not so for Bonhoeffer and Niemoeller.

Dietrich Bonhoeffer instilled confidence in us through a second concern. Somehow this also had its origins in 1930/31, the year he spent at Union Theological Seminary. At that time Jean Lasserre, who later became the secretary of the French section of the Fellowship of Reconciliation, was also studying at Union; and thus France and Germany met there. Bonhoeffer had a profound understanding for the Christian answer to the hostilities and wars between France and Germany. As youth secretary in the ecumenical movement, he brought together students of many nations; the bonds formed in the thirties are still sacred. All this took place in the shadow of a world bent on murder, a world against which Dietrich Bonhoeffer unswervingly preached the gospel of charity, conscientious objection, and reconciliation. The address at the conference at Fanö in 1934 is one of the really great legacies which he has left to posterity. Bonhoeffer told of Philippe Vernier and his courageous life in prison. There in France, before the military court, one of the most talented, deeply pious men testified to charity toward the "sworn enemy" and was sentenced to years of a wretched, damp, and cold existence in a prison cell, both before and during the war. That evoked in us a solemn resolve, and we learned to understand the cost of discipleship.

Later it was my privilege to form a close friendship with these magnanimous French Christians whose testimony in a world of war gave direction to our lives. Fearlessly and in faith, Philippe Vernier and many of his friends carried the burden and our collective guilt for the war. From within prison they showed us the path away from the confusion, from preparation for war, and from war itself. And then, when many of us were interned by the Gestapo in the camps in France and elsewhere in 1940, these friends of the Ecumene brought us consolation, comfort, and courage, gave us food to eat and helped all the camp inmates in times of suffering and persecution.

Jeanne Merle d'Aubigne, Madeleine Barot, Suzanne Aillet-Rennes, André and Magda Trocme, Eduard Theiss, Henri Roser, Suzanne Rette, Jacques Harts, P. C. Toureille, and many others put their bread and even their lives on the line in order to alleviate our need and want.

It was the concern of the ecumenical movement that brought Bonhoeffer to London in 1933. Thus the brotherhood of Christians in Germany and the West was not broken, as the Nazis had hoped it would be. Dr. George Bell, Bishop of Chichester and President of the Ecumenical Council, was a tireless helper moved by a warm sympathy for the suffering of all nations. He translated that into action as he worked and stood with Dietrich Bonhoeffer. The collaboration of the churches on both sides of the British Channel was so close that in 1933 and 1934 telephone calls between Bonhoeffer in London and Berlin were made nearly every day. One fine day the monthly telephone bill exceeded the pastor's salary. When Dietrich, somewhat embarrassed, made the pilgrimage to the telephone office, the authorities said no pastor could pay such a bill—and quite simply cut it in half.

The parsonage in Sydenham was a lovely old house, and Bonhoeffer decorated it with beautiful pictures and prints. Among them were the Isenheim altar for his study, Tersteegen's saying "Ein Tag der sagt's dem andern," and splendid reproductions of other works of art. The furniture and the library, as well as a grand piano, came from Bonhoeffer's home in Berlin. There in London, in 1934, one could often hear him playing the piano, and he gave wonderful concerts together with Eric Seymour, Lawrence Whitburn, and the choirs of both London parishes. I shall never forget a performance of Brahms' *German Requiem*, nor the meetings with Julius Rieger, their families, with Franz Hildebrandt, and with many faithful members of the congregation.

During the London stay, despite telephone conversations with his mother, father, siblings, and grandmother in Berlin, Dietrich still occasionally found life lonely in contrast to the parental home in Berlin, which was always bubbling with activity. One day the question arose of whether a puppy might be a refreshing addition to the parsonage. Bonhoeffer visited a pound for lost dogs, but the poor dogs there were not a very edifying sight. But on a return visit he found a young St. Bernard. I do not know where he came from, but he was a wonderful puppy. He was trained and lived up to all expectations. But he ended tragically: frightened by a cat, he ran into the street and was hit by a car.

Deeply touched by this loss, we came to reflect on eschatology once more. Although our ways of theological reasoning led in different directions, it was always interesting to learn from Dietrich. He often reported on good theologians with whom he did not necessarily agree. Adolf von Harnack held Bonhoeffer in high esteem, and Dietrich had often accompanied the great Professor von Harnack on walks. Shortly before his death von Harnack wrote Bonhoeffer a postcard, whose text I found very moving: "The substance of eschatology is but this: that we learn to understand that we are God's children."

In this period in London—in 1934—we were faced with the question of what our Christian duty should be in this horrible period in history, which was heading more and more toward the abyss. Since the ecumenical bond between Britain and Germany was already firm and secure, Bonhoeffer felt that the work had to be done in Germany from then on. The task, in the face of such a grotesque, diabolical unfolding of power, was overwhelming, and we often felt the need for some entirely new kind of training in order to enable us not only to preach the gospel of the Sermon on the Mount in such a situation but also to live it in such adverse circumstances. Mahatma Gandhi had learned to cope with racial hatred and violence in war and in peace. We had something to learn from him. So it was a great joy when a letter from Mahatma Gandhi arrived in London in 1934 via C. F. Andrews, a British missionary and friend of Gandhi, inviting us to the Wardha Ashram. Preparations were made and details were discussed; it was necessary to prepare for long-term resistance in Nazi Germany and to help our church in this task as Gandhi was helping his people.[1]

But before Christmas 1934, special delivery letters and telegrams arrived in London stating that Dietrich Bonhoeffer was needed in Germany immediately, in order to lead a student seminary. Many well-meaning friends in church leadership were thinking much too conventionally in a situation which demanded new direction. The need of tomorrow made them overlook the overwhelming task of the coming years. Only very few saw that Gandhi's peace efforts very closely paralleled the German problem of the thirties. Much could have been attained had we learned more about passive resistance. It was self-evident to Bonhoeffer that this could not be accomplished without intensive training. Yet he could not evade the pressing call of the church and the students.

Since the seminary now had to be put on its feet, Bonhoeffer seized the idea of training in the form of a community house (von Harnack spoke frequently about the significance of a Protestant monastery). Many discussions were necessary to make this plan of Bonhoeffer understandable. But the idea of a coeducational institution was not at all acceptable to the church authorities. This was strange, because we already had women theology students and married couples in our ranks. Cooperatives were recognized as stable institutions in Anglo-Saxon countries; and especially through the discipline which this seminary established, it could have become a forerunner of the voluntary service camps. Such "work camps"—which included study—proved an outstanding success after the war in the work of reconstruction and in international peace efforts.

Finkenwalde, then, was the seminary in which most of Dietrich's plans became reality. Finkenwalde would not, however, have been Finkenwalde without the good Frau von Kleist in Stettin. She was a very kind and courageous woman who held the Confessing Church together and cared for the seminary. And the grandchildren, Maria von Wedemeyer and her brothers and sisters—still quite small at that time—visited regularly and made a deep impression on us all, and not the least on Dietrich.

No wonder Dietrich later became engaged to Maria. They shared a deep concern for liturgy, a never hesitating devotion to the call of the church, and a deep security in sacred faith. A violent death separated us all from Dietrich Bonhoeffer.

> The past returns to you
> as your life's most living part
> through gratitude, through repentance.
> Grasp in the past God's remission and goodness.
> Pray that God shelter you now and tomorrow.

(WE, p. 286)

Notes

1   When it became evident that the mess in Nazi Germany nullified my visit to India, Dietrich and Julius Rieger still tried to realize the visit.

TEACHING ETHICS AND MORAL DECISION-MAKING IN THE LIGHT OF DIETRICH BONHOEFFER

Marvin Bergman

Introduction

A PERENNIAL QUESTION discussed by philosophers, "How shall I decide?" is a question being raised by increasing numbers of youths and adults. At least theologians and church curriculum writers are suggesting that inquiry and questions related to moral decision-making are a high priority item for many youths and adults today.[1] A review of such curricular materials reveals a three-fold emphasis: 1) a keen sensitivity to the complexity and diversity of moral dilemmas confronting people today; 2) a conviction that theology is a key resource for moral decision-makers; 3) a quest for more effective strategies of teaching ethics and moral decision-making.

One theologian whose work addressed concerns of these kinds is Dietrich Bonhoeffer. For example, he noted that a compulsive regulation of life related to precise courses of training and vocational activity had led to an ethical emasculation of individuals.[2] On another occasion he wrote that "our period, more than any earlier period in the history of the west, is oppressed by a superabounding reality of concrete ethical problems."[3] Apparent to him also was the inability of many church people to deal with the burning practical questions of everyday life.[4] His sensitivity to such problems was matched by a conviction that theology—and Christian ethics in particular—provides a resource that needs to be tapped by young and old. For example, after undertaking a catechetical ministry in the Berlin suburb of Grünewald, Bonhoeffer commented that theologizing was worthwhile only if it had something of great importance to say to the children of Grünewald.[5] Though his life was terminated too early to allow any systematic reflection on a key question faced by teachers in the church, "How does one attempt to assist youth and adults involved in the making of moral decisions?" Bonhoeffer's work does provide a base for Christian educators interested in developing strategies of teaching ethics and moral decision-making. Specifically, Bonhoeffer's work illuminates five questions of interest to teachers in the church: 1) What is meant by "ethical" or "moral"? 2) What is the predicament of a moral decision-maker? 3) What are the foundations of Christian ethics? 4) What are the components of a moral decision? 5) What strategies of teaching ethics and moral decision-making can be identified? These questions will serve as the focus of this discussion, which will explore the Bonhoeffer corpus and give particular attention to *Ethics*.

Defining "Ethical" and "Moral"

When one considers the kinds of decisions that confront individuals, a variety of examples can be cited, such as:

1) Bill and Mary own a 1963 Chevrolet, a car with minimal safety features; they wonder if they should borrow money in order to secure safer transportation.

2) John and Sue learn that their daughter is considering an abortion after becoming aware that her fiancé will not marry her. What kind of advice should they give?

3) While her husband is out of town for an evening, Jane debates whether or not she should watch television or read a book that explores parent-child relations.

Which of these people is involved in making an ethical decision? Isabel Rogers suggests that decisions that involve regulating children's television watching, casting a ballot for President, or deciding what is right for one in a given situation involve making an ethical decision.[6] James Nelson proposes that Christian ethics be seen as a self-critical reflection on the meaning of human responsibility.[7] Such perspectives suggest that a Christian will find himself continually involved in the making of ethical decisions, with each new day bringing a new set of ethical questions.

Bonhoeffer, however, restricts the definition of "ethical" and "moral" in order not to overburden the life of an individual with a sense of the ethical. He emphasizes that the costly grace of God revealed in Jesus Christ sets one on a path of freedom, so that Christian discipleship does not ordinarily involve one in viewing everyday choices in terms of ethical decisions. The ethical is peripheral in daily life until one becomes involved in a disturbance and interruption of life, such as when fellowship in a community is disrupted, a life is endangered, or a moral course of action is not self-evident.[8] It is then that the words "shall" and "should" are seen to confront an individual. Ethical and moral concerns involve an individual especially in concrete dilemmas linked with particular persons, times, and places.[9] For Bonhoeffer, all ethical and moral concerns that may face an individual coalesce in the object of Christian ethics—the commandment of God. Thus a decision that involves such alternatives as watching television or reading a book ordinarily is not an ethical decision but a decision to be made in the context of one's freedom. However, a decision that involves an interruption of human life, such as an abortion, is clearly one that involves a moral dimension.

As the reader may have noticed, no clear-cut distinction between "ethical" and "moral" in this discussion has been made thus far. Bonhoeffer's work reveals a lack of consistency in the use of these two terms, with "moral" sometimes used where "ethical" may be expected. In this discussion I make a somewhat arbitrary distinction: *ethical* refers to the grounds on which a moral judgment is made; *moral* or *morality* denotes the process of making such a choice.[10] There is, of course, some overlapping. For example, in the following discussion of the predicament of a moral decision-maker, attention will focus on both the process and foundations of making a moral decision.

An Analysis of a Decision Maker's Predicament

Bonhoeffer's contacts with people in a large variety of circumstances, ranging from parishioners in Berlin and Barcelona to a circle of plotters, sensitized him to various difficulties experienced in making moral decisions. His own involvement in a number of dilemmas, some of which centered on life and death issues, also served to stimulate a deeper probe of the ethical and moral problems evident in his day as well as the roots of the predicaments facing moral decision-makers.

In discussing moral dilemmas, Bonhoeffer cites a number of problems. He describes the blind obedience to a governmental order as paving the way for many kinds of arbitrariness and disorder.[11] A more significant problem in his view is a blindness to the power of evil, apparent, for example, in six types of moral decision-makers, whom he describes in these ways: 1) the *reasonable* person, who maintains that the use of reason will enable one to solve a moral problem; 2) the *fanatic,* who emphasizes the power of the will and allegiance to moral principles; 3) the person who endeavors to make decisions solely on the basis of *conscience*; 4) the individual who stresses *duty* to a particular command or commandment as the surest kind of guide; 5) the believer in *absolute freedom* as his operating principle in responding to ethical dilemmas; 6) the person who takes his stand on the platform of *private virtue.*[12] All six types are described as Don Quixote figures who ride into endless battles to experience nothing but futility, demonstrating the need to replace rusty swords with ones that are sharp.[13]

Bonhoeffer also pointed out that ethical and moral confusion contributed much to the dilemmas of his day. Individuals who attempted to think of ethics in terms of "How can I do the good?"[14] or churches that attempted to define what is good once and for all he saw to be quite limited in making any kind of contribution.[15] Attempts to focus primary attention on motives, attitudes, and consequences, or attempts to base ethical decisions on positivistic and empirical grounds that aim at eliminating norms while postulating infinitely varying goods—these Bonhoeffer severely criticized as surrendering to the expedient and momentary.[16] He also pointed to distorted theological views, such as attempts to formulate ethics in terms of good and evil and hence to subordinate one's actions to one's knowledge of good and evil,[17] or attempts to divide reality into two parts on the basis of Luther's two kingdoms concept as illustrations of confusion.[18] Also contributing to the confusion of some was a heavy reliance on general moral principles or on general and abstract ethical discourse unrelated to a particular person, time, and place.[19] Bonhoeffer criticized several theologians as well, such as Dilschneider, Troeltsch, and Reinhold Niebuhr, who, he thought, made a number of unwarranted distinctions, such as "moral man" and "immoral society."[20]

Not satisfied with a mere description of theoretical and practical difficulties, Bonhoeffer probed more deeply by using a theological lens to uncover the roots of the predicaments confronting a moral decision-maker. The thrust of his stance is seen in the assertion that "moral difficulties were the first consequences of the *Fall,* and are themselves the outcome of 'Man in Revolt' against God."[21] The Fall is described in the context of mankind's primeval state, which centered in a life that revolved around God's presence, symbolized by the tree of life in the middle of the garden. There Adam and Eve lived in genuine community, in an obedience to God that sprang from freedom.[22] In encountering the Tempter, mankind heard the tantalizing suggestion to go beyond the Word of God for the purpose of discovering a greater, nobler God.[23] The question "Did God say?" clearly drew the issue between two kinds of existence, *imago dei*—Godlike man in his existence for God and the neighbor—and *sicut deus*—Godlike man in his acting out of himself.[24] When the act occurred in which the limit was transgressed, one sees that:

> In the first place the middle has been entered, the limit has been transgressed. Now man stands in the middle, now he is without limit. That he stands in the middle means that now he lives out of his own resources and no longer from the middle. That he is without a limit means that he is alone. To be in the middle and to be alone means to be like God. Man is *sicut deus.* Now he lives out of himself, now he creates his own life, he is his own creator. He no longer needs the Creator, he has become a creator himself, to the extent that he creates

his own life. With this his creatureliness is finished and destroyed for him. Adam is no longer creature. He has torn himself away from his creatureliness. He *is* like God, and this "is" is meant very seriously.[25]

With the relationship between God and mankind being broken, love is turned to selfishness. A person by nature now has a heart that curves in upon itself, with the result that one turns God into a religious object, the neighbor into a thing, the world into material to be plundered, and the self into a creator, master, origin, and interpreter of good and evil.[26] Understanding self according to its own possibilities, one becomes a god against God, dominated by sin, a narcissism of the human will that is expressed in acts that are self-seeking.[27] The power of sin within an individual and a community is such that it is humanly impossible to know the self as a sinner apart from revelation.[28]

Manifestations of the Fall can be seen in the realm of moral decision-making in a number of ways. A decision, for example, may be motivated by an attempt to avoid shame, described by Bonhoeffer as an acknowledgment of the limits that do exist in this world, as well as a hating of the limits that one encounters.[29] Making decisions on the basis of conscience may also become a trap, since conscience may serve as a call to unity with the self instead of with the Center of life. Or conscience may become an accuser, driving one further from God.[30] Guilt, which has the character of one being alone in a state of disunion, also may become a key determinant in a moral decision, driving one, for example, to become one's own creator, one's own judge, one's own restorer.[31] Equally destructive in the making of a moral decision is the propensity of people to pass judgment on each other, with the ultimate criterion being mankind itself, which, of course, can only lead to greater disunion.[32] This can happen especially in the case of one who believes that he is engaged in the doing of the will of God and is called to execute the law, while in reality such action springs from one's own knowledge of good and evil.[33] Another consequence of the Fall is that one may cite God or conscience as the grounds of a moral decision while actually using God or conscience in a very self-centered way.

Convinced that both concrete problems and many kinds of confusion in ethics and moral decision making were symptomatic of the root of the ethical and moral predicament of mankind, that is, rebellion against God and a radical disunion with the Center of one's being, Bonhoeffer directed the bulk of his energies to an articulation of the reconciling work of God as the basis of mankind's liberation and the grounds of Christian ethics. It is to this facet of his work that we now turn, giving particular attention to the foundations of his ethics.

The Foundations of Bonhoeffer's Ethics

When one begins to explore questions related to values, ethical norms, justification of a moral decision, and so forth, attention will focus on ethics, the grounds of one's decision. For Bonhoeffer, the foundations of his ethics were shaped by at least two key factors: 1) a personal experience of the meaning of reconciliation in Jesus Christ; 2) a theological commitment which saw that deliverance from mankind's predicament was possible only through the power of the gospel. His deep interest in writing an ethic reveals an awareness of the importance of articulating the basis of a moral decision. Of course, Bonhoeffer did and would object to viewing ethics as a system. And yet he did identify constituent elements and describe their interrelationships in such a way as to make possible this kind of discussion.

Of crucial importance in ethics is the point of departure, since it is the *terminus a quo* which directs one's search for a responsible decision. In Bonhoeffer's work, it is quite clear that the point of departure is Christology. For it is the work of Christ that addresses the predicament of mankind and provides the grounds of liberation from egocentrism and disunity which lead to confusion and traps of various kinds. The decisive word that marks the distinction between man in disunion and in a state of liberation is the love of God revealed in Jesus Christ.[34] God's love means that the world is subdued, not by its destruction but by its reconciliation in Christ. In the Incarnation God makes himself known as the one who wishes to exist not for himself but for mankind. The Crucifixion points to the reality of the sentence of death that has fallen on the world; at the same time, the cross is the maker of reconciliation and a setting free for life in the world.[35] In the Resurrection God reveals his "Yes," which declares that the law of death has been shattered and that a new creation has begun.[36]

Not only does God's action in Jesus Christ deliver one from the key predicament, but it also places one in a community that serves as the context for decision-making. Though one can note shifts in Bonhoeffer's view of the church between his early and later years, a number of common elements can be discerned. For example, he sees the church existing only by the work of Christ and the Holy Spirit, with Christ being the creator of its life as well as revealing his presence within the Christian community.[37] Not only is the church called as a bearer of revelation, but it is also summoned to express God's new purposes for people, constantly realizing the will of God anew.[38] As a body called to open the eyes of the world to the reality of the love of God, the church has the responsibility of offering concrete instruction in concrete situations. Though the Christian church has no solution for all of the social and political problems of a society, there are countless opportunities for the church to plunge itself into the life of the world and "range themselves with God in His sufferings."[39]

Bonhoeffer also sees that the work of Christ involves nothing less than the reshaping of the very being of man, so that it is Christ's taking form in one's person that supplies the springs of ethical action. Believing that an image needs a living object, Bonhoeffer points out that when the image of God revealed in Jesus Christ begins to mold a human being, a transformation occurs that provides a new outlook, a new direction of will, a new pattern of behavior.[40] Such a transformation occurs only by being drawn into the unique form of the Christ who became a man, was crucified, and rose again. The place where persons are gripped by the power of the grace of God and where Christ takes form among people is the Christian community.[41] What counts in Christian ethics, then, is Christ taking form among us here and now, which negates any attempt to say what is good once and for all.[42]

The thrust of the liberating work of Christ as the point of departure, the Christian community as the context, and the formation of the person—these become more apparent when attention is directed to the significance of the *ultimate* and *penultimate* in Bonhoeffer. The ultimate is seen as that final word in God's address to men, a word beyond which he will not go, the word of the justification of the sinner by grace through faith alone.[43] It is this ultimate which shapes those things that are next to the last—the penultimates. When a clash develops between one and the other, the problem finds resolution in Jesus Christ, through whom those things that are pitted against one another become one. The Christian life, then, allows neither a destruction nor sanctioning of the penultimate as an ultimate; rather, the reality of God's work in Jesus Christ allows one to participate in his work in the world. In fact, what is nearest to God is the need of the neighbor, so that it is the love of Christ that moves one to respond to the hungry and the dispossessed.[44]

The significance of ultimate and penultimate is further sharpened by an examination of the meaning of ethical. For Bonhoeffer, the ethical centers in one's definition of reality, which he interpreted as centering in the miracle of God's reconciliation of the world. Ethics, then, involves one in an inquiry of the realization of this divine reality in Christ, meaning that action which is in accord with Christ can be described as ethical.[45] Here the question of the good becomes a question of one's participation in such a reality. This also suggests that the object of Christian ethics is the commandment of God, which does not consist of a summary of ethical propositions, timeless principles, or abstractions, but of the concrete claim laid on a person by a merciful God in Jesus Christ, which sets one free from disunity for a life of freedom and certainty.[46] Such a commandment is to be seen as an act of God's revelation rather than being equated with the order of creation, for example. This also means that values do not exist in themselves but only in relation to the work of Jesus Christ. Another dimension is that the commandment confronts one concretely in four spheres or mandates: labor, government, family, and the church.[47] Those who exercise authority in these spheres bear the mandate to act as deputies in the place of God, who assigns such a commission out of a desire for the world to become a place for the humanization of man. The key question that springs from the commandment of God and confronts a moral decision-maker is, "What is the will of God?" This, of course, immediately raises questions related to the how of making a moral decision.

Components of the Moral Decision-Making Process

In making a moral decision, one's attention deserves to be directed not only to the foundations of one's decision but also to the process, to the way in which one implements an ethic when confronted by a moral dilemma. Often one will be involved in wrestling with questions related to conscience, the law, principles, intentions, possibilities, consequences, and so forth. Though not addressing these questions in a systematic way, Bonhoeffer did concern himself with the decision-making process, stating on one occasion that a person needs to be concerned with "not only the motive, but also with the object . . . one must devote earnest thought to the consequences of one's action . . . one must ask what are the possibilities."[48] At other times Bonhoeffer dealt with issues related to conscience, the law, and principles, and identified key components of the decision-making process.

Having rejected both a heteronomous stance, in which principles and precepts are imposed on an individual, and an autonomous posture of "rugged individualism," Bonhoeffer posed as the key question in the making of a moral decision, "What is the will of God?" Here the will of God is more than an idea; it is rather "the becoming real of the reality of Christ with us and in our world."[49] Asking about the will of God focuses attention on that reconciliation which has already been accomplished and which seeks to be realized anew in the world. Or one may say that to live in reconciliation with God and men, to live the life of a disciple of Jesus Christ, is the precondition of doing the will of God. Bonhoeffer does not say that knowing the will of God depends on intuition, any first thoughts or feelings, a system of rules or principles, or one's own knowledge of good and evil. Rather, knowing the will of God is possible only on the basis of the revelation of God's will in Jesus Christ and one's union with Christ; this means that one needs to examine what the will of God may be in each situation.[50] Of course, at one time or another one will experience difficulty in discerning the will of God. Bonhoeffer notes:

> We are confronted by unparalleled situations in which we must make a decision, and in which we make again and again the surprising and

terrifying discovery that the will of God does not reveal itself before our eyes as clearly as we had hoped. This comes about because the will of God seems to be self-contradictory, because two ordinances of God seem to be in conflict with one another, so that we are not in a position to choose between God and evil, but only between one evil and another. And here it is that the real, most difficult problems of ethics lie.[51]

However, such problems are not insurmountable for the man in formation. One who has been renewed through conformation to Christ will want to employ the whole apparatus of human power given to him. In a passage that contains Bonhoeffer's most explicit suggestions about the use of human capacities, he wrote:

> Intelligence, discernment, attentive observation of the given facts, all these now come into lively operation, all will be embraced and pervaded by prayer. Particular experiences will afford correction and warning. Direct inspirations must in no case be heeded or expected, for this could all too easily lead to a man's abandoning himself to self-deception. . . . Possibilities and consequences must be carefully assessed. In other words, the whole apparatus of human power must be set in motion when it is a matter of proving what is the will of God.[52]

These suggestions warrant giving greater attention to the potential contribution and place of a number of resources that can be tapped by a decision maker, such as the heart, reason, observation, and experience.

Emphasizing that the voice of one's heart cannot be equated with the will of God, Bonhoeffer saw the role of one's heart in terms of the transformation that occurs through the reality of the love of God in Christ.[53] It is this love that sets the neighbor in the place of the self, with one's concern for the neighbor becoming "man's will for God's will for the other man."[54] Aware of the limitations of reason, Bonhoeffer also saw that reason has a place in the life of a disciple, as, for example, an instrument for perceiving the imperative of the Decalogue in the larger social order.[55] Observation of the facts of a given situation, of possibilities and consequences of particular actions, as well as of social roles and circles of responsibility can provide helpful input in the making of a moral decision.[56] Experience—personal, social, and historical—can provide correction, warning, and sensitivity, illuminating perspectives of realities in life, and thus serve as a means to act in a more decisive and meaningful way.

Another resource that can be enlisted is the law. Bonhoeffer rejects two reponses to the law: libertarianism, which suggests that one is free to totally ignore the law; and legalism, which enslaves one to the law. Response to the law centers, rather, in the Christ who has fulfilled the law and has given a new law, the law of Christ. For it is Christ who restores the lost gift of freedom which provides the ability to respond to God, the neighbor, the self, the law, and so forth.[57] In the ethical commandments of the New Testament and the Sermon on the Mount one sees a demonstration of what God's commandment can be for a person today. However, these are not to interpose themselves between God and the decision maker by becoming fixed moral commandments.[58] In fact, responsible action may involve breaking a law for the sake of service to God and the neighbor, though such a breach of the law must be recognized in all its gravity.[59]

In considering conscience, Bonhoeffer insisted that a distinction be made between two forms of conscience. He saw the first, natural conscience, as a judge that could come between Christ and the decision maker.[60] The second, the liberated conscience, involves a reflection on the self in the light of Christ, who displaces attempts by the natural conscience to confer self-justification on itself and posits a new goal—a summons to a unity with Christ.[61] Since conscience does contain fundamental features of the law of life and serves as a warning against transgression, it is generally not advisable to act against one's own conscience.[62] However, this is not the last word, for Christ is the Lord of conscience, and it is he who sets one free for a life of responsible freedom.

A key characteristic in the life of a disciple is freedom, the foundation of which is the gospel that God in Jesus Christ has bound himself to man, enabling the creature to stand before the Creator and to be free for him and others.[63] Instead of seeing freedom in terms of arbitrary self-will, freedom in and through Christ offers one the liberty to dare to act and surrender the deed to God.[64] Where there is freedom, there is obedience, so that when Christ issues his call, one responds and obeys his concrete command. Specifically, obedience to Christ means that one makes a break with the past and turns to Christ, responding to his call and expressing the reality of faith through obedience.[65] The tension that is apparent between freedom and obedience is resolved in responsibility, which considers the meaning of obedience while also being creative.[66] Or one may say that a life of responsibility is a life in which one lives by responding to the Word of God addressed to one in Jesus Christ.[67] Such responsibility is seen to include both a verbal response, which points to what has taken place in Christ, and a deed, which accepts responsibility for men before Christ, so that one answers to men for Christ and to Christ for men.[68] Responsible action that expresses concern for the brother does not attempt to shun guilt; rather, one will be ready to incur guilt for the sake of the brother.[69]

At this point it is apparent that the key dynamic in Bonhoeffer's ethic, the reality of God's reconciliation of the world in Jesus Christ, and a dialectic involving faith and obedience, shape the direction of the moral decision-making process. By riveting one's eyes on determining the will of God, by responding to the need of the neighbor, by answering the claims of conscience and the law, by employing the full range of human capacities, one is empowered to make a decision. With both freedom and obedience as vital components of responsibility, one is enabled to respond to both God and the neighbor, committing the deed to the gracious will of God.

Some Implications for Teaching Ethics and Moral Decision-Making

Since it is the function of strategy to provide bridges between ethics as a foundation and the moral decision-making process, teachers interested in helping to equip children, youths, and adults to make such decisions find themselves in a quest to develop such strategies. To be sure, teaching is not a simple process that can be easily blueprinted. However, any teaching of ethics and moral decision-making that is based on a strategy linked to an appropriate foundation is likely to be more fruitful than a mere plunge into the act of teaching.

In developing a strategy, it is recognized that the teaching/learning process may be explored from a variety of vantage points, including psychological, sociological, historical, and educational perspectives, with each discipline capable of making its own unique contribution. Following the emphasis of this study, attention will be directed toward taking seriously the contributions of a theological perspective. An examination of Bonhoeffer's work reveals that particular attention to three facets of a teaching strategy is warranted: the formative power of the community, the role of the teacher, and the curriculum.

Already in 1931, Bonhoeffer recognized the significance of community in the teaching ministry of the church. Describing a catechetical class of fifty youths in the Berlin slum of Wedding, he wrote, "I have developed all my instructions on the idea of the community."[70] That he took seriously the importance of developing a community as the context of Christian education is seen in his renting an apartment near the homes of the catechumens, planning weekend retreats with youths, and so forth. Bonhoeffer's great experiment in linking community and pedagogy was, of course, his work with a group of seminarians at Finkenwalde.

To suggest that a community serve as the basis of a strategy of teaching for a catechetical class or a seminary was a bold and radical innovation on the part of Bonhoeffer. And yet, a moment's reflection on his theological perspectives will reveal that there is a basis for placing a significant degree of confidence in the formative power of a community. In a context in which an individual exists in a state of radical disunion from the center of his being, actions that are based on a commitment to the self as the center will result in the individual's being trapped either by an autonomy or a heteronomy. However, when one is a member of a community in which Christ's image is the center, one is given a new image of self, a new direction of will, a new perspective, and a new kind of motivation in which one is moved to act in responsible freedom, seeking the will of God and the good of the neighbor.

That community should serve as the basis of a teaching strategy is not surprising when one remembers, as C. Ellis Nelson has pointed out, that community shapes three key processes within an individual: 1) a sense of personal identity that affects one's relationships with individuals and groups; 2) a perceptive system that provides a world view; and 3) a conscience that rewards and punishes on the basis of values that have developed.[71] By structuring one's teaching of ethics and moral decision-making in terms of a community and its self-identity, value structure, mores, celebrations, and so forth, one will be giving attention to key dimensions in the formation of a decision maker. Such formation can be aided by Bonhoeffer's theological perspectives, which provide a basis for the selection of content. As Nelson has suggested, the development of self-identity, perception, and conscience does involve a content, not in the sense of abstract knowledge or information, but as personal knowledge consisting of thought, feeling, and striving, labeled by some as "sentiment."[72] Particular themes that bear directly on a strategy of teaching include, for example, the image of Christ, discipleship, freedom, responsibility, the ultimate and the penultimate, the will of God, ethics, and conscience.[73]

A related facet of teaching strategy centers in learning through events. Events, which involve both persons and sets of circumstances, furnish a context in which learning takes place and supply realities through which learning occurs. Events are powerful learning experiences since they serve to draw one into thought, dialogue, and activities, all of which contribute to the development of meanings. Events of particular interest in the teaching of ethics and moral decision-making are real happenings within both the Christian community and the larger social order, which can supply a base for exploring questions, problems, issues, and dilemmas involving particular persons and situations. When the case-study approach becomes the focus, such events will serve to help integrate facts, concepts, images, values, feelings, and commitments to reality.

Central to the teaching of ethics and moral decision-making is the role of the teacher. Though Bonhoeffer in his writings did not distinguish in a formal way the role of a teacher and a preacher, for example, his life and work do provide important clues for describing a number of roles in the life of a teacher. The amount of time and energy he invested in developing relationships, for example, reinforces the notion that the teacher as a *personalist* and the quality of his relationships with learners are key factors in the formation of a community. In this context a teacher can function as a bridge in assisting learners to relate faith to the moral dilemmas they encounter. A teacher can also serve as a *provocateur* who becomes a "devil's advocate" in stimulating reflection, discussion, and action that springs from responsible freedom. As a *person in dialogue,* a teacher can reveal an openness to the concerns, problems, beliefs, and values of members of the community as well as to his own questions, doubts, values, and commitments. In working with children and youth, a teacher can also serve as a *link with the home,* becoming aware of the world views, life styles, and value systems of adults, while also providing reinforcement of key values, and, on occasion, confronting students with gaps that may exist between word and deed. The teacher can also function as a *parish midwife,* one who helps interpret events within a parish, serves as a channel of communication between individuals and the community, and encourages meaningful involvement in the life of the Christian community. Not to be overlooked is the teacher's role as a *model,* not in the sense of serving as an exemplary ideal but in the sense of being a transparent person who is also engaged in the quest of making decisions that reflect the meaning of responsible freedom.

Curriculum is also important, and facets of the curriculum that can be briefly explored in this essay include: 1) sources of ethical knowledge; 2) the structure of ethics and moral decision-making; and 3) the nature of the curriculum. The source of ethics in Bonhoeffer's thought—God's revelation in Jesus Christ and the faith that responds to this revelation—suggests, for example, that moral values, instead of being seen as entities in themselves, need to be justified in the light of what is ultimate in all of life. This does not mean that revelation constitutes the only source of knowledge, since reason, experience, observation, and the heart also provide important penultimate kinds of stimulus to one's value structure and decision making.

In developing a curriculum, attention can also be given to the structure of an ethic and the components of the moral decision-making process. In Bonhoeffer's ethics key organizing themes can clearly be identified, including: Christ as the point of departure; the church in the world as the context; formation as the springs of ethical action; the ultimate and penultimate as two facets of Christian ethics; ethics as the realization of God's will for the reconciliation of the world; the commandment of God as the object of Christian ethics. Attention can also be directed to the components of the moral decision-making process, which include: seeking the will of God; reacting to the need of the neighbor; responding to conscience; responding to the law; tapping human resources (such as reason and experience); and acting in responsible freedom.

The nature of a moral dilemma and Christian ethics as a discipline suggest strongly that a curriculum begin with and focus on real events and issues, especially those that confront members of a group and the larger community. Events, reports, biographies, case studies, simulation games, and so forth, can help sensitize participants to the conflicts involved in particular dilemmas, to the grounds of making an ethical decision, to key components in the moral decision-making process, and to possibilities and alternatives.

In this study of Bonhoeffer's ethics I have identified key dimensions of a strategy of teaching ethics and moral decision-making. An analysis of the decision maker's predicament points to alienation and disunity as the source of the dilemmas confronting a decision maker. I have cited God's act of reconciling the world through Jesus Christ as the basis of an ethical decision, empowering one for a life of participation in God's purposes. In identifying the components of the decision-making process, we can reject the postures of heteronomy and autonomy in favor of a Christonomy that moves one to respond to the will of God and the need of the neighbor. A strategy of teaching that reflects basic theological perspectives builds on the formative power of community, which provides the source of one's identity, perception, and conscience. With the person of the teacher being a key in the teaching/learning process, events inside and outside the community are the basic curricula that provide content for a teaching strategy intended to assist individuals in responding to moral dilemmas with free responsible action. Thus the dialectic which relates faith and obedience not only is the key component of a moral decision, but it also becomes the goal of a strategy of teaching ethics and moral decision-making.

Notes

1   Examples of church curricula that focus on moral decision-making are: *Decisions! Decisions!* (St. Louis: Concordia Publishing House, 1972); *The Gray Between Yes and No* (Minneapolis: Winston Press, 1972); *In Response to God: How Christians Make Ethical Decisions* (Richmond: Covenant Life Curriculum, 1969); *Priority: Values in Home and Church* (Minneapolis: Winston Press, 1972); *The Responsible Christian: A Churchly Ethics for Worldly People* (Philadelphia: United Church Press, 1969); *Valuing Christian Values* (St. Louis: Concordia Publishing House, 1973).

2   Bonhoeffer, *E,* p. 251.

3   *Ibid.,* p. 64.

4   *Ibid.,* p. 144.

5   Bethge, *DB,* p. 124.

6   *In Response to God: How Christians Make Ethical Decisions,* p. 21.

7   *The Responsible Christian: A Churchly Ethics for Worldly People,* p. 15.

8   *E,* pp. 266-267.

9   *Ibid.*, p. 270.

10   Such a distinction is suggested by Philip Phenix in his *Philosophy of Education* (New York: Holt, Rinehart and Winston, 1966), pp. 277, 285.

11   *E*, p. 144.

12   *Ibid.*, pp. 66-67.

13   *Ibid.*, p. 68.

14   *Ibid.*, p. 64.

15   *Ibid.*, p. 86.

16   *Ibid.*, pp. 192, 194.

17   *Ibid.*, pp. 18, 25.

18   *Ibid.*, pp. 196-197.

19   *Ibid.*, pp. 269-270.

20   *Ibid.*, pp. 191, 320.

21   *CD*, p. 64.

22   *CFT*, p. 51.

23   *Ibid.*, p. 66.

24   *Ibid.*, p. 71.

25   *Ibid.*, p. 72.

26   *AB*, p. 156.

27   *Ibid.*, p. 162.

28   *E*, p. 155.

29   *CFT*, p. 79.

30   For a fuller discussion of conscience, see *CFT*, pp. 80-81.

31   *E*, p. 110.

32   *Ibid.*, p. 31.

33   *Ibid.*, p. 48.

34   *Ibid.*, p. 49.

35   *Ibid.*, p. 297.

36   *Ibid.*

37   *CS*, p. 97.

38   *Ibid.*, p. 104.

39   *LPP*, pp. 122-123.

40   *CD*, p. 192.

41   *E*, p. 83.

42   *Ibid.*, pp. 86-87.

43   *Ibid.*, p. 123.

44   *Ibid.*, p. 137.

45   *Ibid.*, p. 195.

46   *Ibid.*, p. 277.

47   For a more extended discussion of the four mandates, see *ibid.*, pp. 207-213.

48   *Ibid.*, p. 233.

49   *Ibid.*, p. 212.

50   *Ibid.*, p. 38.

51   "What is a Christian Ethic?" *NRS*, p. 46.

52   *E*, p. 40.

53   *Ibid.*, p. 38.

54   *CS*, pp. 121-122.

55   *E*, p. 341.

56   *Ibid.*, pp. 40, 364.

57   *NRS*, p. 45.

58   *Ibid.,* pp. 45-46.
59   *E,* p. 262.
60   *AB,* pp. 177-178.
61   *E,* p. 243.
62   *Ibid.,* p. 242.
63   *CFT,* pp. 37-38.
64   *E,* pp. 248-249.
65   *CD,* pp. 54-55.
66   *E,* pp. 252-253.
67   *Ibid.,* p. 222.
68   *Ibid.,* p. 223.
69   *Ibid.,* p. 245.
70   *NRS,* p. 150.
71   C. Ellis Nelson, *Where Faith Begins* (Richmond: John Knox Press, 1967), pp. 36, 59.
72   *Ibid.,* p. 213.
73   For a further development of such themes, see Marvin Bergman, "Teaching for Moral Decision: An Analysis in the Light of Dietrich Bonhoeffer" (unpublished dissertation, Teachers College, Columbia University, 1970).